Disruption in Detroit

THE WORKING CLASS IN AMERICAN HISTORY

Editorial Advisors
James R. Barrett, Julie Greene, William P. Jones,
Alice Kessler-Harris, and Nelson Lichtenstein

A list of books in the series appears at the end of this book.

Disruption in Detroit

Autoworkers and the Elusive Postwar Boom

DANIEL J. CLARK

UNIVERSITY OF ILLINOIS PRESS
Urbana, Chicago, and Springfield

Library of Congress Cataloging-in-Publication Data
Names: Clark, Daniel J., author.
Title: Disruption in Detroit : autoworkers and the elusive
    postwar boom / Daniel J. Clark.
Description: Urbana : University of Illinois Press, [2018] |
    Includes bibliographical references and index.
Identifiers: LCCN 2018007677| ISBN 9780252042010 (hardcover :
    alk. paper) | ISBN 9780252083709 (pbk. : alk. paper)
Subjects: LCSH: Automobile industry workers—Michigan—
    Detroit—History—20th century. | Automobile industry
    workers—Labor unions—Michigan—Detroit—History—
    20th century. | Automobile industry and trade—Michigan—
    Detroit—History—20th century. | Detroit (Mich.)—
    Economic conditions—20th century.
Classification: LCC HD8039.A82 U632165 2018 | DDC
    331.88/129222097543409045—dc23
LC record available at https://lccn.loc.gov/2018007677

E-book ISBN 978-0-252-05075-6

To Bob and Bonnie

Contents

Acknowledgments

I offer my deepest gratitude to all the retired autoworkers and their family members who allowed me to interview them for this project. Those conversations were amazing gifts of incalculable value. Running partner Ed Lyghtel and former student Steve Clinton led me to UAW retiree chapter presidents Bob Bowen from Local 849 in Ypsilanti and Bonnie Melton from Local 653 in Pontiac. Bob and Bonnie immediately understood the importance of exploring the experiences of their chapters' members and facilitated many of the interviews at their respective union halls. This book would not exist without them.

A number of students recommended family members for interviews, and at the risk of overlooking someone, I want to offer specific thanks to Greg Miller, Paul Dusney, Marie O'Brien, and Kim Frink for connecting me, respectively, with L. J. Scott, Dorothy Sackle, Ernie Liles, and Allen Leske. Marie O'Brien, who is a superb historian, deserves to be in some sort of Hall of Fame for transcribing the first drafts of the majority of the interviews. She did an outstanding job bringing conversations to life on the printed page, and she has been supportive of this project from the beginning.

Much of my research took place in the Microfilm Room at the University of Michigan's Hatcher Graduate Library. The staff there seemed to practice poses of nonrecognition, even toward those who showed up every day for weeks on end, but they were always extremely helpful when necessary. The cool vibe broke one day during December—I can't remember which year—when a staff member offered me an ornament made of a book jacket cover, one she had made for their holiday party. I cherish it. I also have to thank the last of the old-fashioned microfilm readers, which was far superior to newer models for the type of research I was doing and which held out just long enough for me to finish.

Many thanks as well to the journalists at the *Detroit Free Press*, *Detroit News*, and *Michigan Chronicle*, whose work I read on microfilm. I have relied heavily on their reporting, and I remember feeling shaken when reading about *Free Press* columnist Leo Donovan's untimely death in 1957, and like a friend was moving away when *Free Press* staff writer Robert Perrin left the paper in 1955 to work for Senator Patrick McNamara in Washington.

Thanks to John Beck and Michigan State University's "Our Daily Lives/ Our Daily Bread" lecture series for hosting me twice and offering insightful feedback. Likewise, two appearances at the North American Labor History Conference in Detroit proved helpful, and I especially thank Liz Faue for helping to organize a crucial panel in the early stages of this project. I was honored to be the target of two hours of intense grilling in Chicago by members of the Newberry Library's Seminar in Labor History. It was exactly what a researcher hopes for, and it was the most fun I've had as a scholar.

Oakland University provided a fellowship to launch the project. Within the history department, Todd Estes, Cara Shelly, Keith Dye, and Bruce Zellers always checked in on how my research was going, and no matter what they thought privately, they always seemed to have faith that a book would come from it someday. Todd talked with me at length on many occasions about the project, always with sharp insight, and he alerted me to the Newberry Library opportunity. I appreciated the comments offered by colleagues at a "First Drafts" presentation hosted by my department. Graham Cassano, an accomplished sociologist who specializes in labor, offered particularly challenging feedback. He has also strongly supported this project, in part by producing a wonderful podcast about its oral history component that is available via the website for the journal *Critical Sociology*. The Saturday morning breakfast gathering at Afternoon Delight, in Ann Arbor, especially Bruce Zellers, Sue Zellers, and Beth Yakel, heard me go on and on about what I was finding in my research, and I appreciate their patience, insight, and support. Generations of Phi Alpha Theta History Honor Society members have followed my progress. Most of them understood that my dedication to them slowed down the book but that I also would not have had it any other way. They're celebrating with me.

Darren Clark tracked down all the missing article titles and dates in my mountain of newspaper research. Lesley Chapel helped me get back to basics when thinking through oral history methodology. Quinn Malecki gave the penultimate version of the manuscript a close reading and identified many glitches that had escaped my bleary eyes. Petra Flanagan located most of the rest and brought a needed nonhistorian's perspective to the work. She also believed in the project, and in me, from the start.

The publication process has its suspenseful moments. Laurie Matheson and James Engelhardt from the University of Illinois Press guided me through them, and I'm grateful for their constructive criticism and crucial support. I'm also thankful for copyeditor Jill R. Hughes, whose eagle eyes and rigor significantly improved the manuscript.

Disruption in Detroit

Introduction

How did autoworkers in the metropolitan Detroit region experience the 1950s? Historians have generally portrayed the 1950s as a decade of job stability and economic advancement for blue-collar auto employees, who entered the middle class as beneficiaries of generous contracts negotiated by the United Automobile Workers (UAW) during the heyday of the post–World War II boom. Yet despite all that has been written about the auto industry and the UAW, no research focuses in any sustained way on autoworkers themselves. Instead, most studies have focused on top-level union policies and officials, particularly Walter Reuther, the longtime president (1946–1970) of the UAW.[1] The lack of attention given to actual autoworkers inspired me to launch an oral history project to explore that subject. Although my research focus shifted over time, the goal of learning more about how ordinary autoworkers experienced the postwar years has remained central to this work.

At the risk of simplification, what follows is the composite view of autoworkers that can be gleaned from the existing literature. Most significantly, they made increasingly large amounts of money, as their real wages doubled between 1947 and 1960, mostly because of cost-of-living allowances (COLA) and the productivity-based annual improvement factor (AIF). They also enjoyed new fringe benefits such as pensions and company-paid health insurance.[2] Large numbers of new autoworkers, many of them white Southerners, entered the auto workforce during World War II and the early postwar years and cared little about the struggles during the 1930s to create the UAW. These recent migrants were concerned instead with gaining a foothold in the burgeoning postwar consumer society and were largely apathetic about their union.[3] On the other hand, these same workers offered strong support whenever the UAW launched official strikes, and many of them participated in unauthorized walkouts, called "wildcat strikes," rather than resolve disputes through cumbersome grievance procedures.[4] On occasion, ordinary workers even forced UAW leadership to authorize strikes that conflicted with top-level strategies.[5] It is also implicit in the literature that autoworkers would have rallied behind more radical approaches if top-level union leaders had not offered such a constrained, bureaucratic vision—wages, benefits, and grievance procedures—of what was possible. Indeed, much of the literature about postwar autoworkers contains counterfactual undercurrents, revealing understandable disappointment, decades later, with the way things turned out.[6] On the whole, however, it seems that male autoworkers, who were the vast majority, tended to care more about extra-plant activities, like hunting and bowling, or horseplay on the job than militant unionism.[7]

Another important part of the composite picture of postwar autoworkers is that much of the documented militancy, at least among white workers, was aimed at preventing equal opportunities for blacks in auto employment and housing.[8] The implication is that many white workers, if not most, were overt racists and that all were the beneficiaries of white privilege. In addition to facing persistent job discrimination at hiring offices, black workers were disproportionately affected by job losses from technological innovations and the decentralization of the industry away from Detroit. Over one hundred thousand manufacturing positions left Detroit during the 1950s, and machines came to perform many of the "meanest and dirtiest" jobs, historically reserved for blacks.[9] Although in principle more supportive of racial equality than the union's white membership, top UAW leadership tended to turn a blind eye toward racism in auto plants and within local unions. UAW officials claimed with some justification that they did not make hiring decisions and were therefore not responsible for discrimination at that level, but those same leaders put little pressure on automakers to change their ways and integrated their executive board only in response to pressure and shaming.[10] Most male autoworkers and top union leaders were also sexist, and women activists in the UAW fought hard for workplace equality throughout the postwar years.[11]

Although much of this literature appeared after my project began, we still know very little about actual autoworkers. My initial research goal, in the early 2000s, was to locate and interview ordinary workers, although I wasn't entirely sure what that meant other than that I was looking for people usually referred to as the "rank and file." I did not look for activists or union leaders, although I did interview several people who held local union offices of some sort, and I did not turn down an interview with anybody. My hope was to interview people who had been alluded to in, but largely left out of, the historical literature. This is a purpose particularly well suited for oral history, even though most such projects to that point had focused on union leaders or activists.[12] Finding people to interview was more difficult than it had been in my previous research on Southern cotton mill workers. Although there were potentially thousands of people who could have been fine candidates, they were not clustered in a particular village or neighborhood in metro Detroit where I could knock on doors and hope for the best. A possible entry point, it seemed, was UAW local union retiree luncheons, since most of the people who had been autoworkers in the late '40s and during the '50s were likely to be retired by 2000. An early break came when a running partner, who had been an engineer at the now closed Ford Motor Company plant in Ypsilanti, Michigan, took an interest in this research and got me in touch with the Local 849 retiree president, Bob Bowen. A student later directed me to Local 653 retiree chapter president Bonnie Melton at the Pontiac Motor plant in Pontiac, Michigan. Both Mr. Bowen and Ms. Melton understood immediately the potential importance of interviewing the retirees they led, and both offered crucial support at that stage of the project. Retiree luncheon recruitment efforts involved going table to table, briefly explaining to potential interviewees what I hoped to learn from them. Quite a few interviewees initially assumed that I wanted them to tell me about Walter Reuther or national-level union activities rather than their personal experiences. At first I naively expected that almost everyone at these gatherings would be eager to talk with me. Enough of them were interested that it turned out to be a worthwhile approach, but many more were too busy with their lives to schedule anything else, or perhaps they were skeptical about the sincerity of an academic in their midst. In any case, there was no hope of convincing anyone to be interviewed once the Bingo games and raffles began.

Eventually I conducted interviews with forty-two people, most of whom were born in the 1920s or early 1930s. Many were young adults in the late 1940s, and others reached adulthood in the early 1950s. Relatively few of them were born in metro Detroit. Most came from outside southeast Michigan—for example, from West Virginia, North Carolina, Alabama, Kentucky, Missouri, Arkansas, North Dakota, Minnesota, Illinois, Pennsylvania, Ontario, the Upper Peninsula of Michigan, or the western and northern parts of its Lower Peninsula. Of those who were born in the Detroit area, many had parents who were immigrants, often from Turkey, Poland, or Greece, in the early twentieth century. The majority of those I interviewed were white men, but a disproportionate number, compared with their presence in auto plants in the 1950s, were white women, likely because women generally outlived men and many of those women liked to socialize at retiree luncheons.

Three interviews were with African American men. Victims of race and sex prejudice, black women rarely worked in auto plants in the years I studied. I used a life history approach to interviewing and never asked people to be experts in anything other than their own experiences, including how they came to be autoworkers. Although I took many pages of questions with me into each interview, I hardly ever used them. Doing so would have unnecessarily impeded the flow of conversation, which I managed to do on my own often enough.

Many themes emerged from the interviews, but the most significant one was that job instability and economic insecurity dominated these workers' lives during the supposed postwar boom. Details and circumstances differed in each case, but the broad outlines of most stories were similar. Few of the people I talked with had even a foothold in what historian Lizabeth Cohen has called the "consumer's republic" of the postwar era.[13] Auto work had been unstable since its inception, but that was supposed to have changed during the post–World War II boom.[14] Based on my reading of the literature, I had fully expected to hear stories, at least from white retirees, about how autoworkers managed their newfound prosperity during the postwar boom. But a very different picture emerged through the interviews. Although most of these people *tried* to be autoworkers throughout the 1950s, layoffs were so frequent that in many cases they actually *were* autoworkers only about half the time. A partial list of the positions held by interviewees during auto layoffs during these years includes trailer home washer, cab driver, department store clerk, bank employee, telephone pole installer, promotional event searchlight operator, feed store worker, cyclone fence builder, moving company worker, University of Michigan Law Club janitor, junior high cafeteria worker, insurance repair construction worker, winery employee, trash hauler, chicken farmer, wallpaper hanger, army surplus store employee, barber, berry picker, golf caddy, and soldier. It was no longer apparent that these people consistently held jobs as autoworkers during the postwar boom, which called into question what we mean by the term "autoworker" when thinking about this era.

Despite its strengths as a route to learning about the lives of nonelites, however, oral history is not without complications as a research methodology. Oral historians have long recognized that interviews do not provide a direct window into the past. Instead they tend to tell us how people interpret their experiences at the particular points in their lives when interviews take place. Oral history interviews are a joint creation between interviewer and interviewee, and most of these conversations happen only because of the researcher's particular project. Many factors can influence the thoughts expressed in an interview. These include similarities and differences between interviewer and interviewee in race, sex, and age; the degree of familiarity between the participants; the interviewer's preparation and demeanor; the location and duration of the interview; balky technology; and distractions, from telephone calls to pets.[15] Oral history does not provide objective evidence about the past. However, historians understand that there is no such thing as an objective source that reveals incontestable truth. Almost all documents have some sort of bias in that they are generated for a particular purpose and for an intended audience, which is why historians analyze and interpret them. Historians engage all sources with curiosity, skepticism, and empathy, whether the sources are written documents in an archive or human beings in a living room, but those qualities, especially empathy, are particularly important in oral history. Whether based on written or oral sources, historians' interpretations in some cases would likely be inconceivable, or even objectionable, to those who created the documents or to those who offered the oral testimony.[16] Oral historians have come to see their methodology's subjectivity as a strength, as it allows scholars to analyze, as Alessandro Portelli explains, "not just what people did, but what they wanted to do, what they believed they were doing, and what they now think they did." Many "'wrong' statements," he notes, "are still psychologically 'true,'" and "this truth may be equally as important as factually reliable accounts."[17] So it is important to be aware of, even cautious about, the potential perils of collecting and using oral evidence, but the methodology can still be tremendously useful, and it has been for countless books and articles. Indeed, guidebooks on the practice of oral history analyze the strengths and weaknesses of the methodology while encouraging potential practitioners to get out in the field and conduct interviews.[18]

For this project, oral history helped immensely in revealing a dimension of autoworkers' lives that has been overwhelmed by the postwar boom narrative. The life history approach offered a particular strength. Rather than focusing directly on how interviewees remembered the 1950s, the conversations proceeded mostly chronologically, beginning with childhood. Job instability in the auto industry became apparent as we reached the period in each person's life when he or she attempted to obtain and maintain employment as an autoworker. The instability manifested itself differently in each case, and interviewees responded to it in their own ways. Most of the people interviewed did not know one another, so there was little chance that I was stumbling upon collective lore that had been hashed out and refined over the years. In addition, the theme of unstable auto employment in the early postwar era is not conventional wisdom in the region, or in the history profession, so interviewees were definitely not tapping into cultural mythology about the era.[19]

Nevertheless, I remained skeptical about the oral evidence precisely because these stories ran counter to what was held to be true about the postwar boom. Did these interview findings mean anything? Although it seemed significant that there were so many independent accounts of instability and insecurity, the number of autoworkers employed at any particular time in metro Detroit in the 1950s fluctuated between three hundred thousand and five hundred thousand. My sample, then, was very small, and it seemed possible that I had simply found a few outliers who had failed to take advantage of the period's abundance. How could I determine whether their experiences were representative or atypical? Most of those I interviewed had been young, in their twenties or thirties, during the 1950s. Obviously many 1950s autoworkers were much older than that. It was hardly clear, however, that conducting more interviews would resolve such questions. How many interviews would it take to achieve a representative sample? I wasn't even sure what "representative" would look like, especially since few if any of the older workers during the early postwar years were likely to be alive. Another disincentive for pursuing more interviews, as anyone who has practiced oral history knows, was the enormous amount of time necessary to transcribe the recordings. To address my skepticism about the interview evidence, I investigated Detroit newspapers from 1945 through the 1950s to see if they might corroborate or contradict the oral testimony. I read issues of the *Detroit Free Press* from 1945 to 1960; the *Detroit News* from 1953 to 1958, a range that includes the most and least prosperous years for the auto industry in the decade; and the *Michigan Chronicle*, an African American weekly based in Detroit, from 1949 to 1959.

The newspaper evidence overwhelmingly supported and enhanced what interviewees had recalled. Combining the voluminous newspaper accounts and the oral history evidence, it seemed clear that from the perspective of ordinary autoworkers, the period from 1945 to 1960 was anything but a postwar boom. The auto industry in no way provided stable employment and secure, rising incomes. Everybody knew it, from recent production-line hires to the presidents of General Motors, Ford, and the Chrysler Corporation. There were vast ebbs and flows in auto employment during the decade, along with persistent, unpredictable bursts of short-term unemployment. In only three periods during the 1950s—in 1950, 1953, and 1955—were there several consecutive months of sustained full employment. Most new autoworkers were hired during these brief upsurges, especially in 1953, and those were the employees most vulnerable to layoffs throughout the era. As top UAW officials often complained, these recent hires were an increasingly large proportion of all autoworkers. Many of them had been in diapers during the wave of sit-down strikes that launched the union in the mid-1930s and therefore had no direct experience with the pre-union era.[20] Among these young workers in the 1950s, however, were the retirees I interviewed decades later. It turns out that they were more typical than I imagined. In the end I abandoned hope of conducting a representative sample of interviews and took comfort in that what I had done was suggestive of the complexity that would undoubtedly emerge if somebody had the time and resources to conduct hundreds or thousands more. Of course it is now too late to embark on that mission. Still, newspaper research indicated that my relatively small interview sample was more valuable than the numbers might indicate.

Although much testimony from ordinary autoworkers appeared in the local newspapers, many of the articles pertaining to the auto industry explored subjects that had a bearing on employment without direct commentary from affected workers. Reporters relied on data published by *Ward's Automotive Reports* and by the R. L. Polk Company regarding car assemblies, sales to dealers, and consumer registrations. State agencies provided data about unemployment totals. Union and management spokespersons provided insight and numbers, often comparable and sometimes incompatible, concerning the causes and impact of local strikes and layoffs. If anything, a visiting journalist noted in 1956, the coverage of the auto industry in Detroit's daily newspapers "is so great and so consistently industry-oriented that disgruntled Detroiters sometimes call them 'the three trade papers.'"[21] That was truer for editorial positions than for newsroom coverage. Editorially, both the *Detroit Free Press* and the *Detroit News* believed that Walter Reuther and the UAW were leading Detroit and the nation toward a nightmarish socialist future. At the same time, both editorial boards were unabashed civic boosters, arguing that pessimists, especially those who emphasized the negative effects of automation and decentralization, were misreading clear evidence of future growth and prosperity for the city. Neither editorial board wanted there to be insecurity and instability in the auto industry. The *Michigan Chronicle* generally supported the UAW's larger mission while emphasizing the persistence of racial discrimination within the union, at company hiring gates, and in the larger community. The *Chronicle* did not cover labor events in anywhere near as much detail as the city's daily papers, but it provided insights on the experiences of working-class African Americans, from a black middle-class perspective, that were hard to find in the *Free Press* and the *News*.

However, if any type of source is assumed to be less objective than oral interviews, it might be newspapers. For most of the nation's history, newspapers offered no pretense of objectivity, and none was expected, although there were debates about that quality's desirability as early as the 1830s. For

many journalists and their editors, objectivity became a stated goal beginning in the 1930s, but there was uncertainty about what it meant to be an
objective reporter who filed objective news stories, especially with cultural
influences affecting reporters' sensibilities, the fact that most newspapers
were profit-seeking corporations, and the increased management of news
by government and private organizations. As one scholar put it, for most
journalists objectivity became their "supreme deity," although in practice
the principle remained "a vague point to strive for, like the North Star." In
many American newsrooms in the mid-twentieth century, objectivity meant
repeating what a source said, without analysis, no matter how far-fetched
the remarks, an approach that many journalists later felt had not served the
country well during the McCarthy era. As journalists in the 1960s inserted
their views more overtly into coverage of the civil rights movement and
the Vietnam War, they opened themselves up to renewed charges of bias,
that reporters were unprofessionally, perhaps unethically, taking sides in the
events they covered. Others applauded what they saw as a necessary injection
of moral judgment into the news. In the end, to many Americans the ideal
of objective news reporting no longer seemed definable, let alone attainable,
even though the principle remained a staple of journalistic training. How
much stock, then, should any historian place in newspapers as sources? More
importantly for this project, how reliable are the local Detroit newspapers as
sources?[22]

Newspaper articles have to be treated as any other source, with a combination of curiosity and skepticism, and with an eye toward how they might,
or might not, contribute to answering the historical question driving the
research. For this project, Detroit newspapers indeed helped contextualize
oral interview evidence. The interviews did much to reveal how individuals experienced this era, but they did not provide much understanding of
why the auto industry was so unstable and why layoffs were so frequent.
Newspaper reporters in Detroit asked those questions and provided what in
most cases struck me as plausible explanations, such as materials shortages,
parts shortages, automation, strikes, extreme weather, lack of natural gas,
decentralization, and overproduction of automobiles. They attempted to do
what James Fallows has called "the essence of real journalism, which is the
search for information of use to the public." Detroit journalists engaged in
interpretive and investigative reporting beyond the transcription of official
pronouncements. Indeed, regular beat writers assigned to automakers or
to the UAW often did little to conceal their skepticism and sarcasm when
writing about official news releases.[23] As discussed above, historians expect
sources to be subjective. Yet a lack of objectivity can also involve what is not

reported, even what is not thought of to cover, as much as the manner in which information is conveyed. For example, the daily newspapers, the *Free Press* and the *News*, had huge blind spots regarding race, but the *Michigan Chronicle*, the works of other historians, and interviews helped to compensate for such oversight.[24]

As sources, the local newspapers are hardly perfect, but if historians had to rely only on perfect sources, there would be no works of history.[25] In the case of Detroit newspapers, journalists reported extensively on the auto industry, which was obviously of great importance to their readers. As a national reporter put it at the time, "The fall of a government in France, or a riot in Cyprus, must take a back seat in the Detroit papers if it occurs on the same day that one of the automobile companies issues a press release outlining innovations in next year's model."[26] The daily papers were also fierce competitors. If one of them had misrepresented auto production or unemployment figures, the other would have been sure to criticize them. As it turns out, although instability and insecurity dominated the local newspapers' coverage of the auto industry, the extent of the volatility was most likely underreported, because there was no official recording of short work weeks or underemployment. Being on the job for as little as one hour per week put one in the "employed" column for statistical purposes, and it could take a lot of investigating to determine which plants, out of dozens, or which departments, out of thousands, were operating less than forty-hour weeks. Perhaps the biggest reason for taking these newspapers seriously is that reporting about instability in the auto industry was constant, even though no one, including editors, automakers, business leaders, union leaders, union members, neighborhood shop owners, local and state politicians, or even the civil servants who measured unemployment, wanted that to be true. These constituencies disagreed, often heatedly, about who or what was to blame for unemployment, as well as about what, if anything, should be done. But the fact of chronic layoffs is most important for this project, and on that they all agreed.

Other sources confirm the general pattern of instability and insecurity. Throughout the 1950s the business publication *Fortune* reported on the volatility of the auto industry. The magazine's main focus was not on autoworkers, but it would have been impossible to read the magazine during this era and believe the auto industry was experiencing uncomplicated stability and prosperity.[27] *Ford Facts*, the publication of UAW Local 600 at Ford's massive River Rouge plant, approached the issue from a completely different perspective but reached much the same conclusion. Amid coverage of bowling results and the long-standing feud between UAW president Walter Reuther and Local 600 president Carl Stellato, articles in *Ford Facts* addressed the equally chronic issue of employment instability at the Rouge complex.[28] If one looks carefully, the business history literature on the auto industry also emphasizes instability in this era. As with *Fortune*, the focus is not on autoworkers, but these books highlight the automakers' challenges, particularly shortages of parts and materials in the late 1940s, metals rationing in the early 1950s because of the Korean War, the 1954 recession, the decline of the independent automakers (Hudson Motor Car Company, Nash Motors Company, Packard Motor Car Company, Studebaker Automobile Company, and the Kaiser-Frazer Corporation), unattractive designs (especially by Chrysler), and doldrums in the mid- to late 1950s, culminating in the 1958 recession.[29] Instability for automakers, of course, made life insecure for autoworkers. These sources do not contain well-developed analyses of the industry's volatility, however, which underscores the value of oral history interviews and newspaper evidence.

The labor history literature on autoworkers and the UAW also hints at problems with instability and insecurity. Nelson Lichtenstein wrote that the doubling of real wages between 1947 and 1960 "was not quite enough for an urban family of four to achieve a 'moderate' standard of living, as defined by the Bureau of Labor Statistics (a five-room house, maintenance of a four-year-old Chevy, no savings), but it represented real progress for the generation of autoworkers who had come of age when Depression memories were still fresh." In addition, he argued, "The good pay was not matched by employment security: after 1948 big layoffs and plant closings were a regular feature of automobile employment." Along with a mention of a "brief recession" at the end of the Korean War and the number of years of seniority needed to keep one's job in 1958, that is the extent to which he explored this theme. John Barnard offered a similar qualification of his argument that the UAW successfully "secured wages and living standards against the hazards of a historically volatile industry." "Even in the generally prosperous 1950s," he wrote, "prolonged layoffs during model changes and periodic declines in demand were not uncommon. . . . Despite the industry's general prosperity and an overall increase in auto employment, which peaked in 1955, periodic unemployment and its consequences were still threats to auto workers. The industry still swung back and forth between peaks and valleys of production, creating an underlying anxiety within the workforce." His discussion ends, however, with that provocative statement, and such hints about a possible counternarrative have been largely overwhelmed by assertions of prosperity and security.[30]

Indeed, in a number of recent works that address this period, the postwar boom for industrial workers, especially autoworkers, is a given, and scholarly debates tend to be about why it happened, why it ended, and whether or not there can ever be another such golden age for ordinary workers. In his economic history of the United States since the Civil War, Robert Gordon refers to increasing annual automobile production from 1941 to 1955 as if it had been a linear, upward progression, one that continued into the future, when in fact there were wild fluctuations in yearly car assemblies. As for autoworkers, Gordon claims that they "eagerly bought" the "ubiquitous Chevrolet" and that, in their "transition to solid middle-class status," they were able to purchase a "suburban subdivision house with at least one car, and often two."[31] Marc Levinson also takes the postwar boom for the working class as established fact in his exploration of the global decline of prosperity since the 1970s. In wealthy countries from 1945 to 1973, he writes, "employment, wages, factory production, business investment, total output: almost every measure of vitality increased year after year, at a rapid rate, with only brief interruptions." During the postwar boom, he argues, "jobs were a birthright and prosperity a constant," as "unemployment, ubiquitous in 1950, had all but vanished in the wealthy economies by 1960." Jobs were so abundant in U.S. industrial centers, he insists, that hundreds of thousands of African American sharecroppers in the South, displaced by mechanized cotton pickers, moved north and were "absorbed almost effortlessly by factories in Detroit and Chicago." American workers, Levinson insists, "could feel their lives changing, their circumstances improving, from one day to the next."[32] Jefferson Cowie offers a similar assessment in his analysis of twentieth-century U.S. politics. In the auto industry, he writes, negotiations in 1950 "resulted in the security of a five-year contract with cost of living adjustments, health benefits, unemployment, pensions, and vacations." Overall, he argues, the post–World War II boom "was an extraordinarily good time to be a worker . . . not simply because wages were going up to unprecedented levels and inequality was going down but because the future was bright, work paid off, and there was tremendous promise for the next generation."[33]

If one focuses on aggregate statistics regarding overall performance of the auto industry in the early postwar era, especially on corporate profits and on the difference between wage and benefit packages in, say, 1950 and those in 1960, it can be argued that the auto industry boomed and that autoworkers experienced a steadily rising standard of living. The problem is that people who worked in auto plants did not live their lives as aggregate statistics or in hindsight. It would have been of little consolation to autoworkers when laid off in 1949—or during the Korean War, or in 1954, 1956, 1958, and various other times—that Labor Department statistics comparing 1960 with 1950 would look good at some point in the future. People moved in and out of auto work throughout the decade, usually with little control over the timing. Factors such as parts and materials shortages, deep recessions, low seniority, overproduction of automobiles, the weather, and military service made auto work an uncertain prospect. So did authorized and unauthorized strikes in auto factories, strikes in other industries, and even plant explosions, all in addition to automation and decentralization. Perhaps one of the biggest reasons for widespread auto layoffs in the 1950s is that few autoworkers, the elite of blue-collar employees in the country, could afford to buy the new cars they manufactured, a marker of middle-class status. Obviously, then, neither could lesser-paid members of the working class. As one autoworker journalist declared, "The corporations must be made to understand that in order for workers to buy their products they must have incomes—not meager incomes on which they can barely exist but sufficient to give them purchasing power."[34] According to aggregate economic data, and undoubtedly for many Americans, the postwar boom was real and lucrative. For Detroit autoworkers, however, the boom remained elusive, even though their alleged prosperity has lived on in historical literature.

This book challenges only a part, albeit a significant one, of the composite picture of postwar autoworkers sketched above. Left intact is the sense that many workers felt little or no allegiance to the UAW in the 1950s, although this obviously changed over time, since so many interviewees continued to attend UAW retiree luncheons. There were also plenty of unauthorized wildcat strikes. There were certainly racist white workers and racist hiring practices, and nothing in this book challenges the reality that many thousands of black workers lost their jobs because of discrimination, low seniority, automation, and decentralization. Far fewer women worked for auto companies in the late 1940s and 1950s than had during World War II, and those with auto jobs often experienced harassment from male coworkers. Beyond work, lots of autoworkers indeed loved to go deer hunting and fishing. All of this, however, took place in a context of persistent instability and insecurity.

Some clarifications at the outset are in order. Unless otherwise specified, the term "Detroit" refers to the metropolitan Detroit region, specifically Wayne County and parts of neighboring Macomb and Oakland counties to the north. That was the main designation used by the Michigan Employment Security Commission (MESC) and its predecessor, the Michigan Unemployment Compensation Commission (MUCC), for calculating unemployment statistics, in part because it allowed inclusion of huge plants like the Ford

Rouge, officially in neighboring Dearborn; the Dodge Main plant, in Hamtramck, completely surrounded by Detroit; and Pontiac Motor, in Pontiac, about twenty miles northwest of the city. Moreover, although automakers and suppliers built numerous plants in newer Detroit suburbs during this period, workers at those facilities experienced instability and insecurity as well. Prospects were worse for African American Detroiters left behind by decentralization, but conditions were far from stable and prosperous for those who managed to gain employment in these new outlying factories.

Although this book cites them frequently, the MESC's (and MUCC's) unemployment totals were approximations at best. They were reached through a combination of assessing unemployment claims and surveying a few dozen employers, usually monthly, and a much larger list of employers on a quarterly basis. Those figures were used to make best-guess estimates, even though the totals were conveyed as objective truth. Nevertheless, the unemployment numbers mean something even if they are not precisely what experts claimed they were. They are useful for comparative purposes and for establishing general trends. In large part the MESC figures had to be estimates, because it was impossible to know how many autoworkers were employed at any time. There were so many auto-related workplaces, each with fluctuating employment totals, often on a daily or weekly basis, that any number would have been immediately outdated. Moreover, as noted earlier, one was considered to be officially "employed" if assigned as little as one hour per week on the job. Underemployment was a chronic problem, as acute at Big Three (GM, Ford, Chrysler) automotive company facilities as at smaller parts suppliers, yet it was one that remained invisible in official statistical analyses.[35]

Just as it was impossible to calculate the total number of employed or unemployed autoworkers, it was difficult to determine how much autoworkers earned. Wage rates, of course, were set by contract, but historians have been guilty, as economists were in the 1950s, of assuming that annual earnings could be calculated closely enough by multiplying the hourly wage by a forty-hour week and about fifty weeks a year. In reality, layoffs were so common in the auto industry that it was misleading to assume any correlation between hourly earnings and monthly or annual incomes. Hourly wage rates meant nothing to people who were out of work.

It is also worthwhile to note that throughout most of the era under consideration, Chrysler was Detroit's largest employer and most directly affected the local economy, followed closely by Ford. Both of those companies usually had somewhere between 70,000 and 130,000 local employees, depending on the particular moment (peak employment for both was during 1955). In contrast, General Motors had a relatively small blue-collar presence (30,000–40,000) in Detroit throughout most of the 1950s. By the last years of the decade, however, GM's expanded production at its Willow Run facility, west of Detroit, along with reductions in Chrysler and Ford employment in southeast Michigan, meant that each of the Big Three had somewhere around 70,000 area residents on their payrolls, whether or not those workers received regular paychecks. In addition, until their demise or consolidation in the mid-1950s, the independent automakers Hudson, Packard, and Kaiser-Frazer, with their suppliers, employed far more Detroiters—at times over twice as many—than did GM.

This book is organized chronologically, in large part because of lessons learned about living in real time from interviewees. It would be difficult to understand the full impact of employment instability and insecurity during these years if the various causal factors were analyzed in isolation. For example, it mattered to workers that unemployment caused by a parts supplier strike came on the heels of a coal strike that indirectly shut down their plant, or that a three-week bout of unemployment because of cold weather came after numerous layoffs resulting from steel shortages, or that the thousands of layoffs caused by an explosion at a transmission plant came at a time when automakers were already cutting back production due to lack of sales. Context and contingency, which are important for understanding the past, would be hard to grasp if the argument were structured topically. Since this book is ultimately about instability and insecurity in the auto industry and how workers coped, it makes sense to try to view events as workers experienced them. This approach also consistently reinforces the book's thesis. When workers and journalists remark, as they often did, about how the industry was wracked by chronic employment problems, it rings true; these are not just sour-grapes comments of peculiarly disgruntled commentators.

Although by most accounts the postwar boom ended sometime in the 1970s, this book concludes in 1960. In large part this is because the oral history interviews, the original core of my research, focused on the 1950s and ultimately set the parameters for the manuscript. By the time I discovered the recurrent theme of instability and insecurity in the interviews and then followed up with the newspaper research, it was far too late to go back and try to extend the project's chronological scope. If I were to cover the rest of the so-called postwar boom, it would mean essentially starting from scratch, with a new set of interviewees, on a project of size and scope comparable with this one. The period from 1945 to 1960 is important enough to study in its own right, however, because in the reigning narrative those years marked the heyday of the UAW, when lucrative contracts allowed autoworkers to enter the middle class and enjoy their high wages and benefits. That narrative, it turns out, is deeply flawed. Fine-grained research on the 1960s and 1970s has yet to be done, but if nothing else, this book challenges the existence of a postwar boom for autoworkers. If the boom began in the 1960s, it could hardly have been a *postwar* boom unless it had a very long fuse, and it could not have lasted very long given the oil crises and increased foreign competition in the 1970s.

As mentioned above, quite a few interviewees assumed that I wanted them to tell me about Walter Reuther and top-level UAW policy. Often they apologized in advance for not being the best informed on such topics. It was evident that many of them had never considered themselves to have been historical figures or to have anything substantial to add to our historical understanding. Of course they had much to offer, and this book is rooted in that vantage point. Therefore, it is not a history of the UAW or of top union leadership. UAW officials, especially Walter Reuther, appear throughout, and UAW policies certainly have a place in the argument. But despite contractual gains, the UAW was unable to tame the volatile auto industry, and because employment was so unsteady, wage and benefit improvements proved elusive for workers. There is nothing wrong with exploring the perspectives of top-level UAW officials. Indeed, such research has been essential to the development of labor history. But this project shows that we can't fully understand what happened in this period, and that our sense of things can actually be distorted, without sustained attentiveness to the experiences of ordinary autoworkers.

It is ironic that while I thought the newspaper research might provide a contextual framework for the oral history interviews, the oral evidence, although interwoven throughout, now complements a newspaper-driven narrative. When using interview material, I have taken some liberties with the order in which words were spoken, often consolidating thoughts expressed on a subject into a single quotation. I have eliminated many false starts to sentences and a lot of filler words—"um," "uh," "whatnot," "and such," "you know"—but I have been as faithful as possible to the meaning of what each person said. I have also represented the speech patterns, syntax, and grammar of each individual as carefully as I could while making some editing choices for clarity and readability. I have chosen not to try to convey slang. Even if the word sounded like "wanna," "gonna," or "drivin,'" I wrote "want to," "going to," or "driving." After I had figured out how I wanted to convey the oral evidence, I found that Alessandro Portelli had already explained my approach far better than I ever could.[36]

1 Shortages and Strikes, 1945–1948

Although Detroit had earned the nickname "The Arsenal of Democracy" for its contributions to the Allied victory in World War II, employment in its war factories had peaked in late 1943 and the postwar era brought employment instability. Shortages of crucial materials such as coal, iron, steel, copper, aluminum, and glass made auto production, hence employment, sporadic. Those shortages were compounded, and often caused, by strikes in major industries. Both authorized strikes and unauthorized wildcat walkouts in parts and assembly plants in the auto industry contributed to ongoing instability. Cold weather, hot weather, and federal credit regulations played roles as well. As a result, autoworkers experienced persistent layoffs. Although auto companies managed to earn profits during the early postwar years, production totals were nowhere near what they had anticipated. In late 1948 no one in the industry thought that the postwar boom had arrived.

* * *

With the end of the war in Europe and successful, if brutal and bloody, campaigns against Japan in the Pacific, there were reasons to be hopeful about a quick transition in Detroit from wartime production to civilian car and truck manufacturing. By mid-August 1945 the federal War Production Board eliminated production quotas, and automakers predicted that they would soon reach an annual assembly rate of five million vehicles. Government sources estimated that enough steel could be diverted from military to civilian use in the remainder of the year to launch a postwar boom, including half a million passenger cars, as well as millions of toasters, electric irons, refrigerators, and washing machines.[1] Yet there were also reasons for concern. Manufacturing workers faced layoffs while factories retooled. Veterans were returning in increasing numbers and needed jobs. Moreover, although city leaders had long predicted a mass exodus when peace came, few of the hundreds of thousands of people who migrated to Detroit for wartime jobs appeared to be leaving. Instead, would-be autoworkers streamed to Detroit even after Japan surrendered.[2]

Women workers were affected disproportionately by postwar changes. Over 250,000 women had worked in Detroit's factories in November 1943, the peak month during the war, but more than 50,000 of them had been let go by September 1945. A year later only 67,000 women remained in auto plants. Most women who took wartime defense jobs had once been waitresses, sales clerks, domestic workers, and such, and they expected to continue working after the war. A survey conducted in Detroit auto plants near the end of the war by the Women's Bureau of the U.S. Department of Labor shows that 75 percent of women workers wanted to hold industrial jobs in peacetime, and that 85 percent of them absolutely had to find jobs to support families.[3] Ford's Highland Park plant, however, provided an example of harsh postwar realities. In late 1944 nearly 6,000 women were employed there, the peak total at that factory, but in November 1945 fewer than 300 remained, and laid-off women picketed the plant, claiming that since the war had ended, 2,200 men with no seniority had been hired while over 5,000 women with seniority remained unemployed. Highland Park Local 400 president John G. Carney defended the protesting women against plant managers, who argued that postwar tractor production was too arduous for women, apparently unlike the tractor jobs they had competently performed at Ford's Rouge plant during the war.[4]

Individual women experienced the transition in a variety of ways. Margaret Beaudry had worked on water pumps during the war at Pontiac Truck and Coach, known to locals as "Yellow Cab," and had wanted to keep her position. "But I also knew that when the war was ended, we might not get a job," she recalled, "because the men that were over there, they had to come back to their jobs." She left Yellow Cab on her own, however, to join her husband, Marvin, who was still serving in the military near Spokane, Washington. There Margaret worked in an egg factory, separating whites from yolks. It did not pay as well as Yellow Cab, she noted, "but it was *easy*." When Marvin was discharged, he and Margaret returned to Michigan's Upper Peninsula, where both had been raised and where he hoped to make a living painting houses. Margaret stayed home with their baby, wishing she could "have gone out to work," she remembered, "but jobs weren't that easy to get up there." Katie Neumann had hired in at a Fisher Body Corporation factory shortly before the war ended and was laid off two months later. Her husband had a position at the Dodge Main plant but was out of work frequently as factories converted to civilian production. Katie was eager for paid employment, because they had purchased a house during the war and did not want to lose it. "Our payments were forty dollars a month," she recalled, "and it was even hard to make that." During her layoff from Fisher Body she managed to get a job in the Pontiac Motor foundry, which tended to hire only black men and white women. Dorothy Sackle, however, found only temporary jobs for several years after having been laid off from a Plymouth plant at war's end.[5]

Even if one avoided reconversion layoffs, employment was often erratic because of strikes at plants that supplied parts to the auto industry. Every auto company relied on extensive supply networks for the thousands of parts, large and small, that went into a car. Parts manufacturers, in turn, required supplies of raw materials, such as coal, iron, steel, copper, aluminum, and glass. Disruptions at any stage of these complicated supply chains could stall assembly operations and ultimately result in significant unemployment. For example, Ford production at its flagship Rouge plant was jeopardized in late August when forty-five hundred workers went on strike at the Kelsey-Hayes Company, which supplied wheels and brake drums. The Kelsey-Hayes dispute stemmed from what the local union considered to be unfair firings of workers who had forced a foreman out of the plant in April. Although the National War Labor Board (NWLB) had ruled in favor of the company, Kelsey-Hayes workers stood their ground on the picket line, inadvertently shutting down the Rouge, and by mid-September, fifty thousand Ford workers, forty thousand of them in metro Detroit, were laid off. Henry Ford II complained that because of the Kelsey-Hayes conflict his company had produced fewer cars in a month than he expected to roll off assembly lines every three hours. No matter how one felt about the strike, it had resulted in tens of thousands of layoffs. As soon as this conflict ended, a nationwide coal walkout threatened all stages of manufacturing. Every auto manufacturer was affected by these dynamics, which constantly prevented full production, hence full employment. In early November total postwar auto production had reached only 19,136, a meager start toward the 500,000 vehicles the industry hoped to build by the end of the year.[6]

By mid-November, however, optimism had returned. Business leaders announced that reconversion to civilian production was nearly finished and that expansion of production, as quickly as possible, was now realistic and necessary to remain competitive. These hopes were quickly dashed by a glassworkers' strike. In addition, a walkout of lumber mill workers in the Pacific Northwest meant that wood separators, essential for car batteries, were in short supply.[7] Facing the impact of steep postwar inflation, General Motors workers also struck, on November 21, demanding a 30 percent raise, no increase in car prices, and a requirement that the company grant the UAW access to its financial records if it claimed that meeting these demands was impossible. Since GM was a major parts supplier for both Ford and Chrysler—indeed, GM was the largest parts supplier for the entire industry—its strike was yet another reason why all auto production was jeopardized. In addition to these threats, Ford endured strikes from fifteen other suppliers, which meant layoffs for forty thousand workers, most of them in Detroit. Henry Ford II conceded in mid-December that his company's production would fall fifty thousand vehicles short of the eighty thousand he had predicted would be built by the end of the year. He emphasized that there had not been "a single unauthorized work stoppage" in his company's plants since the war ended. Nevertheless, he lamented, "Ford Motor Co. production is limping, instead of galloping along, because of insufficient supplies—parts and materials."[8] All Detroit automakers confronted versions of this crisis. Ford's low production and enormous layoffs coincided with the GM strike. Nationwide, over two hundred thousand GM workers were off the job in late November, around thirty thousand of them in Detroit and another sixteen thousand in nearby Pontiac, Michigan. As it turned out, however, GM's production would have virtually stopped in early December regardless of the UAW strike because of the unresolved conflict in the glass industry. Chrysler was also operating at greatly reduced rates. "If we had been in full production of new cars, the glass shortage would have stopped us," conceded a Chrysler spokesman.[9]

Heading into 1946 the postwar boom in autos had failed to arrive, employment remained unstable, and autoworkers scrambled to get by. Pent-up demand for cars still existed, experts maintained, and the reconversion process inside factories had been largely completed, but the auto production process was so complex, with so many potential points of disruption, that it proved impossible for the industry to gain traction. As a result, autoworkers lived precariously. Striking GM workers faced especially difficult circumstances. The Michigan Unemployment Compensation Commission cut off a potential source of relief by ruling that no one on strike, or who was laid off because of it, was eligible for unemployment benefits. Since there was no UAW strike fund, GM workers were largely on their own. War bond redemption rates were well above national averages wherever GM workers lived. Early in the strike many autoworkers went deer hunting, more seriously than usual, for food. By mid-January 1946, however, most GM strikers had exhausted their savings and cashed in all of their bonds.[10] They displayed mixed emotions about the conflict. Most understood that their wages had not kept pace with inflation and believed that a raise was necessary. As one local union officer at a Detroit Chevrolet plant explained, "The take-home pay during the war was only 40 or 45 bucks a week. After the war it was about 35. How can you get ahead on pay like that?" World War II veteran Stanley Stasik, thirty, insisted that the union's demands were justified but admitted that he thought differently while overseas. Enthusiasm for the postwar cause was clearly tempered by financial hardships. Most strikers had started out with enough in reserve to hold out, at most, about two or three weeks, not two or three months. "I was just talking to a fellow on the picket line," said Albert Winters, forty-three, in January 1946. "His wife is going to have a child. He's behind in his rent. There's sickness in his family." "We've had to tighten our belts—tighten 'em a lot," John Geiger, twenty-six, added. "I don't know how some exist." Winnie Rowland, thirty-two, reported that of the Detroit Cadillac plant's 350 remaining women workers, "almost all of them have exhausted their funds."[11] After twenty-three months overseas, World War II veteran F. L. Wolff expressed bitterness that after returning to Detroit and landing an auto job, "I worked two weeks and three days and was laid off when the GM strike was called." Moreover, by taking that position he had become ineligible for twenty-dollar-a-week federal benefits available to returning soldiers. Wolff struggled to support himself, his wife, and their two children on his one-time-only mustering-out pay of two hundred dollars for his military service and about sixty dollars he had been able to earn as a part-time janitor.[12] Aware of situations like Wolff's, Bud Weber held off on reclaiming his job at Pontiac Motor, preserving his eligibility for military benefits after he returned from service during the GM strike. He was married and had a child on the way, though, so he would have preferred a steady job.[13] Gene Johnson had served in the U.S. Army during World War II and had returned to Pontiac Motor in 1945, but in early 1946 he reenlisted in the military to support his wife and child rather than remain on strike.[14] The GM conflict, like all layoffs, forced workers to tap into emergency reserves, if they had them, or to find some other way to survive.

Continued materials shortages ensured that Detroit unemployment was widespread and long-lasting, regardless of the GM strike. The glassworkers' conflict was not resolved until well into January, and alternative sources could not meet demand.[15] Yet even if glass supplies had been ample and secure, a steelworkers' strike, which began on January 21, prevented almost all auto production in Detroit. No matter how much metal an automaker had stockpiled, car assemblies depended on whether or not every other manufacturer in each of its supply chains had enough steel and in the right varieties, of which there were dozens. Most companies had only about three to five days' worth on hand. Ford, which made more of its own steel than its competitors, immediately laid off fifteen thousand employees when the strike began. Unable to get crankshafts and connector rod bearings from its steel-strapped suppliers, automaker Packard issued layoff notices to eight thousand workers.[16] General Motors, of course, was already shut down because of its own strike, but it would not have been able to manufacture vehicles even if it settled with the UAW. Indeed, it appeared that GM had no incentive to reach an agreement, because it would not be able to produce anything either way and it was not responsible for paying unemployment benefits as long as the strike lasted.[17]

Chrysler and Ford workers were heavily affected, although in different ways, during this unstable period. Because Chrysler had stopped production due to the glass shortage, the company had small supplies of steel on hand. When glassworkers returned to their jobs, Chrysler seized the opportunity and recalled nine thousand workers to duty in early February. "We will be able to operate a little while," announced a company spokesperson. "Just how long we can't tell." Meanwhile, Ford produced virtually nothing. Vice President of Manufacturing M. L. Bricker explained that parts shortages stymied any auto assembly plans. One holdup was the lack of upholstery tacks, a casualty of the steel strike. This was "one of many" instances, Bricker complained, "but it shows how failure far down the line can accumulate until it reaches the point where production stops." Whenever the steel strike ended, he predicted, it would take at least three more weeks for parts supplies to reach assembly plants in numbers large enough to resume vehicle production. He was correct. U.S. Steel settled with the United Steelworkers in early February, and three weeks later some thirty-eight thousand Ford workers who had been laid off for more than a month were set to return.[18]

When the GM strike appeared to be over in mid-March 1946, it was possible again to envision some sort of postwar boom, albeit a much smaller one than industry analysts had once anticipated. "The automobile industry is ready to move forward," declared *Free Press* auto beat writer Leo Donovan, while reporting a huge downward revision of the industry's 1946 production goal from six million to three million vehicles. The slow resumption of operations at GM plants underscored the need for cautious optimism. After 113 days the UAW and GM reached an agreement that was ratified by an overwhelming majority of strikers. UAW local unions, however, had the right to remain off the job until issues pertaining to their specific plants were resolved, and workers in twenty-two GM facilities, many of them crucial to supply chains, stayed on strike. Consequently, most GM workers remained idle for at least two weeks beyond the national strike settlement, and many stayed out much longer.[19]

Contentious issues at the local level continued to cause widespread lay-offs at many auto companies. In early April 1946, for example, second-shift trailer drivers at a Briggs Manufacturing Company plant refused to work after management replaced one of their fellow workers, a World War II vet-eran who had served four years overseas, with someone the union members called "incompetent." The trailer drivers stopped working, which meant that no auto bodies left the Briggs factory for Chrysler assembly lines at the automaker's Kercheval and Plymouth plants. With auto bodies piling up, production halted at Briggs, and without those parts the affected Chrys-ler facilities stopped their lines. The result was twelve thousand laid off at Briggs and five thousand more at Chrysler. Almost any group of workers had the ability to bring supply, production, and assembly chains to a halt in such ways—even if they did not intend to do so before taking action—and exercising such power often seemed to make sense when frustrations were high. It was a tough reality, though, that many thousands of fellow workers laid off by such walkouts might not appreciate the missed time, especially if they were far removed from the problem's source. This particular layoff lasted only a couple of days, but it was another interruption with lost pay for a significant number of Detroit autoworkers.[20]

Such unauthorized wildcat strikes affected job stability for many Detroi-ters. Sometimes the issues seemed baffling to outsiders, but they were almost always of great importance to those directly involved. For example, in March 1946 at a Chrysler plant, 40 employees on the framing line refused to work because their seats had been removed. The seats had not been there long, and they were not really seats; they were boxes that had been lying around the plant until workers who appreciated the comfort chose to sit on them. When a cleanup crew removed the boxes, the framing line workers refused to do their jobs, and soon all 2,000 employees in the plant were sent home. Although it is impossible to know how the other 1,960 laid-off workers felt about this matter, they missed work and lost pay at a time when employment was already uncertain. A few weeks later, 80 metal finishers quit in the middle of a shift, forcing the layoff of 4,400 workers at the closely connected Chrysler Kercheval and Jefferson Avenue plants. Management claimed that one worker had been disciplined for loafing and that others had supported his laziness. In contrast, UAW Local 7 president Tom Cunningham argued that the workers walked out because of inadequate ventilation in their department. In another thorny dispute, 850 workers at the Briggs Mack truck plant went on strike in early May to protest what they called "excessive production standards." As a result, 6,500 employees at Mack and another 2,500 at the Chrysler Plymouth Division, which relied on auto bodies from Mack, were also sent home. Briggs

Local 212 officers complained of "two months of indignities and Hitler-type methods" at the hands of management. Company officials claimed they were only enforcing production standards that had been agreed upon in recent contract negotiations. Whatever the truth in these conflicts, production was easily disrupted, and in each case thousands of autoworkers missed time on the job.[21]

While UAW local unions tussled with management, persistent shortages and strikes continued to affect employment and production. Ford had all of its eighty-nine thousand employees on the job for only one week in April 1946. "Shortages run from motor blocks to nails," a Ford spokesman grumbled. "A total of 36 parts supplier plants are out on strike." And just as Ford resumed operations, a national coal miners' strike threatened auto production. The impact of that walkout on auto work depended on dwindling stockpiles of coal at each auto-related factory and, perhaps more importantly, at steel mills, which had to cut operations. Among the most pressing needs for automakers were simple yet vital items such as screws, nuts, bolts, and washers. Packard assembled automobiles only nine days during the first three months of 1946 because of a lack of bearings.[22]

The coal strike ensured that stability would not arrive anytime soon. Ford shut down operations by the second week of May, idling nearly 100,000 workers in the Detroit area. Chrysler was able to run a few extra days. GM had more coal on hand, because none was used during its long strike, but parts shortages made that stockpile irrelevant. The federal government set priorities for scarce coal supplies, and auto manufacturing was not high on that list. In 1946 the vast majority of the nation's freight moved on trains, which were powered by coal. Trains, then, received supplies but not to haul auto parts. Officials gave top consideration to public health and safety, so hospitals were a top priority. Electrical plants also received coal before auto factories. Even if auto plants had been deemed essential, a ban on Great Lakes shipping, to conserve coal, meant there would be no iron ore heading from the Mesabi Range on the western shore of Lake Superior to steel mills in Pennsylvania, Ohio, Michigan, Indiana, and Illinois. These limiting factors made life difficult and insecure for Detroit autoworkers. Over 120,000 Chrysler, Ford, and GM employees were laid off because of the coal, steel, and parts shortages. Thousands more at Briggs and other suppliers were also out of work. Fresh off their long strike, most GM workers had long since exhausted their financial reserves. Ford encouraged its workers to consider this layoff to be their annual vacation so that it might be possible to have uninterrupted production when conditions permitted. Chrysler pretended to be comparatively healthy, claiming that only 10,000 of its 70,000 Detroit employees were laid off before dropping the pretense and closing its facilities.[23]

It is hard to imagine how so many workers and their dependents made it through this period. Unemployment compensation was helpful, at twenty dollars a week plus two dollars a week per child for up to four children. "I stood in that unemployment line a lot of times," Bud Weber recalled of the early postwar era. "They'd just lay you off." But those who had started work within the past year or who had interrupted job histories, which included many in the auto industry, were ineligible for these benefits. Quite a few laid-off autoworkers traveled to stay with relatives, often in West Virginia, Kentucky, Arkansas, or northern Michigan, who had either never migrated to Detroit or who had returned home after giving it a try. Most who were out of work looked for whatever odd jobs they could find, a task made more difficult by the large numbers of people in the same circumstances. Corner grocery stores extended credit when possible, medical bills went unpaid, and rent, mortgage payments, and utility bills piled up.[24]

The lofty production goals that had been announced when Japan surrendered seemed wildly optimistic in mid-1946. Industry experts had anticipated the production of six million passenger cars in the twelve months following Japan's surrender, but after eight months the total remained below four hundred thousand. Kaiser-Frazer, a new auto company that many thought would help boost the industry's total to record heights, had produced only sixteen prototype vehicles by May 1946. There was more bad news for the auto industry in early June, when 70 percent of domestic copper production was held up by strikes. Cars required large amounts of copper, for radiators as well as electrical wiring. There were no substitutes, and plenty of other industries coveted the now scarce metal. As a result, auto production fell even further behind shrinking expectations. It was especially galling since industry observers maintained that there was consumer demand for ten million new vehicles.[25] As a Packard official complained, auto production was constantly held up "by one aggravating little thing after another." Considering the wide-ranging consequences of shutdowns at his company, he noted, "more than 60,000 persons in the families of Packard's 2,000 dealers and their employees are deprived of their main source of income every time the final assembly line halts. Add to them the thousands of others in the factory and related industries—and the total becomes staggering."[26]

Sporadic, short-term, local conflicts also continued to force layoffs throughout the region. Thousands of workers in Detroit's auto plants refused to stay on the job during heat waves. Auto factories tended to be hot to begin with, and there was no air conditioning in the 1940s. Skilled tradesmen struck three tool and die plants to protest the removal of doors from toilet stalls. They resented the lack of privacy and management's argument that the time spent opening and closing lavatory doors would be better spent on the job. Another sixty-five hundred workers, this time at Dodge Main, lost a day on the job when eleven hundred of their fellow union members, mostly veterans, celebrated the first anniversary of Japan's surrender.[27] These types of conflicts, and subsequent layoffs, never disappeared and sometimes resulted in tens of thousands out of work.[28]

There were no reprieves. A seventeen-day coal strike in November and December resulted in tens of thousands of auto layoffs in Detroit, in part because freight trains could not operate without their primary fuel. The cycle repeated itself. The coal walkout created another lag in steel production, which in turn extended autoworkers' layoffs. Automakers had abundances of some parts and scarcities of others, which meant few cars could be produced until the coal strike ended, steel mills had enough coal to operate, steel reached parts factories, and parts were delivered to assembly plants. Frustrated by delays, false starts, and unpredictable conditions, Ford and Hudson laid off eighty-two thousand Detroiters for an extended, unpaid holiday vacation. On New Year's Eve the entire first shift at Chrysler's Jefferson and Kercheval body plants left for lunch and never returned, and only one hundred out of three thousand showed up for the second shifts. Thousands of Briggs workers also took the afternoon off, against company wishes, to begin celebrating early. A Briggs spokesperson blamed the employees for this instance of "retarded production." More likely, workers had become so accustomed to intermittent employment that they took a few hours on their own terms.[29]

*   *   *

In early 1947 few auto industry observers expected the postwar boom to arrive anytime soon, although automakers insisted that the potential for one still existed. Indeed, Chevrolet claimed to have over a million unfilled orders for new cars. But the persistent barriers to full production and full employment had not been resolved, and nearly a quarter of Detroit's estimated 444,000 would-be factory workers were laid off in mid-January.[30] In addition, strikes in Detroit continued to disrupt production chains. Union members reported that the conflicts involved production speedups, overbearing foremen, and unfair warnings, while managers cited lazy workers and irrational responses to reasonable workloads. It was difficult to get to the truth then, and impossible now, but each instance resulted in thousands of people out of work up and down supply networks.

Layoffs were so persistent that in March 1947 Walter Reuther demanded of GM a guaranteed forty hours of employment for anyone called in to work at the start of a week. For many months, Reuther noted, autoworkers had rarely worked full-time and were lucky to get twenty-five to thirty hours a week. "The worker must hold himself available," he declared. "He cannot seek other employment, nor can he claim unemployment compensation even though he may be getting paid for only a few hours' work each week." No doubt this demand exasperated GM management, which pointed to strikes by UAW members and materials shortages caused by strikes in other industries, not the company's unwillingness to offer full-time work, as principal causes of intermittent employment.[31]

But contrary to what business leaders thought, the postwar strikes were not irrational roadblocks to prosperity. The tensions between workers and foremen continued the sorting-out process, begun during the mid-1930s, of determining how much influence workers would have over crucial job-related issues, including pay, but also job security through seniority rights and some say over the content and pace of workloads. In many cases the root issue was dignity. Maybe an auto executive thought it reasonable to remove doors from toilet stalls, for example, but clearly the affected workers did not. The larger, industry-wide strikes addressed serious economic concerns. The cost of living skyrocketed after wartime price controls expired. Wages did not keep pace, and even if they had, erratic employment reduced earnings.[32]

Middle-class aspirations proved as elusive as steady work. If GM had granted Reuther's demand for steady, forty-hour work weeks, the average UAW wage of $1.31 per hour would have produced just over $50 a week in pretax earnings, or a little more than $2,500 per year. Yet at this time economists and industry leaders calculated that a monthly income of $400 was necessary to purchase even the lowest-priced new vehicle. The inability of vast numbers of industrial workers to buy new cars might have explained much of the disparity between the relatively low number of passenger vehicles produced in 1946 (2,155,924) and the much smaller number of such cars actually sold by dealers (1,185,196).[33]

The auto industry's volatility affected Chrysler and GM contract negotiations with the UAW in the spring of 1947. With employment so intermittent, the union had little leverage, and GM quickly shrugged off Reuther's demand for a guaranteed forty-hour work week. In 1947 there was no talk of a strike like the long one that had ended just over a year earlier. Indeed, a walkout would have relieved GM of its unemployment compensation liabilities much more than it would have hindered the company's sales. In the end, UAW members at GM received a total compensation increase, on average, of fifteen cents an hour. A couple of days later, Chrysler and the UAW signed a similar contract but for two years instead of one. Chrysler president K. T. Keller pointed to record earnings during the first quarter of 1947 as proof that "the Corporation's operations can now be considered as fully re-established on a peacetime basis." He hoped to lock in predictable labor costs to ensure continued profitability.[34]

It quickly became clear, however, that the industry's new contracts could not resolve persistent steel shortages, which remained a fundamental barrier to a postwar boom for autoworkers. The auto industry's production pace, even though well below what it ultimately desired, soon exhausted available steel supplies. For its part, the steel industry was actually booming during much of 1947, reaching a record peacetime rate of 93 percent of capacity nationwide during the first three months of the year.[35] But there was massive demand for steel output in many sectors of the U.S. economy, especially for the cold-rolled sheet variety automakers needed most to build cars. Steelmakers told auto executives to stand in line, be patient, and expect no more than what they were receiving, as their precious metal was essential for construction, appliances, ships, planes, and trains. Production of sixty thousand new railroad freight cars, necessary for economic growth in all sectors of the economy, took priority over automobiles. Ironically, one factor that reduced supplies for the auto industry was the huge amount of steel required to build new steel mills. The petroleum industry presented another such conundrum. If the auto industry were to expand, more oil would be required to produce and operate those vehicles. Yet the petroleum industry lacked enough steel to build the rigs, pipelines, tankers, and barges it needed to meet any increased demand. Conditions might worsen before they improved, experts warned. Indeed, the proposed Marshall Plan called for diverting steel from U.S. markets to help rebuild Western Europe.[36]

Steel shortages affected automakers, hence employment, in many ways. High demand meant increased prices for scarce supplies, which necessarily boosted the cost of new cars. It did not help that postwar automobiles were significantly heavier than prewar models and that most of the added weight came from steel. Costs increased considerably as well for tools, dies, and presses, largely made of steel, and those expenses had to be passed on to consumers. At the same time, inflated prices for housing, food, and clothing reduced household disposable incomes and thereby affected the ability of consumers to pay for new cars, if not to hope for them.[37] General Motors managed to purchase adequate quantities of steel, at least for the short run. Ford was not as severely affected as its competitors, because it made so much of its own steel. It did experience significant production disruptions, however, when its foremen struck in hopes of gaining union recognition.[38] Packard was still producing on a limited schedule, but it was doing far better than during the first quarter of the year, when it operated only twenty-eight of the sixty-three available working days. Even Kaiser-Frazer produced a decent number of vehicles in May. Yet Chrysler continued to do poorly for lack of steel, and nearly fifty thousand of the company's employees were laid off.

Lines stretched for blocks outside unemployment offices as those affected resorted to their secondary support systems.[39]

Sporadic unemployment persisted at other auto companies for reasons not always related to steel. These included excessive heat, extreme cold, and even the use of a particular type of cockroach spray that incited the pests to attack workers.[40] Missing a day here, a week there, a month on occasion, and often even more made it next to impossible for workers to predict earnings and plan for the future. Because of the continued instability in auto production, many skilled tradesmen left Detroit for what they hoped would be more lucrative opportunities elsewhere—for example, in the emerging aircraft industry. Auto analysts feared that a developing shortage of tool and die workers, pattern makers, carpenters, electricians, metal finishers, and maintenance mechanics would hinder future prospects. In late 1947 openings in the skilled trades in Detroit auto plants were plentiful, but there was very little demand for unskilled or semiskilled production workers. This was particularly bad news for African Americans and white women, who were effectively barred from the skilled trades, but it was not especially comforting for white men either, because there were nowhere near enough apprenticeship positions or available jobs to accommodate the large number of them who were unemployed or underemployed.[41]

Given the high annual turnover rates for the auto industry's entry-level positions—estimates were in the 40 percent range—if plants were running, there were almost always some jobs available. Paul Ish, a native of Pontiac, Michigan, remembered being placed in an assembly job, the most common entry-level position for whites, soon after hiring in about this time at Pontiac Motor. "They were always short of help over there," he recalled. "So I went over there and I worked up on second floor of Plant 8 putting brackets on horns before they went on the car." Before long, his foreman stationed him "in a pit" from which he fastened molding to the underside of each car. "I worked down there for probably a month or so," Ish remembered, "and then I ended up above, putting hoods on the cars as they come down the line. Well that about killed me." The weight of the hoods and the pace of the line over an eight-hour shift—"they were running fifty-two an hour at that time"—wore him down. For such reasons, some entry-level positions had annual turnover rates as high as 400 percent. For those who remained, Ish recalled, "everybody was waiting for the line to shut down" because of some mechanical problem or parts shortage, and when that happened, with joy and relief they would all "hoot and holler." As an African American, Joe Woods faced a different set of possibilities. An Alabama native, Woods hired in at Pontiac Motor "on May 7 of '47" and quickly surveyed the segregated landscape. "They put all the blacks in Plant 6, in the foundry," he said. "And if you got in the main plant, you got a job on sanitation." African Americans, Woods noted, "didn't get no production jobs, unless it was a job that didn't nobody want." Of the two options for blacks, Woods preferred sanitation. "I was blessed that I didn't get in the foundry," he said. "I got in the main plant as a chipper and a sweeper," cleaning up the metal debris from parts-stamping operations. "I couldn't have stayed in the foundry," he insisted. "I would have quit."[42]

Also African American, World War II veteran James Franklin returned from duty overseas to take a job in the Rouge plant foundry. He settled in, he recalled, "on the bull ladle, where you would take your cup, catch some of the iron when you was pouring it into your mold." Then he would crack the metal and check to make sure that it was tempered properly, "from the top to the bottom." Unsatisfied at the Rouge, Franklin took a job in 1946 at upstart Kaiser-Frazer, where he was allowed to bid on jobs outside the foundry. He progressed rapidly from materials handling, which was exhausting, to stock chaser, "where you run stock all over where it's needed" to keep the lines running. He quickly advanced to inventory checker, managing the stock chasers. If certain parts were in short supply, it was his job to prevent a line shutdown by noticing far enough in advance so that more arrived before anything ran out. "It was a high degree of responsibility," he emphasized.[43] Franklin's quick climb up the job ladder demonstrated what could have happened for more African Americans if given the chance, but most black autoworkers remained trapped in foundries or in menial positions supporting white production workers and therefore had limited opportunities to gain access to auto work.

Adding to insecurity, all newly hired autoworkers were on probation for their first ninety days, after which they received seniority and accompanying protection under UAW contracts. Before the ninety-day mark, probationary workers could be let go for any reason, and when the industry was unstable, as it was throughout the mid- to late 1940s, they were often fired before achieving seniority. New workers could be found easily, and companies did not want to expand payrolls, and subsequent unemployment responsibilities, without some certainty that more employees would be necessary for the foreseeable future. Large numbers of new hires, both black and white, lost their jobs this way.[44] Others, like Don Hester, were fired because they had trouble showing up on time. A native of Pontiac, Michigan, who had grown up on farms far from the city, Hester admitted that after he was hired at Pontiac Motor, he "couldn't get up in the mornings. Living down here in the city was a whole bunch different from living in the country. I was trying to burn the candle at both ends, hanging out with the guys." Before he completed his ninety-day probationary period, Hester remembered, "they let me go. Yeah, I lost that first job, and I was out of work."[45]

Despite dynamics that hindered steady production and employment, total U.S. auto production in 1947 was the third largest in history, topping 1929 and 1937. Chrysler posted all-time record sales and profits in 1947. GM reported a peacetime record for sales and an enormous increase in net income over 1946. In addition, unemployment in Detroit at the end of 1947, as measured by the MUCC, was as low as it had been since the war. Statistics like these laid the foundation for the notion of a postwar boom in the auto industry.[46] The aggregate numbers, however, failed to reveal that layoffs, short weeks, and uncertain income had been the norm for Detroit's autoworkers.

* * *

In early 1948 auto industry officials anticipated another record postwar year, with output of as many as six million new vehicles, steady employment for autoworkers, and occasional overtime pay.[47] But high hopes were quickly thwarted by cold weather throughout the Great Lakes region. Record demand for natural gas strained the supply from the single pipeline through which it was transported from Texas and Oklahoma to Michigan, as well as to most of Indiana and Ohio and much of Pennsylvania and New York. Officials suspended industrial use of gas and gave priority to the increasing number of households that had switched from coal to gas for heat. Some Michigan companies, such as Ford, produced much of their own gas, but within days of the cutoff Chrysler and GM facilities were closed completely, and unemployment in Detroit was as bad as during the worst times in the Great Depression. Resumption of auto work took time because of reduced production in coal mines and steel mills, a result of the gas shortage, and subsequent industrial curtailment from New York to Indiana. After three weeks off the job, tens of thousands of Detroit workers were desperate. Briggs employee Jessie Goe, sixty-four, had spent his savings on food and furniture payments and waved his empty wallet in front of onlookers. Another Briggs worker, Floyd Curtis, forty-one, had exhausted the financial reserves it had taken him eight months to accumulate. Although Ford averted the worst of the gas-crisis layoffs, the company planned major changes for its 1949 models and laid off twenty-five thousand Rouge workers for up to six weeks while updating machinery. Any hopes for a year of steady employment were already dashed.[48]

Despite persistent disruptions, automakers produced a postwar monthly record of 490,000 vehicles in March, but more troubles loomed. The United Mine Workers launched another strike that gradually created a familiar ripple effect throughout the national economy. Coal shortages hurt steel production, and railroad shipments were curtailed, affecting supplies of parts and materials. When the federal government ordered national freight train service to be cut by 50 percent, automakers tried their best to get supplies via trucks and ships, but there was no way to replace the volume normally carried by rail. Although the coal strike ended in mid-April, it took nearly another month to restore production to March levels. In response, General Motors closed operations for two weeks, laying off nearly forty thousand Detroit-area workers, and Chrysler president K. T. Keller glumly warned stockholders that production would be hampered for several more months.[49]

Additional disruptions appeared likely as contract negotiations faltered at the Big Three automakers. The UAW had demanded what amounted to a fifty-cent-an-hour increase from Ford. Thirty of those cents were to go toward a straight wage increase, and the rest would support programs like a medical plan, pensions, and a three-week paid vacation. The union's demands of Ford far exceeded those made of GM (twenty-five cents an hour total) and Chrysler (thirty cents an hour), which outraged Ford officials. Ford vice president John Bugas argued that higher wages would only accelerate inflation, resulting in fewer new car purchases and additional unemployment. Since Ford already paid a higher average hourly wage ($1.53) than GM ($1.42) and Chrysler ($1.43), Bugas warned, his company would propose a wage cut instead of an increase.[50]

Chrysler workers made the first move, however, by striking for a contract. At the time, Chrysler operated eleven plants in Michigan, ten of them in Detroit, employing sixty-five thousand people. The Chrysler walkout caused an immediate shutdown of operations at Briggs plants, and industry analysts estimated that an additional fifty thousand Detroiters would be out of work if the conflict dragged on, which seemed certain. Most Chrysler strikers appeared to support the action, although a sizable number of them conceded that they lacked the resources to stay out for long. Ineligible for state unemployment benefits and with no financial support from the UAW, striking Chrysler workers, like their GM counterparts two years earlier, were on their own.[51] Many wives of Chrysler workers assumed larger roles as wage earners. Some families leaned on relatives for help. Others were already supporting members of their extended families. "Besides my children, I have my father and aunt to look after and we're paying $17.50 a month for a new icebox," said one mother of seven. "I don't know how we'll ever make it now." Elizabeth DuVan, seven months pregnant, worried about medical expenses. "We'll have a large hospital bill in a couple of months," she noted, "and I don't know where we'll get the money to meet it."[52]

GM settled without a strike. The sides agreed on a wage increase of three cents an hour, improved health benefits, and, out of the blue, a mechanism for keeping up with inflation. If the cost of living, as determined by the federal Bureau of Labor Statistics, rose by a certain amount—1.14 points on the bureau's scale—GM workers would receive an additional penny per hour. If the cost of living went down by the same amount, workers would lose one cent an hour, but hourly wage reductions during the life of the contract would be limited to five cents total. The Bureau of Labor Statistics used 1940 data to create a baseline index of 100.2. In April 1948 the index was 169.3, meaning the cost of living had increased 69 percent in eight years. GM claimed that its proposal (nicknamed COLA, for cost-of-living allowance) would "promote prosperity and stability and protect and improve standards of living" for its workforce.[53] Shortly after, Chrysler and the union reached a similar agreement, although without a COLA clause. Despite their contract settlement, many Chrysler workers did not return to their jobs right away because of wildcat strikes at Briggs and a contract strike at the Budd Company, both major suppliers. The Chrysler settlement, it turned out, had not brought steady employment. Neither had the GM agreement. The corporation shut down in mid-June because of the long-term effects of the coal strike, and nearly thirty thousand of its Detroit employees were once again off the job.[54]

The inability to sustain full employment irritated auto executives as well as their workforces, and stricter federal credit regulations were partly to blame. Economists warned of a disturbing rise in consumer debt across the nation, fueled by an increasing percentage of car purchasers who relied heavily on credit. The Federal Reserve Board sought to rein in the binge by strengthening "Regulation W," an inflation-fighting directive that originated during World War II. The board had eased credit requirements in 1947, but the 1948 upsurge in debt prompted it to order that automobile purchasers make down payments of one-third the selling price and pay off loans within eighteen months. This meant more substantial down payments and steeper monthly installments, putting purchases of new cars out of reach for many consumers and certainly for most industrial workers. Indeed, a study by auto financing companies showed that only those with family incomes in the nation's top 14 percent could afford new cars under the revised Regulation W. It was even difficult for many potential purchasers to buy used cars. For autoworkers it made little sense to commit to relatively high monthly payments when employment was so volatile. Indeed, in the month after the revised Regulation W took effect, used car sales in Detroit plummeted and many used car dealerships closed. Industry observers understood that a healthy used car market was essential to sustain new car sales. Shoppers wanted to trade in their old vehicles for maximum values, but the offers they received were low in large part because of Regulation W's negative impact on demand, which in turn discouraged new car purchases. On the other hand, as the Federal Reserve pointed out, the likely alternative was a credit bubble and inflation, followed by some sort of crash.[55] Auto industry analysts estimated that there was an unmet demand in the range of 4.5 million vehicles, which at the automakers' current sluggish rates was about a year's worth of production. And although steel shortages remained the largest impediment to production, tight credit did not help sales.

While the credit controversy raged, a production disruption at the plant level tested the limits of solidarity among workers in tough times. In early September, 170 guards at Briggs plants, members of the independent United Plant Guard Workers of America (UPGWA), went on strike, hoping to gain fifteen minutes of paid time to prepare for work once on site. UAW members refused to cross the UPGWA's picket lines, halting production at Briggs plants and quickly forcing the shutdown of most Chrysler and Packard operations. Fifty thousand Detroiters were immediately laid off. When the plant guards and Briggs management held fast to their positions, one hundred thousand Detroiters up and down the affected production chains were out of work. With employment having been so unstable, many autoworkers soon had second thoughts about observing the UPGWA picket lines, and UAW leaders pressured the plant guards to give up. "We are returning to work because we realize so many others have been affected by our dispute," explained UPGWA president James McGahey.[56]

Despite intermittent production, automakers earned record profits during 1948, and official employment levels reached postwar peaks. Total industrial payrolls in Detroit for 1948 reached an all-time high of over $1.530 billion.[57] If one looked only at these official statistics, it would be easy to conclude that these were boom times for Detroit autoworkers. The catch, of course, was that total employment figures did not translate into steady jobs for autoworkers, who had experienced tumultuous swings in employment and persistent economic insecurity. National Association of Manufacturers president Morris Sayre warned industrialists in Detroit that volatility in the auto industry was a serious national concern. "Security represented by the steadiest job possible is the first concern of every working American," he declared, and the free enterprise system might not last unless each employer considered "every unemployed worker as our personal problem." Despite any favorable economic data, by the end of 1948 autoworkers had yet to experience a postwar boom.

2 The Era of "The Treaty of Detroit," 1949–1950

The 1950 contract signed by GM and the UAW, called "The Treaty of Detroit" by *Fortune* magazine, looms large in accounts of postwar U.S. labor history, because it seemed to ensure steady employment, increasing wages, and improved benefits for autoworkers. That contract, however, was signed after a year of national recession marked by intensifying competition in the auto industry, with production speedups and strikes, new efforts at automation (the replacement of jobs with machinery), national coal and steel strikes, and increasing unemployment for autoworkers. Despite the recession and disrupted production, most auto companies prospered in 1949. But for workers the Treaty of Detroit and comparable contracts with Chrysler and Ford were efforts to achieve some semblance of stability and predictability in a volatile industry, not the confirmation and continued promise of the postwar boom. Chrysler workers, for example, gained their pension plan in 1950 only after a 104-day strike, during which one hundred thousand Detroiters were out of work and struggled to meet basic needs. The contracts appeared to have a positive short-term effect, as auto sales soared in early to mid-1950, especially when Chrysler's strike ended, in the closest thing yet to a postwar boom. But the onset of war in Korea threatened auto industry prosperity as the government allocated strategic resources for military purposes. By the end of the year, employment instability had returned in force as many workers, including tens of thousands of new migrants to Detroit, were forced to rely on secondary support networks.

* * *

In early 1949 total employment in Michigan was declining and national demand for new cars was weakening. Economic indicators could not account for these drops. On average, passenger cars on American roads were over nine years old, with two-thirds of them built before World War II. Surely those vehicles needed to be replaced. On the other hand, disturbing unemployment trends extended well beyond Michigan and threatened the auto industry. Disregarding ominous signs, automakers boosted production at a pace that would have resulted in topping 1948's output by nearly 750,000 units. Declining demand, auto officials maintained, could be overcome by energetic sales efforts at dealerships, which were required to purchase whatever their franchisor produced. To auto companies, a car was considered "sold" when it was shipped from the factory to the dealer. Dealers went into great debt to absorb high-volume production and had to sell those vehicles to consumers or watch inventories amass on their lots. If dealer stockpiles expanded too much, auto assemblies were reduced, and by the end of February it was difficult to ignore the backlog of unsold cars.[1] Automakers blamed this predicament on tight credit terms. In March the Federal Reserve actually loosened requirements, allowing twenty-one months for the repayment of auto loans instead of eighteen, but industry officials argued that Regulation W was still too strict. Even under the revised terms, complained the Detroit Automobile Dealers Association, "It is almost impossible for the production worker on Ford, Chevrolet and Plymouth assembly lines to buy one of the cars he makes."[2]

Despite intense competition in a tight market, automakers refused to lower prices. To do so would have upset the vehicle-sales ecosystem. For example, if prices were reduced for low-end new models, such as Chevrolets, Fords, and Plymouths, sales of medium-range used cars, such as Pontiacs and Oldsmobiles, would be jeopardized. Why buy a used car, the thinking went, if you could purchase a new one for roughly the same price? A backlog of medium-priced used cars would reduce trade-in values for those models, thereby discouraging sales of new autos in that important sector of the industry. Since costs for engineering, tools and dies, materials, and labor were roughly comparable for all vehicles, higher-priced cars generated the largest profits for automakers. So even though most consumers were unable to afford new cars, reducing prices on vehicles that were most likely to be in demand was out of the question.[3]

The most effective way for automakers to compete, then, was to reduce production costs, which provoked numerous strikes over workloads. Workers at Hudson, Briggs, and Chrysler experienced the most lost days.[4] UAW leaders charged that automakers intentionally incited conflicts by ignoring complaints about harsh working conditions, thereby limiting production and inventories via strikes instead of layoffs and avoiding liability for unemployment benefits. Automakers disagreed. "The current disputes over production standards have generally been provoked by insistence of the union that more men than necessary be used to man some of the new machines," explained a management representative. Inefficiency could no longer be tolerated, he insisted, because "the day of competition has returned to stay in the auto industry."[5] The largest workload strike erupted in the "B Building" of the Ford Rouge plant in May. At issue was a proposed speedup of the final assembly line, which, Local 600 charged, had been moving incrementally faster for months. Was Ford's planned new rate within contractually acceptable limits, or was it excessive? The formal grievance procedure had failed to resolve the question to anyone's satisfaction. The core dispute in this case was not so much about the regular speed of the assembly line, but rather the pace at which it operated when making up for the inevitable breakdowns and delays that occurred during each shift. As motor-line employee Teddy Winston insisted, "The company has been getting away with murder on these speedups." Local 600 members voted overwhelmingly to strike, pending approval of the UAW's International Executive Board (IEB). But when the IEB hesitated, irate Local 600 officials forced the issue by calling a strike anyway.[6] The IEB's reluctance stemmed in part from awareness that most UAW members were already in precarious economic circumstances and that it was possible there would be a strike later that year for a new contract at Ford. Two possibly lengthy strikes would likely lead to more economic hardship than most workers could tolerate. By its standards the UAW's strike fund was large, about a million dollars as opposed to nonexistent. But because the Rouge plant was essential for Ford operations nationwide, well over one hundred thousand UAW members would be affected if the plant shut down. The strike fund could not stretch far under those circumstances.[7]

As the speedup strike passed the two-week mark, all Ford operations stopped, and Walter Reuther encouraged Rouge workers to find other jobs until there was a settlement. Detroit resident and former Rouge employee James Oliver Slade noted that, including strikers' families, at least a quarter million Detroiters were directly affected by the Rouge conflict. He warned that so many "ill-fed, ill-clothed, ill-housed in this community can do none other than increase crime, delinquencies and generally unwholesome conduct for many persons who ordinarily would behave as law abiding citizens." With little money left in its budget, Detroit's welfare department braced for an upsurge in cases. One had to prove indigence and no means of support—no savings, no war bonds, no assets, no car—to qualify for city welfare benefits.

If a family of four met those standards, and only eight out of a thousand Ford applicants were approved, they would receive about fifty-five dollars every other week, a little less than half of average Ford wages, in exchange for forty-five hours of work on city projects.[8] The loss of Ford workers' income had a staggering effect on the local economy. Neighborhood grocery stores and movie theaters fared reasonably well, but restaurants, drugstores, and bars saw business drop immediately. Furniture and appliance sales declined noticeably. The Detroit Street Railway lost ten thousand dollars a day for lack of ridership. As happened during many layoffs, rents and mortgages went unpaid. Under Michigan law, homeowners had eighteen months to make up any missed payments before facing foreclosure. Landlords, however, could evict tenants at any time for any reason, although during layoffs they had generally offered extensions, figuring that when the tenants returned to work the back rent would get paid. But with the region experiencing a housing shortage, State of Michigan Circuit Court judges in Detroit braced for a wave of strike-related eviction hearings. As it turned out, Ford and the UAW reached an agreement after twenty-five days, without settling the core dispute, and it took an extra week or two before full production resumed, because supply chains had to be restocked.[9]

While the Ford strike dominated the news, confusing economic data appeared. In a time marked by record auto production and employment levels, the state's jobless total rose to over two hundred thousand. It was difficult to believe that production records could be set, given the number of strikes and supply shortages in the preceding months. And record employment levels could be deceiving, since they included thousands of Detroiters on "short weeks," marked, according to the MUCC, by "cuts in weekly working hours, spotty one-and two-day layoffs and intermittent production shutdowns." Automation was partly responsible for increased production and decreased employment, yet many industrialists were reluctant to invest as heavily as possible in new technology. Automakers knew that steel shortages and high demand for new equipment could increase the cost of machinery, which often forced them to settle for piecemeal upgrades even though improvements in one area could succeed only if every related process kept pace with expanded productivity. After all, auto production was ultimately limited by the least available part.[10] In 1949 one crucial constraint was auto bodies, which could not yet be manufactured quickly enough to support the productive capacity of assembly lines. Yet there was also the example of new chemical-dipping techniques for polishing bumpers, which eliminated many jobs but also solved the problem of having to sell bumper-less cars with IOUs, which had been a common practice when sales boomed. No matter what, though, auto manufacturers always looked for ways to decrease the number of workers in each department, which contributed to rising car output with increasing unemployment.[11]

Those out of work or underemployed were forced yet again to turn to secondary survival strategies. Bud Weber, for example, found a job as a part-time janitor at the post office in Drayton Plains, outside of Pontiac, in an area increasingly populated by whites leaving or avoiding the city. Alternative employment in suburbs was virtually impossible for African Americans, and given the intense job segregation in Detroit and Pontiac, laid-off black autoworkers always had fewer options than whites. Many blacks tried to find temporary employment as butlers or porters, and most of them faced further disappointment. "Our office is jammed with people every day," remarked the owner of Jones Employment Service, "but we just don't have the jobs to send the people out on." The abundance of temporary job seekers led to depressed wages. If they could find service positions, African American men who were laid off from auto work were lucky to make twenty-five dollars a week, well less than half what they could earn in a factory. Black women often received only fifteen to eighteen dollars per week as maids, about half of what they were paid in defense plants during World War II.[12]

Aware that high unemployment gave the UAW little leverage entering contract negotiations, Ford maintained that it was in the workers' best interest to accept an eighteen-month pay freeze. Hoping to lower production costs, automakers had little control over prices for materials and parts, so they focused primarily on cutting expenditures for labor. "The postwar buggy ride of ever higher wages, costs and prices is over," Ford's John Bugas warned. Yet autoworkers had barely a toehold in the postwar consumer society, and driving their wages downward, UAW officials cautioned, was bound to have a negative impact on the entire economy. "The textile and shoe industries are depressed because insecure auto workers and other workers cannot buy garments and shoes with their present wages," Walter Reuther observed. "It is further apparent that textile and shoe workers will not be customers for Ford autos until they have their own purchasing power restored and increased." Ford's proposed solution for long-term prosperity, Reuther warned, would "drag other industries and perhaps the whole economy down with it."[13]

Disgusted with the prospect of more pay for autoworkers, Detroit Board of Commerce executive Harvey Campbell argued that those who built cars had become lazy and dependent. "Take a look at the employment records every Monday," he emphasized. "Too big a percentage of workers don't show up at all. They work four days and make enough money to enjoy themselves for the next three days." If autoworkers found themselves in tight economic circumstances, he insisted, it was their own fault: "Poverty has become a profession—welfare a career." Campbell assumed that if autoworkers were just ambitious enough to show up every day, they would prosper. Some evidence in mid-1949 indicated that Campbell's point contained a kernel of truth. Bureau of Labor statistics showed that autoworkers were earning record weekly pay of $68.90. Moreover, according to the Board of Commerce, the city's industrial workers enjoyed higher wages than their manufacturing counterparts anywhere in the nation. By these measures it seemed clear that opportunities existed for autoworkers with good attendance records to attain economic security without pay increases.[14]

But once again, statistics indicating high wages and steady hours proved to be misleading. In August unemployment in the city reached eighty-seven thousand, about 7.5 percent of the workforce. Caution ruled in factory personnel offices, and hiring stopped at most smaller plants. Some jobs were available at larger facilities because of high turnover rates for entry-level positions, but foremen were increasingly picky, rejecting as many as fifteen applicants for every opening, often for reasons besides ability. "As the unemployment lines grow longer and longer," observed a *Michigan Chronicle* editorial, "the old employment formula of selectivity once more begins to take hold," causing "Negroes, Catholics, Jews, men of foreign birth, men over forty and women, to be slowly hired and hastily laid off." Journalist Charles Wartman reported that "the ratio of 100 whites to one Negro, alleged to be the pattern of hiring at the Chrysler Motor Company, is still bringing great screams of protest." To address the unemployment crisis, Detroit municipal departments compiled lists of New Deal–style public works programs—repairing fire hydrants, painting light poles, maintaining parks, and such—and city leaders petitioned the federal government for money to fund them.[15]

A contract settlement between Ford and the UAW in late September eliminated one possibility of a strike, which would have caused widespread unemployment. The agreement included no wage increases. However, the two sides agreed to the first major pension program in the industry, funded entirely by the company. When combined with federal Social Security, the Ford pension would provide retirees with a total of one hundred dollars a month, just over one-third of average, full-time monthly pay at the time. UAW members at Ford could receive full pension benefits when they turned sixty-five if they had at least twenty-five years of service with the company. Management hoped to replace older, less physically capable workers with younger ones and to set a precedent by demonstrating that corporate benefits could meet society's needs, eliminating any momentum for expanding government programs like Social Security. Union leaders hoped that older workers could enjoy a dignified retirement and make way for unemployed younger Detroiters to take their jobs. The UAW would have preferred more generous Social Security benefits for all Americans, but given the Cold War political climate, a private pension plan made sense.[16]

Although the Ford settlement kept tens of thousands of Detroit autoworkers from picket lines, job stability proved elusive nevertheless because of a national steel strike in mid-October. If the steelworkers had not walked out, a simultaneous coal strike would have shut down their foundries anyway. Most auto companies had stockpiled thirty to forty-five days' worth of steel, but they still had no control over supplies for parts manufacturers. As one auto industry analyst put it, having plenty of steel on hand "may not provide any more security than lighted candles on the Christmas tree." Because unsold car inventories were so high, auto officials might have welcomed a shutdown that they could blame on somebody else. For autoworkers, however, a familiar cycle recurred: tens of thousands of them were laid off, the MUCC prepared for an onslaught of unemployment applications, and merchants in Detroit's working-class neighborhoods prepared for yet more hard times.[17]

Contract settlements in the steel and coal industries in November offered hope for an end to Detroit's crisis, but the lag time between resumption of steel operations and significant automobile production was considerable. As Thanksgiving approached, more than 100,000 Detroiters were counted as unemployed, with totals rising to 175,000 by December.[18] "Having barely skimmed through a 'thankless' Thanksgiving, many of the laborers now at leisure in metropolitan Detroit are bitter and baffled over the turn of events," wrote journalist Myrtle Gaskill, reporting on "the long line of workers who jam the unemployment compensation offices each day. There you will find a cross section of humanity whose expressions range from moderate hope to utter dejection." "It takes the little I have accumulated to survive," Edward Lowe claimed. "I don't know what my kids will do," said a worried woman in line. "It takes every penny I make to support them. I've been at the plant since the war—my man was killed in the Pacific. It will take me four months to catch up with what this lay-off has cost me and by then I guess there will be another."[19]

When Detroit automakers announced a gradual return to work in early December, economists and industry analysts quickly forgot the most recent weeks of high unemployment, even if those who were directly affected did not.[20] Indeed, most auto companies declared that 1949 had been a tremendously successful year. Chrysler set new records for production, sales, and net earnings. GM announced peacetime highs for payroll, employment, and profits. Although Hudson and Packard showed reduced earnings compared with 1948, both companies had relatively high profits and voiced optimism that they were well situated for the future. Only Kaiser-Frazer suffered losses.[21] William J. Cronin, head of the Automobile Manufacturers Association, reviewed the industry's accomplishments: "Production moved at a fast pace throughout the entire year, sales kept right on the heels of production, and employes worked longer, steadier and were paid more money than in any year in the history of the industry."[22] Such claims, however, offered a misleading sense of the year for autoworkers, who had missed weeks of employment from steel and parts shortages, speedup strikes, and overproduction. Indeed, a different year-end review marveled over strong output and profit statistics while noting that it all seemed "paradoxical," because each month of 1949 had seen "a disheartening number of strikes, shutdowns, shortages and obstacles to production."[23] Because of these disruptions, many autoworkers had exhausted any financial reserves and had fallen behind on rent, mortgages, and installment payments while running up burdensome tabs with their local grocers. The aggregate economic data gave the impression of industrial stability and financial security, neither of which autoworkers had experienced during the year.

*   *   *

A 104-day strike for a contract at Chrysler dominated the early months of 1950 in Detroit. Negotiations reached an impasse before production could recover from the fall 1949 steel shortage, and when there was no settlement by the January 25 deadline, more than one hundred thousand Detroit-area workers, eighty thousand of them Chrysler employees and the rest from suppliers, were either off the job again or out of work even longer if they had not yet been recalled.[24] The main sticking point was a pension plan. The UAW demanded a program like what had been negotiated with Ford, while Chrysler offered only a promise to do the best it could, without any formal framework or funding guidelines, "backed," as a company vice president put it, "by the integrity and solvency of Chrysler Corp. itself."[25]

Chrysler strikers, of course, were ineligible for unemployment benefits, although those laid off from suppliers, such as Briggs, could now receive weekly checks. In mid-1949 unemployment benefits in Michigan had increased to twenty-four dollars per week, with an additional two dollars per week for each child up to a maximum of thirty-two dollars. To qualify for benefits, however, a laid-off worker had to have earned at least forty-two dollars in each of the previous thirty weeks from that employer. Given the frequency of layoffs and short weeks throughout 1949, this was a difficult standard for many autoworkers to meet. About eight hundred Chrysler strikers a day applied for city relief, but as the walkout neared the three-week mark, only six-teen total had been approved.[26] Overwhelmed with applications, the MUCC tried to match strikers with job openings but found that local manufacturing firms refused to hire them. As an official at the Cadillac Employment Agency explained, "They don't want any Chrysler strikers. They know the men will leave when the strike ends." Some customary opportunities for seasonal work were not available that winter. "Usually at this time of the year we have a lot of requests for coal handlers and coal truck drivers," an employment agent noted. But because of the miners' strike, he said, "there's no coal."[27] Some Chrysler strikers hoped for help from the UAW. The union had recently begun a dollar-a-week assessment of its non-Chrysler membership to bolster its strike fund, which stood to receive six hundred thousand to seven hundred thousand dollars each week. At union gatherings strikers often questioned what was being done with those resources, because the money reached only a small percentage of individuals at the local level. In response, the UAW's Emil Mazey emphasized the arithmetic—there would be enough in the fund for only about six dollars per week per striker. Chrysler workers had to fend for themselves.[28]

Alternative jobs helped a bit. In 1950 Detroit had no snowplows. Instead, streets were cleared by hundreds of temporary workers. With heavy snow in the forecast on a February evening, some two thousand Detroiters, mostly laid-off Chrysler workers, waited for hours, hoping to be among the lucky eight hundred chosen to shovel all night for $1.26 an hour. A Department of Public Works official described the scene as "the biggest line since the depression." One of the hopeful shovelers said he had only a dollar to his name. Another remarked, "My cupboard is not far from being bare." A laid-off Kaiser-Frazer employee said he was desperate for work because he had a "baby on the way."[29] Many women increased their earnings, if they could, during such layoffs. For example, Helen Stanwyck used her dressmaking skills to support her family of seven, and her husband, Tony, who normally worked in the trim department at Dodge Main, helped by riding his bike downtown to buy thread and material. Working steadily, Helen earned $30 to $35 a week, she said, "and it kept us from going behind in our house pay-ments and not get too heavily in debt."[30]

Unloading possessions, begging for mercy, scavenging, and leaving town were also common strategies. Uncertain that they could make monthly pay-ments, a number of striking workers sold their cars for whatever cash they could get. UAW officials met with Detroit Common Pleas Court commis-sioners to ask for leniency in cases involving strikers who faced debt collec-tion and eviction. Large numbers of unemployed workers gathered at the site of an old boat-fueling station on the Detroit River to collect coal, which had once covered several acres of the property in a massive pile and with its weight had sunk into the ground about a foot deep. Hundreds of thousands of Detroiters in 1950 still heated their homes with coal. Facing shortages from the miners' strike, soaring prices, and little or no income, desperate workers hacked out the precious fuel left behind. A steady line of vehicles, sagging under the weight of their cargoes, left the riverside as empty cars and trucks entered. Rather than scrounge out an existence in Detroit, many laid-off autoworkers, white and black, chose to leave the city to stay with friends or family members until plants reopened. Greyhound tripled the number of buses heading south to accommodate them.[31]

John Gibson, fifty-eight, with sixteen years of seniority at Chrysler's Plymouth plant, strongly supported holding out as long as it took to gain a pension plan. "When you get past 50," he said, "you begin thinking more in terms of future security. The young fellows don't feel that way and I don't exactly blame them." Gibson was married and had three children, two of whom still lived at home. He conceded that he had not been able to save much money in the past few years. "I have a little but not enough to last a long time," he noted. He could meet February's $70 house payment, but he was "not so sure about the next one." His wife, in charge of the family budget, had plenty of experience managing finances during tough times. "I think the really hard part," she emphasized, "is after the strike is over and you start trying to catch up."[32]

A fellow Chrysler striker was less certain than Gibson about the merits of the current conflict. "I have been a union member for years," he said. "I believe in organized labor." Nevertheless, he insisted, his concerns and needs were not taken into account by top UAW leadership. He emphasized the economic hardships caused by the strike: "We hope and pray we will get enough overtime so we can pay the bills that have piled up on us while we have been off from work, then by the time we get our bills paid, including the loans at the finance companies, and get our belongings back from the pawn shops, we are called out on strike again." If one calculated on a cost-benefit basis, he insisted, strikes were not always worth it. "A lot of workers, like myself, are getting fed up. All we want is to be able to work steadily so we can support our families. When we strike for higher wages what do we gain? Nothing. It takes us years to make up what we lose while out on strike." Sensitive to such concerns, Walter Reuther explained to a crowd of seven thousand strikers that the walkout was necessary "so our kids can grow up in a better world."[33] But the union leader had no relief to offer in the present.

Stress mounted among strikers as the conflict dragged on with no settlement in sight. Demetry Kolada normally worked at Chrysler's Plymouth plant. He had bought a home for his family of five when World War II ended by exhausting his savings and cashing in all of his war bonds to make the down payment. Since then, keeping his children fed and clothed while being subjected to intermittent layoffs had prevented him from building an emergency fund. As soon as the Chrysler strike began, the Koladas canceled their contract for thirty-five quarts of milk each week. They had meat only on Sundays, and Demetry ate all of his meals at the Local 51 soup kitchen in return for serving tables and washing dishes. He and dozens of other volunteers were allowed to take home any uneaten food at the end of each day. When the Koladas' children all needed shoes at the same time, they applied at the welfare department but were denied. Behind on their mortgage payments, the couple received help from Demetry's mother-in-law. "She has bought up the mortgage," he explained, "and after I get back to work, I'll start making my payments to her."[34]

After seventy-five days on strike, Frank Lubinski and his family were approaching desperation but showed no sign of giving up on the cause. "Feeding and clothing a family of eight on an auto worker's pay is not easy even when you're working steadily," Frank said. "These kids will eat $45 worth of food a week. And milk, they'll drink eight quarts a day if you give it to them. Fresh fruit is something we almost never have, even in the best of times." "Children grow out of things so quickly and they're so hard on clothes," observed Frank's wife, Clara. "I've patched Carol's snow suit so often there isn't room for another patch, and still it's coming apart. It's the same with their dresses and shoes." The children had been able to pay most of their Catholic-school tuition with after-school chores, and Frank did cabinet work at the church and parish house to make up the difference. Suffering from sinus problems, nine-year-old Donald needed regular medical treatments, but those were suspended during the strike so that the money could be used for food. "He comes to us crying in the middle of the night," Clara said, "but all we can do is give him an aspirin tablet." The strain was economic and psychological. Clara was glad that her husband spent his days at the union hall. "He has to get out and talk to somebody or he'd go crazy," she explained. "And it's a relief to me to get him out of the house. He either paces the floor or mopes around with his head in his hands, worrying. He never was one to sit around idle." By this point the Lubinskis were four months behind on their house payments and three months late on gas, electricity, and telephone bills. Altogether, they owed over three hundred dollars. "It was touch and go to make ends meet even with regular paydays," Clara remarked. "Now, with all the bills that have piled up, I don't know how we'll ever get them paid."[35]

Ralph Smith lost his home. A thirty-eight-year-old veteran who met his Irish wife in London during World War II, Smith bought a house in 1948 on a five-thousand-dollar land contract. The Smiths had a four-year-old at the time, another baby was on the way, and housing was very difficult to find. A truck driver for Briggs, Smith had missed a month of work in December 1949 because of steel shortages. He had been back on the job for three weeks when the Chrysler strike began, which forced Briggs to close. Because he was not technically on strike, he qualified for unemployment compensation, which with two children came to twenty-eight dollars a week. The family managed to hang on for three months before falling behind on mortgage payments and being evicted. Police escorted Mrs. Smith and the children to Wayne County General Hospital, which offered food and shelter on a temporary basis. Mr. Smith stayed at a neighbor's home, keeping watch over the family's possessions, which still sat in their former yard.[36]

These were just a few of the nearly two hundred thousand Detroiters who were out of work in Detroit in early 1950, and no one can know for sure how representative they were. It is highly unlikely, however, that many ordinary autoworkers, especially those with families, had been able to meet living expenses and save adequately for unpredictable, often long-lasting layoffs. Although the Chrysler strike was an extreme example, whenever layoffs occurred some version of these survival strategies kicked in, with distinct variables and different outcomes, but all in the context of insecurity and instability. The impact of layoffs continued to be wide-ranging. As one Detroiter observed, "economic paralysis crept over the city," but the hardships were especially acute among the unemployed and shopkeepers in working-class neighborhoods.[37]

For the first six weeks of the Chrysler strike, Ford and GM had been hamstrung by the prolonged coal walkout, but those two-thirds of the Big Three boomed after the mine workers settled in early March. General Motors and Ford hoped to set new production records for the entire industry, with or without Chrysler.[38] By mid-April vehicles rolled off assembly lines at a staggering annual rate of seven million. Industry analysts concluded that since sales of low- and medium-priced cars were especially high, demand must have finally materialized from people in low- and medium-income groups, which could sustain the good times. Even the Hudson Motor Car Company set production and sales records, and with its twenty thousand employees this was of no small consequence for Detroit. To many, the postwar boom finally seemed to have arrived.[39] Yet Chrysler and its suppliers were on the sidelines, with strikers and those on collateral layoffs falling deeper into debt. When the Chrysler walkout ended on May 4, returning workers learned they would not receive paychecks for two weeks, while bills, most of them overdue, continued to arrive. "I'm happy it's over," said Frank Lubinski, but "I can't forget the bank note for $285, the payments on the washing machine, the doctor bill, the three light bills, three gas bills, three telephone bills and four house payments." He had fallen a thousand dollars in debt, he said, "and for a working man, that seems hopeless."[40]

The long Chrysler strike was an example of militancy that resulted in significant benefits, ultimately for hundreds of thousands of workers. In the end the UAW extracted from Chrysler most of what it had demanded from the start: the equivalent of the Ford pension plan. It had become clear that the federal government would not expand Social Security to provide anything near what was necessary for a dignified livelihood in retirement. Average monthly payments to Social Security recipients in 1950 were only forty-one dollars, and about half of all Americans eligible for Social Security that year chose to stay at work because they could not afford to retire. The first to claim a pension at Chrysler was eighty-five-year-old Charles Long, who had been on motor assembly since 1924 and hoped, finally, to "take it easy." Although immediately worthwhile for older Chrysler workers, the pension plan could easily seem remote and extremely costly for many younger ones. Much depended on how connected and comfortable people were with the long-range goals of the union movement as opposed to present economic needs, especially given the industry's volatility. But whether or not they had supported the strike, all Chrysler's manufacturing workers had suffered enormous economic setbacks.[41]

Production at Chrysler facilities resumed as quickly as possible. Parts plants had been fully operational before the strike, feeder lines were full, and partly built cars still sat on final assembly lines. This contrasted with lengthy delays after coal and steel strikes, when supply chains had to be refilled. Although Chrysler's early post-strike contributions helped set an all-time weekly record for vehicle output, the company operated initially at only about 50 percent of capacity, because so many workers had scattered to other states and it took time for them to return to Detroit. As those stragglers arrived, all auto production was threatened by what turned out to be a brief railroad strike, prompting enormous, largely unsuccessful efforts by automakers to arrange alternative modes of transportation for parts and materials and much reflection about the fate of the industry. "The whole career of the car and truck makers since the war has been a series of interruptions in production," wrote a business observer. "The gleaming new machines that do the work of X number of obsolete machines and XX number of men in minus numbers of hours continue to function almost flawlessly," he noted, "until there's a strike. Or a change in the weather. Or something." If not disgruntled railroad workers, he predicted, "it will be something else."[42]

In this context GM and the UAW signed a new five-year contract in May, thus avoiding a strike like Chrysler's. Called the "Treaty of Detroit" by *Fortune* magazine, the agreement guaranteed four-cent-an-hour raises each year above increases in the cost of living, and pensions of up to $117 a month, including Social Security, for retirees at age sixty-five. If GM employees were to work regularly, by the end of the contract they would receive over $700 more annually than under the previous agreement. GM also agreed to pay half of the hospital/medical insurance cost for union members; previously, workers paid the entire premium. In addition, the contract called for a modified union shop, in which all new hires at GM plants would have to join the UAW for their first year but could then quit the union if they desired. For its part, GM wanted to avoid interruptions in production when market conditions were so favorable, and looking to the future, predictable labor costs would help the company unleash its engineers to develop new technology and model designs. The UAW definitely wanted to avoid another walkout, especially one in which it would have had three times as many strikers (about 270,000 nationwide) as the recently ended Chrysler conflict.[43]

Labor peace accelerated surges in auto production and hiring, with unemployment in Detroit dropping from over 225,000 in February to only 44,000 by mid-June. The MUCC noted that because the demand for workers was so high, employers were abandoning their usual practices of discrimination on the basis of race, sex, and age.[44] Recently divorced with three young children to support, Dorothy Sackle benefited from this boom by hiring in at Dodge Main. Despite Sackle's good fortune, however, women continued to be severely underrepresented in manufacturing. At the peak of wartime employment, 259,000 women worked in Detroit's industrial plants. That number dropped to 67,400 after postwar layoffs, and it had risen to only 88,000 by mid-1950. Although more women were employed in the Detroit area in 1950 than during the war, most had been shunted into the service sector. It was uncertain how many women in Detroit wanted to work in factories in the early 1950s, but relatively few had the opportunity because of discriminatory hiring practices. Joe Woods, an African American worker at Pontiac Motor, took advantage of the tight labor market to land a better job in the company's gun plant, where he helped skilled tradesmen dismantle and reassemble military equipment for shipment overseas. He recalled that he was as good at those tasks as the white men who had been through apprenticeships, and that he proved to be more valuable than many of the official white "helpers" assigned to the tradesmen. But despite Woods's successful transfer, racial discrimination in factories was persistent and well understood in the black community. Black women stood virtually no chance of being hired for auto work, unlike during World War II, when they held defense jobs in large numbers. Many black Detroiters were convinced that if not for discrimination, African Americans already in the city could fill any supposed labor shortage during the 1950 boom. Middle-age Detroiters of any race, both men and women, also routinely met rejection when applying for auto work. Declining physical abilities and increasing pension liabilities hindered the chances of older residents, and during the 1950 boom the unemployment rate for those over age forty-five rose to nearly 33 percent.[45]

Celebrating the auto boom, the Detroit Board of Commerce declared that the average industrial worker in Detroit now earned $3,345 per year, still the best in the nation for blue-collar employment. The board's wage calculations, however, assumed steady full-time employment and did not account for strikes or layoffs. For the tens of thousands who had recently missed weeks or months of pay, the record-setting statistic rang hollow.[46] Even if the Board of Commerce's wage figures had accurately represented blue-collar earnings, most autoworkers would still have been, at best, on the fringes of the new car market. According to a survey sponsored by GM and released in February 1950, only 12 million of the nation's 43.8 million families were financially able to purchase a new car. Only 22 percent (2 million) of the 8.9 million families that earned between $3,000 and $5,000 a year, which, according to the board, would barely include an average full-time autoworker, owned new cars. Another 44 percent in that category had used cars, and 34 percent owned no car at all. GM understood that its hourly employees would probably not be able to purchase even the cheapest new Chevrolet. Instead, the nation's largest automaker set high prices for its vehicles, ensuring desired profits even if actual demand for its cars fell as much as one-third short of predictions. Used cars, the company maintained, were available for working-class consumers.[47] Many autoworkers owned cars in 1950, but despite being the elite of blue-collar workers, they played only a supporting role in the viability of their industry by propping up the used car market so that others might be the first purchasers of what they built.

As the auto industry boomed in mid-1950, the onset of war in Korea distorted the domestic economy. In late June, immediately after the conflict began, consumers rushed to purchase both new and used cars, as well as much else, from washing machines to nylons to refrigerators. It was part of a monthlong shopping spree, prompted by memories of World War II rationing programs. Frenzied demand contributed to inflated prices for manufactured goods. Food prices spiraled upward as well. Many wondered if Detroit would reprise its role as the Arsenal of Democracy, its economy humming with war production. Economists cautioned, however, that even if the war in Korea escalated, there would be no sudden employment boost from defense spending in Detroit, in part because it could take up to two years to convert back to military production. In the meantime, auto plants churned out as many cars as possible for the civilian market.[48]

The rush to produce was most urgent, and caused the most problems, for Chrysler and Briggs, which had been strikebound for over a hundred days while their competitors had thrived. During the first two post-strike months, numerous conflicts broke out in Chrysler and Briggs plants, some obviously a result of attempts by the automakers to make up for lost time, while others were familiar examples of shop-floor contentiousness that always seemed to crop up. The ripple effects from these conflicts resulted in layoffs for almost a quarter of Chrysler's blue-collar employees in Detroit, with comparable impacts on Briggs workers.[49] Strikes continued to affect production in non-Chrysler operations as well. A walkout in Muncie, Indiana, at the Warner Gear Corporation, which produced transmissions and overdrives, forced Kaiser-Frazer to lay off ten thousand employees "right when our production is at its peak," a company spokesman complained. This sudden shortage also hurt Ford, Packard, Nash, and Studebaker.[50]

Most of these strikes were unsanctioned by the national UAW leadership and exposed fault lines within the union. Local UAW officers were obligated to inform wildcat strikers that they were breaking the contract and were thereby subject to penalties ranging from suspension to dismissal. As the only directly elected officials in the union, however, most local officers were reluctant to deliver these lines with enthusiasm or conviction. Whether or not they sympathized with wildcat strikers, upper-level UAW officials were in a bind, because they negotiated contracts that promised labor peace by settling conflicts through formal grievance procedures. According to UAW leaders, wildcat strikes undercut their authority at the bargaining table and could come back to haunt workers, since unauthorized walkouts could potentially set precedents for breaking contracts. UAW regional director Norman Matthews offered an example of a typical higher-level response to a wildcat strike, this one at Hudson: "If it is impossible to negotiate a satisfactory settlement of the grievances, the international union will authorize a strike by the Hudson workers once a proper strike vote has been taken and all other provisions of the contract and the international UAW constitution have been properly observed. We cannot and will not condone strikes or stoppages which are called and conducted in violation of those procedures."[51]

In a perfect world, smooth-functioning grievance procedures could resolve almost any conflict. That was the promise of formalized grievance systems, with arbitration of the most difficult cases, which became the norm in industry during World War II. The wartime necessity of maintaining full production made a virtue of settling disagreements without resorting to strikes, even though thousands of wildcat walkouts still took place. In the postwar era, grievance procedures continued as standard features in most union contracts. If a worker believed he or she had been wronged, the first step was to meet with a union steward or shop committee member and the department foreman to try to sort out the problem. Although this stage rarely made headlines, nearly half of all budding grievances (more than 25,000 of 52,146) at GM plants from July 1948 through December 1949 were resolved this way. If the first step proved unsuccessful, both the worker and the foreman wrote out their versions of what happened and testified before a meeting of the local shop committee and management representatives. Again using GM as an example, more than a third of complaints were resolved at this stage. If an agreement still could not be reached, another meeting took place with the worker, the foreman, and two representatives each from the union and the company. This stage settled another 12 percent of grievances in GM plants. The thorny remaining cases went to an "umpire"—each of the Big Three had one—who ruled on them in court-like proceedings. By the numbers, then, the grievance procedures could be viewed as amazingly successful, because the vast majority of problems were indeed resolved without strikes. But wildcat strikes persisted, even if in small numbers compared to the total number of grievances. Some problems were too sudden, too serious, or too persistent for workers to wait for the formal process to unfold. What was of great importance to a particular group of workers, however, could be viewed as trivial or counterproductive by fellow union members in other departments and other plants or, more likely, by the larger public. As autoworker Patricia Cayo Sexton noted, "In the rest of the plant, we in trim were regarded as prima donnas and hotheads. In fact, other parts of the plant got quite tired and angry about being dragged off their jobs so often by trim wildcat strikes." Whatever their merits, wildcats often bedeviled managers, union officials, and many thousands of indirectly affected workers.[52]

While turmoil racked so many auto plants, the onset of war prompted a new wave of migrants to Detroit—over 100,000 arrived between June 1950 and June 1951—who compounded a serious housing shortage in the city. In 1949 housing experts had concluded that there was virtually nothing available in the city for persons of low or average income. Only one-tenth of 1 percent of rental units in metro Detroit were open, and those commanded rents from $85 to $110 a month, well beyond the range of autoworkers. Working-class families, especially large ones, generally found it impossible to come up with down payments for purchasing houses, and many landlords refused to allow children to live in their apartments. In December 1950 the Detroit Housing Commission concluded that 250,000 Detroiters lived in "substandard" housing, defined as "dilapidated" or without indoor toilets, bathtubs, or running water. An additional 500,000 lived in what the commission called "substandard conditions," in which two or more families occupied a unit meant for a single family. Nearly 40 percent of the city's roughly 1.85 million residents, then, endured officially poor living conditions. Comprising about 16 percent of Detroit's population, African Americans were certainly in the worst situation, but no one with limited means who hoped to rent in Detroit was likely to find something livable and affordable.[53]

Also of great concern was whether or not auto plants could absorb the new arrivals, let alone employ those already in Detroit. The return of stricter credit requirements in mid-September was an ominous sign. Total consumer debt, in large part for auto loans, had reached a record high, fueling inflation and prompting the Federal Reserve Board to act. Under the revised Regulation W, the least expensive new car on the market, with a one-third down payment, would require monthly installments of ninety dollars, nearly a third of an autoworker's income. As feared, new car sales declined by 30 percent. A spokesman for used car dealers complained that they were hit even harder and that the tighter requirements took "the working man right out of the auto buying picture." Paul Graves of the Detroit Auto Dealers Association predicted that "the paralyzing effect will now back up through pipelines to automobile factories and suppliers. Obviously, autos can't be built if they can't be sold." Walter Reuther called Regulation W "a grievous blunder" and accused Federal Reserve Board members of "living in a world of banker mentality," of having made "a stab in the dark," with the knife "in the backs of America's low-income families." Local 600 officials complained that "the new restrictions impose hardships on those with the greatest needs while leaving those with the ability to pay completely unhurt."[54]

Apprehension rose while industry officials waited for the federal government to announce its resource allocation plans. Five months after the war's outbreak, government officials ordered nearly a 30 percent cutback on civilian copper use. Without copper, cars would have to go without radiators and electrical wiring, which was obviously impossible. But if the auto industry received all the copper it wanted, military electronics would be compromised, everyone in the household appliance industry would be screaming, and the nation's electrical grid could not keep pace with increasing demand. Steel shortages seemed likely as well. The domestic steel industry had difficulty keeping up with the boom in early 1950, and even if it boosted production by 10 percent, as it planned to do, there would still not be enough to meet both civilian and military needs. In addition, automakers were reduced to pleading with federal agencies for a portion of the aluminum supply normally allocated for children's toys.[55] Fears appeared justified in November when materials shortages led to tens of thousands of job losses, mainly at Ford and Chrysler. Chrysler explained away its thirty-four thousand layoffs as part of a changeover in car models, but the company conceded that it had no definite plans to resume production. Chrysler workers wondered how they would pay for housing, food, or property taxes due at the end of the month, let alone any Christmas gifts. Hopes fell further when the company announced that in a best-case scenario, production would be reduced by 20 percent for the foreseeable future, requiring some twenty-five thousand fewer employees.[56]

Nevertheless, at the end of 1950 automakers and business boosters celebrated record annual production for the industry. Compared with 1949, vehicle output had increased by 28 percent, despite the long Chrysler strike and persistent steel shortages. Indeed, some industry analysts called this a "miracle" that had created "a veritable mountain of wealth." Detroit factories had produced a record 9.8 billion dollars' worth of manufactured goods, and industrial workers' wages pumped an average of 37 million dollars each week into the local economy. The aggregate data was misleading, however, because conditions had not been so wonderful for actual autoworkers. Chrysler employees had missed three months early in the year, many were laid off again in the late fall, and chronic production interruptions occurred at every auto firm. Ford's Rouge plant was currently enduring massive layoffs, and the war in Korea threatened hopes of high production and full employment in the coming year. "There will be disruption in Detroit employment in 1951," the Pentagon guaranteed. Walter Reuther translated that to mean "mass unemployment."[57] On paper, contracts like the Treaty of Detroit promised increasing incomes and greater security for autoworkers, but in the real world unstable employment and inflation brought continued economic insecurity.

3 No Longer the Arsenal of Democracy, 1951–1952

As the war in Korea continued, auto employment in Detroit became increasingly precarious, and persistent inflation made it harder for autoworkers to cope. Government allocations of raw materials did not favor the auto industry, and military contracts tended not to go to Detroit factories, even when awarded to auto companies. Memories of full employment during World War II, when Detroit was the Arsenal of Democracy, motivated tens of thousands of people to migrate to the city despite dire warnings from industrialists, union leaders, and civic officials. In the background, and often hard to detect amid disruptions caused by the war, industrial engineers continued to develop new machinery that streamlined production and reduced the number of workers necessary in auto plants. Wildcat strikes also continued to disrupt remaining operations. As a result, unemployment in Detroit skyrocketed, and it was heavily concentrated in the industrial sector. At one point in 1952, 10 percent of all the unemployment in the nation was in the Detroit area. While economic commentators gushed over the thriving national economy, autoworkers in Detroit faced inflation, rising rents, and bleak prospects, even if they were on the job, but conditions were especially tough for those on layoff. There was no end in sight as federal government officials privileged the war effort over jobs for Detroit's unemployed. Then a nationwide steel strike in 1952 quashed any hopes of an auto industry recovery. Not even top UAW officials knew how their rank-and-file members managed to survive. Yet by late 1952, steel supplies stabilized, the federal government relaxed wartime materials restrictions, and suddenly Detroit's automakers, facing a labor shortage, began recruiting far and wide for new workers.

*　*　*

In early 1951 pessimistic predictions for the auto industry came true. Unemployment in Detroit worsened, in large part because of continuing materials and parts shortages. Chrysler plants experienced the most disruptions, especially when the Dodge Main plant was affected by a strike at the L. A. Young Spring & Wire Corporation, a Detroit firm that manufactured moldings and auto cushion springs. Persistent wildcat strikes also resulted in layoffs. Charles Scrosani, an employee at Chrysler's DeSoto-Warren plant, complained in March that he had not worked a full week for the previous three months largely because of unauthorized strikes, and he blamed local union officers for condoning such disruptive action. By early February, Detroit layoffs totaled nearly 115,000. Then a railroad strike halted freight traffic between many auto plants, and winter storms prevented trucks and planes from picking up the slack. When parts could not be sent by rail from the Rouge to outlying Ford assembly plants, 30,000 more workers were sent home.[1]

Conditions deteriorated to a point where Detroit automakers, union officials, and government leaders collaborated to distribute anti-recruitment notices across the nation. Their message was blunt: "Attention would-be war workers! Stay away from Detroit unless you have definite promise of a job in this city. If you expect a good-paying job in one of the big auto plants at this time, you're doomed to disappointment and hardship." Moreover, the leaders emphasized, newcomers to Detroit would not qualify for either unemployment benefits or city welfare assistance. A Ford industrial relations manager noted in early 1951 that his company employed eleven thousand fewer people than it had during peak times in 1950. "Before we hire any new employes," he emphasized, "we will call back our former employes now laid off. So there is no possibility of a walk-in-job-seeker getting work now or in the immediate future."[2]

Inflation, especially for food, made unemployment particularly painful. "Prices are going up every day," remarked a supermarket spokesperson. In this era, food generally comprised at least 40 percent of a working family's budget, so rising costs made it more difficult for people to meet other obligations even when they were employed. With monthly car payments often in the one-hundred-dollar range, many autoworkers defaulted. "Collections are becoming difficult," noted an auto finance official. Groceries were a higher priority for autoworkers, his agents had learned, especially for those with larger families. Economists debated how well UAW members had fared with respect to inflation. Official data showed that since 1941 the cost of living had increased 82 percent while autoworkers' wages had gone up only 73 percent. But if the cost of fringe benefits was added to wages, workers could be said to have come out ahead, 87 percent to 82. Basic wage rates could be misleading, however, because of overtime pay or shift differentials and, of course, layoffs, which had been chronic. In the end, economists declared that the "average" autoworker now earned thirty-five hundred dollars a year and was either better off or worse off than before, depending on how one defined necessities and luxuries and how much debt he or she had incurred. The experts, however, did not ask autoworkers what they thought as inflation and layoffs soared.[3]

In the near future, autoworkers' economic fate depended on the balance between civilian and military production. Early in 1951 GM, Ford, Chrysler, and Packard all announced lucrative government war contracts, but none of them were likely to result in Detroit-area employment anytime soon. GM's successful bid to produce F-84 Thunderjet fighter planes was good news for those who would build it—in Kansas City, Kansas. Chrysler received a contract for $160 million to build tanks in Newark, Delaware, in a plant that was constructed as part of the government's plan to decentralize military production during the Cold War. The company also won the rights to manufacture J-48 Turbo-Wasp jet engines, but the plant for this project had yet to be built at an undisclosed location. Ford was awarded a contract to produce 4,000-horsepower engines in Chicago. So while job seekers streamed to Detroit, wartime spending created opportunities elsewhere. In February the U.S. Navy chose Packard to manufacture marine diesel engines in Detroit, but that would happen well in the future, because the tooling process began only after the contract was secured. Ford predicted that it would eventually need forty-two thousand workers to meet its defense contracts, which surpassed the billion-dollar mark with a $195 million order for medium-size tanks. Only skilled workers were needed in the short term, however, as the projects were nowhere near the production stage and the tank plant had yet to be built.[4]

One contract would eventually benefit Pontiac Motor, which received the go-ahead to produce a new amphibious cargo vehicle called the "Otter." Pontiac received more good news in April with its successful bid to manufacture medium-caliber cannons for the army, a project that could absorb as many as three thousand workers from car-making operations.[5] Elwin Brown hired in at Pontiac Motor during this period. He had enjoyed a part-time job in the printing business and had no intention of becoming an autoworker, but he was not making much money, and he remembered well his dad's demand that he apply at Pontiac Motor: "Get your ass over there and get yourself a job!"

Brown obeyed and began in mid-February, but he became a victim of the lag time between the awarding of defense contracts and actual production. Laid off after three months, he ended up working at a friend's gas station.[6]

Instability in auto employment occurred for many reasons, including in-plant infractions and vulnerability during probationary periods. L. J. Scott recalled getting a job at Chevrolet Gear and Axle in 1951 after arriving from picking fruit in Florida with "$3.25 in my pocket." Scott had never seen the inside of a factory. "Tall machines and all that noise and stuff around—I'm busy looking at that stuff," he said, and he failed to notice when he walked through a no-smoking area with a cigarette in his mouth. Facing a two-week suspension—"I mean I made a mistake and I had to pay for it"—Scott looked for other work and found an entry-level position at a Chrysler plant. But he was let go before completing his contractual ninety-day probationary period and ended up working at an army surplus store.[7]

Automakers were reluctant to let new hires gain seniority, because parts and materials shortages continued to disrupt production goals. For example, Detroit's Gemmer Manufacturing Company could not supply enough steering gears to keep Chrysler operating, even at reduced assembly rates. More ominously, the federal government announced new metals restrictions—from 50 to 60 percent below existing levels—for aluminum and copper.[8] Immediately, Ford scheduled layoffs for ten thousand workers. Hudson followed shortly with ten thousand layoffs of its own, hinting that twenty-five hundred of those would be permanent. Blaming materials shortages, Chrysler laid off twenty thousand workers "for an indefinite period," and Briggs did the same with eighty-eight hundred of its employees.[9] Still common, as well, were wildcat strikes, mostly over production speedups, which affected supply chains. As one auto industry analyst described the situation, automakers "don't know how many cars they will build during the next six months; they don't know how much unemployment will result from material cutbacks, and they don't know how many new cars will be sold during the July–December period."[10]

Detroit manufacturing was in turmoil. Citing lack of metals, General Motors shut down most of its operations for a week while Ford quietly cut fourteen thousand jobs from its Detroit-area plants.[11] The best bets for steady employment in the auto industry were either as a tool and die maker gearing up for war production or as a production worker for Cadillac, which was by far the smallest GM division but one with a steady, affluent clientele and a mostly high-seniority labor force.[12] Government metals allocations continued to destabilize the auto industry. In September the National Production Authority (NPA) placed limits on the number of automatic transmissions, newly popular and aluminum-based, that automakers could install in various types of vehicles. Expensive cars (priced over $2,500) could all have automatic transmissions, but the NPA allowed only 65 percent of mid-priced cars ($1,800–$2,500) and 35 percent of lower-end cars (less than $1,800) to offer the new technology. These restrictions made sense in terms of national defense. Jets and cars drew on the same finite supply of aluminum, but an average passenger car contained between seven and eleven pounds of the metal, mainly for pistons and automatic transmissions, while a single Thunderjet fighter frame required seven thousand pounds.[13] The new federal order did not have much effect on low-priced autos, few of which had automatic transmissions, but almost all mid-priced cars, such as Buicks, Oldsmobiles, and Pontiacs, had automatics and advertised them heavily. Perhaps consumers would purchase cars with manual transmissions out of a sense of patriotic duty, but even so there was no way to gain access to tens of thousands of alternative parts anytime soon. In November the Michigan Employment Security Commission (successor to the MUCC) stated the obvious: "The smooth meshing of defense and civilian economies in the Detroit area at present appears to be an objective rather than an actuality." And Detroit was long past the point when experts had predicted that there would be a labor shortage because of increased defense work. Instead, more than one hundred thousand Detroiters were jobless, with at least another hundred thousand either underemployed or laid off intermittently without being counted in the official unemployment statistics.[14]

One strategy for boosting auto production involved scouring the country for scrap steel and iron that could be converted to industrial use. Even in good times, as in early 1950, the auto industry depended on large quantities of scrap metal. One out of every two cars made in 1950 relied on the 29 million tons of scrap recovered and reused that year. Much of the waste came from steel mills and iron foundries, but millions of tons in 1950 could be found in outdated steam locomotives, newly replaced by diesel-powered engines. Millions more existed in abandoned farm equipment rusting in barnyards. In hopes of finding even more unused metal, the steel industry's scrap mobilization unit sent seventy-five agents on reconnaissance missions throughout Michigan to see if manufacturers themselves were harboring unused, obsolete, or unwanted machinery. When forced to look, Packard alone discovered 2.5 million pounds of scrap steel in and around its various plants.[15]

Although wartime materials shortages created the bulk of short-term layoffs, new developments in automation also affected Detroit's employment totals. The cutting edge of industrial engineering in the 1940s and 1950s was materials handling, which had historically involved muscle power to move

parts from one stage of production to the next and had been disproportionately assigned to African Americans. Automakers had not hesitated to
purchase new production technologies, such as huge, multistep stamping
presses, but they had been slow to explore using machines to connect the
stages of manufacturing. This was "in spite of the fact," according to Ford
vice president for manufacturing Del Harder, "that nearly 25 cents of every
dollar paid for production labor was being paid for the handling of materials," amounting to $9 billion annually. Harder offered an example of what
he saw as a positive change in a Ford foundry, in which 112 workers, one
hundred wheelbarrows, and twelve cranes had once been required to move
scrap iron. Now the department needed only 36 workers, assisted by power
trucks and hoppers. The company recouped the cost of the equipment in less
than three months and now saved $250,000 a year on that change alone. That
meant, however, that 76 workers had permanently lost their jobs. Chrysler's
newly renovated DeSoto plant required no manual laborers to move parts or
materials; everything was transported mechanically. Meanwhile, advances
in production automation continued. At DeSoto a few machine operators
oversaw the manufacturing of engine blocks, which were milled, drilled,
reamed, and bored automatically, displacing dozens of workers. In the Rouge
plant's piston department, the local union's newspaper reported, "All you see
now are machines, machines, machines! Technology, mechanical hands,
automation, have reduced the workers from 1000 to 265." In piston grinding
alone, the paper noted, "by realigning the machines and by means of a series
of conveyors, 39 of the 42 jobs were eliminated." Variations on these stories
took place in countless departments in factories across Detroit, adding to
the city's unemployment total but difficult to quantify amid the large-scale
layoffs resulting from the war.[16]

Also concealed by aggregate unemployment data were the battles in many
departments to ensure fairness with layoffs and recalls. Under UAW contracts
seniority supposedly ruled, but sometimes the official provisions did not sit
right with those who were laid off. For example, tensions often flared when
only certain departments suffered layoffs, usually because whatever was produced in unaffected areas could be stockpiled or was needed in greater quantities further along in the production process. Sometimes lower-performing,
high-seniority workers were bumped to jobs beyond their current abilities,
or ones that they could not learn quickly enough to meet production quotas,
which some saw as a cunning way by which foremen could dismiss them. If
higher-seniority workers were laid off while those with less seniority in different parts of the plant remained on their jobs, hard feelings could provoke
wildcat strikes and additional layoffs, regardless of the contractual language.

Proposals for plant-wide seniority to correct this problem seemed fair on the surface, but because of inequities in hiring practices those with the highest seniority were disproportionately white males.[17] Even when seniority favored African Americans or women, racism or sexism could trump the contract. In one such case at the Rouge plant, forty women were replaced by men with less seniority, including some who had only recently been hired. The women were desperate to regain their jobs, and two had already lost their homes because of missed paychecks, but Local 600 officers were unwilling to support them. When the women protested across town at UAW international headquarters, officials there apprised them of their formal rights under the grievance procedure, which meant they were once again at the mercy of their unsympathetic local officers.[18]

As the 1951 holiday season approached, around 120,000 people in the area were still officially out of work, many had exhausted their unemployment benefits, countless others were about to, and a good number more were unemployed but had not worked long enough at their current jobs to qualify for any relief. Unemployment was officially at about 8 percent in Detroit, but it was closer to 25 percent for industrial workers, most of whom supported families, which multiplied the number in hardship.[19] Local 600 leaders considered their supposedly lucrative 1950 contract to be a bust, emphasizing that "THOUSANDS OF OUR MEMBERS ARE LAID OFF AND MANY MORE THOUSANDS ARE THREATENED WITH LAYOFFS." A little more than a year after that contract was signed, employment at the Rouge had dropped from 70,000 to 47,000.[20] Conditions worsened when 90,000 more autoworkers were laid off in December because of the government's wartime materials quotas. Ford tried to soften the blow by offering holiday bonuses to those who would have qualified if they had still been on the job.[21] More than twice as many people as usual lined up outside the Federal Building the first day applications were available for 10,000 Christmas-rush jobs at the post office. Hoping to shovel out the downtown area's roads, thousands more stood in line for hours during a heavy snowfall. "These are mostly people who have been laid off," said city official Sam Gentile. "Mostly they're trying to get money for Christmas." Fortunately for those who were chosen, it took several days to remove the heavy snow into waiting trucks to be dumped into the river. About a thousand men who were not selected, however, stormed the front of the line before police intervened.[22]

* * *

Crisis conditions in early 1952 prompted Detroit and state government leaders to plead with federal authorities for relief. Washington officials, however, believed that they were doing a tremendous job balancing military and civilian needs. Defense mobilizer Charles Edward Wilson, former president of General Electric (GE), issued a glowing report on his agency's progress during 1951 and insisted that the nation should stay the course in the new year. Michigan's governor G. Mennen Williams and auto executives complained bitterly, including a scathing charge leveled by the defense mobilizer's namesake, Charles Erwin Wilson, the head of General Motors. "The Government has taken enough steel and copper from the automobile industry alone to fill all defense needs," auto executive Wilson charged, while accusing the former GE leader of favoring the electrical industry. Mobilizer Wilson responded with outrage: "Nobody in his right mind with any sense of fairness would say that." Governor Williams complained that steel and copper defense allocations had boosted production in places other than Detroit. In early 1952 about 12.4 percent of Michigan's manufacturing laborers were involved in defense work, compared with a national average of 38 percent. NPA director Manly Fleischmann explained that "automobiles are less essential than military or industrial expansion." Trying to defuse the situation, the government's Wilson offered a "preferred basis" plan, under which Detroit firms could win defense contracts with bids 10 percent above any otherwise lowest offer. A month later, however, no new military contracts had been awarded for work in Detroit on any basis.[23]

Hollow gestures became the norm. Fleischmann boosted the quota for automobile production during the second quarter of 1952 from 800,000 to 930,000, which was cause for celebration in Detroit until the realization set in that the increased allowance was not accompanied by any additional metal supplies. "The fact of the matter is that we are being allotted both copper and aluminum for only 800,000 cars," complained Henry Ford II. When Fleischmann came up with an extra million pounds of aluminum for auto production, no one in the auto industry was fooled. Without commensurate copper supplies, the increase was meaningless.[24] Frustration grew in Detroit when defense mobilizer Wilson's task force announced to Michigan's congressional delegation that "dispersing the Detroit labor force" to areas with higher levels of defense-based employment was on its list of preferred strategies. Michigan senator Blair Moody immediately objected, insisting that "you can't move men around like checkers." It turns out, however, that many Detroiters, perhaps more than twenty thousand of them, had already adopted this strategy, some heading back either to their home states or to someplace else where employment prospects seemed brighter. Most of those who left for war-related jobs were young, single men, not those with families or significant seniority. It was all very distressing for Detroiters, who still prided themselves on having been the Arsenal of Democracy in the not-so-distant past. As one observer put it, this was a "strange combination of war and peace."[25]

Some experts failed to comprehend what was happening in the city. When *Business Week* editor Gabriel Hauge spoke before a meeting of advertisers in Detroit, he predicted boom times in 1952. Defense spending would be greater than in 1951, he explained, consumers had saved $20 billion in 1951, twice as much as they had in 1950, and "if they spend in large amounts, the seams will split." There were rumblings in the audience, however, because this rosy picture did not accurately describe the city in which he was speaking. Indeed, 10 percent of all the unemployment in the United States in early 1952 was concentrated in the Motor City. "Detroit is the squall area on the nation's economic weather map," Hauge conceded. "I am talking, of course, of the nation as a whole. I am confident, however, that the problem here will be worked out in due course."[26] Civic leaders put a positive spin on their economic woes. Detroit's Board of Commerce admitted that Detroit was "one of the isolated thorns in the nation's generally-rosy economy," but insisted that since recent unemployment totals had been nearly eighty thousand anyway, these times were not all that much worse and did not compare with the depths of the Great Depression. Also on the bright side, the board reported that aggregate savings in Detroit banks were higher than the previous year. Economists speculated that workers with high seniority were banking their paychecks in case they were the next to be laid off. Yet virtually all industrial workers in Detroit, skilled and unskilled, lived paycheck to paycheck, and many were still trying to pay off debts incurred during previous layoffs. It was far more likely that white-collar Detroiters had boosted local savings totals.[27]

The suffering in blue-collar neighborhoods was serious. Mack Plantier, thirty-six, married with four children, was laid off in mid-December 1951 from his job inspecting bearings at the Rouge plant and survived on unemployment pay of $140 a month. "I was bringing home around $73 a week," he reported in early January 1952. "Groceries alone cost us $25 a week. . . . We just got the gas and electric bill. The house payment is due pretty soon. It's $45. I've been tramping around looking for a job to tide me over." Finding nothing, all he did, he said, was "sit around the house. That's what gets me. I'm used to working. I don't feel right, just sitting. I get to arguing with the kids and the missus." "Mack prowls around here like a lion in a cage," his wife added. "The children get on his nerves and Heaven knows, he loves them dearly. It's just resting that's getting him." Furniss Todd, forty-eight years old with a family, had been a machinist at Ford since 1928 but also had been laid off since mid-December. "We cut the milk down from a quart a day to a quart every two days," he noted. "We send a little money to the telephone and the electric companies to let them know we're in good faith and hope they'll carry us." John Manion, twenty-eight, was unmarried and still on the job as an inspector at a Chevrolet plant but only for four days a week. "There's plenty of us single fellows who have as many responsibilities as the married men," he insisted. "I'm taking care of my mother, and an uncle who was hurt in an auto accident. I have to earn $230 a month before I can see any of it. When I lose as little as a day's work it's more than I can stand." Manion had waited in line to shovel the city's streets. So had Simon Daniels, forty-six, with three children. "My rent is $8 a week and I'm behind. Me and the wife are living on beans and potatoes. It's a long time since we bought a pork chop." Calvin Thurman, twenty-nine, with a wife and a ten-year-old daughter, found temporary jobs as a short-order cook, as a bootblack, and in a laundry. "All of a sudden there just wasn't any work," he said. "I don't understand it." Most of Detroit's unemployed did whatever they could to make a few dollars, selling vacuum cleaners door-to-door, washing windows, or possibly helping out at service stations, but most fell further behind on bills and installment payments. Top-level UAW leaders were as baffled as anybody as to how their membership survived while they were out of work. To find out, they commissioned a survey.[28]

Many secondary jobs came by way of recommendations from friends, clergy, or even foremen, which increased advantages for white workers. Whites owned more businesses than blacks did and were therefore more likely to be connected to job opportunities through social networks. In addition, many local shops refused to hire African Americans, further cutting off potential safety nets. In Pontiac, for example, some laid-off autoworkers found short-term employment at places like Lewis Furniture or Neisner's variety store, both of which were charged by the local NAACP chapter with job discrimination in the 1950s. Nevertheless, many whites had great difficulty coping with layoffs, and when offered a chance to make some money or to gain greater security, they did not ask questions about any possible racial bias behind their good fortune. Gene Johnson left the military in 1952 and returned to joblessness in Pontiac. Before long he was hired as a taxi driver, a position largely off-limits to blacks. Paul Ross was laid off from his nickel-plating job in 1952 but scratched his way into an accelerated skilled trades program because of his work on a pipe gang in the navy during World War II. No African American would have been afforded such an opportunity.[29]

MESC officials did their best to quantify the unemployment crisis. Director Max Horton conceded, however, that his agency's calculations were really just informed guesses, derived from regular surveys of five hundred large companies in the Detroit metropolitan area. At one point the MESC admitted to losing track of thirty thousand laid-off workers. "They can't have all gone fishing," an agency spokesperson said. "No doubt some have left the State, others have entered the service and some have gone to work at plants not covered by our reporting service. But there are still thousands which just can't be accounted for." In the end, unemployment figures were approximate numbers, at best, to be compared over time rather than to be considered accurate depictions of any particular moment. Horton asserted that "strikes, shortages, booms and busts" in the past few years made it impossible to label any period as "normal."[30] The commission did not hesitate, however, to call early 1952 the worst for unemployment in Detroit since the reconversion to civilian production after World War II. Thousands of autoworkers saw their jobless benefits expire and were therefore no longer even monitored by the agency. About two thousand job openings were listed through the MESC, but mostly for positions like metallurgist and mechanical engineer. "The main call is for hot-shot designers and machinists," an employment agent said. "We could place all of those we could get." Unfortunately for the tens of thousands of people looking for work, demand was low for unskilled jobs.[31]

As unemployment worsened and benefits expired, Detroit's welfare system strained to handle the increased load. By early 1952 the city's three shelters for homeless families were filled beyond capacity. The housing market remained extremely tight in Detroit, and since plenty of landlords refused to rent to anyone with children, many families had great difficulty finding places to live even in good economic times. Those with the most children—and this was the baby boom era—faced the worst prospects when seeking apartments and had the most difficulty keeping up with rents. It was not surprising, then, that many residents in Detroit's homeless shelters were members of large families.[32] Despite budget shortfalls, the welfare department relaxed its rules by allowing recipients to keep their cars and telephones for ninety days, but many laid-off autoworkers sold their cars whether or not they intended to apply for welfare, because they needed cash and could not afford to operate them.[33] During this period of extreme unemployment, Detroit police reported sharp increases in crime, especially robbery, auto thefts, and larceny. Neighborhood grocers told of regular customers, who were desperate, out of work, with hungry children, showing up with cheap guns and useless masks to steal from cash registers, which often contained more IOUs than money. "If these men could tell about when they'll get back to work," speculated the chief of detectives, "it would relieve their worries." Nevertheless, in the midst of this crisis the Detroit Board of Commerce claimed that the "typical" Detroit factory worker earned more than ever—$2.04 cents per hour, or $81.60 for a forty-hour week. Reality told a different story, as tens of thousands of factory workers were either unemployed or underemployed, but if they had been working full-time, they would indeed have made record amounts of money, and presumably much of the chaos would have been avoided.[34]

The military continued to siphon off a number of the area's workers, both unemployed and employed. Detroit led the Midwest in enlistments for the navy, the marines, and the Women's Army Corps. According to military officials, the first months of any year were generally good for recruiting. "The men wait to spend one more Christmas at home before signing up," an officer explained. There seemed no doubt, however, that in early 1952 unemployment spurred many to join. Only 40 percent of February recruits had jobs. Those who enlisted could generally choose their branch of service, which prompted many who expected to get drafted, almost certainly into the army, to act preemptively.[35] It was common for those who received draft notices to have their working lives disrupted. Elwin Brown remembered the precise date: "July 23, 1952." He had been recalled to Pontiac Motor after a three-month layoff and despite low seniority had maneuvered his way into a fairly good job, inspecting pin bearings on crankshafts. But he soon found himself in Korea, training troops on the Browning Automatic Rifle. Joe Woods was also drafted away from a position at Pontiac Motor to serve in Korea. His duties were familiar ones for blacks in the military, including engineering support on bridges and construction work, in his case on an air base west of Seoul. L. J. Scott had finally landed an auto job, but within a few weeks he was drafted and spent the rest of the Korean War as a cook at Fort Gordon in Georgia. Don Hester's military service probably saved his auto career. He had joined the naval reserves in 1950 and had to report to Chicago for two weeks of training each summer. In 1952 those two weeks came at a perfect time, near the end of his ninety-day probationary period at Pontiac Motor. Hester would almost certainly have been let go before he acquired seniority, like those who were hired with him, but by contract no one could lose a job while fulfilling military obligations. When he returned from Chicago, he had seniority rights.[36]

When the United Steelworkers voted to strike in early April, there appeared to be little hope for recovery in the auto industry. Then, in a controversial move, President Truman seized control of the unionized mills and prohibited any walkouts while the courts considered the constitutionality of his action. The case wound its way through the legal system until June, when the U.S. Supreme Court finally overruled Truman. Detroit braced for the worst.[37] Ford was in better shape than its competitors, yet company officials understood

that their thousands of suppliers were as dependent as ever on a function-
ing steel industry, so they phased out assembly operations before shutting
down completely in mid-July.[38] Chevrolet laid off nearly 15,000 employees
at its Detroit facilities. Additional cuts followed, including 5,400 at GM's
Gear and Axle plant in Detroit. Nearly 70,000 of Chrysler's Detroit-area
employees were out of work by mid-July, and 24,000 Briggs workers joined
them. The total number of jobless Detroit autoworkers increased rapidly to at
least 150,000 in mid-July. Only Pontiac Motor escaped relatively unaffected,
largely because of defense contracts.[39]

This latest round of mass layoffs underscored the volatility of auto employment. There had been optimism in the spring that car production would
rebound, labor reporter Robert Perrin reminded his readers, but by late
June, "with no steel to feed the State's hungry industrial plants, the jobless
rolls are growing by the thousands daily as manufacturers scrape the bottom
of their supply barrels." James McGuire had heard the positive employment
forecast for Detroit while working in a West Virginia coal mine and headed
for the Motor City. "You find out that Detroit is the only place that's capable
of hiring people," he recalled the wisdom at that time. "And what happens
is, I came up here during a steel strike." Six weeks into the steel walkout the
MESC calculated that Detroit unemployment had risen to 240,000, and
agency officials conceded that their figure was probably too low. Making
matters worse, iron ore freighters were grounded, having nowhere to unload
their cargoes. Since there were only so many ships in service on the Great
Lakes, there would be no way to ramp up deliveries when the steel strike
ended, which was critical because ice would eventually end the shipping
season. "Most of the 1953 models are still underground in the Mesabi range,"
remarked a despondent Detroit auto dealer, referring to the iron-rich area
on the shores of Lake Superior. "When this city hits the skids it hits pretty
hard."[40] After the steel strike ended on July 24, auto analysts anticipated that
it would take up to six weeks to approach normal assembly levels, whatever
that meant. Indeed, auto industry layoffs actually increased the week after
the steel truce, eventually reaching an official total of 250,000 in Detroit.
It appeared that the vegetable and fruit canning industry was likely to get
priority over automobiles for new steel supplies; otherwise a significant portion of the nation's crops would go to waste. In a best-case scenario, parts
plants would resume production first, followed by the reopening of assembly
operations in mid-August, with residual effects from the steel strike lasting
indefinitely.[41]

Some autoworkers were clearly fed up. As one UAW member explained
his view of the situation:

I have been a union man since 1938 and have saved as much as possible. I have a bank account and I have purchased $1,600 worth of Government bonds. Due to inflation my bank account and my bonds are worth about half what they were. Even though my wages are high, I find it difficult to buy the necessities of life because of high prices.

I have lost months of work due to strikes in my factory. I have lost a lot more time because the company I work for has plants in other parts of the Country and when any of those plants strike, we have to go on strike, too. I have lost other time due to steel, coal and railroad strikes and every time any of the plants supplying my factory with parts go on strike, I again lost time.

All the increased wages I have received through my union have not paid the money back that I have lost from strikes. Besides higher prices for everything, my taxes are now higher and one wonders where and when will it all end.[42]

There is no way to tell how many workers shared this level of exasperation, but even if an autoworker maintained steadfast faith in the UAW and in the larger union movement, this description of instability in the auto industry and precarious economic security was still accurate.

Then, suddenly, conditions improved dramatically as steel supplies increased, and Detroit seemed primed for boom times. The federal government began to ease war restrictions, and it appeared possible that quotas could end the following spring. Automakers were ready to compete with one another, they said, rather than with the government and other industries for basic supplies. "Twelve long years of hot and cold wars, controls, materials shortages, substitutes, inflation, expansion, tensions, strikes, storms and turmoil are coming to an end in the auto industry, apparently, with the end of the 1952 model car production," wrote business reporter Leo Donovan, conveying the automakers' mood with more than a hint of sarcasm. One concern was that to ensure a spring boom, the industry needed more workers right away to build up parts inventories. In mid-September Detroit auto firms hoped to recruit at least twenty thousand unskilled and semi-skilled workers, in part by posting fliers in the same states from which they had discouraged migration a year and a half earlier. This was a rare postwar period when auto jobs were there for the taking, automakers had enough parts and materials to run full speed, and plenty of overtime hours were available. In addition, a number of defense projects, long in the planning stages, were finally ready to begin production.[43]

Ernie Liles benefited from this upsurge in production. After helping build the Bull Shoals Dam in his native Arkansas, Liles had tried making a living by leading fishing expeditions on the new backwater lake. Otherwise, he recalled, "there was no work down there," except maybe "pumping gas for little or nothing." By the early 1950s a number of Liles's relatives had already moved to Detroit. "They didn't want to be farmers no more," he said. "I had three uncles work for Chevrolet. They worked in forge there at Gear and Axle. I had a cousin who worked at the same place. Then my grandfather, he come up here and went to work for Hudson." So Ernie joined them. "Come up here on September the fifth, hired in at Chevrolet Gear and Axle," he remembered, "to be a press operator." He applied in the morning, had his physical the same day, and worked that night.[44]

Despite improved employment prospects, inflation continued to threaten autoworkers' economic security. By July 1952 prices in Detroit had increased almost 11 percent since the start of the Korean War. The cost-of-living escalator clause in UAW contracts had helped to some extent, but most workers felt they were falling behind, especially when taking into account the long stretches of unemployment so many had experienced. The largest price increases in 1952 had been for food, in part because of a serious drought. Even residents of Birmingham, Michigan, a relatively affluent suburb, complained loudly about rising costs. Working-class neighborhoods, where most of the recently unemployed lived, were hit even harder, especially when the Consumer Price Index reached a postwar peak in the summer of 1952. Walter Reuther and GM president Charles Wilson agreed that the cost-of-living clauses in UAW contracts were not responsible for the national inflation rate. Yet autoworkers knew that as soon as they received pay increases, prices rose in the neighborhood stores where they shopped.[45]

Blue-collar workers received another jolt in October when the federal government ended wartime rent regulations. Immediately, the Detroit Area Rent Control Office, set up to handle complaints, was overwhelmed. "Our phones have been ringing all day," said Director Morton Barris. "All but one said their landlords were boosting the rent 25 per cent or higher." Monthly rental for one complainant's house, for example, increased from $58.50 to $74.50. A low-end apartment now went for $45 a month instead of $31. One tenant who had rented a place for $35 a month was now asked to pay $5 a day. The larger the family, the greater the difficulty meeting higher rent obligations, especially with the rising cost of food. But that assumed such families had places to live. "Even if one can find a place to rent there is always a big question," reminded Detroiter Irmgard Bobak. "Have you any children? If one can answer 'no,' he is lucky and can rent a flat or house. But if one must answer 'yes' he might just as well save himself the trouble of asking, for 90 per cent of the people will not take renters with children." The Detroit Real Estate Board encouraged landlords to be "moderate and just," but now that controls were lifted, property owners could do as they pleased. With thirty days' notice a tenant could be evicted for any reason or for no reason at all.[46]

In this context the UAW asked General Motors to reopen their five-year contract, the Treaty of Detroit, signed before the Korean War began. The union hoped to increase by a penny the "annual improvement factor," designed to account for productivity gains, to five cents per hour per year. It also insisted that GM incorporate into workers' base pay most of the cost-of-living increases received so far and to limit any possible wage decreases, if there happened to be downward trends in the Consumer Price Index, to five cents an hour over the contract. In addition the UAW wanted to increase monthly pensions for its retirees to account for inflation. The strategy was clear. If GM agreed, then Ford and Chrysler would have to do the same. And the timing was no coincidence. The economic pain for workers was real, and General Motors wanted no disruptions as it maximized production to compensate for the steel strike.[47]

It made sense to push for gains when auto production picked up, because it was never clear how long relatively good times would last. "Anyone who has been around the State for the past few years," noted *Free Press* reporter Robert Perrin, "knows full well that sooner or later the bottom is going to drop out of the job market again." Based on Perrin's reading of the postwar years, it was guaranteed: "Michigan citizens might just as well add the unemployment crisis to death and taxes as the only sure things in our world." Earlier in the year, he recalled, joblessness in Detroit had been nearly two hundred thousand, and it had been close to three hundred thousand during the steel strike. Those episodes could be added to a long list, including postwar reconversion, the natural gas crisis, recurrent metals shortages, the 1949 recession, and the 104-day Chrysler strike, as causes of the largest waves of postwar unemployment.[48]

Now, however, the call was out for thousands of new workers to come to Detroit. This was nothing new. According to a 1952 University of Michigan survey, two-thirds of Detroiters over the age of twenty-one had been born somewhere else, having moved to the city, most of them as adults, because of real or imagined demand for their labor. "Idle labor reserves have dropped so low that many plants are unable to staff their second-shift operations," the MESC announced. Michigan employers worried that prospective laborers might find newer industrial regions, especially on the Pacific Coast, more attractive than Detroit. "We are hiring all the men we can find," said Charles Williams, personnel executive for Packard. "We don't care what color they are."[49] Many employers, however, continued to care about race. A number of

African American men agreed in late 1952 that they were not as likely as usual to be bypassed in favor of white job seekers at major automotive plants, but they maintained that discrimination had by no means ended. And African American women experienced little improvement in their dismal chances at hiring gates, even at factories like Ternstedt, on Detroit's west side, that had a largely female workforce.[50] Given the disproportionately high rate of unemployment for blacks, in good economic times and bad, it stood to reason that there was an underutilized labor reserve already in Detroit. In 1952 the African American population in Detroit was roughly 300,000 out of nearly 1.8 million people in the city. Blacks who sought work in the auto industry, however, had learned over the years that what they desired made little difference in hiring offices. "A vast source of untapped skilled, semi-skilled and unskilled labor is going stagnant," wrote Detroiter Earl Clemens. If there really was a labor shortage, he concluded, "let it occur for reason only of a true lack of takers for jobs."[51]

While debates continued about the labor supply already in the city, thousands of new auto industry recruits appeared at Detroit's train and bus stations. Elbert Garner, who had moved to Detroit from Tennessee and found a factory job, brought his wife and seven children to join him in October and spent all of his savings on an apartment and groceries. There was nothing left for clothing. Back home, Mrs. Garner said, "The children usually get out and pick cotton to earn money to buy shoes. But there isn't any cotton up here. It's just the blamed cold, or we could get by for awhile." Recent arrivals often went straight from the train station to hiring gates, without having a place to live. Some had lost contact information for relatives and wandered around the city hoping to locate them. Although some would-be autoworkers, like Gene Johnson, gave up on the Detroit employment roller coaster and returned home—in Johnson's case, to Missouri—tens of thousands of people migrated to the Motor City.[52]

If one considered the most favorable economic information, those new arrivals to Detroit were likely to find good jobs and prosper. Despite all disruptions in auto employment, 1952 had turned out to be the fourth-best year in history for vehicle production, and Michigan led the nation in manufacturing payrolls. The economy was on the upswing, and industrial leaders held this to be proof that the United States could win the Cold War while sustaining a booming consumer economy.[53] At least until its last few months, however, 1952 for most autoworkers was a cruel year, filled with unemployment, uncertainty, and economic strain. One piece of economic data flattened the peaks and valleys of everyday life but still revealed much about where autoworkers stood in the early 1950s. The median family income for

Detroiters in 1952 was $4,550. If an autoworker made $2.00 an hour for forty hours a week and was employed steadily for fifty weeks during the year, that worker's annual income would have been $4,000, well below the median. Yet few autoworkers had experienced anything like steady employment, and the few weeks of overtime in the fall hardly made up for the weeks, and in many cases months, of layoffs earlier in the year. Only about 10 percent of autoworkers, the skilled tradesmen who were kept on payrolls to keep them from bolting for more stable work, had any hopes of earning incomes above the median.[54] During the Korean War, Detroit had not reprised its role as the Arsenal of Democracy, pumping out war materiel and providing full employment for all who sought it. Instead, the war years had been anything but stable and prosperous for Detroit autoworkers. By the end of 1952, however, the economic rollercoaster appeared to be on the upswing even as the war remained mired in a stalemate.

4   A Post–Korean War Boom, 1953

The upsurge in auto production that began in late 1952 continued well into the new year, surpassing mid-1950 as the best approximation of a postwar boom. The end of government wartime controls on industrial materials created the free market conditions that auto executives had long coveted, and Detroit automakers experienced acute labor shortages in early 1953. Thousands of migrants from outside Michigan headed to Detroit for auto jobs, but not enough to fill available openings. Despite the labor shortage, intense debates occurred as to whether or not women could or should enter the industrial workforce in great numbers. Employers continued to relent a bit on racist hiring practices, however, and they were willing to provide jobs to middle-age men who were normally considered well beyond productive usefulness. Yet even during the boom there were concerns about the future. Production was so high early in the year that UAW leaders predicted both a significant drop-off and widespread layoffs in the fall. With the end of the Korean War, Detroit workers who had finally settled into military-related jobs wondered what would happen if the government canceled those contracts. An enormous explosion in August at GM's transmission plant in Livonia, just west of Detroit, led to tens of thousands of layoffs in the area and much additional disruption to workers' lives. For a month or two, the fallout from that tragedy masked tens of thousands of unrelated layoffs resulting from declining auto production. Business leaders offered the theory that those affected were "marginal" workers—women, African Americans, the old, the partially disabled, and Southern migrants—none of whom should be considered real Detroiters or actual autoworkers, and whose fates should be of no concern. Although UAW officials and business leaders disagreed about what the future would bring, the many thousands of new migrants to Detroit, along with residents who signed on for auto work during the boom, found themselves in precarious circumstances as the auto market slackened, layoffs increased, and housing options in the region continued to be few and expensive, especially for workers with children.

*   *   *

The auto industry indeed boomed in early 1953. Assembly lines ran full bore, supply lines remained stable, and auto employment climbed to a record post-1945 level. In early January total factory employment in Detroit reached 736,000, the highest since World War II, and over 100,000 more than in nonmanufacturing sectors. Automakers' optimism soared in mid-February when the federal government ended the metals rationing system. After defense needs took first claim, all remaining metals would be available in a rough-and-tumble free market with no production quotas.[1]

To take maximum advantage of these rare circumstances, however, automakers needed tens of thousands more unskilled laborers in addition to those already recruited in late 1952. Detroit business leaders continued to worry that the rise of industry across the country, in part because of the decentralization of auto production, drew potential workers away from the Motor City. The dismal housing situation in Detroit also discouraged new migrants. "There is a big turnover among those who come here, get a job and then spend their week-ends trying to find a place big enough so they can send for their families," explained a Chrysler official. "After a few weeks of this, a worker will quit and go back home." An even bigger deterrent, automakers maintained, was the persistent instability of their industry, which, according to one report, was "so well recognized that potential workers know that today's hiring boom can become tomorrow's layoffs." Thousands of onetime Detroiters had left the city and were unlikely to return.[2] Persistent high turnover rates, especially for entry-level positions, also plagued automakers. According to one manufacturer, after a day or two on the job, most new autoworkers said something along the lines of "Factory work is harder than I thought. I've got a few bucks saved up, so nuts to that kind of labor."[3] Turnover rates remained high, and possibly even worsened, when the economy heated up and jobs were plentiful. In March 1953 one auto company representative revealed, "We are afraid to say that we ever have enough workers." In addition, although first jobs in the auto industry were usually on final assembly or parts production, in the years since World War II those positions were often unavailable, because workers with seniority claimed them during layoffs. This meant that many Detroit youths had little experience with auto work and were unlikely to meet the industry's needs as production surged.[4]

The Detroit labor shortage never became acute enough to fully overcome the industry's aversion to hiring more women, which, according to a Chrysler personnel director, would be an absolute last resort. "Women can do some jobs much better than men," he conceded. "But married women, for example, are not too satisfactory. They usually are trying to raise a family and their attendance is not regular." The MESC agreed that women were unreliable workers, largely because they had to stay home whenever their children were sick. Men's absenteeism rates were just as high, officials admitted, but men generally missed work in a predictable pattern—Mondays to recover from weekend drinking binges, or the day after payday. In contrast, "Junior's colds," which kept women from work, followed no particular pattern. Chrysler management also argued that it would be too difficult to provide restroom facilities for women. In addition, since state law prohibited women from lifting more than thirty pounds on the job, management claimed that they were "not flexible enough in the plant." Auto manufacturers insisted that most jobs they offered were so arduous that only men could do them, although if automation experts were to be believed, many positions were now less physically demanding than the defense jobs that women had handled well during World War II. A larger percentage of married women held jobs outside the home in 1952 than had done so at the peak of employment during the war. The UAW's Women's Department strongly encouraged automakers to hire more women, and the MESC asserted that resistance was based mainly on prejudice on the part of hiring personnel and among union members. Walter Reuther also encouraged auto companies to hire women, but this was never a major cause for top-level UAW officials. In any event, automakers mostly resisted any pressure. Rather than target potential women workers, they focused recruitment efforts on young, recently retired, and mildly disabled men.[5]

No doubt many women did not seek auto work, but a significant number would likely have jumped at the chance. Edith Arnold and Margaret Beaudry, both married, reentered the nonautomotive workforce in 1952 but hoped to be hired at auto plants. In the meantime, Arnold ground coffee at an A&P grocery store and Beaudry returned to a job she had held previously at Neisner's, a local variety store. Undoubtedly many single women were also interested in exploring auto work, especially given the wage disparity between UAW jobs and the domestic service, secretarial, and clerical positions open to them. A GM experiment in Flint, Michigan, indicated that many women indeed hoped to be autoworkers. After advertising for two hundred women to fill "men's" positions at its Fisher Body and Chevrolet plants, the company was "swamped" with applicants. Plenty of jobs in auto plants, including those reserved for men, did not require brute strength after all. Women in Flint cleaned car windows, polished auto bodies, installed rubber strips on doors, tested water seals, and also ran punch presses and other heavy machinery without trouble. Most of the new women hires were married, and most were parents. "I have two children," responded Donna Nivers when asked why she took an automotive job. "We are buying a car and paying for a home. Aren't those enough reasons for my getting a job?" Chevrolet local union president Anthony O'Brien remained unconvinced. "An emotional problem arises when women leave their housework to work on an assembly line," he insisted. "They may work very hard in their homes, but it is different work in a plant where they are not their own bosses and have to meet production schedules set up for men." A Chevrolet official, however, thought the plant might have no choice: "Within the next two months there will be openings for nearly 4,000 new workers. Our employment offices are open six days a week and are not able to get enough men for the jobs. We have to hire women."[6]

Similar to the situation in Flint, when the new Lincoln-Mercury plant in Wayne, just west of Detroit, added a second shift, the company announced that it would hire women for positions previously off-limits to them and for more traditionally female jobs, such as working with upholstery trim. Four hundred women applied immediately. Sixty were hired, most of them married and between twenty-two and thirty-five years old. A number of them already had children. It made economic sense for these women to seek auto jobs, which paid close to two dollars an hour, far more than what they could earn in sectors of the economy traditionally reserved for them. But the trend concerned MESC officials, who argued that hiring women was bad for business. Women, the agency insisted, got more upset than men if there were any changes in their jobs and had to be "coddled" and "persuaded" to do new things. Using more measurable scales, MESC officials conceded that women had exceptional records concerning safety and production and generated less scrap on the job. Women had also proven themselves able to handle huge punch presses, lathes, and milling machines, which led some industry analysts to admit that the ability to do most factory jobs might not be related to sex at all. Extremely high turnover rates for men in entry-level auto jobs supported that theory. Some city leaders saw potential benefits in hiring more local women. During the next economic downturn, they argued, a laid-off woman could "go back to her kitchen and the family breadwinner is not lost." However clueless about the circumstances that propelled women into the paid workforce, this kind of thinking had the potential to help them overcome barriers.[7]

Edith Arnold left her job at an A&P supermarket for a position at Pontiac Motor during the early 1953 boom. She liked her job grinding coffee, but even though her husband, Don, was an electrician in an auto plant, she recalled that they "weren't getting ahead. We were just breaking even, payday to payday. Like everybody else. I guess I wanted more." Edith insisted to Don that it would be a good idea for her to hire in at an auto plant. "Paid better money," she pointed out. But he was opposed. Indeed, he had disapproved of her decision to work outside the home at A&P. She eventually persuaded him about the merits of auto work, in part with the promise of more expensive cigars and "good whiskey instead of belly-rot." He consented, and she reminded him of those advantages whenever he had second thoughts. Edith's job became essential when Don was laid off for a year, but she had barely made it through her first morning. "The day I hired in," she recalled, "it was so noisy in there, I thought, boy, one hour of this, I'm going home." A coworker yelled at her, "and I couldn't hear what he was saying." She was miserable, she remembered. "But three hours later I was getting better at it. I thought, I guess I'll stay until noon." The hollering man, it turns out, "was breaking me in on the job, telling me what to do, how to do it. So about noontime, I thought, well, it ain't so bad. I guess I'll go to work the next day. And the next day I thought, well, I guess I'll do another day. By the third day, I'm all broke in." That first job was operating a drill press for rocket heads, part of a military project. "I *liked* the job," Edith remarked. "These things were heavy, but I learned how to do it and not hurt my body doing it." As she described her work, a rocket head would arrive on a conveyor line "and we'd grab the handle, pull it out, and just flipped it over, one at a time onto the drill press." They'd fasten it in place "and push a button. The machine comes down, and drills three little holes on the side of it, and then automatically turns off." The tricky part for Edith was grinding the metal burrs off the edges of the holes. "I'd take off more than needed to come off. I couldn't stop it quick enough. I was not good at that. But there would be two people that would change off, back and forth, do this and then do the other. And they'd just leave me on the drill press."[8]

Margaret Beaudry also had to overcome resistance from her husband to take a job in an auto plant during the 1953 boom. "He didn't really want me to work," she recalled, even at Neisner's, where she already had a job, "but he knew that the money helped. He just didn't want me to work." She told some white lies to ease his anxiety, suggesting that she wouldn't stay on the job for long. "I said, 'I'll just use all my money and we'll get a brand-new car, and then I'll quit.' Oh, that sounded good to him. That was a way of getting him to let me go." She secretly applied at Pontiac Motor in January

1953 but did not hear back for several months, even though a female friend of hers was hired on the spot. Beaudry grew tired of waiting and convinced another friend to accompany her to the hiring office. "We were in line at 4:00 in the morning," she remembered. "And she never got called, but I did. I got called this time. So I got hired in on May 11th of 1953. Oh, I was happy." Her husband, Marvin, felt otherwise. It helped that Margaret and Marvin were usually on different shifts. That way there was always a parent around to care for their daughter. As backup, Margaret's brother and her sister-in-law, who stayed home full-time, lived in an apartment just below theirs, and both were willing to babysit if necessary. Margaret was impressed that Marvin looked after their daughter in the evenings, when she was at work, and assumed other parental duties. "I mean, he curled my daughter's hair," she remarked. "She must've been a good kid, because she just sat there and it took him an hour to do her hair when I was gone to work. Of course my husband was a perfectionist, so it was done right!" Margaret's first job was on the final assembly body line. "Oh, god, what a job!" she recalled. But she was thankful for her union committeemen. "I used them, too! They were there whenever I needed them, because they didn't treat us nice!" She hated, for example, being scrutinized during bathroom breaks, and she fought with her supervisors. Without union interventions, she conceded, "I would've never lasted. Because I couldn't stand that when nobody respected me." Some male coworkers caused trouble as well. "You could always tell how a man treated you if his wife worked," Margaret said. "If his wife worked, he treated you nice. But if his wife didn't work, he didn't treat you nice. We could spot that." A woman being harassed, the logic went, could be your own wife in a different department. Arnold and Beaudry were part of a wave that pushed employment of women in Detroit to a record postwar high of 372,000.[9]

While many in Detroit took advantage of the 1953 boom, Elwin Brown and Ernie Liles missed it because they had not yet completed their military obligations. Brown had entered the service the previous July, and Liles was drafted in February, so both were away on duty during this steady stretch of employment. Don Hester found hiring conditions so favorable in early 1953 that when he received a three-day suspension for participating in a wildcat strike, he quit. "Turned in whatever tools I had," he recalled. "I punched out, and I went downstairs, went outside, went right up to the employment office. 'You're hiring?' 'Yes, sir, yeah, sure we're hiring.' 'Yeah, I'd like to get me a job.' 'OK.' Signed right back in. Next morning I go back to work, same place, ten cents an hour less." At the time, he did not care that he had lost some wages or his seniority. He quickly made up the dime an hour, and he had seniority again after ninety days. James Franklin benefited from the hiring boom in 1953 after he lost his job at Kaiser-Frazer when the upstart automaker floundered. After seven years away, Franklin returned to the Rouge foundry, vulnerable for having lost so much seniority but happy to be employed.[10]

Although many African Americans continued to disagree, the MESC declared that racial discrimination at industrial hiring offices had essentially disappeared. It is likely that during this window of opportunity more blacks than usual were hired and that some—although not James Franklin—were offered jobs previously not open to them. For example, Ford promoted a black worker, Steve Ayler, from garage work to truck driver. Ayler was the first to break the color barrier for that position, but it took courage. White truck drivers threatened to strike if Ayler remained in his new job, while black workers in the garage warned that they would walk out if he was removed. African American women also finally broke through racial and gender barriers in the Rouge plant's pressed steel department, in plastics, and in the axle and motor plant.[11] There were indeed new opportunities, then, when labor was in short supply, but market forces hardly eliminated prejudice.

The labor shortage benefited middle-age Detroiters who were too young to retire but who had been largely shut out of factory employment. The MESC reported that the unofficial ban on hiring anyone over forty had "gone by the board." Nevertheless, Detroit factories still needed more workers. A campaign to lure recently retired autoworkers back to their plants helped a bit. Some retirees resumed auto work because they could barely survive on their pensions, especially with the rising cost of living, but also because of high medical bills and, for some, boredom.[12]

Contributing to the labor shortage, migration to Detroit was not as heavy as anticipated. Southern recruiting grounds, the MESC said, were producing a "mere trickle" of migrants to the Motor City, and some areas were experiencing labor shortages of their own, prompting Tennessee, in the midst of a nuclear power plant boom, to ban efforts by employers to lure its residents to another state. Automakers, of course, had helped create the labor shortage in Detroit by building new parts and assembly plants in other parts of the country in order to be closer to emerging markets.[13] The 1953 boom, which despite labor shortages resulted in second and third shifts in many Detroit plants, tended to mask the industry's exodus from the Motor City. When asked, automakers insisted that decentralization would have no negative impact on either Michigan or Detroit. "The heart and the brain, and the bulk of the brawn, of the industry are here and will remain," a local automotive official insisted. Plenty of evidence supported that view in the first quarter of 1953. Auto production was 54 percent ahead of the comparable period in 1952, and Detroit factories were humming.[14]

Concerned Detroit leaders, however, looked at their city and saw outmoded industrial facilities, often three or four stories tall, which would need to be single-floor factories with huge parking lots to meet future manufacturing needs. Only about a third of Detroit's available industrial space (1,000,000 square feet out of 3,000,000) had any potential use, and all but 10 percent of it was already on the market, with no takers. Chevrolet's decision to build a new plant in Livonia, a new suburb just west of Detroit, illustrated the problem. This facility, designed to build springs and bumpers for GM's best-selling models, was slated for a 130-acre site, far larger than anything available in the city, with much of it dedicated to an employee parking lot big enough to hold two thousand cars. The construction of better roads and more housing in the suburbs, Detroit officials feared, would hasten the decline of the city's industrial base. Many suburbanites, however, welcomed new plants. When Ford announced that it intended to transfer its main Lincoln-Mercury assembly operations from Detroit to a new plant in Wayne, enthusiastic townspeople harvested corn from the 50-acre site before construction began.[15]

More immediately, the health of the auto industry in Detroit was threatened by the possibility of an end to the Korean War, less than a year after defense and civilian production had become reasonably synchronized. By 1953 about 20 percent of autoworkers were not building civilian vehicles. Instead, they depended on defense contracts for their jobs, and it was not clear that the civilian economy could absorb them if their positions disappeared. In April the U.S. Department of Defense canceled Ford's contract to produce jet engines for the navy. Packard had seen its jet engine orders reduced by a third, and Chrysler lost its jet engine work before manufacturing began. In June the air force withdrew over $200 million worth of contracts with Kaiser-Frazer, jeopardizing close to ten thousand jobs in the company's Willow Run facility. When the government announced that defense spending in Detroit would be reduced by 75 percent, fears of job losses intensified, as did a sense of betrayal, because the secretary of defense in the new Eisenhower administration was the former General Motors president, Charles E. Wilson, who seemed to be turning his back on the city.[16]

UAW officials voiced concern that the auto industry might be heading toward a recession no matter what happened with defense contracts. Production through the first four months of the year had been at such a frenetic pace, Walter Reuther argued, that it could not possibly be sustained. Ordinarily automakers hoped to assemble 55 percent of their annual production in the first half of the year, but in 1953 they aimed for 60 percent, a plan that Reuther called "economically unsound and morally wrong," guaranteeing mass layoffs in the fall. In response, executives from GM and Chrysler insisted that high production was necessary to meet the backlog of demand for new cars. "As you know, the customer controls our volume of production," GM president Harlow Curtice lectured the UAW president.[17] Ultimately, the production bonanza's biggest obstacle was indeed demand, in this case the inability or unwillingness of consumers to buy new cars. By late August the number of unsold vehicles on dealers' lots reached 600,000, a post–World War II high, as opposed to 175,000 a year earlier. Consistent with that trend, automakers began to scale back their steel orders, which was generally a prelude to lay-offs. Nevertheless, the Michigan Association of Manufacturers insisted that there was nothing to worry about, that the biggest threat to the economy was "depression talk."[18]

Despite troubling signs, the months-long boom helped the UAW succeed in reopening five-year contracts with the Big Three and extracting economic gains. Nineteen of the twenty-four cents an hour that autoworkers had received in cost-of-living increases since the program's inception were rolled into their base pay, which meant that no matter how low the consumer price index might fall in the future—and postwar deflation was a possibility—those nineteen cents could not disappear. The annual improvement factor, compensating workers for productivity gains, was increased from an automatic four cents an hour to five. The contract reopening also addressed skilled workers' concerns about wage compression by granting them an additional ten cents an hour, and it boosted pensions for retirees.[19] Yet it remained uncertain whether or not auto industry employment would be stable enough to take advantage of these gains.

No one expected the next calamity to befall Detroit's auto industry. On August 12, while welders conducted routine repairs on the conveyor line at GM's transmission plant in Livonia, a spark hit a line of spilled oil, igniting a fire that tracked like a fuse until it hit a vat of cleaning chemicals, which exploded. Within minutes the entire factory, 1.5 million square feet, was in flames, with steel beams and brick walls twisting and melting as they collapsed. To Dorothy Pekala, "It looked like a tornado. There was black smoke all over the place." A nearby businessman said it "looked like an atom bomb—a great mushroom of smoke." Residents of Warren Township, twenty miles away, could see the plume. Amazingly, only four workers were killed. Two more were seriously injured, and nine were hospitalized for smoke inhalation and burns. Firefighters from every nearby community sped to the plant. Once there, they hesitated to enter because of underground oil storage tanks, and they were limited in what they could do from the outside, because water pressure in the new suburb was low. Housing and industry had outpaced infrastructure.[20]

GM tried to remain positive, but the explosion exposed the lack of safety precautions in auto plants, and the loss of Hydra-Matic transmissions imperiled the company's assembly of midsize and luxury cars while disrupting employment for tens of thousands across metro Detroit. The year's record-setting pace meant that few automatic transmissions were in stock at assembly plants. As a result, all eleven thousand Cadillac workers in Detroit faced layoffs, as did many of the seventeen thousand employees at Pontiac Motor, which installed Hydra-Matics in over 85 percent of its vehicles. A number of independent automakers, including Hudson, Kaiser-Frazer, and Nash, also relied on Hydra-Matics. GM scrambled to restore its productive capacity. It had just transferred the last of its Hydra-Matic operations from its old Riopelle plant in Detroit to Livonia. It now hoped to send that work back to the city, but not enough equipment had survived the explosion. Ford offered assistance to its rival, making available its former Lincoln-Mercury plant now that it had shifted operations to its new factory in Wayne. Packard indicated that it might be able to modify its Ultra-Matic transmissions to make them functional in GM vehicles. By adapting Buick's Dynaflow transmission for Cadillacs and Oldsmobiles and Chevrolet's Powerglide for Pontiacs, GM could soften the blow, but there was no way to ramp up production quickly enough to meet all of the company's needs. GM eventually leased a huge part of Kaiser-Frazer's Willow Run plant, which had formerly produced military aircraft, in hope of resuming production as quickly as possible.[21]

In the meantime, former transmission factory workers lined up by the thousands for unemployment benefits. In all, GM laid off 25,800 workers after the explosion, but the company tried to help by keeping 35,000 on the job to conduct unscheduled, and most likely unnecessary, inventories in various plants. Walter Reuther challenged governments at all levels to treat the incident like a natural disaster. Republican senator Homer Ferguson convinced the Federal Housing Administration to relax foreclosure requirements for anyone out of work as a result of the Livonia inferno. Within a month of the disaster about 800 of the 10,000 transmission plant employees had found jobs with other companies. About half of the factory-less workers remained on unemployment benefits and wondered if their jobs would reappear. A couple of thousand of those displaced were new hires who had not yet completed their probationary periods. According to Local 735 president Michael Loverich, they would have to "wait their turn," as priority for recalls would go to the 5,500 workers with seniority. A number of jobless workers left the state. Others exhausted their savings and found whatever work they could—for example, in a nearby tool plant, brickyard, or box factory. Many expected the Livonia plant to be rebuilt, but obviously that could not happen quickly.

If their jobs moved temporarily to Willow Run, they would face commutes of fifteen to twenty miles, significant by 1953 standards, which undermined decisions to rent or buy homes in Livonia. Few were willing to contemplate what they would do if for some reason the transmission jobs never returned.[22]

James McGuire hired in at the Livonia transmission plant days before the explosion. Before then he had pieced together a living. After the 1952 steel strike he had found work at both a Fisher Body plant and the Ford Highland Park facility, violating the UAW contract by simultaneously holding two union jobs. At Highland Park, McGuire worked on half-inch-thick steel bomb casings, making sure they were balanced. At Fisher Body he helped install headliners, the fabric on the car's ceiling, in what would become Chevrolets and Cadillacs. He did not dare give up either job, because no one knew when or where layoffs might occur next. Indeed, before long he was laid off from his Fisher Body position, but he managed to land a new second job at Dodge Main during the early 1953 boom. At Dodge he used refrigeration skills he had acquired through earlier training to install air-conditioning equipment in new models. McGuire remembered exactly how many air-conditioning units his crew installed, 356, because he kept count until he received a layoff notice that summer. He was able to stay just long enough to train his replacements, who had higher seniority but no experience with air conditioning. Feeling vulnerable with only one auto job, McGuire hired in at the Livonia transmission facility. Then came the explosion. Back to one full-time job, he decided to follow transmission work to the new GM Willow Run operation, and to make things geographically manageable, he transferred from Ford's Highland Park plant to its Ypsilanti factory, keeping two full-time positions, undetected, for the better part of four years.[23]

When GM announced in November that it did not intend to rebuild the Livonia plant, workers had difficult decisions to make. Some with significant seniority took jobs at GM's alternative transmission facility at Willow Run, despite the distance. In their view they would be risking too much by starting over somewhere else. "We moved here last Thanksgiving from Detroit so my husband wouldn't have to drive so far," explained Mrs. Andrew Johnson. "But several of the employes have a share-the-ride plan working so it makes it easier. We expected that the plant was going to be rebuilt. This certainly is a blow, but there is nothing we can do about it. My husband is 54 and he can't just quit like younger fellows can." Many others, however, left GM, hoping to find work closer to their Livonia homes.[24] When GM formally purchased the Willow Run facility, ending any hopes of a rebuilt plant in Livonia, emotions were still raw. "GM has shown disregard for thousands of workers living in Detroit," charged UAW Region 1 codirector Mike Lacey. "Daily transportation to Willow Run costs our workers from $1 to $2. That's a good chunk out of their hourly wages." The UAW's GM director, John Livingston, complained that the Willow Run purchase would hurt "hundreds of workers who are faced with heavy mortgages on homes they bought near the Livonia plant based on GM assurances of 'permanency.'"[25] Perhaps the angriest workers in the region were laid-off Kaiser Motors employees (Joseph Frazer left the company in 1953), who had been displaced earlier because of the loss of military work. They had bitterly protested that government decision, and now they opposed GM's takeover of their former plant, which effectively made their layoffs permanent. Local 142 officials sent a telegram to Secretary of Defense Charles Wilson: "Do you have a few little old defense contracts lying around that you could give to the thousands of laid-off Kaiser Motors unemployed workers, now that you are taking care of your bosom buddies, General Motors, with all of the Government facilities at your command?" At a minimum, laid-off Kaiser employees wanted priority for temporary jobs moving aircraft machinery out of their former plant, and they blocked the process until they won that demand.[26]

Former Kaiser employees had few alternatives, because the boom was fading. The Livonia explosion had occurred in the midst of, and had obscured, a general reduction in auto production. Although total unemployment remained low compared with the worst stretches since World War II, it was trending in the wrong direction, and hiring in Detroit plants had virtually stopped.[27] A month after the Livonia blast, Plymouth and Briggs, which had no connection to the GM transmission plant, announced the "indefinite layoff" of twenty-two thousand employees, supposedly because of a shortage of interior upholstery. UAW leaders considered the excuse a ruse to deflect attention from declining production. The plants had pushed employees to reach record output early in the year, charged Norman Matthews, director of the union's Chrysler department, and since then "tens of thousands of workers have been working only three or four days a week, some of them less than 16 hours." Chrysler did not deny the accusation but pointed to market forces during the first half of 1953. "We cannot afford for ourselves or for our employes to fail to do all we can to supply a market when it exists," explained a company vice president. "And we obviously cannot afford to let competition supply that market instead."[28]

Despite warning signs, industry leaders and boosters declared that all was fine. "People will have automobiles," declared GM's Harlow Curtice, who saw no possibility of dwindling demand for new cars. Benjamin Fairless, chairman of the board of U.S. Steel, insisted to the Economic Club of Detroit that he could not see a recession, "even with a telescope." The only economic danger, he insisted, was pessimism that could "predict" the economy into a tailspin. Ford vice president Ray Sullivan reinforced that message. "It's no secret that a good many businessmen find factors which disturb them in the current economic outlook," he told an audience in Cleveland. "But this is no time to lose confidence or courage." There was a simple explanation, he said: "We've left behind the somewhat hectic and unhealthy flush of the postwar market, and are moving into more normal, competitive conditions. This actually should be good news to all of us who believe in the private enterprise system."[29] In October, *Detroit News* business writer Ralph Watts declared triumphantly that Walter Reuther's predictions of mass unemployment in the auto industry had "failed to come true." Indeed, he emphasized, the five millionth passenger car of the year had just been built. A few weeks later, however, Watts reported that automakers planned a 25 percent reduction in output.[30]

Despite business leaders' assurances, the auto industry appeared to be heading toward another crisis. Unsold inventories of new cars continued to rise. When unemployment in Detroit approached eighty thousand, Max Horton of the MESC put a favorable spin on the development by noting that this was still *below* the post–World War II average. One industry analyst observed approvingly that "for the first time in the postwar period these car makers are letting up on production of their own accord" rather than because of materials or parts shortages. But no matter how the situation was portrayed, tens of thousands of Detroit autoworkers were once again laid off, and there were no recalls in sight. The Detroit Board of Commerce's John Stewart acknowledged that production was scheduled to be reduced in 1954, down to 6.5 million vehicles from 1953's 7.5 million, but he insisted that conditions would "not in any way resemble a recession." He was not concerned, he said, because those most likely to be laid off were "housewives" and other "marginal workers," not part of the "normal" labor force.[31]

The "normal" labor force, however, had increased by tens of thousands— some estimated the total to be in the hundreds of thousands—from late 1952 through mid-1953 in response to the high demand for autoworkers in Detroit. New migrants strained the already inadequate housing supply, and when layoffs mounted in mid- to late 1953, homelessness and desperation increased as well. In the summer of 1953 anywhere from ten thousand to eighteen thousand Detroit families were evicted from their apartments. The lowest rents in the city were about sixty dollars a month for a single room without a kitchen or a bathroom, and often without a window. Unexpected layoffs, more mouths to feed, and medical emergencies were common reasons for missing payments. Constantly rising rents contributed to evictions, as many landlords thought they could get more money from someone else. In addition, the beginning phases of highway construction through the city and the Gratiot Redevelopment Project leveled vast tracts that included many rental units, disproportionately affecting African Americans.[32] Public housing was scarce and of limited help to those who still had jobs but had difficulty finding affordable apartments. Robert Lee Jones, a well-paid worker at Briggs ($2.05 an hour), was evicted with his wife and children, ages five and two, from the Brewster-Douglass public housing projects because he earned too much money. The only affordable apartment he could find, at fifty dollars a month, was a side building, probably once a barn, that had one sink, in the kitchen, and a toilet but no bathtub. "I've only been in here a couple of days," Jones remarked. "They said they'd put in a tub pretty soon, and maybe a washbowl in the toilet room. I found this place through friends and some of my wife's relatives. It isn't as good as the project, but it was the best we could do. There's no ice box yet. I have to get one mighty quick for the children's milk." Ford worker Cotty Mott lived with his wife and five children in the second floor of a condemned house that had a leaky roof and a single gas burner for heat. They had been there for six years because the space was affordable, only fifteen dollars a month paid to the city, and they could find nowhere better on their budget. But they were evicted as part of the slum clearance program in the Gratiot area. "All who qualify can be cared for in permanent public housing," insisted Detroit Housing Commission official Mark Herley. "I guess maybe they're trying," responded Mrs. Mott. "With our five children, no one wants us very much. One thing for sure. We'll have to get out by cold weather. The windows all are broken out. We have only that one little gas heater, and that won't keep the children warm."[33]

Robert and Margaret Veitch and their two girls (fourteen and five), recent arrivals from Alabama, also had difficulty finding a place to live. It had proved much easier for Robert to land a factory job. "This is the best we could find," Margaret said, opening the door to their ten-by-ten-foot apartment above Jefferson Coney Island Lunch and Lincoln Credit Jewelry. "We eat, sleep, cook and live, if you can call it that, in this one room." The apartment came without running water, or a bathtub, or a toilet. It included a window view of another building six feet away. "We pay $15 a week for this," Mrs. Veitch said. "Of course, that's furnished," she mentioned, pointing out a chair, a dresser, a bed, and a stool. A hot plate served as a kitchen, a bucket as a sink, to be filled from the bathroom down the hall that they shared with three other families. "I hope this isn't going to be for long. But it doesn't look too good. I've been hunting for another place ever since we got here. There just isn't a thing. My husband brings home better than $75 a week, but we can't find anything we can afford."[34]

For working-class Detroiters, having children in the midst of the baby boom continued to make it very difficult to find housing. "Can't something be done about landlords who refuse to rent to people with children? Also about those who ask exorbitant rent that it is impossible to pay? How can anyone save to buy a home and raise a family when landlords raise the rent as often as they please?" asked one angry resident. "We've applied 15 different times at vacancies, but when they see our two babies they say 'no.'"[35] "My daughter, who has one child and is expecting another shortly, is looking for a place," explained another frustrated Detroiter. "Will she have to do something desperate before some 'kind' landlord will take pity on her? Every ad she answers is the same—no children."[36]

One way to avoid no-children policies, of course, was to own one's home, but precarious economic circumstances made that increasingly difficult. Most autoworkers, especially new hires, could not save enough money for the down payment necessary to obtain a traditional mortgage. If they wanted to be homeowners, they often had to buy houses on land contracts, which required lower down payments and higher monthly installments for much shorter periods of time than did conventional loans. The seller retained ownership of the property until the buyer paid off the contract, with the final installment often being a large "balloon" payment. Meeting those obligations seemed possible when workers had steady paychecks, especially when plants ran overtime. And when government rent controls were in effect, landlords often converted leases into land contracts so they could receive higher monthly payments. When layoffs mounted in late 1953, however, many home-buying autoworkers found themselves falling behind and the Detroit Circuit Court saw significant increases in foreclosures. "Until recently we rarely got more than two or three land contract foreclosures a day," reported Court Commissioner A. Tom Pasieczny, "but now it's not unusual for me to get as many as 35 in a single day." Pasieczny observed that those facing foreclosure were disproportionately black Detroiters. "Nobody would rent to them with children," he explained. "The husband got out of work and no money came in sufficiently to pay food bills, clothing costs and big monthly notes." Sellers were not required to foreclose on delinquent buyers, but much depended on how pressing the seller's financial needs were and on how easily a paying tenant or different purchaser could be found.[37]

Even fully-employed skilled workers could experience housing difficulties. The Looten family—with six children ages one to thirteen—was evicted in August 1953, despite having a tool-and-die maker as its breadwinner. "The landlord wanted his place, and there wasn't much we could do," Mrs. Looten said. "We put our furniture in storage and tried to get a furnished place after we couldn't get anything else by the time we had to get out." They found a short-term solution at the city's temporary housing shelter. "Last Sunday, we went all through the ads. The best we found was one with eight rooms that sounded about right. But the rent was $125 a month," she said. "We can afford up to $85, but that's our limit. Meanwhile, we're here. I suppose we should be grateful but the place is horrible. I try to spend as much time across the street in the park with the children as I can."[38]

Circuit Court commissioners handled an increasing docket of eviction cases. In one example, a couple and their four children were kicked out of a one-room apartment, with a bathroom shared by five other families, for which they had paid twenty-one dollars a week in rent. Their landlord had found new tenants, a family with six children, who agreed to pay twenty-five dollars a week. Judge William Krueger determined that this was fully legal. "With rent controls killed," he said, "there is no protection for the tenant. Rents can be and are as high as the traffic will bear. Even if the rent is paid, a landlord can evict any tenant any time." An evictee outside Krueger's court-room described his circumstances: "Sure I got a job. And I got a wife and five kids, too. I make good dough, but making that rent ain't easy. I get sick. I lose a couple of days. Maybe the shop is down a couple more days. I'm late on my rent. Do they wait? Not much. If I can't pay on the button, they'll get somebody who can." He had paid his rent on time for two years, he said, was late the next month, and was told he had "seven days to get out."[39] Several tenants, including laid-off Chrysler worker Albert Butler, won reprieves after they testified that their landlord had not provided heat for the past year. Their dilapidated building had been cited more than thirty times for inadequate plumbing, faulty wiring, and lack of fire escapes. Originally designed as a duplex, the house had been subdivided into thirty-three units, most of them single rooms, with several families sharing each toilet. Although the tenants won, their building was slated to be razed.[40]

City shelters again overflowed with hardship cases. The Stone family of eight (with a ninth on the way) had lived in the city's Scotten Shelter since early 1951. Mr. Stone, a press operator, was laid off from Ford in 1948. "He's 53 now and he's hard of hearing," Mrs. Stone said. "It isn't easy for him to get a job. And most of the jobs they offer pay only $70 a week. That isn't anything these days." Mr. Stone hired in with Packard in October 1952, but after four months, his wife noted, "he got laid off and it was the welfare again. No, we never tried to get into the city projects. There just isn't any use trying to find a place. If you make a week's pay, they all jump you for what you owe. What's the use of trying?" Mr. Stone searched for odd jobs every day. "Once in a while he gets a job washing dishes in one of the restaurants along Fort,"

Mrs. Stone said. "Then they let him bring some food home. None of the kids has had breakfast yet," Mrs. Stone admitted, at 11:00 A.M. "School? Yeah, the twins, they're the oldest, they'll go to school for the first time this fall. But they're not going 'less they have clothes. And they sure ain't got 'em now." Mr. Stone's hearing impairment, which was common for press operators, had not been a liability during the hiring surge in late 1952. In the tight labor market of late 1953, though, a disability made it very difficult to find work. When personnel departments could be picky, job seekers with a physical problem rarely passed medical examinations, even if the disability had no bearing on the job in question. In tough times a missing eye, a nonfunctional ear, or a lost limb generally eliminated chances of industrial employment, despite a study of Michigan factories showing that workers with physical disabilities, compared with the able-bodied, were higher performing, more efficient, had lower absenteeism rates, and were generally more loyal to their employers. The study concluded that "the physically handicapped person is a second-class citizen at the employment gates." This was an especially critical issue given the number of disabled veterans, from both World War II and the Korean War, and the frequency of serious accidents in industrial plants. Many of the lighter jobs that would have been well-suited for someone with a physical impairment were reserved for high-seniority employees nearing retirement.[41]

As an increasing number of autoworkers faced hardships, experts continued to disagree about the future of the industry.[42] Of course Walter Reuther had been warning for months that a recession, possibly a depression, would result from what he saw as the irrational burst of early-year production. Citing high dealer inventories, Senator Paul Douglas (D-Illinois) predicted in November that an industrial recession would soon reach Detroit "in full force."[43] Chrysler president L. L. Colbert, however, saw things differently. "The whole economy is at the beginning of a great era of growth, not at the end," he insisted. Millions of prewar cars were being scrapped, he noted, and new car buyers reentered the market every three to four years.[44] Henry Ford II predicted that 1954 would be the greatest year ever for the industry, and President Eisenhower promised that there would be no "boom-and-bust America" during his administration.[45] *Free Press* financial reporter Kenneth Thompson agreed, citing rosy predictions by leading economists and dismissing people like Reuther and Douglas as "gloomsters."[46] The gloomsters pointed to contradictory evidence. The Federal Reserve Bank of Chicago reported in December that unemployment in Detroit had recently increased by fifty-five thousand. Even the Detroit Board of Commerce predicted that forty-five thousand more Detroiters would soon lose their factory jobs. But the board discounted its data by reinforcing the developing view that those affected would be "marginal" workers, not primary breadwinners, but rather "youths, oldsters and housewives who took jobs during the abnormal employment bulge last spring and summer." Another affected group, it noted, would be recent migrants, mostly from the South. "A large part of this group is continually on the move," the board reported. "When jobs grow scarce, they go elsewhere or return to their home communities." Economic prospects for skilled workers, those on salaries, and professionals looked solid. The demand for skilled office help—stenographers, typists, office machine operators—also remained strong, as did forecasts for those in retail sales. In this optimistic projection, then, everybody could expect to do well except for unskilled and semiskilled autoworkers, the bulk of the industrial workforce in the Motor City, few of whom considered themselves to be "marginal."[47]

Times were indeed getting more difficult for working-class Detroiters. When Chrysler laid off another ninety-two hundred workers just before Christmas, it was actually a relief for many of the newly jobless. As the UAW's Norman Matthews remarked, Chrysler workers' savings "have been reduced to nothing by virtually continuous short work weeks since July of this year." For those who had been scheduled for fewer than fifteen hours a week, unemployment benefits, while they lasted, were likely to be more lucrative than their jobs. Business leaders preferred to emphasize the Detroit Board of Commerce's aggregate data, which showed that in 1953 the "average" Detroit factory worker earned eighty-nine dollars a week and kept well ahead of cost-of-living increases. Although the figures claimed to account for overtime pay and shift premiums, they remained uninfluenced by layoffs, short weeks, illness, injury, rising rents, or many of the other factors that affected "average" earnings and expenses for autoworkers. Walter Reuther offered examples of two Detroit plants, one in which workers had been on the job only ten days in a month and another that had operated only six days. Everyone on the payroll at these two factories was considered "employed." If one multiplied their hourly wages by forty hours a week, one would come up with statistics like those provided by the Board of Commerce, but for the workers in question those numbers bore little resemblance to their lived experience.[48]

5 A "Painfully Inconvenient" Recession, 1954

While the nation experienced a recession in 1954, Detroit's automakers responded to the difficult economic conditions in starkly different ways. Ford and GM ignored all warning signs and ramped up production, while Chrysler, Hudson, and Packard cut back auto assemblies and laid off large numbers of workers. Tens of thousands of these unemployed autoworkers resorted to their secondary support networks, yet many industry officials and civic leaders denied there was a recession, accused negative thinkers of causing any problems, and tried to convince all who would listen that volatility in the auto industry was normal and should not be of great concern. Seeking scapegoats for high unemployment, many Detroiters blamed Southern white migrants and working women for the industry's difficulties. Concerns about the effects of automation also intensified as overall auto assembly totals remained high, mainly because of continued high production at Chevrolet and Ford, without significantly reducing the large number of unemployed workers. Some UAW members in the skilled trades, however, benefited from automation, because they helped design and implement the new machinery. Still, predictions that there would be a booming need for skilled workers seemed overly optimistic and ignored the racial and gender barriers to the trades. Jobs in the skilled trades were no solution for the vast majority of autoworkers, who continued to struggle and often resorted to desperate measures to survive. Although booming production continued from two of the Big Three, automakers could not figure out how to sell the cars they produced. One thing auto companies would not consider was increasing the wages of autoworkers to allow them to become new car purchasers. The demise of the independent automakers, particularly Hudson and Packard, further worsened the unemployment situation in Detroit. In addition, efforts by the Big Three to produce more of their own parts contributed to the demise of major suppliers, which resulted in thousands more layoffs. After a near total shutdown of the auto industry in the fall of 1954, production again began to increase rapidly, this time even at Chrysler. But with continued high levels of unemployment during this upturn, business and civic leaders discouraged anyone from moving to Detroit for auto jobs. Although autoworkers who were called back appreciated employment, many remained concerned about how long the upswing would last.

* * *

Conditions in early 1954 made the "gloomsters" seem prescient. In January there were at least one hundred thousand unemployed Detroiters, 7.4 percent of the area's workforce, but most likely double that number for industrial laborers. Some twenty thousand workers at the Dodge Main plant were laid off, and thousands more Chrysler employees continued to experience short weeks, in part because of the unattractive styling of the company's 1954 models. Many of the jobless had exhausted their twenty weeks of unemployment benefits, and most of the others were near that limit. Local union officials at Chrysler plants pleaded with finance companies to hold off on repossessing their members' cars and appliances. Hudson sent home forty-five hundred of its twelve thousand Detroit workers, and grave concerns were expressed about the company's viability. The same was true for Packard, which laid off seventy-eight hundred. Several thousand former Kaiser workers were still without jobs, and defense contracts continued to disappear from the Detroit area.[1]

Yet optimists did not concede defeat, because in early 1954 both Ford and GM were operating at nearly full throttle, trying to gain an early edge in the annual production contest between the leading brands. Certainly autoworkers at those companies appreciated their steady work, which was indeed evidence against a recession. Still, sales of new cars were sluggish. Ford dealers complained that they had to purchase far more cars than they wanted or risk being "de-franchised." The company, however, insisted that dealers had to be more aggressive in pursuing purchasers. With color televisions entering the market at a thousand dollars apiece, a Ford official warned, "There's competition for the pocketbook."[2]

Hardly prospective new car purchasers, laid-off autoworkers had to figure out how to survive. "I have not worked more than three days a week for the last three months," said George Hughard, who had eleven years of seniority at Hudson. Billie Alvis was part of the hiring surge in early 1953, arriving from

West Virginia with his wife and young son. He had worked as a press operator at an auto parts plant but had been laid off since mid-December. "There's no sense in returning to West Virginia," he remarked. "The job situation is the same there." Eduardo Vazquez had worked on the assembly line at Hudson. "It doesn't look good," he said, "but I have been laid off before. I think I can find something." Henry Caldwell, also laid off from the Hudson assembly line, was as upbeat as possible: "I've got three children, but I have been able to meet the bills so far. But, I can't miss too many paychecks. Unemployment compensation isn't enough."[3] Many jobless autoworkers shifted quickly to their secondary support systems. Whenever he was laid off, Don Hester did construction work for an insurance repair company, getting paid in cash so he could continue to receive unemployment compensation. Thomas Nowak latched onto a construction crew putting finishing touches on the new Ford plant in Wayne. Margaret Beaudry still took shifts at Neisner's. Unlike Billie Alvis, Emerald Neal left for West Virginia, as he always did when laid off, this time finding work in a machine shop until the owner abruptly closed it in response to a union organizing campaign. Gene Johnson, as usual, went back to driving a taxi. The split with the cab company, he remembered, was "fifty-fifty," and a good day meant making fifteen dollars on a twelve-hour shift. Elwin Brown was discharged from the military during the 1954 unemployment crisis and looked for work in his wife's hometown, Evansville, Indiana. Finding nothing, he contemplated taking a position with Halliburton, in the oil business, but decided against it because of his wife's concern about the likelihood of constant relocations.

L. J. Scott left the military in 1954 and returned to layoffs at Pontiac Motor, but that was not his primary concern. While in the service, Scott, an African American from Alabama, had become friends with a white lieutenant from nearby Plymouth, Michigan, but things turned sour when Scott, a cook, refused to allow the lieutenant special dining privileges. The lieutenant retaliated, Scott said, with arbitrary chores and punishments, and for several weeks after being discharged Scott was obsessed with seeking revenge. "I was completely messed up," Scott remembered, to the point where he purchased a gun and checked out locations where the lieutenant liked to go. "That's craziness," he recalled. "I could have been in all kinds of trouble." Eventually he cooled down, but there was still the problem of making a living. He considered opening a television repair business, but he would have to pass trigonometry and chemistry tests to get licensed and he had not finished high school, so he had to tough it out, waiting for opportunities at Pontiac Motor and picking up odd jobs. Laid off at the Rouge plant, James Franklin managed to find a job at a Chevrolet factory in Flint, fifty miles north, and he lived there with his brother during the week. Franklin eventually quit his Flint job because of poor working conditions, especially for black men, lack of support from his local union, and the stress of being away so much. He and his wife held firm religious beliefs that the man was head of the household, yet his job in Flint kept him from home.[4]

Business leaders and boosters scoffed at news that workers were suffering. Henry Ford II insisted that "unemployment in Detroit doesn't amount to a hill of beans." Any layoffs, he said, would be "only temporary." GM's Harlow Curtice declared that pessimists were "planting fear in the minds of the public" and that "the result might be the very condition we seek to avoid." MESC director Max Horton complained that of the one hundred thousand workers from outside Detroit who had migrated to the area during the 1953 boom, only seven thousand had left—although he did not explain how either number had been calculated or where he thought the recent migrants should have gone. Total employment in Detroit had fallen by ninety-nine thousand since June 1953, yet it was still higher than it had been in June 1952. The difference, according to Horton, had to be recent migrants. Without them, he claimed, there would be no recession in the Motor City. A *Detroit News* editorial indicated that mass layoffs were part of life in Detroit and nothing to get too worked up about. "Alternate periods of feverish activity and of lull are as old as auto manufacture," the paper declared. Former GM president Charles Wilson reinforced that general view. "I would not worry about Detroit," he said, while announcing the government's rejection of defense contracts for Motor City manufacturers. "The business is never good in winter. Come spring and everything is going to be all right."[5] After the U.S. Department of Labor classified Detroit as a "distressed area," the *News* defensively conceded what most autoworkers knew full well: "It is a fact, however unfortunate, that the industry is and always has been subject to violent fluctuations, both seasonal and otherwise. It has had need of a labor force that is readily expandable and contractile, and this need to a degree has been accommodated by the working habits of Detroit families. . . . An understanding of this is indispensable to understanding the peculiarities of life in Detroit.[6]

Most of the actual unemployed were unsatisfied with these interpretations. Ted Kaleniecki, for example, was tired of hearing responses to mass layoffs like "nothing to fear," "nothing to be alarmed about," "pretty normal," and "we're in better shape than some people think." "In Heaven's name," he wrote, "how can anyone who is still drawing a paycheck have the gall to make and repeat such cheerful statements to 110,000 persons who are combing the City from one end to another in search of work? It really rankles me." Kaleniecki had only recently lost his job, but since then his perspective on the security of auto employment had changed. "My eyes have never seen so many unhappy and worried people than in these two weeks," he wrote.[7] Desperation was apparent in MESC lines. Referring to his weekly unemployment benefit, Bill Barnes explained, "Half of my $27 is going for rent, have to pay it or out we go. I was earning $81 [weekly] at Briggs, shut down Dec. 4. . . . I'm three payments behind on car and furniture." William Tannous experienced similar pressures. "I just can't make out," he said. "I have two children, one five, the other three." He had borrowed nine hundred dollars since he was laid off in December, and fortunately for him, the rent on his public housing unit was reduced from sixty dollars to twenty-eight dollars a month. "But still, what can I do with this check?" he asked, referring to his twenty-seven dollars in unemployment pay. "We need that much for food alone. Besides the kids haven't been feeling well. I owe the doctor money." Dorothy Collins was laid off from Chrysler in January, two months after her husband lost his job with the same company. They and their two children relied on friends and relatives for food. Elva Hedbloom, unmarried with no children, had been laid off from Chrysler since November. "I'm on my own," she said, "but I can't live on $27 a week. It is a good thing I have dates who take me to dinner." Walter Sneddon, laid off from Hudson for two months, offered some perspective. "At least things are better than the 1929 depression," he said. "We didn't get anything then."[8]

Responding to a Labor Department survey that called unemployment in Detroit "moderate," Alex Fuller of the Wayne County CIO Council fired back, "This thing is real, real rough. Nothing is moderate to a man who is laid off and stops getting a paycheck." Conditions worsened when automakers reduced production goals for the first quarter of 1954 by 12 percent. Chrysler's Plymouth plant felt the pinch, with 5,800 workers laid off out of a peak force of 11,500. Packard sent home another 3,800, and despite Harlow Curtice's optimism, 9,000 Detroit Chevrolet workers went on short weeks.[9] One of those who remained on the job at Packard through much of 1954 was Boyd Braxton, twenty-nine, who supported his wife, Lola, and nine children under the age of six, including four-year-old twins. The youngest were newborn triplets. Although Braxton was officially still employed, he worked only a day or two each week through September 1954 before being officially laid off. For most of the year his family faced eviction. Since their apartment was unheated, during the winter Boyd and Lola occasionally ran the oven for warmth, and by the summer their electric and gas bills were long past due. "Things will be better when they ever call my husband back to work," Lola said, "but it's awful tough going right now."[10]

Whenever times were tough, many looked for scapegoats, and Southern white migrants to the city were frequent targets. Martin A. Larson, president of the Small Property Owners of Detroit, called Southern whites "a fundamental threat to our community." "Most of these people come up here from the south, without a dime and sometimes literally without shoes," he complained. "Even though they come with large broods of hungry children, they expect to obtain cheap rental housing, free education and police protection, and, whenever an easy income gives out, to live on handouts from the community." Moreover, he claimed, "these people are prone to violence and vandalism."[11] Although Welfare Superintendent Daniel J. Ryan also blamed migrants for the city's troubles, he criticized manufacturers for luring them to Detroit in the first place. "I hate to say I told you so," he said, "but as long as a year ago I said that if Detroit industry didn't stop recruiting workers in every hamlet, village and crossroad in the country it would get us into trouble."[12]

Married women with jobs also received much of the blame for the city's economic troubles. "All my life I have been taught that the man is the breadwinner and sole support of his castle," wrote an unemployed Detroiter. "Recently I was laid off from my present employment," he claimed, because of "women who refuse to stay home like a good mother should and rear their offspring properly." World War II veteran Walter Grogan also blamed women for his circumstances. "In my opinion it is the working wife who is partly the cause for present unemployment, high prices, juvenile delinquency and even disrespect for the marriage laws," he wrote. "Bar any wife whose husband is working from the factory and let man again be head and wage-earner in his home." Another angry Detroiter described working wives as "pathetic gluttons. How many working women could be replaced by men? Why should a family's bills mount so high that both must work to pay them? . . . Maybe we would have less juvenile crimes and fewer divorces or broken homes if the mothers would stay home and the non-mothers would seek activities in the community to take up their spare time." Bill Thomson, a UAW member at American Standard Company, was outraged that any wives had jobs while men were laid off and wanted Walter Reuther to know about it. "How many greedy and Godless 'Working Wives' are keeping jobs from these unemployed men?" he asked. "How many of these uncultured females are protected from dismissal by the CIO-UAW?" In response, the president of Bill Thomson's UAW local, Henry Sommerfeld, voiced concern that Thomson's views might be taken as the union's official position. "We believe in protecting the job and seniority rights of all workers, including those who happen to be 'working wives,'" wrote Sommerfeld. "If it were determined that married women do not need work as much as men, then it would naturally follow that single men do not need work as much as married men, that men with two children do not need work as much as those with six children, that older men who own homes do not need work as much as younger men who do not—and so on and on."[13]

Working wives, of course, knew that their circumstances complicated any caricatures or wild generalizations. Even *Fortune* magazine noted that for a working-class family to achieve middle-class income status, it would most often require a "supplementary" earner, usually the wife, although the publication warned that counting on those wages as a constant "would be dangerous." "The vast majority of women in the factories need those jobs for the same reason a husband does, to support a family decently," explained a working married woman. "I know, because I am one of them and am mighty proud to be able to make good money." A study by personnel departments at Detroit factories confirmed that many working wives were the sole support for their families. That was the case for Dorothy Sackle, who was divorced by 1954 and would have advised against counting on a husband to be a faithful provider. Anyone familiar with auto work in postwar Detroit knew that no one's job was so secure that it could be taken for granted. Edith Arnold and her husband, for example, alternated between being on layoff or medical leave and usually lived on one income even though both were officially full-time autoworkers. Katie Neumann had to stay on the job at Pontiac Motor if she and her husband, who was frequently laid off from Dodge Main, were to make their modest mortgage payment. If a working wife had an employed husband and sacrificed by giving up her job to an unknown man, she might not be able to find auto work when her husband was laid off, sick, or injured. And what about good old American striving? "I can't see why so many people protest when a woman becomes ambitious enough to try to supplement her families' income," wrote a working wife. "True, a television set might be considered a luxury, but there are other things that are really necessities, such as refrigerators and stoves, which really take a hunk out of savings."[14] Many women on layoff in early 1954 reported to MESC offices for unemployment benefits and waited for recall notices. When asked if she would prefer to remain at home, Geneva Yelland snapped back, "Not me." She had worked for fifteen months on a small assembly line at Chrysler's Eight Mile plant before becoming jobless. "My husband is a cushion builder at the Chrysler Mack plant," she explained. "We were both laid off about two weeks ago. With rent and food prices as high as they are I cannot get back to work soon enough." Alice Stovall, a laid-off riveter at the Chrysler Mack plant, said she wanted to go back to work "because I cannot afford not to." Her husband, she explained, "is a gas company maintenance worker and is still employed but we have two daughters, 2 and 7, and need the money I earn to live."[15]

While Detroiters argued about who should be working, statistics showed, counterintuitively, that rising unemployment was accompanied by high levels of overall auto production. Chrysler, which had purchased Briggs in 1953, was responsible for the largest percentage of Detroit-area layoffs, while Ford offered overtime on many of its shifts and everything in the Chevrolet and Cadillac networks ran full tilt.[16] But fewer workers were required to meet that production in 1954 than in previous years. A major reason, it seemed, was automation, which continued at an uneven but relentless pace, especially throughout the Big Three's plants. One of the year's main developments, a "colossus" machine to produce engine blocks, came from the Cross Company. This innovation allowed a single operator to produce finished engine blocks from hunks of steel at a rate of one hundred per hour. The machine cost two million dollars, was 350 feet long, and contained 646 tools that performed 540 separate operations and 112 automatic inspections of each engine block in progress. It could replace anywhere from thirty-five to seventy-five jobs that had been reserved for white workers. In heat-treat departments, unprocessed steel now moved from step to step with a magnetic crane—ultimately to produce doors, panels, hoods, and fenders—thereby eliminating physically grueling materials-handling positions that had been reserved mostly for black workers. Bumpers were now dipped into chemical vats by overhead conveyors, instead of people, to achieve their polished shine.[17]

While workers and union officials had profound reservations about the results of automation, many business leaders celebrated such technological innovations and discounted concerns about job losses. Speaking to the Society of Automotive Engineers, Dodge president William Newberg declared, "The economics of automation are harsh, but simple: Automate or die." Sure, there were naysayers, Newberg noted, but he dismissed workers and union leaders who "regard automation as a nebulous bogeyman who is after their jobs." Likewise, Henry Ford II accused critics of demagoguery. "If I were a union leader today, I too would doubtless be raising the roof about automation," he declared. "If you want to stir people up, sometimes you've got to scare them." But "obsolescence is the very hallmark of progress," he emphasized. "The faster we obsolete products, machines and antiquated ways of working, the faster we raise our living standards and our national wealth." Automakers, Ford suggested, should "concentrate on making obsolescence palatable to people." Only then, he thought, would workers "cheerfully put up with the sporadic irritations and upsets that go along with the free competitive system."[18]

While not necessarily cheerful about it, a number of skilled tradesmen benefited from automation. The Cross Company's engine block machine, for example, was produced mainly by its workforce of skilled UAW members. Les Coleman's job as a skilled worker also involved developing the technology that eliminated production bottlenecks—and jobs. "I felt sympathetic towards those people that would be put out of work if we did the automation," he recalled, "but I *knew* that this was coming." Some of the most challenging, stimulating union jobs involved designing machines that caused unemployment for other UAW members, which created a dilemma for individual workers and the union. "A lot of us were against it," Coleman explained. "If you're in the union, your heart is with these people!" The Automobile Manufacturers Association insisted that autoworkers would still be necessary in the future but that they would be "shifted progressively into jobs that require less muscle and more brains. The unskilled laborer is going to be less and less in demand in the automotive industry." Automakers agreed that there would be a growing need for people to design and maintain the machines that were replacing so many unskilled and semiskilled workers.[19]

Counting suppliers, nearly 20 percent of Detroit autoworkers were in the skilled trades, but gaining the necessary qualifications to enter those professions was hardly easy. Despite what seemed to be constant demand for skilled workers, apprenticeship programs restricted entry. Union officials blamed companies for this, since managers ultimately determined who was accepted into these training programs. Automakers, in turn, accused the UAW of limiting the number of available spots, presumably to maintain the higher status and pay that skilled workers enjoyed. To be eligible for apprenticeships, which were usually four years long, an applicant had to be white, male, and a high school graduate. He also had to pass a mechanical aptitude test, display competency in mathematics, and be "generally intelligent." World War II veterans were exempt from age limits, but, otherwise, men entering the trades had to be younger than twenty-one and not facing military service. Apprentices received eight thousand hours of on-the-job instruction in fields like toolmaking, wood or metal patternmaking, machine repair, welding, and electrical work. They also had to attend school several hours a week and were responsible for their tuition, which could amount to hundreds of dollars over the four years. Rarely could an apprenticeship seeker show up at a plant gate and be accepted into a program. Recommendations generally came from current tradesmen, and there were usually long wait lists.[20]

A Packard apprenticeship program official explained the pressures faced by prospective skilled workers. On the one hand, such jobs had a reputation for being relatively secure and could therefore help tradesmen avoid the financial traumas so common in their neighborhoods. On the other hand, the social prestige of skilled work had diminished over the years. "Parents are the greatest deterrent to an expanded training program for tool and die makers, a program vital to our future survival and our continued industrial prosperity," bemoaned Herbert Murrer, president of the National Tool & Die Manufacturers Association, before a Detroit audience. "They fail to recognize the dignity of men working with their hands. They oppose their children entering into skilled trades like tool and die making or machine tool operation. They don't want their sons to get their hands soiled or nicked. School teachers also aid and abet this intellectual snobbery by relegating high school students with lower I.Q.s into vocational schools as though they were some form of inferior person." Moreover, established skilled workers often lacked enthusiasm for mentoring apprentices. Skilled work was not immune to layoffs, and it was common for those who trained others, as one apprenticeship official put it, to "fear for their own jobs" when training potential competitors. In addition, by 1954 skilled workers were grumbling about wage compression that had reduced the financial advantage for going through an apprenticeship. In 1947 tradesmen had enjoyed a 55 percent pay differential over unskilled laborers, but that gap had shrunk to 37 percent by 1953. As the wife of a skilled tradesman observed, all recent wage increases had gone "to the unskilled worker or young college engineer." Indeed, most of the UAW's bargaining energy had been expended trying to lift standards for the unskilled majority of its membership.[21]

L. J. Scott had fleeting hopes of becoming a skilled tradesman. Once while on layoff he took a series of career aptitude tests. "I made my best test on tool and die," he recalled. That posed problems, however, because everybody in Detroit knew that blacks were not accepted into the skilled trades. Scott told the test administrator that he figured he had better not pursue an apprenticeship: "I said, 'Tool and die—I can't work at that because they ain't got no black tool and die out there. It's all white.' Then he said, 'I think you're making the right decision.'" In contrast, Paul Ish was an underwhelming, white candidate for trade school but nevertheless became an apprentice in 1954. Although his work at Pontiac Motor had been satisfactory, his high school record was far from stellar, and trade school involved academic coursework as well as practical training. Ish conceded that his father-in-law "hounded" the head of the trade school, "trying to get me in. It's who you know, not what you know a lot of the times. But after you got in, then it was up to you to cut the mustard." In addition, being in an apprenticeship program offered a high degree of protection against layoffs, because training, unlike production, was not linked with fickle consumer demand.[22]

In the end, the skilled trades were no answer for the vast majority of unemployed autoworkers, whose secondary support networks frayed as layoffs worsened. The official number of jobless Detroiters hit 140,000 in early March. In April only 1,000 of over 30,000 in the Dodge Main workforce were still on the job, and 60 percent of those laid off would soon see their unemployment compensation eligibility expire. The Detroit Police Department blamed high unemployment for a 56 percent increase in burglaries over the previous year (1,869 to date in 1954). Most suspects, according to one detective, were either jobless men or teenage boys whose parents could no longer afford to give them allowances. Detroit experienced over twice as many robberies (629) as in the first two months of 1953, as well as a 22 percent rise in stolen cars (1,104 in 1954). Some of the robbers were caught at grocery stores and gas stations where they had been regular paying customers when employed. One unemployed factory worker shot a deer out of season to supplement his family's diet, but he was caught, convicted, and fined $25. Sam Wood had arrived in Detroit from South Carolina with his wife, Jessie, and their six children during the early 1953 hiring boom, and he had worked steadily as a machinist until the fall. Beginning in November, however, sickness and layoffs had reduced the family's $5,000 savings account to $150, and there was no indication that Sam would be returning to work anytime soon. He snapped, took a shotgun, threatened to shoot his two youngest daughters (ages four and seven months), then killed his wife while she was making lunch for the family. He shot himself as well but survived.[23]

Many other unemployed autoworkers also acted desperately, if within the law. Many wives of laid-off black autoworkers resorted, reluctantly, to domestic service. A couple of months after James Craft was laid off from his grinder job, he, his wife, and their six children, ages two to fifteen, were evicted from their rented house. Having nowhere to go, they spent three weeks living in an old hearse. James managed to find some odd jobs, like selling balloons, but he had not made enough money to pay for housing, assuming they could even find a landlord willing to rent to such a large family. Times were so tough that pawnbrokers stopped accepting television sets and radios. "You'd think the depression was on the way these people trot in there every day with heavy television sets to pawn!" reported one shop owner. "We can't take any more. We'd have to go into the television business to redeem our loans if the pledgees didn't return for their pawned goods."[24]

While autoworkers struggled, the main problem faced by automakers was whether people would purchase cars off dealers' lots, where inventories were parked at an all-time high. There was no doubt that the industry could produce record numbers of vehicles and could force dealers to buy them, but how many cars could those dealers sell, and at what profit margins? Research conducted by the nation's leading independent auto loan company, C.I.T. Financial Corporation, showed that the average new car purchaser earned between $400 and $450 each month and made installment payments of $76.19. Even with steady employment, autoworkers making $2 an hour would earn well short of this income threshold and would still barely qualify as viable used car customers. Yet automakers were not inclined to raise wages to make their employees potential new car owners. If anything, manufacturers hoped to reduce wages, lower the prices of vehicles, and thereby help dealers boost sales.[25]

By far the largest of the Big Three, GM established the size of the new car market and pricing for the industry. The company's economists determined what they would charge for their various models, with a goal of a 20 percent profit. Then they estimated the national demand for their products at those prices, with enough flexibility that profits would be ensured even if plants ran at less than two-thirds of capacity. Ford and Chrysler priced their cars according to GM's benchmarks, knowing full well that if they tried to compete on price, GM could easily undersell them and put them out of business. The only thing holding GM back from doing this was fear of federal antitrust suits. GM consistently and intentionally set new car prices that were well out of the reach of most blue-collar Americans, including UAW members, who were among the best paid in the working class. The Big Three's transportation solution for their workforces was captured in a slogan attributed to GM: "A good used car is the answer to the American public's need for cheap transportation." In 1954, however, it was evident that the automakers had miscalculated demand for new cars, and many disgruntled Chevrolet salesmen, who, unlike GM, had to compete on price, called for serious cutbacks in auto production, with some advocating a two-month shutdown of the industry. Automakers realized that they had to reduce the burdens they placed on franchisees, because many dealers had overextended their credit lines and simply could not pay for any more cars. But of course that meant slowing down or stopping assembly lines.[26]

Many dealers coped by "bootlegging," the term used for the unloading of unwanted new cars by selling them at cost, or marginally above cost, to out-of-town used car dealers. These used car businesses, then, could offer the same products as franchised dealers in their communities but at lower prices, in part because they avoided corporate "destination charges" that inflated prices of vehicles in the official selling system. Although some bootlegging

had occurred during previous booms, it became rampant in 1954, and automakers had little control over the situation. "We've gotten down on bended
knees to the dealers, begging them not to sell their new models to used-car
dealers," explained a Big Three official. "And they tell us, when we trace a car
back to them, that they sold it to a school teacher or some legitimate person
who took it to a used-car dealer right away."[27] This sparring between automakers and their dealers underscored the reality that not enough Americans had
the money, or the inclination, to purchase new cars, which forced dealers to
move their inventories any way they could. Each bootlegged car, of course,
had already been counted as a sale by its manufacturer and had been fully
paid for by a dealer, if only on shaky credit. Automakers made money while
autoworkers and auto dealers dealt with a recession of crisis proportions.

Significant shifts in the auto industry also worsened Detroit's unemployment situation. Between 1953 and 1954 independent automakers, such as
Hudson and Packard, lost nearly half of their remaining market share as well
as sizable defense contracts. They could not afford much of the newest technology and could no longer compete with the Big Three, especially with the
end of materials quotas that had effectively guaranteed them a certain portion
of auto sales. In 1954 the only way for the independents to survive appeared
to be through mergers. Hudson and Nash-Kelvinator combined in January
1954 to form American Motors Corporation, which had a negative effect on
Detroit employment. With five plants on the east side of the city, Hudson
had recently employed over 15,000 production workers, but that number
had dwindled to 8,000 by the time of the merger. Nash-Kelvinator produced
automobiles, mainly in Kenosha, Wisconsin, and in 1953 the company had
sold about twice as many cars (150,000) as Hudson. Four months after the
merger, American Motors announced that it would be consolidating all auto
operations in Wisconsin, which meant layoffs for about 4,600 additional
Detroiters. A despondent Walter Reuther described the UAW leadership's
reaction to the company's announcement: "We just sat and listened while
they explained."[28]

No one knew what would become of the remaining Hudson workers,
including those who had been laid off the previous year. Because there had
been so many cutbacks, especially affecting those hired in the 1952–1953
surge, only the most senior Hudson employees were still on the job, and
most of them were over fifty years old. "This is a terrible thing," remarked
Henry Flowerseed, who had thirty-one years of seniority. "So many of us
are older men who thought we were safe." "This is rough on me," said David
Penner, fifty-eight, with eight years of seniority. "For the last seven months,
I've been working only three days a week." "Some of the workers have homes

half paid for and are buying a car," noted Joseph Boyd, fifty-four. "What is going to happen to them? How will they find new jobs?" Andrew Busuttil, with eight years of experience at Hudson and two young children, lamented, "I couldn't possibly leave Detroit. When my wife and I heard it over the radio at the breakfast table, I said to her 'Well, it looks as though I'll have to go out and get another job.' But I don't know where to go." Kay Grence was a widow with sixteen years at Hudson. "I'm terribly worried," she said. "Most of us women in this department have worked here many years. We're getting along in years and are going to have a bad time trying to find work anywhere else."[29]

Detroit's Packard workforce was also threatened. At its postwar peak the company had employed about twenty thousand people in the city, but by 1954 layoffs had reduced that number to eleven thousand, comprised of the oldest and most senior of the workforce. Still, the company hoped that transferring operations to an efficient, one-story plant in Utica, a northern suburb, would reduce operating costs and help it compete in the midsize market. Packard completed its long-range plan in June by merging with Indiana-based Studebaker, and its workers were wary. "Jobs are scarce in Detroit," said John Capello, a Packard worker since 1924 who had been laid off for nine weeks. "You have to be a tool and die specialist just to run a drill press. Skilled hands are doing unskilled labor." "I lived on my savings and unemployment compensation for nearly six months," reported Albert Church, twenty-seven, who was hopeful that the merger would preserve jobs in the area.[30]

Chrysler's takeover of Briggs marked another significant shift in Detroit auto work. Motivated by a desire to redeploy employees who had been assigned to vanishing defense work, and to control supply chains, automakers decided to make more of their parts in-house, which resulted in reductions at many parts makers. The F. L. Jacobs Company, for example, cut its workforce from twenty-four hundred to eighteen hundred. Rockwell Spring & Axle closed its Detroit plant and consolidated operations in Chicago when automakers began to produce more of their own seat cushion springs.[31] This trend proved fatal for Detroit operations of a large, east-side employer, the Murray Corporation. Murray's Detroit plant had long supplied auto bodies to Ford, which decided in the early 1950s to make them itself. In 1953 Murray had employed nine thousand workers in the city, two thousand of them women. By mid-1954 the company's workforce had dropped to twelve hundred. Charles Phillips, sixty, with a wife and five young children, had worked at Murray for twenty-six years. "Where in the world will I go?" he wondered. "I'm able-bodied; can do a job. But they don't even have to ask my age. They can tell by looking at me." Worner Jacoby, fifty-six, lost his right arm in a press accident shortly after starting work at Murray in 1922. "No one will hire me, either because I'm too old or because I'm handicapped," he said. "It was my painful experience to say good-by to several hundred of my friends with whom I had worked for over 25 years," remarked Art Willcocke. "Some were broken in health, some had fingers, hands or legs missing—sacrificed to Murray production. Hundreds were too young to cash in on the pension plan, but 10 years too old to be hired at another plant."[32]

There were indeed few viable employment alternatives in 1954. Despite the heated competition between Ford and Chevrolet, overall auto production fell well below 1953 levels in the first half of the year (from 3,893,369 to 3,514,000). That trend was not uniform. Ford set all-time production records during that period while Chrysler did poorly. But even though the performances were uneven, they added up to serious problems. As Walter Reuther declared in July, "The figures cannot hide the tragic fact of mass unemployment in America's basic industries and in the nation's major industrial centers."[33] The lack of jobs in Detroit had a profound impact on young people. Although almost anyone could get a factory job in Detroit during the employment boom in early 1953, those who were just starting out had the lowest seniority and were the first to be let go when conditions worsened. In 1954 most of those hired the previous year were on layoff, and it was almost impossible for young Detroiters to find positions in the auto industry. As a consequence, gang activity, mostly involving whites, increased. "With the employment situation the way it is right now, a young man doesn't stand a chance of getting a decent job, if any job at all," argued Detroiter Phyllis Robinson. "When a boy—or young man, to be more specific—can go out and get a job, you'll have your cure for young hoodlumism." An older Detroit man echoed that reasoning. "What is happening to us?" he wrote. "I had to start work when I was 14 and I had no time for teen-age hoodlumism, but today, with our modern production system, there aren't enough jobs for the breadwinners, let alone the teen-agers. Imagine what would happen if all the boys in service were home." A. M. Moakley discussed the job crisis with a group of Korean War veterans, all of them out of work, one of whom had a "kid brother," a "June graduate from high school. He's tired too with a bitterness that will grow worse with every negative shake of the head, and every forgotten employment application. He hasn't been in the army yet, but when he goes, he has a lot to fight and hope for, hasn't he?"[34]

An industry survey suggested that conditions were not likely to get better over time, because auto-related jobs in Detroit were indeed disappearing, for reasons other than automation. In 1954 only 30.8 percent of American cars were assembled in the area, down from 35.8 percent only a year earlier. Although this statistic appeared to confirm that decentralization had resulted in a permanent shift in the industry away from its birthplace, Detroit boosters argued that automakers were also investing billions of dollars in southeastern Michigan for new plant construction, plant expansions, and machinery upgrades. The most optimistic of Detroit officials even predicted a return to the city of wayward factory operations that had moved to the suburbs. However, no examples of such movement could be found.[35]

With the auto industry so erratic, it seemed nonsensical to outsiders when workers interrupted rare stretches of employment by striking. Nevertheless, wildcat walkouts occurred repeatedly throughout 1954 and one of them, concerning workloads in the Dodge Main trim department, set off intense public debate. At first the conflict attracted no more attention than any of the dozens of ordinary wildcats. About 5,500 workers were sent home after three men were disciplined for, as the company put it, "failure to carry out their work assignments." The workers considered themselves victims of the company's efforts to de-skill their jobs and then demand excessive workloads on the newly repetitive tasks. Supporting the three who were disciplined, trim department coworkers walked out, then refused to return the next two days. Soon Chrysler's Detroit auto production was shut down and 45,000 of the company's workers were laid off. Together with the long-term unemployed, the total number of jobless Detroiters suddenly approached 170,000.[36] In response, the *Free Press* voiced exasperation. "What troubles us most gravely," an editorial read, "is the long-term damage to Detroit as a place to prosper, whether you are a production worker, management man or merchant. Accumulatively, affairs such as last week's strike hurt Detroit's reputation. And when its reputation goes, hope of an ever-building prosperity goes with it."[37] Overlooked in the editorial was a Chrysler announcement, which appeared during the wildcat, of a model changeover process that was expected to last six to seven weeks. Since World War II, however, automakers had learned how to reduce changeover times to a week or even less. This plan more closely resembled the prewar pattern of prolonged summer layoffs to retool, but it was in response to slow sales, not technological complexity. Although layoffs would be staggered, Chrysler insisted, all of the company's employees would miss several weeks' worth of pay.[38] The *Free Press* editorial staff appeared not to care about the loss of income from this model changeover, which dwarfed the impact of the Dodge Main wildcat strike and stemmed from overproduction and slack consumer demand. Autoworkers and their sympathizers pointed this out. "You make no mention of the layoff to come in August," reminded W. A. Gallimore. "No tears for the lost time then," and apparently no damage done to the city's reputation either. "During the three years I have lived in Detroit there has been considerable clamor raised about the man-hours lost during strikes," commented Buddie Tidwell, who was drawing unemployment benefits while laid off. "According to the noise, great damage has been done [to] the American economy because of these strikes. If this is true, how about the man-hours lost during the widespread layoffs that are in progress right now? . . . Don't tell me there is a difference, for in both situations production is halted, amounting to the same thing."[39]

For autoworkers, non-strike layoffs were the bigger threat. In late August, Chrysler's lowest seniority workers had been laid off for over a year, and twenty thousand of them had seen their status reclassified as "permanent." The *News* editorial staff noted that as long as unpredictable consumer demand drove the auto industry, there was no way to avoid boom-and-bust cycles in the Motor City: "The resulting ups and downs of industry employment constitute an agonizing human problem, and a painfully inconvenient one for the automotive centers." There could be no expectations of predictable employment or income.[40]

Despite these larger economic forces, many people considered unemployed autoworkers to have been responsible for their own fates. Speaking in Detroit at a press conference prior to a hundred-dollar-a-plate Republican Party fund-raiser, secretary of defense and former GM president Charles Wilson chided those who had relied on unemployment benefits during the recession. "I have lots of sympathy for those without jobs," he said, "but I have always liked bird dogs better than kennel-fed dogs. The bird dog is one that will go out and hunt for its food. The kennel-fed dog is one that waits until it is brought to him." Clearly, he implied, a large number of Detroiters during the year had simply lacked the initiative to find jobs. In response, Walter Reuther demanded that the secretary resign if his comments accurately represented his views. The UAW leader took Wilson's words to mean that the secretary would have unemployed autoworkers "abandon life-long savings invested in homes, take their children out of schools and wander like gypsies over the face of the United States seeking jobs that do not exist." In any event, the sixteen hundred in attendance at the banquet apparently felt like bird dogs as they cheered the secretary's announcement that $42 billion in defense contracts remained to be awarded and that many could go to Detroit firms.[41]

Although it was devastating for autoworkers, the near total shutdown of the industry in the late summer facilitated the industry's rebound later that year. One way or another, dealers were able to clear most of their remaining 1954 models to make room for 1955s. With new body styling, automatic transmissions, V-8 engines, superchargers, power steering, air conditioning, automatic windows, and three-tone paint jobs available in their new offerings, each of the Big Three expected booming sales in 1955. Chrysler began the production surge in late September and expected to exhaust its recall list and hire new workers by November. Pontiac Motor spent millions expanding its facilities and hoped to dominate the midsize car market. Ford hoped to solidify its position as the new number-two automaker behind GM. It would take some time, however, for the automakers' ambitious plans to be fully realized. Supply lines had to be filled before assembly lines could run full tilt.[42]

Detroit officials hoped that the estimated 40,000 people who left during the 1954 recession, and any potential migrants, would not be lured back to the city by news of increasing production. The *Free Press* declared that the area had a "labor surplus that cannot be successfully absorbed in the near future" and that unnecessary labor had to be "distributed to localities where it can be effectively utilized."[43] Any migration to Detroit, according to this view, could jeopardize the city's already tenuous employment situation. In November, Mayor Albert Cobo warned anyone considering such a move that they stood "practically no chance of finding employment in Detroit in the foreseeable future." When unemployment remained at 120,000 in mid-November, despite production increases, Detroit Board of Commerce official Harvey Campbell suggested that many of those still without jobs should leave town. He wanted to know how many of them were "actual citizens," and not merely those who had filled the demand for labor during the 1953 boom.[44] The campaign to discourage migration to Detroit rankled many recent arrivals. "I wish someone would tell exactly why we came here," wrote one Southerner. "We didn't come here with the idea of being a burden on the state of Michigan. We came here to work."[45] It remained difficult to define who was an "actual citizen" of Detroit. If one came to Detroit when the auto industry needed workers, did that make the person a Detroiter? Did it make that person an autoworker? Such questions remained significant, because in late 1954 thousands of people, including Emerald Neal in West Virginia, ignored the pleas of Detroit officials and streamed into the city. "Looking for a job, I stood in line at Dodge's for hours," wrote a disgruntled resident. "I've paid taxes in Detroit for over 10 years," he complained, but a new migrant from Alabama was hired before him. And there were still plenty of instances of whites, possibly new arrivals, being hired before blacks, possibly Detroiters since World War II or earlier, especially at Dodge Main, Cadillac, and Great Lakes Steel.[46]

As auto production rebounded in late 1954, layoff-weary Chrysler workers debated whether or not to strike over a variety of issues, ranging from speedups, discrimination against women with seniority, and the removal of lockers, to grisly losses of hands and fingers at the DeSoto plant.[47] It was an advantageous time to threaten a strike, because Chrysler management feared interrupted production. The entire industry was on a frenzied pace, and industry observers salivated over the prospect of producing to capacity, perhaps ten million or even twelve million cars a year.[48] A sizable number of disgruntled UAW members, however, were in no mood to miss anymore days, no matter the severity of the grievances, and especially if they were in plants indirectly affected by possible walkouts. By 1954 a substantial majority of autoworkers had not been part of the organizing campaigns of the 1930s and had experienced anything but steady work since World War II, often for reasons they hardly understood. It was difficult to know, for example, what was really going on in a body plant when facing a domino-effect layoff at Plymouth assembly—or vice versa. In 1951, before the enormous influx of new workers to Detroit in 1953, Walter Reuther had told the union's executive board that "reaching our membership" was the "most serious problem we have. Half of the membership . . . are people who came into our Union after its original struggles were over, and they do not appreciate what it used to be like in these plants before we had a union." In 1954 one such UAW member called himself one of "30,000 pawns" in his union's struggle with Chrysler. Union leaders, he insisted, had "forgotten what it is like to be out of work and have bills pile up all around you until you are frantic with worry." This union member wondered what his organization stood for. "Instead of worrying that the company may not provide work for us," he pointed out, "we now have to worry about OUR union keeping us on the street. . . . Grievances, they tell us. Is this reason enough for you to leave your jobs and go out on the streets for only God knows how long? Is it possible that we might not think that the so-called grievances are worth what we shall all lose?" A worried wife could not understand the strike votes either. "A short time ago the unions were crying 'Give us work!'" she recalled. "Now they want to strike." Many of those directly affected by the brewing conflicts, including those with longer seniority, tried to explain what was at stake. "'Who wants a strike?' Certainly not we men who voted for it," responded Robert McGill. "But we were using the only weapon we had to try to right some of the wrongs in our plant." Nevertheless, such justifications often failed to convince those who were either unemployed or recently had been recalled. "I went in the service before World War II—came back a married man and ran smack into union trouble because I had no seniority," an angry Detroiter complained. "How well I remember the strikes during World War II. The excuse given was to assure us that we would return to something decent—what a laugh!"[49]

No matter what people thought about the possibility of strikes, a number of Detroiters questioned whether or not the high rate of production, even after a year filled with layoffs, was ultimately good for autoworkers. Walter

Reuther cautioned that the record output was unsustainable as long as the country had "an unbalanced economy in which a few are prosperous and the many are in need." It was obvious that the United States had the technology and the labor necessary to produce unprecedented wealth, he noted, but the problem was how "to get purchasing power in the hands of the people to consume that wealth." After months of layoffs and short weeks, more autoworkers than usual were in no position to buy what they made. "We are working from nine to 12 hours a day. We don't mind the extra loot as we have lots of fun spending it," admitted Jim Basden of Local 212. "But I shudder to think what is going to happen later on. A saturation point is inevitable."[50]

6 "The Fifties" in One Year, 1955

To the extent that historians have considered the 1950s to be the golden age for the auto industry and for autoworkers, 1955 is most likely the template for that conclusion. The year began with virtually all auto plants operating at or near capacity, with multiple shifts, and with predictions from business leaders that the good times would last indefinitely. Nevertheless, there were still large numbers of unemployed Detroiters, and autoworkers and UAW leaders feared that excessive production early in the year could mean layoffs by fall. While production hummed at record rates, automakers and the UAW engaged in contract negotiations, with union leaders demanding a guaranteed annual wage (GAW), which, if it worked, would result in more regular employment for their members. The GAW was controversial within the union and vilified by the business community. Avoiding strikes while production and employment were at such high levels, the UAW and automakers settled on a compromise, supplemental unemployment benefits (SUB), which addressed to some extent the hardships workers experienced during layoffs. To outside observers, autoworkers now had high wages, pensions, medical benefits, and protection against layoffs, making them among the leading members of what was called the "labor aristocracy" in America. The reality for autoworkers had been quite different, of course, as employment instability had undercut access to the jobs that supposedly provided elite status, and nobody knew yet how well the new SUB system would work. But more than any other year in the decade, 1955 saw high production, low unemployment, record profits for automakers, and the highest payrolls ever for the industry. Only pessimists, it seemed, focused on the large numbers of new cars that went unsold or the credit bubble that appeared to be financing auto purchases. To auto industry boosters, 1955 was more than the best year since World War II. It was "The Best Year in All History."

* * *

"The automobile industry is in a highly optimistic mood about its own prospects in 1955 and the years beyond," declared William Cronin of the Automobile Manufacturers Association. "The consensus among economists, government officials and business leaders is that, barring unforeseen disruptions, the bountiful and busy economy of the United States will continue on its upward way for generations." A. W. Zelomek, president of the International Statistical Bureau, largely agreed, declaring that "1955 will provide American industry with the greatest opportunity of any year in history," adding that "this applies particularly to the automobile industry." The key was aggregate purchasing power. Nationwide, Zelomek reported, consumers started the year with "close to 200 billion dollars in liquid assets" that would ignite the economy. With this statistic in mind, he concluded that the 1954 recession had been "little more than an inventory readjustment period." Automakers produced cars accordingly. After a dismal year, all Chrysler divisions operated on overtime in early 1955. Ford had fared much better in 1954 and hit the ground running in January. GM president Harlow Curtice predicted that his company's 1955 sales would be "the highest in our history." Walter Reuther, however, claimed that automakers might have to manufacture "plastic consumers" if they wanted to sell all of the cars they were producing. Anyone predicting that 1955 would be a boom year, he said, must be smoking "king-size marijuana cigarets." The *Free Press* editorial staff appreciated the automakers' optimism far more than the UAW leader's warnings. "One suspects that short of his own Utopia nothing can look good to Mr. Reuther," they wrote. "One may suspect, too, that Mr. Reuther feels that until such time as the machinery of government is completely controlled by him and his followers there can be little reason for encouragement."[1]

Reuther's critics had significant evidence on their side. Chrysler's Plymouth plant highlighted the stark contrast with 1954. Whereas the factory had operated either on a part-time basis or not at all a year earlier, in 1955 it was buzzing with activity inside and out. Two shifts of forty-five hundred workers ran on assembly, and three shifts produced parts to keep the final lines running. Twenty-seven miles of conveyor systems moved materials through the plant, while more than fifteen hundred machine tools stamped, bored, and finished parts. City buses clogged nearby streets at shift changes, and workers parked their cars wherever they could. Trucks and train cars delivered frames from Midland Steel and Budd; bodies from the Mack plant;

hoods and fenders from the DeSoto stamping and the Nine-Mile press plants; transmissions from Kokomo, Indiana; tires from Goodyear; cylinder blocks from American Foundry in Indianapolis; and batteries, generators, and ignitions from Electric Auto-Lite in Toledo. Each day trucks and trains hauled away twenty-three hundred new cars along with tons of scrap steel. The plant consumed over 165,000 kilowatts of electricity daily and a million cubic feet of natural gas. Coordinating all of this posed immense logistical problems for Plymouth president John Mansfield, but he insisted he would "much rather have the ones we have now than those we had a year ago." Plymouth was indicative of the entire auto industry, which saw total production in mid-February approach two hundred thousand a week, a pace that would shatter previous annual records by nearly 25 percent. Auto boosters crowed.[2]

Although Detroit-area unemployment dropped by nearly half in early 1955, that still left eighty-five thousand people out of work. The MESC estimated that even with ramped-up vehicle output, the jobless total in the area would remain stuck at about seventy-five thousand for months. Working-class Detroiters understood this. All news reports claimed "that Detroit is having a big auto boom and that jobs are plentiful," noted Edward Klien. "I have been unemployed since August, 1954, and cannot find a reliable job since the company where I worked folded up. I know the shops are working long hours, but they aren't hiring any new help. There is plenty of unemployment in this country, even though the auto plants are busy." Many of those still out of work were older residents who once had high-seniority union jobs at places like Hudson or on now canceled defense contracts. "I would like someone to tell me what a man 50 or over is to do to make a living for his family," wrote an unemployed Detroiter. "I am 58, in good health and able to do a good day's work. I have been out of work for nearly one year. I was a turret lathe operator but will take anything I can get. I have been everywhere I know or where I hear about hiring. But most places will not talk to an old man even if he gets past the outer office which is hard to do, believe me. I have seven years before I can get Social Security. What am I to do until then? Starve?" The unemployed had their critics, however. To the despondent, jobless, fifty-eight-year-old, a fellow Detroiter paraphrased the secretary of defense: "Are you a kennel or a hunting dog?" "I cannot believe it is impossible for these men to support their families," proclaimed another disgusted Detroiter. "What in the world is the matter with some people? Are they lazy, ignorant or just too stupid to help themselves?"[3]

Despite similar surges in production, the 1955 boom differed from the previous one. In 1953 automakers had hired almost anyone available, including women and older Detroiters. They had also aggressively advertised around the country to fill vacant positions. In 1955 there was no out-of-state recruitment, and there remained a large reservoir of unemployed residents, even though total employment was at near record levels. Even the hundreds of thousands at work in auto plants had to wonder if their positions were secure. It was common for automakers to schedule more production in the first half of the year than in the second, but the pace in the early months of 1955 seemed especially torrid. Referring specifically to the annual competition between Ford and Chevrolet, UAW official Douglas Fraser remarked, "No matter which corporation wins the auto production race, auto workers are bound to lose."[4]

With Big Three contracts expiring later in the year, UAW leaders suspected that automakers hoped to create a stockpile of unsold vehicles in case negotiations stalled, especially over the contentious guaranteed annual wage, which the union hoped would create greater stability for autoworkers. The UAW had long argued that auto production had been erratic and cyclical in large part because automakers believed production had to be highest in the first months of the year to prepare for the vaunted "spring selling season." Every year, then, output in the second six months was automatically less than in the first half, so unemployment and short weeks were built into the auto production cycle before accounting for shortages, strikes, weather, model changeovers, and all the other factors that prevented steady work. If companies were forced to guarantee their workers a particular annual wage, UAW leaders reasoned, auto officials would find ways to maintain regular employment throughout the year, thereby minimizing production extremes. UAW leaders began planning for the GAW as soon as the 1950 contracts were signed, and in 1953 UAW research director Nat Weinberg had warned the American Management Association, whose members opposed the GAW as unworkable and quasi-socialist, that autoworkers would get the GAW "just as surely as they got pensions." Automakers were by no means willing to concede, but strike-fighting inventories would have to be quite large. There were far more combinations of colors, styles, and options than in the past, which meant more models than ever needed to be displayed for potential customers. Although GM denied that production rates had anything to do with strike protection, Weinberg pointed out that by the industry's own calculations its current rate of production would meet annual goals in just over eight months. What were workers supposed to do then? *Fortune* magazine concurred with Weinberg. "The major auto companies are still roaring down the straightaway in their fierce production race," the business publication noted in March 1955, "but they will have to start applying the brakes soon," because "the present production pace cannot be maintained much longer."[5]

Whether or not the production boom was intended to be bargaining leverage, Big Three contract negotiations and the fate of the proposed GAW
dominated local news. The UAW's plan would work in conjunction with state
unemployment systems. Each auto company would contribute money into
a fund, managed jointly with the UAW, to supplement standard unemployment benefits and provide the equivalent of full-time pay for those on layoff.
The long slide into recession during the second half of 1953 provided UAW
leaders with a perfect example of why they thought the GAW was necessary.
Autoworkers "don't want to be paid for not working," Reuther emphasized,
"but they don't want to be penalized for not having a job." Ultimately, the
UAW maintained, the GAW was really about guaranteed *employment* to
ensure a guaranteed wage. The purpose of this stability, according to a sympathetic reporter, was to eliminate "the fear of being thrown out of a job on
a moment's notice, and never being sure, from one week to the next, where
the rent and pork chop money is coming from. That is the greatest evil of the
modern industrial system and nobody's been able to lick it satisfactorily."[6]

There was disagreement within the UAW, however, about whether the
GAW was the best strategy to resolve the unemployment crisis. Carl Stellato,
president of Local 600 at the Rouge plant, spoke for those who supported
a thirty-hour work week with forty hours of pay as a better way to provide
full employment. A shorter week would spread available work around to a
larger number of people, but the plan would be viable only if it involved no
loss in pay. Reuther and fellow GAW backers believed automakers and the
larger public would strongly oppose a demand that called for ten hours of pay
without commensurate time on the job, so to them, the "30-40 plan," as it was
nicknamed, was likely to amount to a 25 percent wage reduction. Although
Reuther was irritated by internal opposition to the GAW, he acknowledged
that the thirty-hour week had a measure of support when he added it to his
list of priorities: "We've got to nail down the annual wage and then we will
go after the short work week."[7]

The GAW had plenty of wholehearted supporters. "We do not want any
so-called pay for leisure, we want guaranteed employment year 'round," commented one UAW member, who was tired of worrying "about shut-downs or
lay-offs because orders have been caught up or the market is packed." Edward
E. Tennent, twenty-seven, who worked at Ternstedt, focused on the potential
long-term significance of the GAW. "When you can count on steady work,
you can plan ahead," he said. "I'd rather have a guaranteed wage than a pay
increase." African American minister, activist, and columnist Horace White
strongly objected to GAW critics who charged that workers were inherently
lazy and had to be "prodded to produce." Such assumptions, White insisted,

"show very clearly that there is a certain amount of snobbishness on the part of the opponents to the guaranteed annual wage. . . . The industrial worker wants the same kind of security and stability for his family that any other American wants. He will respond to this security with the same amount of integrity and honesty."[8]

UAW arguments in favor of the GAW emphasized that the plan could help counter the impact of automation. Sensitive to accusations that they opposed progress, UAW leaders argued that they did not oppose future automation and did not want to turn back the clock on technological improvements. The GAW, they claimed, would stabilize purchasing power for the hundreds of thousands of autoworkers still likely to be necessary in the coming years, and without it, boom-and-bust cycles would intensify. To the UAW, then, the GAW was a matter of "social responsibility." Local 174 member Charlie Buber agreed with that reasoning. "Big business, in the process of making these rapid revolutionary industrial changes, shows only concern for their profit and loss statements," he wrote, and "does not concern itself about the social and economic chaos it creates."[9]

Noting that GM's Harlow Curtice had earned $686,000 in 1954, an hourly rate of $342, Walter Reuther appealed for a sense of fair play. "Management has two sets of moral and economic values," he said. "One is for itself and the other is for the worker." Such arguments prompted support for the GAW from the liberal National Religious and Labor Foundation. The more mainstream Methodist Church also supported the GAW. And early in the GAW campaign the UAW received a religious endorsement of sorts from Father Charles Coughlin, the famous 1930s radio preacher who first supported and then opposed the New Deal before undermining his career with anti-Semitic rants. Throughout the 1950s Coughlin remained the lead pastor at the Shrine of the Little Flower in Royal Oak, a suburb just north of Detroit. Apparently still a mesmerizing speaker, he received a long standing ovation from an overflow crowd after defending the GAW—and claiming credit for having come up with the idea during the Great Depression.[10]

Some rank-and-file UAW members, however, voiced concerns about the GAW. One warned that to keep workers busy, "the hard-earned lines of job demarcation will have to be eased, to permit men to be worked out of classification with the resultant discord as the working force is moved from car production to parts production during the slack season." It was unclear how that would be worked out equitably and which wage would prevail when such shuffling took place. In addition, if a GAW plan truly replaced all of a jobless worker's wages, there would be an inversion of the layoff and recall process. Traditionally, higher-seniority workers stayed on the job and those

with less seniority were laid off, collecting unemployment benefits if eligible
and resorting to secondary support systems. With the GAW, higher-seniority
workers might prefer to be laid off first and receive full pay, leaving those with
less time on the job to toil for their income. As one skeptical union member
put it, the GAW would produce a "select class of people, who because of one
day less seniority, can loaf and get paid while the rest of us have to work."
Others focused on the pragmatic question of whether it would be worth it
to go on strike to obtain a GAW. Many Detroit autoworkers were still recov-
ering from extended layoffs in 1954 and could hardly summon enthusiasm
for another stretch without paychecks regardless of how they felt about the
worthiness of the cause. Others favored the thirty-hour week: "I don't think
a guaranteed annual wage would create any more jobs," said Keith Moore,
thirty-four.[11]

Business leaders and boosters harshly criticized the GAW. As the U.S.
Chamber of Commerce declared, "Security is sought at times at all costs,
regardless of its resulting stultification and stagnation." For the individual
worker, the chamber argued, "the incentive to work would be lessened, and
in some cases destroyed, and unemployment for some would be a desir-
able situation." Frank Rising, the general manager of the Automotive Parts
Manufacturers Association, emphasized that the GAW would provide incentives for companies to keep full-time employment at bare-bones levels,
to subcontract jobs, and to schedule overtime rather than hire new personnel. National Association of Manufacturers official Charles Sligh Jr., stated
boldly, "If companies accept the guaranteed wage plan as written, it will
mean the end of America as we know it." The *Free Press* also considered
the GAW to be an abomination. The quest for income security, an editorial
argued, invariably led down the slippery slope to totalitarianism: "Absolute
job stability is like absolute security. It could only be had by rigid Government control of every man's part and opportunity in the economic system.
And it seems to us that nothing but complete Government control of the
entire economy—including telling the citizen when he may buy and where
he must buy—could make the guaranteed annual wage possible." This was
similar to the argument made by the Michigan Manufacturers Association,
which called the GAW a "foreign, socialistic nightmare." Ford's John Bugas
quipped that his company would support the GAW "if only somebody would
come up with a good plan for GAP, or guaranteed annual profits." Chrysler
president L. L. Colbert emphasized that a GAW was only feasible in certain
industries in which "the same number of products will be produced each
year." That might work for soap or laundry detergent, he suggested, but he
did not think the automobile industry was "stabilized sufficiently to make

accurate forecasts for the coming year, and regulate your production to these forecasts." A company could store millions of bars of soap, he pointed out, but "you start talking about building and storing automobiles until you can sell them and you are talking about a different thing altogether"—which, ironically, was how many dealers, who bore the burden of overproduction, saw the current system.[12]

In the end, auto industry officials opposed the GAW because they knew their business was too volatile to guarantee anything like steady jobs for a whole year. The likelihood of stringing together consecutive years of full employment seemed like a fantasy. The UAW's plan for guaranteed yearly wages was ultimately defensive, an attempt to create stability for its membership in a period marked by huge swings in employment and massive investment in automation. As one industry observer put it, "There have been so many job 'crises' in the State, that the citizens have learned to take them pretty much in stride. But familiarity has bred no great fondness for the wild fluctuations." While auto executives claimed to empathize with their employees who suffered from this instability, they did so while trumpeting the marvels of competition in a free market economy. Autoworkers had ample opportunity to achieve stability, they insisted, with retraining or relocation.[13]

The positive aspects of a free market economy seemed apparent through the first half of 1955. By early May second shifts were common and unemployment in Detroit had dropped to forty-eight thousand, just 3.2 percent of the metro area's workforce. Pontiac Motor produced more passenger cars by the second week of April than it had in all of 1954. Chrysler was also booming. The company earned more in the first two months of 1955 than it had in all of 1954 and produced nearly twice as many vehicles in the first quarter of 1955 than it had in the same period the previous year. That news overshadowed Plymouth's announcement that it planned to increase production by 28 percent yet saw no need for additional hiring.[14]

L. J. Scott appreciated the good times. "Fifty-five was a *boom* year," he recalled. "I bought me a '55 Star Chief Pontiac. My second car. My first new one, though. Oh, I was feeling good. Things were looking my way, because in '55 you could work all you wanted to. I worked a lot of overtime." He was also single and saving on rent by living with family members, which made purchasing a new car possible. Thomas Nowak also benefited from the boom. After staying at Kaiser Motors until the bitter end, in 1955 he hired in at Ford's Wayne plant, where he had recently worked on a construction crew. Unsure about the stability of auto employment, he hedged his bets by taking a second job handling baggage and cleaning planes for American Airlines at the Willow Run airport. With three children and a fourth on the way, he explained, "I had to hustle." He worked days at the airport and evenings at the Mercury plant, with forty-five minutes between shifts to drive the ten miles from Willow Run to Wayne. Nowak rarely saw his family, and he eventually exhausted himself. "I run off the road a couple of times," he recalled. So he quit the airline job after three and a half months. The Mercury job paid more and he liked it better. In addition, after his eight hours on the assembly line, he often worked overtime, using his skills as a repairman. "That's where I was making a lot of my money for my house," he noted. After missing the 1954 recession while in the military, Joe Woods returned to Pontiac Motor in 1955 and was allowed to run a production job on the engine block line that, before he left for Korea, would have been off limits to a black man. The thrill wore off quickly, however, even though he liked the steady pay. "All I was doing was checking the bore numbers and sizes, make sure everything was correct," he recalled. "You could just sit up there and go to sleep." Elwin Brown definitely valued the relative stability at Pontiac Motor in early 1955. His pregnant wife, Mary, had decided to stay behind in her hometown of Evansville, Indiana, when he was recalled near the beginning of the production upturn. The unpredictability of auto work and the lack of a family support network in Pontiac had made her reluctant to leave, but boom conditions eventually convinced her to join her husband. The upturn also allowed James Franklin to have no regrets about leaving his job in Flint to be back with his family in Ypsilanti, because he was quickly rehired at the Rouge, where he had worked twice before. Edith Arnold missed the 1955 boom as she recovered from surgery, but Margaret Beaudry, Katie Neumann, and Dorothy Sackle had all the work they wanted. Paul Ross found ways to make more than his wages from auto work during these times. "What I did is run a check pool," he said. "Everybody gets a check once a week, and you had a number on it." Players in the pool would pick their best five numbers as if they were a hand of cards. "Everybody that wanted to play, they'd pay a dollar, and whoever got the best poker hand won the money," minus Ross's cut. "I made my car payments and stuff on that," he remembered.[15]

Automakers emphasized these bountiful times when warning of the dangers of strikes over new contracts. "We believe our employes are just as eager as we are for the continuation of what has been a generally happy and profitable period," Henry Ford II claimed. "We wish we could be sure that all union leaders feel the same way." Ford was especially concerned because if the UAW held out for the GAW, his company would most likely be the strike target. Since Ford had only about a third as many employees nationwide as GM, fewer union members would need relief. It also did not make sense for the UAW to focus strike preparations on Chrysler, even though that company was also much smaller than GM, because its contract expired a few months after Ford's and GM's. Eager to maintain uninterrupted production but not prepared to concede on the GAW, Ford offered to allow union members to purchase company stock at half price when the privately traded automaker went public, which it was scheduled to do in the near future.[16]

UAW officials criticized the stock plan, as did rank-and-filer Michael Turfe, twenty-five. "I've never worked a full year yet," Turfe said. "If a man is going to be laid off for a month or two, how can he afford to buy stock, no matter what the price, or get ahead at all?" "We could not buy any stock in the company," insisted the wife of a Ford worker. "We have three children."[17] A Ford stamping plant worker's wife showed exactly how her husband's pay of $4,582.28 had been spent the previous year:

Telephone	$ 78.53
Gas (including heating for six months)	119.03
Oil (six months)	69.21
Water (six months)	15.78
Car insurance	63.00
Rent and house payments	870.00
Washing machine	60.00
Interest	44.00
Union dues	30.00
Insurance for children	80.48
Blue Cross (surgical, no medical)	70.00
FICA and Income Tax	415.62
Husband's insurance	41.68
Doctor bills, X-rays, medicine, etc.	528.00
Milk	175.00
Church and contributions	200.00
Food ($25 week)	1,300.00
Screens and storm doors	42.00
Husband's transportation to work	120.00
Total	$4,421.93

"That leaves $180.35," she calculated. Yard work ate up some of that total, as did shoes for their two daughters, ages ten and eleven. Their car, used sparingly, still burned fifty dollars in gasoline for the year. In the end, forty dollars for the year was available for clothes for the children and family entertainment. "Will you please tell me what we are going to use to buy stock with?" she asked. According to a tax preparer, who had helped hundreds of Ford workers with their returns, "Not one family—where the wage earner was under 45 years old, had any funds for investment. Practically all had a 'hefty' portfolio of mortgages on everything that could be mortgaged," he explained. "If a man hasn't the money to take advantage of the offer then the opportunity does not actually exist for him." Compared with Chrysler employees, Ford workers had experienced a bonanza year in 1954, but even with relative prosperity—and what appeared to be full employment at the stamping plant—a stock plan made no sense. On the eve of the strike dead-line, the UAW proposed a binding secret ballot of Ford workers: rank-and-file union members would settle the issue by choosing either the company's stock option plan or the GAW. Ford backed down and the deadline passed without a formal walkout, although wildcat strikes erupted throughout the company's plants.[18]

For all the controversy over the GAW, the outcome of negotiations seemed anticlimactic. Shortly before a revised strike deadline—a few days after the original one—Ford and the UAW reached an agreement on a three-year contract. On the biggest issue, the GAW, the two sides settled on what was essentially an improvement in unemployment benefits. The company agreed to contribute toward a fund that would eventually supplement what workers already qualified for through state-run unemployment compensation pro-grams. The existing state system in Michigan provided from roughly a third to just under half of take-home pay, depending on a worker's specific job and number of dependents. With the new supplemental unemployment benefit, a laid-off worker would be eligible to receive 65 percent of take-home pay for the first four weeks of idleness and 60 percent for an additional twenty-two weeks, both far short of the UAW's ultimate goal of 100 percent for a full year. Since employers also funded the state unemployment programs, in effect Ford would pay for the entire benefit package, with one check coming from the state government and the other directly from the company. Back-ing off on years of declarations that no contract would be signed without a full-fledged GAW, Walter Reuther called it a "good agreement" that "provides the principle upon which we are going to build the guaranteed annual wage." Although just a beginning, he emphasized, SUB would "provide workers and their families a greater measure of security against the hardships and hazards of unemployment."[19]

Ford officials also spun the compromise as a victory. As a company spokes-man explained, downturns in the industry were so frequent that something had to be done, but the company wanted to be sure that any plan included "enough differential between the man who is working and the laid-off worker so that the man on the job would not feel discriminated against." In addition, total unemployment pay for any worker had to "be low enough to provide him with an incentive to look for another job in the event of a long lay-off." The company thought that it had hit that sweet spot with the 60–65 percent mark, insisting that "its greatest responsibility to its employes is for the short-term layoff." At a cost to the company of five cents per hour per employee, a fund of $55 million would be built up over several years. Depending on the frequency and duration of layoffs, that sum might or might not be adequate. "There is no such thing as a complete guarantee," the company emphasized.[20]

Most business leaders and industry boosters harshly criticized the settlement, with some charging that Ford officials had gone insane. NAM's Henry Riter was livid, insisting that by giving in on the GAW even a little bit, Ford had steered the nation down a road "leading to a socialistic state and controlled economy." *Free Press* editors largely shared this view, although they breathed a sigh of relief that the UAW's full GAW proposal, which they termed "a thing of unlimited dangers," was defeated. "The question is whether once the start is made in such a revolutionary direction these safeguards and limitations can be maintained." Syndicated business columnist Sylvia Porter warned readers that the UAW-Ford settlement, "in one of the most violently seasonal of industries," meant "the increasing probability that over the long term, our cost of living is going up and the buying power of your dollar is going down." Most economists seemed to think that the SUB compromise would contribute to what was becoming known as the "Century of Inflation." Many auto industry analysts agreed, arguing that the only way now for carmakers to keep a lid on prices was through increased automation. As one expert noted, "Lower production costs will have to be achieved to keep retail prices from higher rises." University of Michigan economist Paul McCracken, however, did not share the dire views. "This does not sound the death knell of the free enterprise system," he argued. In effect, he explained, Ford would divert about $50 million of potential purchasing power into its SUB fund to be released as actual spending when the economy needed it most.[21]

Plenty of Ford workers had negative reactions to the agreement, especially at the Rouge plant, where support had been strong for the 30–40 plan. "If some of you would keep quiet I could explain these things to you," Local 600 president Carl Stellato snapped at hundreds of Rouge workers who had gathered to hear the settlement terms. "You don't boo things that give you security." Stellato was aware that Ford had refused even to discuss the 30-40 plan. Indeed, at a post-agreement news conference, personnel director John Bugas laughed at the thought of the thirty-hour week. Nevertheless, many low-seniority workers remained skeptical that the new SUB provisions would be enough to help them weather economic downturns. Skilled workers were the most vocal opponents of the new contract. Traditionally they had been relatively protected from layoffs and were therefore the least likely to benefit from SUB. "The union promised the skilled workers a 30-cent package increase and then backed down and settled for much less," complained Ignie

Mitskavich, a toolmaker. As Mitskavich noted, the SUB plan did nothing to address wage compression that continued to reduce the economic advantage of belonging to the trades. A skilled maintenance worker at the Rouge accused union negotiators of selling tradesmen "down the river for nothing."[22]

Some of the complexities of the contract settlement could be found in the case of Jim Covert, fifty-five, who lived in Dearborn and had worked at the Rouge plant for thirty-three years. In 1955 he was a final inspector on a motor assembly line and stood to earn about $4,700 if he worked full-time. His job was to check the width of a particular hole in connecting rods as they passed by him. His gauge would read red, yellow, or blue, and he marked each rod accordingly, about three thousand times a day. He agreed that his task got "a little monotonous—you begin to see connecting rods in your sleep." But at least it did not involve much physical exertion, something his doctor had told him to avoid after a heart attack three years earlier. There was no possibility of going back to his previous job, lifting sixty-pound crankshafts twenty-five hundred times a day. Covert had a wife and two adult sons. They had purchased their home during World War II and paid far less on their mortgage in 1955 than they would have had to pay in rent for an apartment. Covert had favored the thirty-hour week and full pensions at fifty-five, precisely his age. The new SUB plan did not interest him. "With my seniority," he explained, "I haven't been laid off at all since 1948." SUB might have been better suited for his two sons. Charles, twenty-three, had worked in a Ford glass plant but gave up on auto work after being laid off for two months. Donald, twenty-two, had recently been laid off for six weeks and calculated that the new SUB pay would have given him only an extra $4.25 for the first four weeks and $1.00 for each additional week of his time off. "He's not impressed," Covert said. Whether or not Covert was typical of Ford workers, his story showed that in 1955 only the highest-seniority Ford workers seemed to have experienced any job stability in recent years and that there was much skepticism about SUB.[23]

Workers like Jim Covert were what intellectuals had in mind when they analyzed the new "labor aristocracy." "Its founders are the United Auto Workers," proclaimed Sylvia Porter. "Its heart lies in Detroit—and its elite are those who work for the auto giants." If you were in this group, the argument went, you were among the highest-paid industrial workers in the country, you could receive a pension when you retired, you only had to pay half the premium for hospitalization and surgery costs, you had a cost-of-living clause to protect you against inflation, you got a paid vacation, and with the new contract, you received triple-time pay for working on national holidays. You enjoyed all of that, plus you now had added economic protection in case of layoffs. All of that was technically true. "Our workers certainly are in a preferred position in the country," bragged a Ford official when asked how his company's benefits compared with those of other employers. "We're about tops in the country," agreed a UAW spokesman. "And we haven't stopped yet." *Fortune* magazine gushed about the rise of the "Detroit middle class," calling it "one of the most quiet and orderly overthrowings of an old established order possible to imagine."[24]

But this comparison with the mass of nonunion workers in the country, and even with most who were unionized, did not accurately depict the experiences of the vast majority of autoworkers since World War II, few of whom would have considered themselves to have lived the lives of the elite. Even the most aristocratic members of the UAW, the skilled tradesmen, were hopping mad in 1955. Few unskilled workers had received anything resembling steady work since the war, which undercut the significance of high hourly wages. Indeed, many had only begun auto work in 1953 and then were promptly laid off, often for an entire year. Medical expenses still bankrupted working-class families. The cost-of-living clause seemed to trigger higher prices even though it was supposed to account for existing inflation. Moreover, relatively few of the hundreds of thousands of autoworkers had been able to retire, and those who received pensions generally found them inadequate, especially with high inflation. This became apparent to Ford officials, somewhat embarrassingly, when they summoned the press to cover a celebration for their ten-thousandth retiree, Jim Wolfe, sixty-five, who had worked at the company for over thirty years. He and his wife, Annie, could expect pension and Social Security benefits totaling $151 a month, less than half of what he had earned before retirement. "It is going to be a tight squeeze," Wolfe told the audience, which included Ford executives, top UAW officials, and local media teams assembled in his front yard. "But my oldest boy, Jim, 37, has a concrete business and maybe I can help him out." Wolfe, who had never owned a car, told the gathering that he was "ashamed of my house. That's the real reason I retired. . . . It's a frame house, and you know what happens when you let them go for a while. I've been working afternoons for seven or eight years now, and that kind of a job is all bed and work. You never have time for anything around the house."[25]

Skilled workers at GM, the peak of any "labor aristocracy," observed the settlement at Ford and wanted none of it. They staged wildcat strikes while their contract negotiations were under way, resulting in ten thousand layoffs in Detroit and sixty thousand nationwide. "We're always the last to be laid off anyway," explained Harold Frye, spokesman for a group of striking skilled workers in Flint. "We'd rather have more money and have some other problems straightened out than agree to the same thing the union got from Ford." For many skilled workers it made sense to form their own locals, separate from the unskilled and semiskilled, a reversal of the 1930s-era "industrial union" approach, which maintained that for maximum leverage the entire workforce should belong to the same bargaining unit. "We feel that's the only way we can get real representation," Frye insisted. Yet just three days after the GM skilled-worker wildcat wave, the company and the UAW reached an agreement almost identical to the one signed by the union and Ford.[26]

Business boosters were generally appalled. "The magnitude of what's just happened in Detroit is beyond the mental reach of any man to comprehend," declared the *Free Press*. Reuther was able "TO KICK IN THE DOOR TO-WARD GAW AT FORD—AND THEN WALK RIGHT INTO THE ROOM UNHINDERED AT GM." Business leaders feared "that Big Labor might be able to push those limits up near the Utopian Reuther goal of paying a man as much for not working as for working." Industry analyst Stanley Rector warned that 1955 would be seen "as the year Reuther performed a hysterectomy on the goose that laid the golden eggs." Regaining his equilibrium a few days later, *Free Press* publisher John S. Knight conceded that the UAW was "right in saying the new contracts will give the auto makers more incentive to schedule manpower and production more evenly. The factory worker will become a better credit risk, buy a little more from downtown stores on time, splurge a little more on recreation and vacations. Steadily, but surely, his personal economic roller-coaster will flatten out. The ride will be less thrilling. But more satisfying." Perhaps Knight accepted the UAW's calculation that the full-fledged GAW would have added only twelve dollars to the cost of a new car, or 4 percent on the average of three hundred dollars' worth of labor that went, into each vehicle.[27]

For all the debate concerning the new SUB plan, over 134,000 GM workers struck the first day under their new contract to protest the lack of progress on resolving local issues. Pontiac Motor, for example, was completely shut down because of disagreements over time schedules and working conditions. This resulted in layoffs at the Fisher Body facility in Pontiac, a main supplier. UAW officials pleaded with members to stay on the job, with some success, but four days later over 65,000 GM workers, including thousands at Detroit's Fleetwood and Fisher Body plants, were still at home because of strikes and resulting parts shortages. Workers at the Fleetwood plant made a number of demands, including the reinstatement of morning and afternoon coffee breaks, something the relentless production pace no longer allowed. Cleanliness was also an issue. "I have to lie and cheat every time I want to wash my hands," insisted welder George Selby. "I don't think a man should have to crawl to his foreman for permission to do that." Women workers complained about filthy conditions and demanded that GM provide them with gloves. In addition, a number of union members wanted smoking areas and more convenient locations for time clocks.[28]

With Chrysler negotiations looming, warning signs indicated that the auto boom had passed its peak. Automakers had already ratcheted back output, most likely, as UAW officials had predicted, because of the breakneck pace during the year's first quarter. If the industry's annual production forecasts were still accurate, the boom from January to March portended as much as a 40 percent reduction during the second half of the year, significantly larger than the customary target of a 10 percent differential. Overtime hours began to disappear, and unemployment crept upward with the elimination of many second-shift operations. In May the number of unsold cars nationwide reached a record 840,000, almost a quarter of a million above the previous high. Huge inventories alone were not necessarily critical, because they could be reduced quickly with strong sales. But as purchases declined, dealers became desperate, and now familiar accusations of bootlegging flew in every direction.[29] To unload 1955 models before the 1956 lines were introduced, some dealers offered incentives like television sets, mink coats, washing machines, refrigerators, trips to Paris, or shares of stock in uranium companies, while others used hard-nosed and duplicitous tactics to get consumers to buy. Debt had fueled the boom, and some economists argued that the nation's prosperity was all a credit bubble waiting to burst. Altogether, auto loans had increased in June by $576 million to an all-time high of $12.5 billion, amounting to half of all the country's installment credit. In August the General Motors Acceptance Corporation (GMAC), the company's car loan division, sent stern warnings to its 18,500 dealers to stop offering "easy credit." Too many purchasers, the GMAC said, were paying more than "they could comfortably afford." In addition, with long repayment periods offered by dealers, there was greater likelihood that the amount owed on vehicles would be greater than their market values, a condition ripe for repossessions. The National Automobile Dealers Association did not mince words, telling its 32,000 members "to put a stop to crazy credit and start back on the road to sanity."[30]

As concerns increased in the auto industry, the Eisenhower administration declared 1955 to be the "biggest ever" for prosperity in America. Detroit headlines concurred, with one declaring in early July that 1955 had already qualified as "The Best Year in All History." Until that point unemployment rates had been low, inflation appeared to be under control, and income and production totals were at all-time highs. Economic experts also offered rosy interpretations of recent history. Government spokespeople asserted that Americans' personal incomes had "never stopped rising," even during the year and a half of recession that began in mid-1953. Moreover, the U.S. Department of Commerce claimed that the 1954 downturn was not as bad as it had previously thought. Total economic activity, the government agency announced, had dropped only about 1 percent from 1953 to 1954, which to economists meant the recession had made little impact on the country. For some Detroiters, these statistics made sense and outweighed any concerns about the future. Automakers had produced a record number of cars during the first half of 1955, surpassing some post–World War II annual totals. GM's success was increasingly important to Detroit autoworkers, because the largest carmaker had greatly expanded facilities and employment in the area. Counting its Pontiac and Willow Run operations, GM had nearly 73,000 workers in metro Detroit in mid-1955, nearly double its total from five years earlier. Total industrial payrolls in Detroit reached all-time highs in 1955, even though total employment remained 10 percent below that in 1953. Largely because of fringe benefit costs—for unemployment benefits, medical insurance, and pensions—auto companies preferred offering overtime hours to its existing workforce, by operating on six days a week or for more than eight hours a day, before hiring new employees. But there were still an estimated 683,000 manufacturing workers in metro Detroit, and they provided much of the purchasing power that sustained the area's 638,000 nonmanufacturing employees.[31]

Since these conditions could easily be considered the foundation for a continuing boom, from Chrysler's perspective it made sense to reach an agreement with the UAW and not risk a profit-wrecking strike. Chrysler had done far worse than Ford and GM during the 1954 recession, by its own admission because of "stodgy" car designs that no longer appealed to consumers. The company had also begun an aggressive, long-term process of expansion and retooling, including the introduction of state-of-the art automation in many plants. Business observers gave much of the credit for Chrysler's comeback in 1955 to its president, L. L. "Tex" Colbert, who had gained his reputation managing Dodge's B-29 aircraft manufacturing in Chicago during World War II. After the 1954 debacle, Colbert pledged to regain lost market share. Through the first eight months of 1955 he kept his promise, as Chrysler met its goal of 20 percent of domestic auto sales. A strike could undercut this progress. Autoworkers at Chrysler were no less eager to avoid a shutdown, and the two sides settled in the middle of the night on September 1. The contract's SUB provision was essentially the same as Ford's and GM's, and skilled workers received the same wage increase that had provoked anger earlier that summer. Shortly after the Chrysler settlement, American Motors and most remaining major parts suppliers, including Kelsey-Hayes, Budd, Borg-Warner, and Eaton, also signed contracts that included SUB clauses.[32]

In many ways, including unprecedented production, record numbers of workers, high wages, overtime, and contract improvements like SUB, 1955 is the reason why so many people have looked on the fifties as a prosperous decade for autoworkers. End-of-year production figures confirmed this assessment. Nearly 8,000,000 passenger cars were produced. Adding trucks, the total reached 9,190,692. General Motors set new vehicle assembly records. Chrysler reported record production and sales, as well as a 440 percent increase in profits over 1954. Ford's output, sales, and profits were its highest ever, and for the first time the company's total payroll topped a billion dollars. Across metro Detroit, the addition of second and sometimes third shifts boosted the total number of autoworkers despite the long-term trends of decentralization and automation. Aggregate income for Detroiters and the volume of local shopping made statisticians forget the previous year and a half of recession.[33] Along with a few months in both 1950 and 1953, 1955 *was* the 1950s as many have come to understand the decade.

Yet there were problems with this glowing assessment of the industry's performance. A number of skilled tradesmen, perhaps 20,000 of the roughly 300,000 skilled UAW members (out of a total union membership of some 1.5 million), formed a secession organization, the Society of Skilled Trades, as they continued to protest what they called "discrimination" against them in contract negotiations. The union could not afford to lose these critical members, and automakers feared that if tradesmen struck, they could prevent the timely introduction of 1956 models.[34] African American autoworkers, who surely saw the irony of skilled workers complaining of discrimination, observed that automation had eliminated many of the materials-handling jobs traditionally reserved for them even while some new opportunities had arisen, especially early in the boom. Women continued to have difficulty breaking into auto work. Of the 391,000 working women in Wayne, Macomb, and Oakland counties in mid-1955, only 34,000 had jobs in auto manufacturing. The frustration for some women who tried to be autoworkers was lessened a bit because the auto-wage-fueled prosperity created thousands of clerical and secretarial jobs and drove wages upward as businesses struggled to fill those positions. At one point an experienced secretary who typed sixty words a minute could earn almost as much as an unskilled autoworker, without the noise, grime, and potential dangers.[35] No matter the sector of the economy, future prosperity in Detroit depended mainly on the auto industry, and layoff totals crept upward in the last half of the year, as did unsold dealer inventories. Unemployment increased more quickly during the holiday season, prompting harsh criticism from affected workers, who wondered whether this was a minor blip or an indication of worse to come.[36]

7 "A Severe and Prolonged Hangover,"
   1956–1957

Although automakers voiced optimism that the banner year of 1955 would become the norm, layoffs increased in early 1956, largely because nearly a million of the record number of vehicles produced had yet to be sold by dealers. As a result, auto companies scaled back production. SUB benefits, at the heart of the 1955 contract settlements, were of little help, because the programs were not fully funded and most unemployed autoworkers could not meet eligibility requirements. Instead they struggled, as always, to cobble together secondary support systems. Making matters worse, many laid-off autoworkers had gone into debt during flush times in 1955 and were now saddled with mortgages, rents, or installment payments without regular income. Although automation continued to affect overall employment, it played a less noticeable role given the vast unemployment caused by overproduction in 1955, the demise of more parts manufacturers, the loss of remaining Packard jobs, and the continued threat of decentralization of the industry away from Detroit. Throughout 1956 and 1957, Detroit floundered while the national economy thrived. More accurately, Detroit's working-class residents suffered from unemployment as well as insecurity on the job caused by the ripple effects of layoffs. Wealthier Detroiters shared in the nation's prosperity by shopping intensely at leading downtown department stores while many businesses in autoworkers' neighborhoods faced bankruptcy. State, local, and UAW officials pleaded for help from the federal government, but none was forthcoming. Federal officials and automakers saw no need for government intervention and blamed autoworkers, with their high wages and generous fringe benefits, for their own predicament. In late 1957 economists declared

an official recession, and the rest of the nation began to face what Detroit's
industrial workers had long experienced.

* * *

In early 1956 the warning signs of the previous year proved accurate, as
production cutbacks and layoffs accelerated in Detroit's auto plants. The first
to be let go had been hired in the 1955 boom, followed by waves of those who
had become autoworkers in the 1953 upturn. Ford's Mercury Division cut
2,450 workers, including 700 at its Wayne plant. Among the newly jobless at
that facility was Thomas Nowak, who had hired in during the 1955 boom after
trying without success to be an autoworker throughout 1954. He had no idea if
he would ever be recalled. Placing the layoffs in perspective, Mercury officials
noted that after these cuts the division still had nearly 19,000 employees, 4
percent more than were on its payroll in January 1955.[1] Many autoworkers
who were not on layoff were affected as well by the return of short time, for
example three- and four-day weeks at Ford, and random total shutdown days
at Chrysler. GM president Harlow Curtice was quick to dismiss speculation
that the industry was returning to the doldrums, insisting to banking and
industrial elites that 1956 would be "another big year." At least 7.5 million
vehicles would be produced, he claimed, and there was "every indication
that full employment will continue." These were bold predictions, especially
since over eight hundred thousand cars built in 1955 remained unsold.[2]

Other industry observers foresaw troubled times, largely because of the
automakers' success in 1955, when revamped styling made new cars allur-
ing and cheap credit made them seem affordable. As an auto sales manager
explained, "Lots of people bought new cars in 1955 when their economic
condition dictated that they buy used cars. We'll pay for that this year." A
Detroit survey showed, unsurprisingly, that if new cars were less expensive,
more people would buy them. Yet autoworkers, among the best-paid industrial
workers, were still only marginal candidates to purchase new cars, and according to automakers, UAW wages and benefits stood in the way of building
more affordable vehicles and increasing sales. Poor quality, resulting from
the rush to assemble as many cars as possible, also hindered efforts to reduce
1955 inventories. One unhappy dealer complained that the cars on his lot were
like "do-it-yourself kits that I have to put together at my expense to keep the
customer happy."[3] For a host of reasons, then, dealer inventories continued to
rise to more than 900,000 cars. Carl Fribley, president of the National Automotive Dealers Association, remarked that the entire industry was suffering
from a "severe and prolonged hangover" caused by its "king-size binge during
1955." With so many unsold vehicles, automakers reduced operations, and

in mid-March unemployment in Detroit reached 120,000. This represented 8 percent of the metro area's total workforce—as usual, about double that if considering only manufacturing employees—and approached the recession levels of March 1954. Acknowledging the industry's grim prospects, Chrysler Local 212 president Pat Caruso warned, "Some of our members, who had a good year in 1955, won't work on this model or the one next year."[4]

Significantly, none of the autoworkers laid off in late 1955 or early 1956 were eligible for the UAW's new supplemental unemployment benefits. It took time to build up the SUB funds, and the earliest date for any benefit distribution was June 1, 1956, still months away. In addition, during the prosperity of mid-1955 the UAW and automakers agreed that to be eligible for SUB, workers had to be on company payrolls as of May 2, 1956, a month before payments could begin. With the downturn in the industry, tens of thousands of workers were laid off before May 2. Even in June the SUB accounts would be seriously underfunded, probably only a quarter of projected maximums. As things stood in early 1956, SUB funds would be able to help an unskilled autoworker with $7.18 a week for four weeks, on top of regular unemployment benefits, and $3.32 a week for the remainder of eligibility, which would be welcome but hardly significant assistance. There was also a good chance that if unemployment worsened, the funds would be exhausted within a month.[5]

Although there had been some modest upward revisions in regular state unemployment benefits over the years, for the most part those laid off in early 1956 faced the same circumstances that jobless autoworkers had confronted since World War II. Thousands lined up at Detroit's MESC offices, welfare claims jumped, second jobs and odd jobs helped a bit, and many left the state to wait for recall notices. L. J. Scott, who had bought a new car during the 1955 boom, recalled that prosperity and steady work "didn't last. It didn't last." Money was always tight for Dorothy Sackle, but the frequent post-1955 layoffs were especially difficult. "I remember when things were really rough," she said. "I was working, and my boy said to me, 'How come these people have oranges and we don't?'" At one point Sackle sought assistance from the Detroit Welfare Department. "I had to cash in bottles to get twelve cents for the streetcars to take me downtown and tell them I needed help," she remembered. She received minimal assistance and some useless advice. "They gave me six dollars," she recalled, and told her, "'You have to go to Friend of the Court.'" It was her ex-husband's responsibility, they said, to support his children. The problem, though, Sackle emphasized, was that "he wasn't very good at paying child support—at that time it was twenty-one dollars a month, for three kids." Even that amount, if she had received it, would not have been enough to stave off a crisis.[6]

There were countless variations in circumstances, all made painful by lay-offs. Bascom Ely, forty-seven, had landed a job as an assembler at Chrysler's Mack plant near the end of the 1953 boom, and he, his wife, and their four children, ages two to seventeen, had lived in a two-room, second-story flat. "My wife can't climb stairs and I couldn't afford the rent for most first-floor places," he said. "One day, the baby fell out of bed and burned its neck on an exposed heating pipe. I knew then we had to get out." With steady employ-ment in 1955 and take-home pay of eighty-six dollars per week, Ely moved his family into a four-room apartment for ninety dollars a month. "I knew we couldn't afford it," he said, "but by scraping, I figured we could make it." A week after settling in he received his layoff notice. Because he had also been laid off another time that year, he was eligible for only sixteen more weeks of state unemployment benefits and, of course, no SUB payments. A laid-off Chrysler employee identified as "R.E.H.," twenty-six, provided another example of how autoworkers coped in these times. Like Ely, he had been hired at the tail end of the 1953 boom. During prosperous 1955 he had purchased a new car and a house, with payments of nearly eighty dollars a month due on each that together consumed half his wages. R.E.H. and his wife were expecting their first child when he was laid off in January 1956, and because of earlier periods of joblessness his unemployment compensation eligibility was about to expire. Fortunately, his wife found an office job, but it paid half as much as auto work. The couple cut back where they could, but they quickly depleted their two hundred dollars in savings and seventy-five dollars in war bonds. When not in the military, William Mazinkowski, forty-five, had worked for the Murray Corporation from 1933 to 1954. After the parts supplier closed, he had no job and his seniority was worthless. In his forties, he was on the outer edges of employability. Early in the 1955 boom, however, Mazinkowski landed a job at Dodge Main and worked steadily until he was laid off in February 1956. With little seniority, he gave up on waiting for a recall notice from Dodge and took a job at the Stroh Brewery, which lasted three months before he was laid off again. "No job in sight, no seniority anymore and funds running very low," he described his situation.[7]

With their spending, people like Bascom Ely, R.E.H., and William Mazinkowski were largely responsible for Detroit's prosperity in 1955, but now they were saddled with debt and anxiety. Many economically comfort-able observers viewed them, and their enablers, as irresponsible. "How are we going to protect men (and women) of this type against themselves," scolded columnist Sylvia Porter, "and thus protect our entire economy against their extravagant spending and borrowing?" Auto dealers, lenders, and retailers, she complained, did not seem willing to say no to any prospective customer. A Detroit labor journalist had predicted this type of moralizing seven months earlier, before the boom fizzled. Robert Perrin asked his fictional autoworker, the French immigrant "Pierre le Travailleur," why he seemed glum when times were so good. "We factory workers, when we are in the money, are coaxed from all sides to buy the cars we build, television sets, disposal units—all on unlimited credit," Pierre replied. "When times are bad and the bills come due, we are berated for not being like the petit squirrels and storing nuts in the hollow tree for the cold winter."[8]

Another blow to Detroit employment came with the end of operations at the Motor Products Corporation. A longtime supplier of window moldings and ventilators for Ford and Chrysler, Motor Products was caught in the same squeeze that had claimed other parts makers. The buyers' market for cars in 1956 forced automakers to cut production costs, including demanding price reductions from suppliers, making profitability impossible for companies like Motor Products. Employment at the company's Mack plant had dropped considerably since the peak of the 1955 boom, and in 1956 the last thirty-eight hundred employees were let go.[9] Detroiters saw warning signs as well when the Rheem Manufacturing Company announced that it would produce auto parts in California. While Michigan's share of final auto assemblies hovered between 30 and 40 percent of the national total through the mid-1950s, California had risen to second place. Parts factories in Michigan and Ohio still supplied most assembly operations outside the Midwest, but shipping costs, especially to the West Coast, were increasingly expensive. It made sense, then, to relocate parts production. If the Rheem experiment proved successful, Detroit stood to lose a significant number of jobs.[10]

These developments led to soul-searching questions. "Can the area continue to depend upon the automobile industry as a major source of employment?" asked the Detroit Metropolitan Area Regional Planning Commission. "And will the industry continue to grow and expand its production facilities here? Will the automobile industry decentralize to such an extent that Detroit will suffer from its loss?" Journalist Charles Wartman worried that if decentralization trends continued, "Detroit ten years from now will no longer be the Motor Capital of the world." Black autoworkers, he recognized, stood to suffer the most: "The Negro worker is going to be the first and hardest hit. Although considerable seniority has been built up by many of them, the overall effect will be against them." Even when industries moved only as far as the Detroit suburbs, Wartman observed, black workers were "placed at a disadvantage. For the most part housing restrictions have made it extremely difficult if not impossible to move near their jobs. Commuting is both expensive and in winter hazardous. . . . The Negro worker may find himself forced to start over again to establish himself in the industry."[11]

Another jolt of anxiety hit Detroit with the announcement that sixty-five hundred of the city's remaining Packard workers would lose their jobs. Packard's merger with Studebaker had not proved profitable, and the company was about to combine with the Curtiss-Wright Corporation, which focused mainly on military aircraft. This improved the employment prospects for workers at Packard's defense-oriented Utica plant, but the company's remaining Detroit auto production would be consolidated in Studebaker's South Bend, Indiana, facilities. At its postwar peak, Packard had over thirty thousand workers in Detroit, but in mid-1956 only about eighty-five hundred were still on the job. On average, they were fifty-two years old with at least twenty years of seniority. "What can I do now?" wondered Charles Binning, sixty-five, who had put in forty years with the company. "Luckily, my wife and I live alone now. Our children are married and on their own, of course. But—is my pension still good? Can I retire now? Or, can I get another job somewhere?" Emil Wilde, fifty-eight, with thirty years of seniority, mulled over the situation faced by many of his coworkers: "We are old Packard families with deep roots here, we have no other place to go, most of us are too old to get other jobs—so tell me, please, what are we going to do?"[12]

With its economic woes, Detroit was an outlier during a year of national prosperity. Based on trends through the first six months, *Fortune* magazine predicted that 1956 would be the best year for business in U.S. history, with a few key exceptions, including the automotive industry. Nationally it was true that employment was up and unemployment was down. According to the U.S. Commerce Department, total manufacturing employment had increased by 150,000 during the first quarter of 1956, despite "reduced activity in the motor vehicle industry." Also running counter to national trends, inflation in Detroit jumped .4 percent in March, four times higher than the national figure. Detroit prices continued to rise at nearly double the national rate in June—1.3 percent versus .7 percent. Food and medical costs appeared to be the major culprits, but the existence of relatively high inflation still confounded economists who expected to see declining prices in a region with high unemployment.[13]

Although the auto industry as a whole was underperforming, the experiences of individual carmakers varied. Despite Ford's declines in production and employment, the company still reported its second-highest quarterly earnings ever in early 1956. In spring 1956 only 43,000 workers were on the job at the Rouge plant compared with 65,000 employees a year earlier, although only 3,085 people were on official layoff. GM's sales to dealers were about the same as they had been in the record-setting first quarter of 1955, even if the company's employment levels had dropped. Most severely affected was Pontiac Motor, where 4,500 out of the workforce of 14,000 were on indefinite layoff. Six thousand more were on short weeks. Chrysler was in the worst shape of the Big Three, with production down by 23 percent and profits down by nearly two-thirds over the comparable period in 1955. Roughly half of the 46,000 workers at Chrysler's Dodge Main plant and in its Automotive Body Division (formerly Briggs) facilities were on layoff.[14]

Auto industry woes became a serious state issue, if not a major concern for the federal government. In May, Michigan governor G. Mennen Williams asked President Eisenhower to declare Detroit a critical unemployment area, giving the metropolitan region an advantage in bidding for defense contracts. The government obliged, but no jobs followed. Instead, administration officials rubbed salt in Detroit's wounds. Referring to high unemployment in the auto industry, White House aide Howard Pyle coldly remarked to reporters, "The right to suffer is one of the joys of a free economy, just as the right to prosper is." Walter Reuther retorted, "Laid-off workers in Michigan and elsewhere would be far more impressed by concrete action on the part of your administration to get them back to work than the sending of court jesters to tell them that suffering is really a joy."[15] Treasury Secretary George Humphrey sparked further outrage that summer when he called the auto industry's doldrums a "refreshing pause," at a time when monthly auto output was equal to the weekly production of a year earlier and when Ford announced that its model changeover period would last for nearly seven weeks, with prolonged layoffs for all seventy thousand of its Detroit-area workers.[16]

Many would-be autoworkers considered alternatives. Elwin Brown remembered that he "thought about being a policeman" or finding "some job in government" because it would be more stable. James McGuire thought he had put auto work behind him. After being laid off from both of his UAW jobs in 1956, he found a maintenance position at the University of Michigan's Lawyers Club. At one point McGuire received employment recall notices from both GM and Ford, but he "quit them both." The varied duties and his level of responsibility at the Lawyers Club appealed to him more. Besides, maintenance was steady work. "I was enjoying myself," he recalled. While once again spending much of his time on layoff in West Virginia, Emerald Neal remained hopeful that he would return to full-time work at Ford. But others might have moved on with their lives. Ford officials reported that they "had to call an average of two people" to fill openings from attrition. "About half of those called did not respond." No one could tell if the nonresponders had given up on auto work.[17]

Confusion was also evident in assessments of the impact of layoffs on local commerce. If joblessness caused such serious problems, it seemed that the proof should come in reduced levels of business activity and increased numbers of struggling store owners. "Instead we have a situation where business seems to be good as a rule," observed one civic leader. "I have yet to meet up with many businessmen who are pessimistic or not confident in the future." Milton Spencer, a marketing professor, conceded that mass unemployment amid solid business activity was "one of the great paradoxes of our time." Detroit's Retail Merchants Association reported that during the first four months of 1956, total sales at the city's major downtown department stores, such as Hudson's and Kern's, were nearly 10 percent above comparable 1955 figures and that these stores were a "fairly accurate barometer" of overall commercial activity in the city. Such observations, however, did not take into account working-class neighborhoods. White-collar workers were on salary and were much more likely to shop at the thriving downtown department stores. Autoworkers rarely shopped at Hudson's and Kern's, and businesses in blue-collar neighborhoods experienced huge declines in sales from the 1955 boom. Furniture store manager Morris Kane, whose shop was near a Chrysler plant, reported a drop-off of 50 percent. "When people don't have money," he said, "they don't buy, even at bargain rates." Antoinette Bruguglio's bakery was also hit hard. "I figured pastry sales would drop," she said, "but they're even buying less bread." Appliance salesman James Affhalter pointed out that "it only takes one or two sales a week to mean the difference between profit and loss." He was closely attuned to each prediction about employment levels in Detroit factories. So were bar owners, whose traffic picked up immediately when workers were recalled or went from short weeks to full-time. "The blight of empty store fronts in neighborhood shopping centers has spread throughout the city," declared one report. "Any conservative estimate of the total number of unused stores in Detroit would run in the thousands."[18]

There were conflicting indicators as well in the fall. On a positive note, nearly 20,000 Detroit-area autoworkers returned to their jobs when Ford and Chrysler completed their model changeovers. Ford reported that most of its recalled workers, more than 12,000 of them, had been laid off for nearly ten months. In Pontiac, 5,900 GM workers with seniority returned and 230 new employees were hired.[19] The good news was tempered by the impact of decentralization. Although Ford still employed about 70,000 in the metro Detroit area, it now had about an equal number of hourly workers in its plants outside the region. In addition, auto production totals were still 20 percent below the automakers' original projections for the period. More jobs, then, were available, but nowhere near enough to absorb the large numbers of unemployed Detroiters—or autoworkers anywhere in the nation. The U.S. Department of Labor reported in mid-October that employment levels in the auto industry had been "one of the chief exceptions to an otherwise generally abundant job situation." Despite these troubles, 1956 maintained its status as the third-best year in automotive history. To be sure, the figure was padded by more than eight hundred thousand vehicles left over from 1955, but increasing fall output and aggregate sales numbers demonstrated that 1956 was a good year for automakers. Still, Ford's production was down about a quarter from 1955, and Chrysler's decreased by 34 percent. Even GM's best-selling division, Chevrolet, reported an 11 percent decline from 1955, while the midsize Pontiac brand took perhaps the largest hit of all, a 43 percent reduction.[20]

The annual figures received boosts from ramped-up production in the fall, which provoked new workload disputes, something that surprised outsiders given the recent history of bleak employment in auto plants. But wildcat strikes occurred whenever factories operated. Earlier in the year most such strikes had occurred in response to speedups intended to maximize efficiency and reduce labor costs during a serious sales slump.[21] In the fall most of them occurred because of speedups motivated by the chance to sell more cars in a suddenly expanding market. One such conflict at Chrysler's Nine Mile press plant revolved around unfair promotions to the "gas welding" classification and ultimately resulted in the shutdown of nearly half the company's Detroit operations. The strike ended quickly, according to Local 869 president Earl Walters, because of pressure from Chrysler workers outside the affected department. After months of missed paychecks, many autoworkers had little patience with the problems faced by others. "We thought 1954 was rough but this year we are finding out what rough really is," remarked an autoworker's wife in December. Counting on that frustration, Chrysler management criticized the wildcatters for "jeopardizing the welfare of other Chrysler employes and the entire economic community."[22]

Those who clung to auto jobs often experienced instability from frequent moves to new positions. Layoffs prompted rounds of "bumping," in which higher-seniority workers claimed the jobs of those lower in rank, often in departments from which the longer-term employees had once escaped. "I went to *every* plant there was," Margaret Beaudry remembered, "because they go according to seniority." At first she was moved to Pontiac Motor's Plant 7, operating small presses to make parts. She was amazed at the intricacy of the process. A piece of metal entered a line and was passed from press to press, each one refining the shape as it gradually became the desired part. Beaudry helped produce headlights, control arms, flywheels, and much else. Despite the massive pieces of equipment in the room, she recalled, the work itself "wasn't heavy" and was probably easier than what her previous position entailed. But operating small presses was dangerous. "You could get your fingers taken off," she said. "If you followed safety rules, you wouldn't have to worry, but there was several people that lost their hands, and if a new woman came in she got the hardest job every time." Before long Beaudry was sent to Plant 9 to install spark plugs on a circular line called the "merry-go-round." "I didn't have no say about where they put me," she recalled. "I was just lucky I had a job. And the union didn't have anything to say about it, either. The only time a union rep could do anything about what job you got would be if it was a hindrance to your health, like maybe the fumes or something." Beaudry's low seniority caught up with her during another round of layoffs in late 1956. Thanks to her sister she got a job in the bookkeeping department at Community National Bank. Along with occasional shifts at Neisner's, that helped Beaudry get by, although she worried that her layoff might last so long that she would have to hire in from scratch at Pontiac Motor. Edith Arnold also experienced frequent transfers. "They shoved me around thinking that I would quit," she recalled. "I worked in every plant except the foundry. I was glad *afterwards*," she insisted, but "I didn't like it at first." There was a silver lining to Katie Neumann's transfer out of the Pontiac Motor foundry because of low seniority. Although her last job there—documenting the amount of scrap metal produced—was pretty good, tragedies in the department haunted her. She recalled a time when a coworker "had his fingers cut off. They wanted me to get that glove with the fingers in there, and I wouldn't do it." Another time, she remembered, when a repairman was working on a large machine, "somebody pushed a button, and the guy got smashed in it. And that was it. I was there that day, but I wouldn't go to see it. That was one of the worst ones that I can remember." In addition, she said, during these tough times there was a movement by some men to rid the foundry of women, or at least to send Neumann back to the tougher job of handling sand and molten metal. Layoffs and bumping forced the issue, and Neumann ended up at the gun plant, never missing an opportunity to tell her coworkers that "everybody should take and work in the foundry. They'd appreciate their job now."

In the midst of these 1956 cutbacks, Don Hester staved off a demotion to the assembly line by successfully challenging the seniority of a fellow worker who was initially allowed to stay on vehicle repair, what Hester considered a "cush" job fixing minor problems that occurred during assembly. Bud Weber had been assigned to military work, on production of the "Otter," an amphibious cargo carrier used by the U.S. Marine Corps, but when orders tapered off, he recalled, "They shipped me to the rocket job. I was just like an extra. Like a pinch hitter or something. They didn't lay me off. They just moved me around." He was afraid to refuse any transfers, assuming that management would respond, "Well, then, get the hell out of here!" The constant shuffling of jobs in this era affected Tom Agorgianitis's home life. He had a son with serious health problems and liked to take over for his wife, Angie, when he came home from work. Continuous bumping often resulted in his having to change shifts for lack of seniority. If he worked second shift, he explained, "I'd be heading to work and the kids are there. Get back and they're in bed. And the work falls all on the wife." Still, he said, "the worst one that almost did me in was the third shift. You get that extra money," he noted, referring to the modest increase in pay for working nights, "but to me it wasn't worth it." Job instability and insecurity marked the era then, although not always with layoffs.[23]

Even those who remained fully employed during this period had a difficult time making ends meet. Elwin Brown recalled that his family had no financial reserves. He and his wife "lived from paycheck to paycheck," he recalled, despite being frugal. "I wondered if I was going to have enough gas to make it to payday." Even with fairly steady work, Les Coleman remembered, "It was really kind of rough. Skilled tradesmen, they're making more, but what can I say? I don't recall ever having a lot of money. I didn't buy any extras or anything. All my money went for clothes for the kids, school, things like that. It was quite a few years before I started living fairly comfortably. Probably in the '70s." Years later Ernie Liles insisted that things were not that bad. Still, during some layoffs his family traveled to the west side of Michigan to pick fruit, only to find that they "couldn't ever make no money berry picking." Other times they went back to Arkansas: "Sometimes we'd even go down there and pick a little bit of cotton."[24]

In an unexpected twist, layoffs at Detroit auto plants became entwined with Cold War developments. B. B. James, a marine who fought at Iwo Jima in World War II, had hired in at Chrysler's Mack plant in June 1951 and had survived the peaks and valleys of Chrysler operations since then, but was laid off in March 1956. James had used up his twenty-six weeks of state unemployment benefits by October. Because he was laid off before May 2, he had never qualified for SUB payments. There was little chance he would be called back to Chrysler, because his most recent job, building seat cushions in the trim department, had been moved to a different factory where his seniority was useless. His secondary support system for himself, his wife, and their two children included odd jobs and increased bitterness when he learned that five hundred Cold War refugees from the recent Hungarian uprising had been guaranteed employment upon arrival in the United States. It turns out that only a handful of those positions were in auto plants, but James would have taken just about any job by the end of November, and as a veteran he considered himself as worthy of assistance as any newly arriving Hungarian.[25]

The tens of thousands of disgruntled, unemployed autoworkers had their critics. "Where there's a will, there's a way," one woman insisted. Her husband, she pointed out, had "held four jobs in the past 15 years." Another local citizen was more sarcastic, recommending that "these 'starvers'" look in the want ads. "In this section I found, in last Wednesday's paper, at least 200 jobs offered to men, women, elderly couples, high school students, etc. As a man who has changed jobs several times in the last couple of years (twice the factory moved), I used that section several times. Sometimes I tried for weeks, but I finally got a job." Assessing this flurry of letters, another Detroiter commented that the hostility expressed was "significant chiefly because it reflects the insecurity felt by American workers, even at a time of prosperity." Indeed, two hundred jobs would hardly have made a dent in the ranks of the unemployed in Detroit.[26]

Those most likely to be jobless were African American, young, old, female, formerly employed by defunct parts suppliers, with low seniority, displaced by automation, or left behind by decentralization. In short, just about everybody was vulnerable. Even highly qualified job seekers had difficulties getting hired. "I can tell you why a young man of 19 with training in the mechanics trade can't find a job," explained Kenneth Filary. "No experience. All want ads call for experienced men, and how do you get experience if they won't hire you? What good is it to go to trade school?" Many younger workers were frustrated with seniority systems that prevented them from gaining a foothold in the auto industry, and a number of laid-off older workers complained that the UAW did little to help them get back on their feet. Some even believed that the UAW, not automakers, laid off workers. UAW public relations director Frank Winn addressed criticisms from older union members, pointing out that significant union gains, such as seniority, transfer rights, health insurance, pensions, SUB pay, and vacations, benefited them most. Nearly half of all UAW members, he noted, were over forty years old and could not be ignored.[27] But only the luckiest of younger UAW members, and few of those who were older but recently hired, were able to stay on the job long enough to enjoy any sort of security from these contract provisions. As always, unemployed Detroiters were left to scrounge for odd jobs or positions that paid, at most, half of what they had made when they worked in auto plants.

Instability and insecurity continued to dominate the lives of autoworkers in the third most successful year in the industry's history.

*   *   *

Business observers and autoworkers worried that 1957 could be a replay of 1956, when the national economy had boomed to record levels while at the same time certain sectors, like automobiles, experienced recession-like conditions. Indeed, according to the MESC, average auto industry employment in Michigan during 1956 dropped to about four hundred thousand, the lowest total in ten years and one hundred thousand fewer than in 1953. The situation seemed paradoxical. As John Stewart of the Detroit Board of Commerce said, "With national income and purchasing power throughout the United States rising faster in 1956 than in 1955, there appears to be no economic justification for either a rise as great as the 39 per cent recorded in 1955 or the 25 per cent drop in car and truck output in 1956." While "all signs point to an upward trend in business and industrial activity in the Detroit area," he noted, there were no guarantees given the counterintuitive relationship between economic indicators and the health of the auto industry. Although the board of commerce's official position was that Walter Reuther and the UAW were the equivalent to, and maybe part of, a Soviet conspiracy to undermine the United States, Stewart did point out that "an even distribution of car and truck production over the 1955–56 period would have given each year record high output, with a steady high level of factory employment in the Detroit area." This, of course, had been the premise behind the union's guaranteed annual wage. In the real world, however, employment levels had been anything but high and steady.[28]

Chrysler was especially eager to rebound after a disastrous 1956. To that end, the company engaged in a wholesale reengineering of its plants and a reconfiguration of jobs within them, which included the elimination of 20,000 positions. Rumors of such a massive cut had been widespread among Chrysler's workers, but with so many of them laid off in 1956 it had been impossible to count how many jobs were gone for good. It was clear in early 1957, though, that the cuts were real, and with so much disruption, conflicts were bound to arise. At the DeSoto Warren and Wyoming facilities, local union officials reported that they had "3,000 people with up to five years [seniority] still laid off," while the 5,400 workers on the job were "putting in nine-hour days."[29] It did not seem fair that some worked overtime while others were still jobless. Adding to insecurities, no Chrysler employees received word that their positions were among the 20,000 eliminated. Instead, laid-off workers waited, often in vain, for recall notices. Although most workers on the job willingly or grudgingly accepted their revised assignments, a sizable number engaged in wildcat strikes. Indeed, top union leaders reported that "there are more strikes pending over production standards in Chrysler Corp. plants than in the rest of the UAW combined." In one example, Dodge Main trim department employees on the first shift walked out but received no support from national leadership. UAW vice president Norman Matthews acknowledged the justice of the trim department workers' complaint, but he denied authorization for a legitimate strike because more than 22,500 people would be laid off within a day if it continued. Most UAW members still suffered from the hardships of 1956, and many were upset with any missed paychecks, even if those in other departments or plants had been treated unfairly. Few Chrysler workers in 1957 had ever experienced stable employment, and a large and increasing number of them had low seniority and no long-term connection with the UAW. Behind with their bills, many of them were not interested in hearing lectures about the union movement of the 1930s or the importance of maintaining solidarity with workers across town.[30]

Inflation had much to do with workers' reluctance to embrace calls for solidarity that meant sacrificing wages. As Leo Orsage of Local 600 remarked, "You can't win because prices outrun wages every time." Orsage did not oppose wage increases; instead he wanted the federal government to "curb this menace" by controlling prices, as it had during World War II. "We auto workers are reduced to a treadmill existence," he said. "Many find it hard to keep body and soul together. Some hold two jobs. Quite a few have to send their wives to work to help support the family. Children start working before they finish school." Twenty-eight-year-old Stanley Vasko also focused on his family and his budget. In 1954 Vasko bought a small house in a new working-class development in East Detroit. A GI loan provided the down payment, and savings went toward secondhand furniture, a refrigerator and stove, windows, interior painting, and landscaping. All of this seemed affordable during the 1955 boom, but in 1956 Vasko was laid off for a total of five and a half months, and unemployment compensation was the family's main source of income. "You can't call it a living," Vasko said. "You just stay home and spend as little money as possible." Vasko had steady work in early 1957, but it would have to continue for many months, perhaps years, before he could overcome his debt and inflated prices to get ahead.[31]

Consumers like Leo Orsage and Stanley Vasko were expected to propel the next auto boom. America's "new middle class," according to Columbia University marketing professor Ralph Alexander, consisted of those making from $4,500 to $15,000 a year, an increasing number of whom, he said, were "semi-skilled and unskilled workers." They would not be looking for luxury models, Alexander reported to the National Association of Automobile Dealers. "They are just removed from the lower-income class and therefore are less used to finer things. They are less impressed by elaborate-looking automobiles and they have no false pride about where they buy their cars."[32] Alexander's data seemed convincing. By calculating annual earnings from hourly wage data, one could indeed place a large number of autoworkers in the "new middle class." But this arithmetic exercise bore little resemblance to reality. If Stanley Vasko earned his $2.32 hourly wage forty hours a week throughout the year, without interruptions, he would barely creep over Alexander's $4,500 middle-class threshold. Five and a half months of missed paychecks in a year obviously affected that equation. Inflation, as described by Leo Orsage, also had a negative impact on working-class purchasing power. And the twenty thousand workers permanently laid off by Chrysler were obviously unlikely candidates to buy a new car. If blue-collar workers purchased new cars, or in many cases even used ones, they risked repossession of their vehicles and poverty for their families. Miriam Hewlett, a Detroit recorder's court official, saw about five thousand such cases a month. "These families get so far in debt they don't know where to turn," she explained, "and when it gets to be too much for the husband, he walks out. . . . I wish Dr. Salk would invent a vaccine for this car craze." Easy credit, she insisted, "has to be stopped somehow." Yet easy credit was the only way that those on the lowest rungs of the new middle class—indeed, those throughout most of the middle class—could seriously contemplate purchasing a car. "We are supposed to be living in an age of prosperity," observed Circuit Court Commissioner William Krueger, "but it isn't reflected in court."[33]

Although automakers tried their best to emphasize only positive news, they ultimately conceded that conditions were dire. As GM president Harlow Curtice admitted to shareholders, "For the second successive year, the historical spring rise in sales has failed to materialize." Industry publicists offered the hopeful theory that the spring selling season would arrive in the fall. For all of its hoopla about its revamped factories, Chrysler had barely kept pace with its 1956 production numbers, in part because of the poor quality of its products. Ford tried recruiting potential purchasers with a "motorized circus," which performed in stadiums across the country, while company vice president Walker Williams lamented that the industry's "greatest problem is distribution—the sale of what we can so easily produce." Statistics bore out that analysis. Total auto output for the first six months of 1957 was the second highest ever for that period, trailing only 1955, yet nearly eight hundred thousand unsold vehicles still sat on dealers' lots.[34] No matter what happened in the near future, long-term industrial employment trends in Detroit indicated decline. According to MESC data, the number of manufacturing jobs in

Michigan had peaked in 1953 at 1,266,000. Just over half a million of those were in the auto industry, with anywhere between 100,000 and 200,000 of them held by recent migrants to Michigan. In 1957 Michigan's total manufacturing workforce was actually smaller (1,075,000) than it had been during the 1954 recession (1,088,000). Between 1953 and 1957, total employment in Michigan's auto industry shrank by 153,000, to around 400,000. Whereas in 1953 there had been slightly more manufacturing than service-sector jobs in Michigan (1,266,000 to 1,215,000), the order quickly reversed, and by 1957 industry overall employed 200,000 fewer people. Of course these snapshots did not capture the complexity of employment in Detroit—there had been plenty of peaks and valleys in those four years—but they supported the conclusion that opportunities in the auto industry were diminishing in the mid-1950s.[35]

The last five thousand autoworkers to lose their jobs at Packard—on average over fifty years old with twenty-five years of seniority—had immense difficulty finding manufacturing employment and looked for alternatives. Thaddeus Slubowski took out loans to start his own delicatessen after spending more than twenty years with the company. He was proud, but nervous, about taking this leap. Almost all of the one thousand women who left Packard headed to the service sector for the types of positions—clerical, sales, waitressing, and so forth—traditionally reserved for them. Walter Lumpkin, who had twenty-eight years of seniority, began selling food door-to-door and hoped for steadier income as a janitor. Louis Rokoczy found a job delivering mail. As a skilled worker Rokoczy had earned an hourly wage much higher than what the post office offered, but he found that carrying the mail was more consistent and less stressful work. No longer affected by sporadic layoffs, his annual income as a mail carrier approximated what he had earned at Packard, and his wife, Gertrude, made up the difference with a job at a bakery. Many unemployed autoworkers, however, were too old to be considered for new jobs. The unstated rule seemed to be that women over thirty-five and men over forty-five had only a small chance of being hired. "If they get interested, they ask your age," explained a former Packard assembly-line worker. "They're polite enough after that. They just tell you that there is nothing doing today."[36]

Automakers blamed high wages for the industry's woes. Ford vice president T. O. Yntema argued that more consumers would be in the market for new automobiles if not for persistent wage inflation, caused by union contracts, which he termed "Public Enemy No. 1." The UAW, he declared, "threatens operation of the free market system." American Motors Corporation president George Romney echoed this view. "The excess power of unionism," he complained, "has accelerated wage increases to the point where they now exceed the ability of American industry to meet them through increased

efficiency." This, he said, was America's "number one problem." If only autoworkers earned less, the argument went, more people could afford to purchase
new cars. That line of reasoning had merit. Most Americans were indeed
hit hard by inflation and were saddled with debt on installment purchases,
mainly for furniture, appliances, and new or used automobiles, not to mention homes. The result, as a study by the National Thrift Committee and the
insurance industry showed, was that the "average American family" was "90
days from disaster." Lowering inflation might help, the report suggested, but
it might not be enough. "Many families have little or no reserve in the form
of savings, to tide themselves over an emergency that suddenly cuts off current earnings," reported one of the researchers. This caused "marital strains
between husbands and wives, plus anxiety and tension among children," not
the confidence in the future necessary to boost new car sales.[37]

The expense of operating an automobile also dissuaded many Americans
from purchasing new ones. The editors of *Changing Times* magazine calculated the annual cost of owning and operating a new car, assuming five thousand miles of travel, to be $575. They concluded that "only an above-average
income family can drive its car 10,000 miles annually without seriously lowering its standard of living," and warned that anyone who earned only $5,000 a
year—the outer reaches of income for a fully employed autoworker—should
stay out of the new car market. Any upswing in sales, then, would have to
come from middle-class professionals, a growing but still relatively narrow
slice of the American population, who earned considerably more than these
so-called blue-collar elites.[38]

If confidence in the future indeed had anything to do with salvaging the
auto industry, it took a blow in November when the United States was officially declared to be in a recession. Unsurprisingly, given that news, business boosters were apoplectic when Walter Reuther declared that the UAW
would push for sizable wage increases in 1958 negotiations with the Big Three.
Raises were necessary, Reuther argued, to boost purchasing power "and restore needed economic growth." Autoworkers, he said, should have increased
earnings with shorter work weeks to allow more people to have jobs. "We
don't lack capacity in the auto industry," he noted. "We lack customers." In
response, National Association of Manufacturers president Milton Lightner
insisted that union gains since World War II had wrecked the economy. To
Lightner, it took a lot of gall for Reuther to deny this reality and "justify
demands for still higher wages and fringe benefits" while claiming that the
union had "only the interests of the nation at heart." The UAW, in turn, blamed
auto companies for the high cost of new cars, charging that automakers had
led a "campaign to raise prices to swell massive profits," a practice that remained "unchanged in the face of mounting unemployment and declining

purchasing power." The union claimed that GM set its prices for 1958 models to ensure healthy profits even if the company operated only 180 days during the calendar year.[39]

The positions were strident because auto production was slowing and economic forecasts remained ominous—seventy thousand autoworkers, including fifty thousand at Chrysler, received layoff notices the week before Christmas. "Normally we hand out about 1,200 checks daily," commented Herbert Rosenbloom, assistant manager of the MESC's Schaefer-Schoolcraft office, in mid-December, "but we are getting many more people in this week because of big auto layoffs." Neighborhoods surrounding MESC branches were overrun with parked cars blocking driveways, preventing customers from shopping at local businesses, and trapping delivery vehicles. "The only real solution," sighed an MESC spokesman, "and it's an impossible one—is full employment."[40]

Automakers and boosters emphasized that, despite everything, 1957 was the fourth-best year for production and the fourth time that the industry had produced more than six million cars. Ford highlighted its first victory over Chevrolet in their annual competition. Chrysler trumpeted its 20 percent market share for the year along with record sales and earnings six times greater than they had been in 1956. *Free Press* editors claimed that total auto industry output for 1957 did "not exactly support" any "sour picture of the Country descending into the economic doldrums." Maybe official statistics showed that there was a recession, the editors conceded, "but it still takes a vigorous economy to support that kind of motor car production."[41]

Throughout 1957, conditions in Detroit continued to run counter to national trends, especially for autoworkers. Despite a national recession that began in the last quarter of the year, on the basis of gross national product, total employment, and overall industrial production, 1957 outpaced 1956 to become America's newest "best year ever." Secretary of Commerce Sinclair Weeks declared in late December that "no new year ever started with the economy on such a high plateau as today." In contrast, according to the MESC, Detroit experienced "continuing serious unemployment, high payment of jobless benefits and concurrent reduction of manufacturing employment to the lowest point since 1949." To the extent such things could be determined in the midst of wild daily, weekly, and monthly fluctuations, the MESC calculated that average auto industry employment in 1957 was 395,000, well below the peak of 503,000 two years earlier.[42] In effect, autoworkers in Detroit had been in their own regional recession since 1955.

8 The Nadir, 1958

In 1958 conditions in Detroit's auto industry went from bad to worse. Unemployment reached staggeringly high levels, often over 15 percent, easily double the national rate. Rampant inflation intensified the problem. Well over 250,000 Detroiters were without work most of the year, and when the Big Three shut down for three months, more than 300,000 were jobless. Conditions were far different from those of 1955, when the UAW and automakers had signed their current contracts amid a production and employment boom. Those agreements were set to expire midyear, but in 1958 the union had no leverage to push for any proposals to combat joblessness. Automakers and autoworkers did agree that conditions in Detroit were dismal, and it was obvious that the prolonged loss of autoworkers' income had serious ripple effects throughout the region's economy. Secondary support networks were more important than ever for laid-off autoworkers, thousands of whom left the city. Detroit became a prime destination for investigative journalists, who tried to make sense of the economic devastation they observed. Still, some business leaders thought that autoworkers, benefiting from lavish UAW contracts, had it too good. Desperate times also brought a resurgence of scapegoating, particularly targeting married women with auto jobs. Since the UAW saw no point in striking—most of their members were out of work anyway—the Big Three let their union contracts expire, and walkouts followed in many auto plants as workers and managers sparred without any formal rules. In any event, contract settlements did not bring peace. Skilled workers were especially upset, as two-thirds of them were laid off by late 1958, and all of them felt disrespected by wage compression that had devalued their apprenticeships. There were no easy solutions to the crisis, and industry forecasts pointed to a grim future.

*   *   *

The national recession hit Detroit especially hard. The New Year began with over 120,000 jobless Detroiters, and Democratic congressman John Dingell, who represented a large section of the city, reported that unemployment was "the overwhelming concern" of his constituents. State unemployment funds for over six thousand Michigan companies were already overdrawn, and automakers planned massive new layoffs. By February, Detroit unemployment approached 200,000. As one national journalist noted, unlike in 1954, the auto industry was not poised to help the nation emerge from the current recession, which was "discouraging not only for Detroit but for the whole economy."[1] Nearly 10 percent of the city's stores and offices went out of business. "It appears that our commercial fabric is falling apart," lamented the city's planning director, Charles Blessing, responding to a report that bankruptcies and blight wracked downtown Detroit and had "taken hold in almost every other section" of the city. "I can't remember the last time I had a decent day's intake here," lamented Jack Haddad, who owned a supply store for factory workers on the city's east side. "And I've been here a long time." Haddad counted eighty-eight vacant storefronts in the few blocks north of his business. The recession also nearly bankrupted the UAW, which ran a deficit of over four hundred thousand dollars for lack of dues from unemployed members, who numbered 450,000 nationwide by mid-April.[2]

The industry's instability affected how UAW officials approached 1958 contract negotiations. With unemployment rising rapidly, union leaders backtracked on their 1955 promise to push for the four-day workweek. Given automakers' resistance to that demand, insisting on it would likely lead to strikes, and with poor market conditions any of the Big Three would probably be willing to hold out for a long time, during which UAW members would be ineligible for unemployment benefits. UAW leaders also still feared a public backlash against the notion of autoworkers being paid for the equivalent of forty hours while working far less, especially after the Soviet Union's successful launch in 1957 of the *Sputnik* satellite, which prompted calls for all-out American effort to regain the upper hand in the Cold War. Nevertheless, the Rouge plant's Carl Stellato and Dodge Main's Pat Quinn remained strong supporters of the shortened workweek, in large part because their gigantic plants had been extremely hard hit by layoffs, and their memberships, with little to lose, were open to drastic measures.[3]

In this context, Walter Reuther proposed a system under which an automaker's profits, before taxes, would be divided as follows: 50 percent for the company, 25 percent for hourly and salaried workers, and 25 percent for customers as rebates. Along with a substantial wage increase, Reuther argued, the profit-sharing program would boost purchasing power and lower the net cost of automobiles for consumers. The UAW leader also insisted on the necessity of both increasing SUB pay to reach 80 percent of gross income instead of 65 percent of take-home pay, and extending eligibility to fifty-two weeks instead of twenty-six. These changes, he argued, would move the program closer to the original goal of the guaranteed annual wage, would provide incentive for stable production, and would help maintain greater purchasing power in economic downturns. Within the UAW, a number of locals offered support for the profit-sharing plan, Carl Stellato and Pat Quinn continued to push for the thirty-hour week, and American Motors and Studebaker-Packard workers laughed at the notion of profit sharing, since their companies had not made money in years. In the end, Reuther's plan won 90 percent approval at a carefully orchestrated UAW convention in January 1958.[4]

Auto executives blasted the UAW's profit-sharing plan. GM's Harlow Curtice charged that the union's proposal was "foreign to the concept of the American free-enterprise system," in that the UAW "would bargain, not only for employes it represents, but also for salaried employes, shareholders and customers." Ford president Ernest Breech accused Reuther of an "appeal to class warfare" by insisting "part of management's job be turned over to him so that he can increase still further the already dangerous degree of monopoly power he possesses."[5] The *Free Press* weighed in, editorializing that the UAW's plan "underscores Mr. Reuther's strong leaning to a Socialistic leveling." The paper's David Lawrence complained that the UAW "asks to have all the workers given the status of 'owners' even though they do not contribute a nickel to buy plant and equipment or risk anything, as do the investors who must take losses of dividends when business is bad." The UAW, he claimed, "wants labor to share in the profits" but "has omitted to say anything about sharing in the losses." This, he said, "comes nearer to wanting to confiscate somebody else's property than anything union labor has ever proposed." The *News* offered a similar critique, insisting there was "little likelihood that auto workers ever will achieve quite the degree of income security" that they sought. "Theirs is a risk-taking industry, whose annual billion dollar gamble with a fickle public taste has no counterpart anywhere on a comparable scale. As long as the industry retains this character, it would seem inevitable that workers must accept some share of the risks."[6]

UAW leaders fought back. When asked why autoworkers only wanted *profit* sharing, without risk if auto sales slumped, the UAW's Leonard Woodcock responded, "Workers have been sharing the losses of this industry for many years." Indeed, short weeks and chronic unemployment always accompanied slow sales and brought economic losses, often severe, to production workers. Autoworkers could reasonably claim that they bore the largest share of risk in a volatile industry, especially since they often experienced repeated layoffs even when automakers prospered. Reuther also pointed out that under the UAW's proposed profit-sharing plan, an average GM worker would have earned an additional $6,000 total from 1947 to 1956, while under the actual GM profit-sharing plan, executives split $635 million during those same years, with nearly $4 million going to Harlow Curtice. "We are somewhat at a loss to understand the kind of mental and moral gymnastics required to see nothing but good in a profit-sharing plan for executives and nothing but bad in the extension of this principle to workers and consumers," Reuther insisted.[7]

Both management and union officials agreed, however, that Detroit was experiencing mass unemployment and that there would be no easy solutions. Government estimates indicated that every one thousand factory jobs created another seven hundred positions in the service sector. It was no surprise, then, that unemployment lines were populated by beauticians, shoe salesmen, gas station attendants, and grocery clerks in addition to tens of thousands of laid-off autoworkers. According to the MESC, jobless Detroiters and their families "have not been panicked by the situation. They have grown accustomed to periodic layoffs and prolonged strikes and are generally a resourceful lot." Those directly affected by the roller-coaster ride of auto employment often felt otherwise. One jobless autoworker, for example, kept count of how often he had been forced to be resourceful. "In 16 years of working at these auto plants," he wrote, "I have actually worked seven years, eight months and three days. The rest of the time I have been laid off, sent home on strikes, etc. This time I have been off nine months and have not made five cents." He had heard enough about the postwar economic boom. "The so-called free enterprise system is a fake and a fraud," he argued, "because we who have to depend on it for work to eat, are laid off more than half the time." Adopting a different tone but telling the same story, B. E. Pierson remarked that although things needed to be replaced in his home, "I will make them do until I can be assured of some steady employment for at least a year—which I haven't had for some time." A *Michigan Chronicle* editorial offered a blunt assessment of working-class life: "In the ruthless wake of unemployment come mortgage foreclosures, repossessions, creeping hunger and naked terror. Here we have earnest, hard working people being nailed to an economic cross right now in the richest nation on earth."[8]

Unemployed Detroiters had few options in the area. Defense contracts would provide at best a few thousand jobs but a year or two in the future.[9] Detroit's Department of Parks and Recreation announced that it could provide full-time work for twenty-six hundred unemployed residents planting trees, clearing brush, and performing other maintenance tasks, but it had no money in its budget and no hope of getting any. Since this downturn was, as some economists called it, a "hard goods recession," women tended to have better employment prospects than men, especially if they were young and good-looking. "I, a woman of 55, cannot answer ads that state 'attractive and not over 35,'" a laid-off autoworker with seventeen years of seniority complained. There were some openings for "top-notch typists," "first-grade secretaries," and clerical workers with experience at data processing. Beyond that, job listings were largely for highly trained engineers, accountants, medical technicians, and, given the baby boom, schoolteachers. Few unemployed autoworkers were qualified for any of these positions.[10]

As in previous downturns, many unemployed autoworkers questioned whether or not to remain directly connected to the auto industry. Mirko Bakic, a father of one with another child due, had worked as much as possible for seven years as a machine operator at Chrysler's East Jefferson plant. His most recent layoff had begun in November 1957, and in March 1958 it appeared that he would not be recalled until late fall at the earliest. Bakic considered taking courses in electronics. Laid off in early January 1958, Floyd Mourer decided in February to try his luck as a taxi driver. But after a short time on his new job, his cab broke down. Citing poor business, his employer chose not to repair it. "I'm worried," Mourer said, "because I have to take care of my mother." After getting laid off in March, recalled L. J. Scott, "I didn't know when I was going back or *if* I was going back. And that's as poor as I've ever been in my life. I tried to get a job, car wash and everything. I couldn't find a job nowhere." The answer, Scott decided, was to become self-employed: "I'm thinking if I learn how to be a barber, I can get a job in any city that I go to, cut hair." But he needed seventy-five dollars for classes to qualify for his license. He scraped together the tuition, mostly from deferred principal on his car loan, thanks to a generous bank. Then he was recalled to Pontiac Motor in November, about the same time that he received his barbering credentials. Like so many autoworkers, he hedged his bets, in his case by returning to the plant and opening a barber shop, handling both jobs for nine years. Meanwhile, James McGuire observed the massive layoffs and turmoil from his position in maintenance at the University of Michigan Lawyers Club, confident in his earlier decision not to return to auto work.[11]

In 1958 nearly every autoworker had to rely at some point on secondary support networks. Elwin Brown had always been able to manage through brief downturns, but this time, he recalled, "I got laid off from March of '58 'til November of '58. That's the longest period of time I was off." At first he had no luck finding an alternate job, although he did claim unemployment pay. But just as those benefits were about to expire in August, Brown said, "the preacher's son asked me, 'Why don't you go caddying with me?' I caddied right up until the snow fell. That's when I got called back to work. Right in the nick of time." Although he ultimately made it through, he and his wife had been evicted from one apartment because they could not make the rent and had to move two more times, including from a friend's place, because they had an infant daughter who made "too much noise." Les Coleman was laid off for weeks, even though he was a skilled tradesman, and survived by working twelve-hour shifts at the Argus Camera Company in Ann Arbor, not far from where he lived in Ypsilanti. Emerald Neal was out of work for a year. "I did every kind of job you can think of," he recalled. "Most of it was with a company putting up cyclone fences, and they didn't have power posthole diggers. Hand operated—and the soil in this country is hard rock clay. We dug those things all day long. The guy sent us out on a job, no money to buy gas, didn't pay us half the time." Gene Johnson thought he had mastered his layoff routine, but with six children and out of work for eleven months, 1958 was especially tough. Although he went back, as usual, to driving a cab, for the first time he found it worthwhile to draw unemployment compensation, even though the amount was reduced to account for his taxi earnings. In 1958 he even received SUB payments, although he remembered that it "wasn't very much at all." While on layoff Margaret Beaudry worked as much as possible at her fallback location, Neisner's. Her husband, Marvin, had steady work with Pontiac Motor because he was in charge of painting show cars, so their situation could have been worse. Edith Arnold and her husband, Don, were both out of work for a year in 1958, and she found a job in a junior high school cafeteria. "I worked out on the line during the lunchtime," she recalled. "I had my own little cart—apples and cookies, and frozen ice cream bars." She enjoyed the sociability of the job. "I could yak with the kids, and you get to know them, and they get to know you." When she worked the cash register on the regular lunch line, however, things were different. "Little pats of butter were supposed to be two cents. And they got these little pats of butter *hid*—oh, those kids were slick—and then the manager comes along, she's yakking at my shoulder, you know, 'Hurry it up. Hurry it up.' You can't hurry up everything like that. I didn't like that. When she'd leave me alone, I did fine." Edith found it ironic that this was the type of job her husband preferred her to have, to shield her from the rough culture in an auto plant. Yet at the junior high, she recalled, she "heard more dirty jokes than I ever did in the shop." It was worse than Pontiac Motor, she insisted, "by far!"[12]

Unable to find alternative jobs, tens of thousands of people left the city, mostly heading south, hoping to be recalled in the future. Indeed, layoffs in 1958 were so severe that displaced autoworkers often flooded their home communities, even though most of their relatives had long since moved north. The population of Harlan County, Kentucky, for example, rose from fifty-two thousand in 1957 to seventy thousand in 1958, mostly because of returning migrants from Detroit and Flint. The conditions that had forced so many to leave in the first place, they found, had not improved. If anything, during the national recession in 1958 there were even fewer opportunities in Harlan, which had long been dependent on coal mining. No matter how excited remaining relatives and neighbors were to see them, laid-off autoworkers taxed limited supplies of food and shelter. A quarter of Harlan County residents were already on some sort of government assistance, whether unemployment checks, Social Security, Aid to Dependent Children, or as recipients of emergency federal food rations, what locals called the "cheese program." The Salvation Army had to close operations in Harlan because so many people needed help and so few could make donations. Those seeking refuge in 1958 often crowded into relatives' homes and in many cases settled into old tobacco-curing barns. According to the local school superintendent, "Most of our people believed the optimistic speeches and headlines about the recession being a figment of the imagination. They stayed on up north, hoping for a job that wasn't there. They spent what little they had saved and they came home completely broke, down to their last dollar." "Many of these people lost their washers and refrigerators in northern cities and left them behind," noted a Harlan resident. "The finance companies took them away." There were still two daily round-trip buses between Harlan and Detroit in 1958, but only the southbound coaches carried many passengers.[13]

Despite all the contrary evidence, many business leaders insisted that the unemployed were "willingly idle" because they could supposedly live comfortably on unemployment benefits. As Gannett newspaper executive Frank Tripp put it, collecting handouts "from the state or Washington" was "the philosophy of a new labor bloc that 50 years ago would have been classified as leeches." Tripp was certain that unemployed workers sat back in comfort and did not seek low-wage "miscellaneous jobs," which, he said, "was the rugged way that past depressions blew themselves out . . . and brought prices down to levels that forestalled inflation." Instead, he insisted, "shameless people, whose fathers would have starved first, offer themselves as vassals of the state, pawns of the politicians, dependents fed by neighbors, as truly as their mothers once fed tramps on the back porch." The problem, he said, was that unemployed Americans were simply not hungry enough. "Aren't we the lucky ones? Oh yes," responded Mrs. T. White to charges like Tripp's. "We are in this racket—not working and collecting unemployment compensation. My husband has repaired washing machines, screens, windows and even was paid $1 for fixing a doorbell. And besides we collect $49 a week compensation. In order to live it up like this," she said sarcastically, "we have had to cancel our children's doctor and dental appointments in order to be able to make our house payment (land contract). Ah, this is the life! Ever try it?" Of course many unemployed autoworkers had exhausted any unemployment benefits, and eligibility was soon to expire for thousands more. Others were on short weeks, earning less from being employed than they would have if they received unemployment benefits.[14]

The impact of unemployment on Detroit's families could be assessed in part by how stay-at-home wives of autoworkers managed to run their households. The consensus of one informal survey was clear. To do their jobs, housewives reported, they needed their husbands to have "a regular five-day work week and some hope of a full work year." Describing her husband's recent work history as a grinder at the Plymouth engine plant, Mrs. Reginald Pelletier said, "Twice, in the past three months, he has had a five-day week. We are lucky when he now works three or three-and-a-half days." In 1957 his pre-tax earnings had been forty-seven hundred dollars, well above what he made in 1956, but barely providing a toehold in the middle class, supposedly inhabited by blue-collar elites. What she really supported, she said, was the guaranteed annual wage: "Steady work makes sense to wives and children." In a similar vein, Mrs. Bernard Hyden, whose husband had worked at Dodge for forty-two years, said she would trade any sort of wage increase or profit sharing for steady paychecks. What she wanted for her husband, she said, was "just work. I'm not greedy."[15]

Many women, however, voiced conflicting views. "Cut a few cents off the hourly wage" if that would help "more men" get jobs, suggested a woman with fifteen years of seniority as a small parts assembler at the Rouge plant. "Let men retire with social security at 60 and give the younger ones a chance. I'd step aside to help." In contrast, Mrs. John Smellie, whose husband worked at the Rouge plant, looked at women autoworkers as the cause of her distress. "Women were needed in factories during the war but they refused to come out afterwards when men needed the jobs," she said, offering a widespread but obviously contentious view of the past. "Men with families deserve those jobs now. When has this country been troubled by as much juvenile delinquency as at present? Send working mothers back home." Leona McCabe agreed. Referring to married women with jobs, McCabe remarked, "We have three on our street within a half block, no children and both working, the women in factories taking a job from a husband and father. Get these women out of the auto plants." Polly Cowan, however, contended that the financial contributions from married women were essential. When she married her husband, Everett, she did not intend to work outside the home, but she took a beauty course while he was in the service, and they both agreed that she should work for a year to help them get established before they had children. Everett's job at an auto supplier proved to be unsteady, including a ten-month layoff in 1958, so Polly continued to work and her income was often all the family had. "It isn't really a question of deciding how to spend the money," she said, referring to her wages. "It's just a question of who has enough—to fix a nine-year-old boy's teeth or a car the same age. Something's always breaking down."[16]

Some Detroiters viewed the challenges faced by autoworkers' families with little sympathy. "I am one of thousands of small business men who are having a hard time to make ends meet," wrote Mr. A. Dunn. "We receive no benefits when times are tough." Unlike the significant amount of money he had spent starting his business, he remarked, "most workers have only to buy a pair of gloves twice a week for their investment and they make $5,000 working only 40 hours each week. Fifty per cent of their wives work so their income is at least $7,000 a year. Why don't they put away a little for a rainy day?" Although Dunn's hardship was most certainly real, his arithmetic hardly matched the experiences of Detroit autoworkers, many of whom would have been lucky to earn seven thousand dollars in two years. Moreover, most small business owners in Detroit ultimately relied on autoworkers' spending.[17]

Nationally known for his doorbell-ringing, interview-based journalism, Samuel Lubell visited Detroit in April to assess the city's unemployment crisis. He found that by wide margins, including 80 percent of those under age thirty, Detroiters feared unemployment and inflation more than they feared the Soviet Union. "With relatively little seniority or developed skills," Lubell explained, "younger workers seem least secure in their jobs. They also have plunged deepest into debt to buy new homes and autos." Inflation tended to be the bigger concern for older residents, who worried that they might not ever be able to retire. Many younger autoworkers hoped that those with higher seniority would leave their jobs and make room for the next generation. "They ought to make everyone over 50 retire, so younger fellows can get jobs," a twenty-eight-year-old laid-off autoworker said. "That would give a man 25 years of work. That ought to be enough for anyone." "You don't know what it is like to be over fifty!" responded an older, unemployed worker. "No one will give you a job. They look at your hair and if it's a little gray, you're too old. If you've saved up a few dollars, how long do they last with prices like they are?" Lubell observed that "to many people the unemployment statistics still seem remote and impersonal." But that was not true in working-class neighborhoods. As his reports were published, unemployment in Detroit rose to 265,000, over 17 percent of the workforce.[18]

Syndicated columnist Joseph Alsop also toured Detroit that month to learn more about the recession's impact. What he saw was "the cruel letdown of a vast army of industrial workers by the system they have been taught to trust implicitly." In the Dodge Main union hall, Alsop saw a Southern migrant who faced repossession of his car and hoped for help. When a crane and elevator-hoist operator named Richard asked if there were any new leads on jobs, Local 3 vice president Pete Telisky replied, "Boy, you can't buy a job in this damn town." Richard faced mortgage payments of $75 a month to keep the house he had grown up in. That became impossible in 1958 with only $42 a week in unemployment benefits. Richard found short-term work as a janitor. His brother, now seventeen, had no luck. "They ain't even hirin' boys in stores," Richard said. "We only got another 11 weeks of benefits to go, and after that there'll be nothing but the welfare." When he toured autoworkers' neighborhoods, Alsop observed that their circumstances appeared "grimmer and more poignant, for one actually sees the furniture and the washers and the cars and the homes that are in danger. You see the children 'who drink water now,' and the harassed wives who 'don't know how we can manage much longer.'" Everybody, he observed, was "obsessed by the thought of the end of 'the 26 weeks' (of benefits), which all these people spoke of with a sort of defeated dread." A couple named John and Jeannette were among them. John had eleven years of seniority and Jeannette had seven, both with Chrysler, and together they brought home $160 a week when they worked full-time. They had a mortgage on their home and had purchased furniture, a washer and dryer, and a television on credit. Then Jeannette was laid off in September 1957. Remaining optimistic, they borrowed $200 to pay for Christmas presents for themselves and their young son. Three weeks later, John was laid off. "If I'd knew that, I'd never of went so deep at Christmas," he reflected. By April they were existing on John's $43 a week unemployment benefits, with three months left. Jeannette's had already run out.[19]

Alsop was torn by what he had learned. Most of those in dire circumstances had "been hard, steady workers," he concluded, but in his view too many had also exhibited "almost total, lotus-eating improvidence." One couple went ahead with their wedding despite the prospective husband's layoff. They bought furniture on credit, hoping he would be recalled in time to make the payments. When no job notice arrived, the couple, expecting a baby, had to go on welfare. According to Alsop, "their whole wretched little apartment smelled of ruin." In another case, before the recession a woman defied her husband and took a job because, she said, "you don't never get ahead unless the woman works." With two incomes, they committed to finishing their attic so that they would have an extra bedroom. But when she was laid off, their installment payments consumed half of their remaining income. Although Alsop saw these autoworkers as having engaged in "short-sighted folly," he conceded that they were in the mainstream of an American culture "that measures achievement not by inner standards but by material objects." He might have also noted that much of the 1950s boom, nationwide, was fueled by credit. The main difference in these cases was the unsteadiness of auto work. Even if conditions improved, Alsop determined, "half the things these people have gained will be lost in the interval," because, as one Detroiter told him, "we just can't meet the payments and feed the kids." If conditions did not improve significantly, Alsop predicted, "the whole pattern of life of all these people will simply fall into squalid ruin."[20]

However autoworkers were perceived, to automakers and industry analysts the cure for Detroit's crisis was positive thinking by potential consumers. A Ford economist claimed that there were plenty of Americans with money to spend, but for some reason they were experiencing "hesitancy in making commitments," which led to "excessive postponement" that increased "the depth of the decline unnecessarily." A group of fourteen business leaders was so perplexed by the situation that they declared "a breakdown in the law of supply and demand." Chrysler's L. L. Colbert told members of Congress that the recession would end quickly if people would simply "wake up and decide they want to buy." Industrialist Harold Ruttenberg insisted that UAW members, by themselves, could "reverse the current recession by getting into new 1958 cars and driving right out of it." He seemed unaware that by mid-March some 230,000 Detroiters, over 15 percent of the area's workforce, had no jobs. The only business showing signs of growth in the city was the MESC, which opened three new branch offices to handle the flood of unemployment claims.[21] No improvement was on the horizon. Despite massive production cutbacks, the inventory of unsold cars dropped by only 10,000 during March, to 854,000.[22] Meanwhile, Detroit's unemployment total reached 275,000. "We are facing an industrial readjustment, a very painful one, on top of a national recession," a Wayne State University economist remarked. "A good year for the automobile industry might bring us back to 10 per cent unemployment." Benson Ford, the younger brother of Henry Ford II, saw high drama in these developments. "If there is no business like show business," he said, "certainly this business of ours runs it a close second for glamour, excitement and adventure. There is no other business with anything like the same elements of risk, big stakes, feverish competition, ecstatic highs and gloomy lows."[23]

In the depths of 1958's gloomy lows, the UAW's profit-sharing proposal disappeared from public discussion, and although the recession gave credence to the union's demand for increased SUB payments, automakers seemed unwilling to divert additional money into those funds. With all Big Three agreements ending either in late May or early June, Walter Reuther backtracked on long-standing policy. If no settlements were reached, he announced, union members would have to work without contracts, something that cut against the grain of union principles. Since so few cars were being produced, the UAW president reasoned, "it would be insane to accommodate the auto industry by calling a strike now." Better to wait for the new model year, he said, when "they will need us to make new cars." Only then, he argued, might a strike provide leverage.[24]

Chrysler, Ford, and GM let their UAW contracts expire. For the time being, no production worker would be required to join the union, and companies would not be obligated to collect dues from employees. There would also be no grievance procedures. As one report warned, freed from the constraints of the contract, the automakers would "not stand for any funny business in the shops."[25] Trouble erupted quickly at Chrysler plants, and managers indeed suspended more than a hundred union stewards and local committee members for what the company called "flagrant insubordination." As was common in tough times, many unionists thought the company provoked conflicts to cripple production while limiting unemployment obligations.[26] Even though no walkout would qualify as an unauthorized wildcat strike—there was no longer any contract to violate—top UAW officials counseled workers to endure abuse and stay on the job, a decision that drew jeers. There were few Chrysler workers left to strike anyway. The major automakers eventually sidestepped disputes by shutting down operations for three months in order to reduce dealer inventories. Although technically Detroit autoworkers were not on strike for a new contract, by early July all of them were jobless.[27]

Most unemployed workers had some version of a story like that of Maria and Fernand Pelo, who struggled to provide for their family of five after both were permanently laid off from a metal shop in January, capping a year of unstable employment. Six months later their unemployment checks—which together had provided $63 a week—had run out, but Fernand managed to bring in $60 a week from a temporary job. They had been scrimping for a long time. Layoffs had been so frequent in 1957 that, despite both being so-called full-time employees, they had earned only $3,200 total for the year. In 1955, when times were good, they had lived it up. "We were both working steady and bringing home pretty near $120 a week," Maria recalled. "But we spent it all as fast as we made it. We went to shows and ate out a lot. We even took a trip to Niagara Falls." The family's finances tightened when their son Joe was born with medical problems involving his leg. "That cost us $1,000," Maria said. "I was sick, too. That took another $1,500." They were unable to save, but they were also debt-free. "Now we can't keep up with anything," Maria lamented. By early July the couple was two months behind in rent for their $65-a-month, four-bedroom, unfurnished apartment. They still owed $100 on a television they bought when times were good, and they needed $45 to keep the encyclopedia set they had purchased for their children. Medical bills continued to pile up. Fernand had cut his arm and had caught pneumonia, racking up $250 in hospital charges. When their three-year-old son, Michael, got sick, doctor bills and medicine cost $175. Uninsured after losing their jobs, they still needed to complete payments to the physician who delivered their five-week-old baby, Carla. "We had to let the Blue Cross expire in January," Maria explained. "They told us it would cost $66 in advance to keep up the policy. We just couldn't do it." Despite their troubles, Maria said, they considered themselves fortunate. "Just about everybody in this neighborhood is laid off," Maria observed. "We feel luckier than lots of people. We aren't going hungry." Their grocer was also their landlord, and he was willing to be patient for them to pay off their debts, but it was difficult for the Pelos to make headway. "I paid $9 for a pair of shoes for my oldest boy," Maria said, "and they lasted only four weeks. Since Christmas I've had to buy him three more pairs of shoes." Although the couple did not own a car, bus fare for Fernand's commute added up. Maria considered looking for a job, but it had to pay enough to be worthwhile. "When I'm working I have to pay $10 a week for a baby sitter and $10 for taxes," she noted. "Then there are union dues, bus fare and lunch money. And I'd need more clothes." All things considered, she concluded, "You don't make much."[28]

Given the rampant inflation in 1958, many UAW retirees, nearly thirty thousand of whom lived in the Detroit area, also had great difficulty paying bills, especially since cost-of-living adjustments did not apply to pensions. Retirees wanted that to change, and top UAW officials had promised to do their best. Thousands of UAW retirees gathered outside GM headquarters to add pressure. "I have to live on $98.50 a month," explained Stanley Kujawski, seventy-one, who began work in the auto industry in 1906 and retired from Packard in 1955. "That's my combined pension and social security—for my wife and myself. My wife's been sick for the last eight years. We have to just

sit at home." Many retirees, along with thousands of other laid-off Detroiters, planted gardens. The city's Parks and Recreation Department created
740 plots, 40 by 50 feet each, in eight municipal parks, specifically to ease
the unemployment crisis. Most gardeners, however, like retiree Anthony
Lichvar, raised vegetables in their yards. "I'm out here nearly every day,"
Lichvar said. "My wife and I get about $90 a month on Social Security and
every penny counts." Barney Gornowicz tended a 35-by-125-foot plot next to
his house. Gornowicz was raised on a farm in Michigan's "Thumb" and had
continued to grow crops, no matter the state of the auto industry. His family
agreed, though, that his homegrown produce was especially valuable in 1958.
Unemployment in Detroit hit the three hundred thousand mark about the
time they picked their first sweet corn of the season.[29]

While those without jobs struggled to get by, those who were called back
after model changeovers engaged in what one GM official called "guerilla
warfare." The triggers were generally local—for example, discipline deemed
unfair by workers, disputes over the order of recalls, or the pace of new
jobs—and were usually confined to a single nook or cranny in a particular
plant. But as always, each conflict quickly resulted in wider-scale layoffs and
led to charges of treachery by each side. Although it was unlikely that top
UAW officials orchestrated the uprisings, as some charged, they certainly
did not mind the appearance of a coordinated effort if it would help with
contract bargaining. Chrysler's Mound Road engine plant was shut down in
early August when workers maintained they were understaffed during early
production for 1959 models. Angry about having to work overtime while
many fellow employees were laid off, forklift truck drivers at the company's
new Twinsburg, Ohio, plant walked out a week later, affecting all Chrysler
operations. Strikes took place as well at Chrysler's Mound Road, Nine Mile,
and Warren plants, and at Ford's Wixom factory. Later that summer the
number of strikes increased, mostly because management refused to observe
seniority during recalls. When Pontiac Motor was hit, GM's Semon Knudsen
accused the UAW of "jeopardizing the jobs of 23,000 innocent employes."
Likewise, the Detroit News referred to rank-and-file UAW members as "pawns
in Walter Reuther's struggle to force upon the nation his doctrinaire approach
to political and economic policies," part of the union leadership's quest "to
become the mahatmas of a perfect society."[30]

If the words of GM officials and the News editors were to be believed,
production workers would have felt liberated without the burdens of contract
provisions regarding workloads and job security, but there is no evidence that
workers would have been happy to accept management's unilateral control
over crucial workplace decisions. Indeed, at Pontiac Motor Local 653, presi-

dent Charles Beach declared that his membership was on strike "because of the cluttered-up grievance procedures over which the management failed to bargain in good faith." UAW executive board member Leonard Woodcock insisted that local members needed no encouragement from top union officials to be upset. With free rein to do as they pleased, he argued, managers assigned skilled workers to sweep floors, forced workers to carry on when a burst pipe had flooded their department, and, just as in the 1920s, prohibited conversations between employees and allowed only limited water breaks during the August heat.[31]

In mid-September Ford broke ranks, as it had done in 1955, and signed an agreement with the UAW. This came only a few hours after Ford workers began a no-work-without-a-contract strike that would have paralyzed the company's preparations for the 1959 model season. The settlement called for no wage increases for production workers, although the productivity-based annual improvement factor (2 1/2 percent or six cents an hour, whichever was greater) and the cost-of-living clause were maintained. Together, these provisions resulted in an immediate nine-cent-an-hour increase for unskilled and semiskilled employees. Skilled workers received an additional eight cents an hour in their base pay—hardly enough, in their view, to counteract the wage compression that they criticized so harshly. The duration of SUB pay eligibility was extended to thirty-nine weeks, up from twenty-six, and benefits were set at 65 percent of take-home pay for the entire period instead of only the first four weeks. Those who were already retired received a modest boost to $2.35 per month for each year served, up from $2.25. Workers left behind by decentralization or automation were to receive a maximum of $3,000 severance pay, depending on length of employment, with the top amount going to those who had put in at least thirty years.[32]

The Ford settlement hardly brought labor peace. Upset with their eight cents an hour, skilled workers at the Rouge vowed to shut down the plant, and the next day only fifteen hundred of the morning shift's thirteen thousand workers showed up. In addition to concerns about wage compression, tradesmen feared that their training no longer guaranteed job security. At this point nearly two-thirds of skilled workers in the auto industry were laid off. Additional disputes over job classifications and seniority provisions rocked specific departments. Such local issues always had to be resolved before national contract agreements took effect, but this time discontent seemed especially severe. Nevertheless, after a week, pressure increased from unskilled and laid-off skilled workers to end the Rouge strike. Local 600 president Carl Stellato empathized with the disgruntled tradesmen, telling them that he was also "not entirely happy" with the settlement, but he insisted that high unemployment had forced the union to do the best it could with its "back to the wall."[33]

Contracts with Chrysler and GM followed quickly. The UAW-Chrysler agreement was essentially the same as Ford's, with a significant exception. A plant-wide and area-wide seniority system for metro Detroit went into effect, under which Chrysler workers with at least twelve years of seniority were placed on an "area" roster. When openings or recalls occurred at Chrysler plants, jobs would be given, on an alternating basis, to those at the top of the area list and those with the most seniority at that particular facility. This was good news for those with high seniority, of course, who chafed at being laid off while those with less time in at other plants were on the job, but the plan undercut prospects for younger workers as so many of them had feared.[34]

The concerns of skilled tradesmen took many by surprise. Long thought to be the most stable and lucrative positions available in auto plants, the skilled trades now suffered from decentralization and mass unemployment, much like other auto jobs. Big Three production remained so low in 1958 that repairmen and millwrights had little to do. Tools and dies did not wear out when they were not in use. Likewise, plumbing and electrical work were largely unnecessary in idle factories. Whereas there had been a chronic shortage of skilled workers during the 1955 boom, there was an excess in 1957 and 1958. For years, advance work on future models had been outsourced by the Big Three to Detroit-area tool and die firms, which in turn subcontracted parts of each order to even smaller job shops. In 1958 non–Big Three skilled tradesmen, when employed, generally earned about $3.52 per hour, which was between $0.35 and $1.00 more per hour than their "captive" brothers who were employed directly by the auto companies. The system broke down completely in 1958. Tool and die shops had sprung up around assembly plants on the coasts and near St. Louis, a natural progression with the decentralization of auto production. In addition, an increasing number of tool and die jobs were outsourced to European firms, with the finished products shipped back to the United States, in sections, to be reassembled. Wages for skilled workers in Europe were often less than a third of those in the Detroit area. As a result, in late October only thirty-five hundred of eight thousand unionized skilled workers outside the Big Three had jobs.[35]

Skilled tradesmen had conflicting ideas about what should be done. Many of those who were military veterans questioned what they had fought for overseas and why they had invested four years in specialized training if it brought no advantages. Others, however, advocated reducing their own wages to keep their jobs. Any skilled tradesmen who demanded wage increases, an unemployed tradesman said, must "have rocks in their heads. They have

already run nearly all the tool and die work out of the city due to high wages."
To him, the arithmetic was clear. "Which is the better income," he asked, "to
receive $3.50 an hour and work four months a year or $3 and work 10 months
a year?" Of course, as another skilled worker pointed out, a wage cut would
not necessarily ensure sustained, predictable employment. "Under a system
of supply and demand such as ours," he replied, "low wages are not a cure for
unemployment nor are they a guarantee for a full year's work." High wages
helped compensate, he said, for "the feast and famine conditions in these
shops." For much of the industry's history, of course, these skilled positions
had been coveted by those excluded from them. By 1958 no women and
only a handful of African American men had broken through the barriers,
an injustice that many had fought to overturn. High unemployment among
white skilled workers in 1958 was no excuse for continued racial exclusion
from apprenticeships, but extensive joblessness created a climate in which
white tradesmen felt more protective than ever of what they considered to
be their hard-earned positions, gained through long apprenticeships that
were decreasing in value.[36]

Contributing to tensions, thousands of autoworkers were upset that they
were still laid off while others who had already been recalled were receiving
overtime hours. "I think this is shameful," wrote the wife of a still jobless
Chrysler worker in November, noting that her husband had been laid off
since January. "Why can't the work be held to 40 hours and get more back
to work?" asked a Detroiter. "I have a neighbor who was laid off in August,
1956, and is still out. He has 17 years seniority at Ford and is a good worker."[37]
Hundreds of laid-off Dodge Main workers picketed their plant, demanding
that fellow union members refuse overtime assignments as long as any of
them remained unemployed. At that point fewer than half of Dodge Main's
pre-recession workforce of eighteen thousand had been recalled. Local 3
president Pat Quinn felt the pressure. He informed those on the job that the
laid-off workers' protest did not constitute an official picket line and that it
therefore could be crossed to report to work. He also conceded that "many
of those laid off will never be called back because jobs have been eliminated."
Angry protesters continued to picket area Chrysler plants, sometimes successfully shutting down overtime operations but more often watching fellow
union members go to work. Frustrated and heavily criticized UAW leaders
had no authority concerning overtime hours in any plants. "It is morally
wrong and socially indefensible for the automobile companies to schedule
overtime work beyond that absolutely required," Walter Reuther remarked
in the midst of the controversy. He urged auto companies "to call back as
many as possible of the unemployed even though their re-employment may

be on a temporary basis. In this way, the benefits of economic recovery from the 1958 recession will be more widely and equitably shared." Company officials responded that they were only doing what union leaders had asked them to do earlier in the year by offering full-time jobs to as many workers as possible and laying off the rest rather than scheduling two or three days of work for a larger number of employees.[38]

By almost any measure, 1958 was a terrible year for the auto industry. Production was down almost two million vehicles from the weak total for 1957, and the MESC concluded bluntly that "the job picture was grim." "I don't think I've had three solid month's work all year," said Dodge Main employee Robert Weatherburn, fifty, in December. "A normal year, I'll make about $5,000. But I'll be lucky if I make half that this year." "This is the worst year I've ever had," concluded fellow Dodge Main worker Ray Czarnecki, thirty-three. "My son came up to me the other day and said, 'That's all right, Daddy. When we get rich, we'll have a lot of things.' Even kids can feel it—I mean the pressure." Confirming the level of hardship in the area, a University of Michigan study determined that 70 percent of blue-collar Detroiters had experienced unemployment or short work weeks in 1958 compared with a national average of 41 percent. Nearly a quarter of working-class Detroiters had lost at least fifteen hundred dollars in expected pay, compared with a national average of 14 percent. The only income category in which Detroit led the nation was the percentage of its jobless residents who had received unemployment benefits. A postmortem on the 1958 recession showed that nearly 60 percent of Detroit's laid-off autoworkers believed they had little chance of ever being recalled to their former jobs or of finding anything that paid comparable wages.[39]

Even the most optimistic predictions for the future seemed grim. On the basis of interviews with seventeen bankers, businessmen, and government officials, the Detroit Board of Commerce maintained that more than 1.2 million more cars would be produced in 1959, payrolls would increase by 11 percent, and unemployment would drop to *only* 150,000, assuming that 25,000 people either dropped out of the work force entirely or left town. This was the most favorable forecast. Others saw little chance for a meaningful recovery. Many auto jobs, it seemed, were gone forever. Chrysler now employed half as many Detroiters—70,000—as it had at the peak of the 1955 boom. Ford's national workforce was down 28,000—to 106,000—from the start of the 1958 model season, with much of that decline at the Rouge plant. According to *Fortune* labor editor Daniel Bell, "What the 1958 recession has done is to emphasize, particularly to the young, that workers do not have middle-class security.

Companies severely hit rarely laid off the white-collar worker," he noted, "but blue-collar workers were laid off in great numbers—and quickly."[40]

The *Free Press* blamed Detroit's woes on the UAW, noting that autoworkers in England earned wages only one-third as high as American union rates, in Germany about a fourth as much as their U.S. counterparts, and in Japan about 14 percent of the American standard. "If America's cost disadvantage continues to increase," the editorial warned, "we must anticipate an accelerated flight of American capital and much more 'sourcing' of parts and products abroad." To the editors, the problem was clear: American autoworkers had been living the high life, and it had to stop. "If we continue the present pattern of inflationary wage increases," they predicted, "the final consequence must be to price ourselves not only out of foreign markets, but out of our own markets as well." The goal, according to Ford's Ernest Breech, was to preserve the "American Dream" from "being stung to death by the wasp of wage inflation."[41] From the vantage point of most Detroit autoworkers, who had experienced unsteady employment at best for several years, who were behind on rents and mortgages, who had difficulty feeding and clothing their children, and whose furniture and used cars were at constant risk of repossession, these were cruel charges.

9 "What IS happening? Which way ARE we headed?" 1959–1960

Despite the official end of the national recession, massive unemployment persisted for Detroit's autoworkers amid huge disruptions in production. Frequent and prolonged layoffs had long since caused safety nets to fray. Most workers had exhausted their unemployment benefits, and few alternate employment options existed in Detroit. The unemployed lined up whenever there were openings, no matter the type of work, and they scrapped with one another, sometimes in violation of union contracts, to maintain access to scarce auto jobs. In contrast with the misery of so many autoworkers, Ford and GM managed to earn healthy profits, despite shutdowns caused by a national steel strike. Chrysler might have profited as well if not for a glassworkers strike that undercut its production. Automakers engaged in post–steel strike exuberance by increasing output, but inventories stockpiled, especially those of midsize cars, and unemployment remained high. The only bright spot in the industry, nationwide, was the trend toward small, fuel-efficient autos. The best chance for any employment in the industry was being part of the supply chains or assembly lines for Falcons, Darts, Valiants, or Corvairs. Even so, steady employment was far from guaranteed. In mid-1960 the U.S. Department of Labor declared Detroit to be in the "worst-off" category for the nation's metropolitan areas. By the end of that year, auto work remained precarious in the Motor City.

* * *

Some signs indicated that 1959 would be a rebound year. Automakers ramped up production in early 1959, Ford earned record profits for the first quarter, and GM and Chrysler also posted significant gains from dismal 1958.[1]

Yet unemployment levels barely changed, with nearly two hundred thousand Detroiters out of work through late February. "We are victims of productivity," declared Manatee Smith from Dodge Main Local 3. "Automation and increased efficiency have chiseled us out of our jobs." Many business leaders continued to argue that a large number of laid-off Detroiters represented "fringe unemployment." The Detroit economy was basically sound, according to that view, even though unemployment might be high. The real problem, the argument went, was a lack of labor mobility, attributable in part to seniority and pension provisions that locked workers into dependency on particular employers, reducing incentives to go "where the jobs were." The *Detroit News* had long argued that the only answer to the area's unemployment problem was "the gradual absorption of the displaced workers by other trades and businesses." Likewise, the *Free Press* advocated the "relocation of surplus labor." MESC director Max Horton reinforced the message: "If I were an auto worker unemployed for the last year or better I would start seeking a job in some other line of work." Of course it was not clear "where the jobs were" for unskilled workers during the 1958 recession, or in its aftermath—Horton suggested picking fruit in western Michigan—but it did seem self-evident that if enough Detroiters gave up on the auto industry and left the area, local unemployment rates would decline to more acceptable levels.[2]

While Detroiters debated their future, Chrysler production came to a halt when a long strike at a key supplier, the Pittsburgh Plate Glass Company, finally affected the auto firm. Although by early 1959 Pittsburgh Plate workers had been on the picket lines for several months, Chrysler had been shut down so often in late 1958 that it still had substantial glass reserves on hand. By mid-January Chrysler's supply ran out, the company shut down most of its plants, and tens of thousands of workers headed into yet another month off the job. Nevertheless, conditions were so bad the previous year that Chrysler vastly outpaced its 1958 production and profits for the first quarter.[3]

Ironically, both the UAW and the MESC contributed to Detroit's jobless ranks. The union continued to suffer from membership losses—down half a million, to 800,000, at the depths of the recession—because of lengthy, perhaps permanent, layoffs. Fewer employed members, of course, meant less dues money, and more than 100 UAW staff members had been laid off in 1958. Another 70 were let go in February 1959. Nearly 700 other union employees, including executive board members, took 10 percent wage cuts to try to balance the union's budget. The MESC's layoffs in March were not a result of decreased unemployment. The number of jobless Detroiters had actually risen to nearly 240,000 even with the resumption of Chrysler's operations, but most of Detroit's laid-off autoworkers had exhausted their benefits.

Only 62,000 of those without jobs still qualified for unemployment checks, and stringing together the eligibility requirement of thirty-nine weeks of full employment in a twelve-month period seemed impossible. With less work at MESC offices, staff members were laid off. Most of them had been so busy for the past year, however, that they easily qualified for unemployment benefits.[4]

The job situation in Detroit was so dire that when the Kroger Company opened a new supermarket on the east side and accepted applications for seventy-five jobs, paying seventy-five dollars a week, six hundred people lined up in frigid temperatures hoping to be among the fortunate. "It was a madhouse when we got here," recalled police officer Jack Gettinger, who was in charge of controlling the crowd. "We thought we were going to have a riot on our hands." Things calmed down quickly when signs reading "No More Help Needed" appeared in the store windows. One of those left on the outside was Ewing Fulks, forty-nine, a laid-off welder who had worked ten years at Chrysler's Outer Drive plant. "I still got four unemployment checks coming, but I'm worried," he said. "I can't find any work, even part time. I've been looking everywhere. I'd take anything." His wife, Goldie, had a job at the local U.S. Rubber plant, or else his situation would have been desperate. J. V. Gann, thirty-five, also lost out at Kroger. He had worked for Studebaker-Packard until the company closed its Detroit operations in 1956. "Steadiest job I've had since was 39 days at one plant," he said. "I've sold my car and the rent on our flat is only $65, but I haven't paid that for two months." Needing to support a family of four, Gann had no income besides disability payments of thirty-six dollars a month from the Veterans Administration for wounds suffered while fighting in Italy during World War II. "I haven't been able to get unemployment compensation for a year and a half," he said. "I haven't given up, though. I guess it's still better here than in Russia." Kenneth Riddle, twenty-six, was laid off from his metal-finishing job at Chrysler's Mack plant and had only been able to find seven weeks' worth of work in the past year. He and his wife, Betty, twenty-two, had bought a house "when work was good," he said, but they had great difficulty making the ninety-five dollar monthly payments. The Riddles had a three-year-old daughter and survived on Betty's store-clerk paycheck of forty-five dollars a week. Betty Wilshire, twenty-eight, hoped for a supermarket position because her husband, John, thirty-one, had been laid off from his auto job in January 1958. "He hasn't heard from Chrysler since," she said. John managed to find work at another plant, but that lasted only two months. The couple had three children, nine, six, and three months. "We've only got two months of unemployment benefits left," Betty explained. "I worked for a while after the baby came, but only part-time—four hours. And that was hardly enough to pay the baby sitter."

Mrs. Fairris Clow, forty-two, was also trying to make up for her family's lost income. Her husband had been a tool-room superintendent at Hudson Motor Car Company and then had been part of American Motors' small remaining Detroit contingent before he was laid off in February 1958. "He's been everywhere and he can't find anything," Mrs. Clow said. "We're living on unemployment compensation." Margaret Gilliam had given up a secure job at Elmendorf Air Force Base in Alaska to return to Detroit to help her mother and her stepfather, who had been laid off for over a year from his job at Ford. "We've been hungry," Margaret admitted. "We're behind in everything. Only thing we got coming in is what I get from day work."[5]

There were countless thousands of comparable stories in the Detroit area, including that of Betty and Bob Haver. "People look at you and think to themselves, 'If I were out of work, I'd find another job in a hurry,'" they commented. "You know you're thinking something must be wrong with you because you have not found a job in 15 months." That's how long it had been since January 1958, when Bob lost his job as a sheet metal worker at B&S Fabricators, which supplied materials primarily to the Ford tank plant just west of Detroit. He had six years of seniority at B&S, having taken a position there after working at another supplier, the Venderbush Sheet Metal Company. "We heard rumors that Ford was going to cancel" its B&S contract, Bob recalled, "but when you've never been out of work, you do not worry too much. You figure you're good and there'll always be a place to work." Before Bob was laid off, the couple had a few hundred dollars in savings; two cars, one of them paid for; and they owned a house, for which they had never missed a payment. They also had four children and a fifth on the way. "We sold a car, stopped bowling, cut all extra expenses," Betty explained, "but didn't really worry because we were sure Bob would go back by February." Betty was furious at the notion that unemployment benefits made people too lazy to look for work. "He tried everything," she said. "Companies rehire their own people before they hire new men. There must be a thousand men for every job." "They say things will get better," Bob noted. "We hear that things aren't bad at all. But I've been to every plant in town and I've answered hundreds of ads, and I know. It's getting worse. I can't see the end of it."

Bob tried selling cars, but that proved futile during the recession. He found a few weeks of work on an experimental sheet metal job, just enough to make a house payment, before he was laid off and dropped to the bottom of that company's four-hundred-man recall list. Their creditors showed no mercy when the Havers asked for extra time. "We couldn't believe their attitude," Betty remarked. The family had to make critical decisions. Their youngest daughter had yet to receive polio vaccinations. "You can't just walk into a doctor's office with no money," Betty explained. "We had the telephone taken out," Bob said, "but put it in again, because we figured we might miss a call to work." The family now relied on government surplus food—rice, flour, butter, cornmeal, dried milk, and, of course, cheese. Bob and Betty could not buy Christmas presents for their children, but a neighbor gave them candy. Another neighbor was a barber and offered Bob free haircuts. A friend who managed to work for two days bought the Havers a ham. "We're living from day to day," Betty said. "The television's on the blink and we don't use the car, but we play pinochle like mad. And we love each other. It's just that we hate to see everything you've worked for disappear."[6]

Robert Hager offered another example of how Detroiters managed during the 1958–1959 recession. Having moved to Detroit from Union City, Tennessee, in December 1955, at the tail end of the auto industry's boom year, Hager had never experienced job stability as an autoworker. "During the past three and a half years," he said, "I've been out more than I've been in." Shortly after his arrival in Detroit he found a job at the GM transmission plant in Willow Run, but almost as quickly he was laid off. After a few months he was recalled, but that stint lasted only ten weeks. He found a job at Evans Products, an auto supplier in Plymouth, Michigan, where he ended up welding bicycles, but he was laid off six times in less than a year. He then landed at the Ford transmission and axle plant in Livonia, where he worked a few months before being laid off in December 1957. From then until the following October, by his own calculation, he had applied for 243 jobs at factories, stores, and shops in metro Detroit, as well as in Chicago and St. Louis. During those months he was single and lived with friends in an apartment rented by landlords who let him run a three-hundred-dollar tab for room and board. He needed his car to look for work, but he could not make the payments. Unlike the Havers' creditors, Hager's bank gave him extra time. He used to collect thirty dollars a week in unemployment benefits, but his eligibility had long since run out. While searching for work he spent time picking corn, hauling sod, and chauffeuring Lt. Governor John Swainson on the 1958 reelection campaign trail. Finally, in October 1958 he was called back to the Ford transmission plant. Confident about his future, he married his fiancé, Patty Ruth, but he was laid off again after five months. Within a few weeks he found a job as a handyman for the Burroughs office machine company, where he still worked in April 1959. Despite all that he had been through, or perhaps because of it, Hager considered himself to be a Detroit success story. "My recent experiences should give confidence to the many men and women who are still without a job," he said. Whether or not Hager's story proved inspirational, it certainly illustrated the instability and insecurity experienced by so many would-be autoworkers.[7]

Older Detroiters, especially those left behind when auto plants closed, rarely experienced good fortune. Jean Velden, sixty, lost his job at Hudson shortly after it merged with Nash. He and three thousand others like him, he said, had been "looking all over for work and with a very few exceptions—no luck. Some of us have taken odd jobs, fixing garage doors or doing anything to stay active." John McDaniel, fifty-seven, became permanently unemployed when Studebaker-Packard ended Detroit operations in early 1957. "The plight of the Packard worker is so disastrous," he said, "that you wonder if some of them aren't going to do bodily harm to themselves." John Kief, fifty-one, had also worked for Studebaker-Packard. "The closest thing I've had to a steady job since then," he said, "was 10 days work at the Michigan State Fair last October." "They don't want to hire old people," explained a woman who would have preferred to work. "If they do, they give you such ridiculously low pay that, by the time you pay transportation, what have you got left?" An estimated 56 percent of former Packard employees, most of them between the ages of fifty-five and sixty-four, were still unemployed in late 1959. About 85 percent of the last to be laid off were over forty years old. None of them had been hired at Packard after 1950. Only 20 percent of them had gone to high school at all, and 65 percent of them were second- or third-generation descendants of European immigrants. Most of them had home mortgages, which made them hesitant to relocate and ineligible for city welfare. African Americans, about 550 of the bitter-enders, had a higher unemployment rate in 1959 than did their white counterparts, but neither group had fared well. No matter their race, almost all of those who landed new jobs found them outside the auto industry and earned significantly lower wages. A study found that many of them were psychologically damaged by their loss of identity both as autoworkers and as part of a workplace community. Such evidence complicated the pronouncement by the Detroit Board of Commerce that the area's autoworkers had enjoyed average earnings of $104.67 a week throughout 1958 and could look forward to 4 percent raises in 1959.[8]

Throughout these months, autoworkers competed with one another for whatever factory jobs became available. In one example, a group of ninety laid-off union members, most of them women, demanded fairness in the recall process at the Rouge, implicating Local 600 president Carl Stellato in the injustice. The protest group's spokesperson, Etta Belle Warren, had sixteen years' seniority at the plant, but her job had run only twelve weeks in the last year and a half. Desperate for a paycheck, she was certain that men with less seniority had already been recalled. Local 600 officials interviewed the protesting women and found positions for seventeen of them. Although Stellato conceded that more of the women might have been unfairly by-passed by lower-seniority male workers, he emphasized that these men had obtained their positions "by virtue of bidding for them after long years of service in relatively tough jobs. I am not about to reward these brothers by attempting to negotiate them back on their old and harder jobs with a pay cut." Ironically, given his reasoning, Stellato accused the women of trying to become "a special privileged group." Local officers obviously had no desire to challenge traditionally sex-segregated job classifications and run the risk of a male rebellion as well. For many years, seniority systems had done much to provide job security and fairness during layoffs and recalls, but they were increasingly under attack as so many desperate, unemployed autoworkers tried to support themselves and their families. Those with jobs, of course, protected them fiercely, even if they had obtained them illicitly.[9]

Another potential problem for Rouge workers was the domestic industry's tentative shift toward smaller, cheaper, fuel-efficient vehicles to compete with foreign imports, especially those manufactured by Volkswagen, which had increased its U.S. sales from 28,000 in 1955 to 160,000 in 1960.[10] When Ford announced that its new small car, the Falcon, would be assembled at the company's Lorain, Ohio, plant, just west of Cleveland, as well as at facilities in Metuchen, New Jersey; San Jose, California; and Kansas City, Missouri, it was a stunning blow to the 10,000 to 14,000 Rouge workers still on layoff. The Rouge would focus on conventional, midsize Fords, which likely meant the loss of still more jobs from that plant if small cars took market share from standard models. "I've got twenty years' seniority and shouldn't have to worry about my job," said one concerned autoworker. "But with these small cars coming you can't tell which way things will go. No one really knows where he stands." Many shared the opinion of a Ford worker who lamented, "We'll be lucky if we get eight months' work a year from now on."[11] When Carl Stellato led hundreds of protesting Local 600 members in front of the Rouge, Ford officials paid no attention. After all, many other UAW members, in Ohio, New Jersey, California, and Missouri, approved of their decision. Although they wanted as much production as possible in their plants, union leaders in Detroit were by no means certain that the Big Three's compact cars would sell. Local 3 president Pat Quinn scoffed at the news that the Chrysler Valiant and Dodge Dart would be built at the Dodge Main: "Look at all the hopes Ford had for its Edsel, and look what a flop it was." "Leave Detroit," Quinn advised a gathering of 4,000 unemployed union members. Anyone with less than ten years' seniority, he warned, should not expect to be recalled to work. For the 230,000 jobless autoworkers who stayed in the area, the UAW set up nine service centers to offer advice on "unemployment compensation, medical care, welfare, garnishments and repossessions, and obtaining surplus food."[12]

For all of the autoworkers' misery, by certain numbers the industry continued to do well in the first half of 1959. GM came "within a hairsbreadth" of its best half year for sales, measured in dollars, and made significant profits ($590 million). Ford reported record profits ($285.9 million), based on vehicle sales to dealers, only slightly below 1955's all-time high. Chrysler boasted that its first half sales of 539,244 autos, 44 percent above 1958's total, offered the "most emphatic proof yet" of its "recovery from the recession."

Big Three executives were concerned, however, about contentious contract negotiations in the steel industry. The United Steelworkers pledged to shut down mills that accounted for 90 percent of national production if they could not reach an agreement by mid-July. Anticipating a strike, automakers ordered as much steel as they could stockpile, even though they had limited control over their destinies. Just as in the past, their efforts would be in vain if their thousands of parts suppliers did not have adequate stocks. With at least twenty types of steel required to make a car, it was nearly impossible to anticipate where shortages might occur and whether or not there might be alternative sources. "We're only as strong as our weakest link," commented an auto official. "If a supplier runs out of steel, we could be in trouble."[13]

As expected, steelworkers shut down the industry on July 15. The main sticking point was the contract's section 2-B, which gave workers a voice in challenging workloads and staffing levels set by steel companies. The union wanted to keep things as they had been, but industry negotiators demanded free rein to set production standards, with no recourse for employees. "Section 2-B is the reason" for the strike, explained a union steward at McLouth Steel's Trenton, Michigan, plant, downriver from Detroit, that employed twenty-six hundred and supplied the auto industry. "If our representatives gave that up, they might just as well not come back." The importance of section 2-B was fresh in the minds of McLouth's workers. Earlier in the year they had complained about more than one hundred safety hazards in their plant, and three workers had been killed on the job in the previous six months. Management's indifference to dangerous working conditions and union objections had led to a strike in January at all three Detroit-area McLouth facilities. Placing faith in management to make wise decisions struck steelworkers as foolish.[14]

As the steel strike entered its second month, the industry's workers scrambled, in ways familiar to their auto counterparts, to provide food, clothing, and shelter. Of course Detroit-area steelworkers, whose production largely went to the auto industry, had honed those skills during the 1958 recession. Many headed back South to wait for a settlement. Others haggled with creditors and looked for part-time jobs. Merchants in downriver steel communities teetered on the edge of bankruptcy.[15] In mid-September, when the steel strike entered its third month, ripple-effect layoffs had been limited mostly to railroad workers, truck drivers, and ore freighter crews that supplied the steel mills, but auto parts plants began to run low on metal. Since these factories generally produced four to six weeks in advance of final assembly, huge waves of strike-related auto layoffs began in late October, eventually reaching at least two hundred thousand. GM shut down completely in mid-November. After the steel strike ended in January 1960, after many twists and turns, automakers estimated that their production had been reduced by 600,000 vehicles, which was probably a blessing for them, because in that time dealers reduced their inventories of now outdated 1959 models from over 900,000 to a more manageable 440,000. In contrast, for autoworkers, and of course for steelworkers, the steel strike meant additional weeks or months without paychecks.[16]

Despite massive unemployment and lost production from the steel strike, both GM and Ford declared that 1959 had been their second-best year ever for profits. Among the Big Three, only Chrysler lost money in 1959, in large part because of the prolonged glass strike before the steel walkout. On the bright side, the company lost less money ($5.4 million vs. $34 million) than it had in 1958.[17]

* * *

Automakers celebrated the end of the steel strike by increasing their production goals and hinting that 1960 could be the industry's best year ever. In late January even Chrysler's plants ran full tilt, especially Dodge Main, because the Valiant and Dart compact cars proved popular. But the rosy predictions for 1960 proved accurate for barely a month. In early February the Big Three ratcheted back production schedules on all models except compacts. It turned out that there were few buyers for midsize cars, which were as essential as ever for overall profitability. Industry analysts blamed the need for retrenchment on "post–steel strike exuberance" that had gone to the automakers' heads. In any event, dealers once again faced increasing inventories, heading toward one million, and profitless sales. These developments demonstrated that the problems that had plagued the industry in the 1950s had not been resolved. Most significantly, the ability to produce cars was still not matched by the means or willingness to purchase them.[18]

Frustrated by so many lackluster years, Chrysler threatened to leave metro Detroit if the company did not receive relief from what it considered to be an excessive tax burden. If the company made good on its threat, as much as 40 percent of the area's Big Three auto employment would disappear. Although Chrysler executives did not mention wage and benefit costs among their complaints, a University of Michigan research team, led by William Haber, concluded that those expenses, along with high unemployment benefit rates, discouraged employers from doing business in Michigan. To the economists, state and local taxes did not seem to be a major contributor to operating costs in Detroit. After all, Chrysler paid only $14 million in local property taxes in 1959. But in tough times the tax burden did spark feelings of ingratitude in automakers, the researchers concluded, and added to "a fairly widespread impression, if not conviction, that Michigan does not offer a 'good climate' for industry."[19]

The best hope for sustained auto employment in 1960 seemed to be working on small cars, which claimed a quarter of domestic sales in the first three months of 1960. Indeed, if not for the booming sales of compact cars, the industry would have been in extremely difficult shape. Finding a job in a supply and assembly network related to compacts, however, was a matter of fortuitous timing and location. The Dart, assembled at Dodge Main, by itself doubled Dodge Division sales in the first quarter of 1960 compared with 1959 (117,859 vs. 53,887). The Chrysler Valiant, the other small car produced at Dodge Main, also sold well (71,586). But total employment at Dodge Main during this surge stood at thirteen thousand—up from a low point of seventy-five hundred in 1959, to be sure, but only about half of 1955's total. GM's Corvair (93,880 sales in the first quarter of 1960) and Ford's Falcon (126,133) were the other main Big Three entries in the small car market. They provided fairly steady work at GM's Willow Run plant and at Ford's Lorain, Ohio, factory. In addition, during the first three months of 1960 American Motors sold over 100,000 Ramblers, which led the domestic small car surge in the mid-1950s and helped bring profitability to the company, for the first time, in the midst of the 1958 recession. Solid Rambler sales provided relatively steady work at the company's Kenosha, Wisconsin, plant, including jobs for a few hundred displaced former Hudson employees from Detroit.[20]

Solid statistics for small car production were little solace for autoworkers assigned to produce midsize models. Employment at the Rouge dropped from thirty-six thousand to twenty-nine thousand in the first few months of 1960 as sales of standard Fords fell 34 percent. Workers in the foundry and the engine plant needed twenty-six years of seniority to stay on the job. "We not only need more work but we want to persuade the company to balance out available jobs," said Local 600's Carl Stellato. "At some Detroit-area plants, for instance, they are working six and seven days a week while high-seniority people at the Rouge, who could do the same jobs, are laid off." Stellato found Ford executives unresponsive to his pleas, perhaps because the company was making record first-quarter profits. Paralleling assembly patterns, companies that supplied parts for compacts thrived while those that contributed to midsize cars suffered. For example, Peninsular Metal Products Company, which had prospered when hood ornaments were in style, lost business when consumers began to prefer bare-bones compacts. Peninsular eventually dropped auto parts production, putting another five hundred Detroiters out of work.[21]

Although output and employment varied considerably from plant to plant, aggregate totals indicated troubles ahead. Despite the popularity of small cars, overall dealer inventories remained above one million in early April, and sales rates indicated that it would take at least several months to make significant reductions in those stockpiles. April, May, and June were supposed to be high-production months, the long-outdated conventional wisdom went, but instead unemployment rose in the auto industry and prospects were not good for early recalls. Making matters worse in auto-dependent communities, another class of high school students was about to graduate into a dismal entry-level job market. Low demand for unskilled workers, which was a growing population with baby boomers about to come of age, caused great concern. University of Michigan researchers did not anticipate anything close to full employment in the next few years. Even if education and retraining were easily available, their report noted, the demand for people with professional and technical skills was not great enough to absorb the large and increasing number of job-seeking Detroiters.[22]

It was no surprise when a study conducted in blue-collar Detroit neighborhoods revealed that "the most constant concern among men who work for a wage in Detroit is the threat—or the grim reality—of unemployment." The reporters found a "general sense of frustration" among factory workers "over their bleak economic future." Even a young GM employee who worked on Corvairs was getting only three days of work a week. "A lot of people are beginning to wonder if we still have a union," remarked a laid-off, fifty-five-year-old Chrysler worker. "The company seems to be able to do what it wants." Conditions on the job could also be brutal. "I used to hear friends at Chrysler complain and I told them it was just because the company was trying to make them work for a change," said a young millwright, who found a temporary job at a major auto supplier. "Now that I've gone to Budd I know it's different in the plants. Speedup! The way they push those old guys is criminal. The company's got us over the barrel." At this point many autoworkers no longer gave priority to higher wages. "Raise the pensions and lower the retirement age," suggested a Ford skilled tradesman who was still two years away from eligibility. "Give the younger men the jobs. The younger men are the ones who buy the houses, the cars and the television sets." There was continued sentiment as well in favor of the thirty-hour-week plan, but there was still no chance that the auto companies would entertain the idea. The U.S. Department of Labor confirmed what jobless Detroiters had been saying when it placed the metropolitan area in the "worst-off" category, indicating "substantial and chronic unemployment," defined as "at least 50 per cent above the national average for three of the preceding four calendar years."[23]

By the middle of the year, auto production remained high, unemployment continued at around 10 percent, and inventories piled up, awaiting buyers. As one report described the situation, Detroit's economy was "a baffling conglomerate of millions of sales, paychecks and layoffs. Clues to the puzzle are found in a welter of statistics, comparisons and indices, which sometimes appear contradictory. What IS happening? Which way ARE we headed?" Downtown department store sales were up significantly, while unemployment remained well above one hundred thousand and the Common Pleas Court processed thousands of garnishment and repossession claims.[24] In another confusing twist, a major Big Three wildcat strike caused minimal disruption in Detroit, highlighting to some extent the effects of decentralization. Ford Falcon production stalled in July when thirty-four hundred workers at a crucial parts-stamping plant in Walton Hills, a Cleveland suburb, struck over unresolved workload complaints. The walkout immediately resulted in the shutdown of a Falcon assembly plant in nearby Lorain, as well as operations in New Jersey, California, and Missouri. Plants in Brook Park and Lima, Ohio, that produced engines for Falcons, also had to suspend operations. Because of subsequent parts shortages, midsize-car assembly plants in Atlanta, Dallas, St. Paul, and in Chester, Pennsylvania, southwest of Philadelphia, were closed. Some twenty thousand Ford workers were laid off because of the Walton Hills strike, but hardly any of them lived and worked in Michigan. Illustrating another key change, when GM significantly expanded Corvair production in September, it required only a modest increase in employment: eighty jobs at Detroit's gear and axle plant, fifty at Livonia's spring and bumper plant, and seventy-five on assembly at Willow Run. Another major Corvair production boost, announced in November, required no increase in the Willow Run workforce of twelve hundred. The 1955 boom had required tens of thousands of new hires to ramp up assemblies, but that was no longer the case. The unpredictability and unevenness of auto work were also evident in mid-November, when *Ward's Automotive Reports* revealed that eight assembly plants were operating on overtime shifts to meet demand while eight others were shut down for lack of purchasers.[25] Even Dodge Main was closed, despite previously strong sales for Valiants and Darts. The company announced that the mass layoffs were a necessary "adjustment to field inventories." As a reporter translated, "This means Chrysler has more cars than customers." Aggregate auto production figures showed a booming industry, with the second-best November ever, behind only 1955. Yet unsold inventories climbed steadily and again approached the million-car threshold. Consequently, short weeks and layoffs returned throughout the Ford and Chrysler networks. Another ominous sign appeared when Great Lakes Steel ordered a ten-day shutdown "for lack of orders" after operating for many weeks at barely over half capacity. Output at Great Lakes Steel, a major supplier to the auto industry, was a reliable indicator of future vehicle production. *Standard & Poor's* confirmed the bad news, predicting that the auto industry's outlook was "not encouraging, for at least the forepart of 1961." *Ward's Automotive Reports* concurred, noting reduced production schedules for the New Year, with "appropriate" layoffs and short weeks.[26] The postwar boom remained elusive.

Conclusion

The postwar boom in the United States is generally held to have lasted for a little over a quarter century after 1945. Detroit autoworkers, however, experienced the first fifteen years of the boom, its supposed heyday, as an era of job instability and economic insecurity. Materials and parts shortages, war, extreme weather, strikes (often in other industries), wildcat strikes in the auto industry, overproduction, lack of demand, decentralization, and automation combined to make the years from 1945 to 1960 anything but increasingly prosperous and comfortable for these supposed blue-collar elites. There was nothing seasonal or predictable about the industry's volatility, as model changeovers could be accomplished in less than a week in the post–World War II era. Everyone from workers themselves to auto executives knew that full-time work was only temporary. Whenever autoworkers experienced anything like sustained employment—for example, in 1953 and 1955—auto production overwhelmed the number of customers, leading to recession-like conditions that were often limited to the auto industry and hit Detroit's working-class communities ferociously.

As it turns out, the very concept of "autoworkers" is problematic. There was no consistent body of people who could be classified as autoworkers during these years. Instead, people periodically entered and left auto work, often with little control over the timing. There was always high turnover in entry-level positions, and there were huge waves of hiring, especially in 1950, 1953, and 1955, that churned the population of autoworkers. The mass migration of job seekers to Detroit, especially when times were good but also when those making the journey thought the Detroit economy *should* be booming, prompted intense debates as to who was an autoworker and who was a Detroiter. During the Korean War, when unemployment skyrocketed in Detroit, the city's board of commerce insisted that most of the jobless were recent migrants, that they should not count as unemployed autoworkers, and that they should leave the region.[1] But two years earlier when the auto industry needed additional workers, Detroit's manufacturers advertised for them out of state, and tens of thousands of people responded by moving to Detroit and getting jobs in auto plants. Were those new employees officially autoworkers? Were they Detroiters? Did they view themselves as a floating labor force, to be summoned and discharged as auto manufacturing needs shifted? Or did they hope to make new, permanent lives as autoworkers in southeastern Michigan? What about the hundreds of thousands who had migrated to the city during World War II? At what point did those recruited to the auto industry become Detroiters and autoworkers? Were previously rebuffed African Americans, women, those over forty, and the moderately disabled, who were prized by automakers during the 1953 production upturn, actual autoworkers, or were they "fringe" populations to be hired and laid off as needed?

Heated debates over these questions persisted throughout the 1950s, especially during the downturns that followed each period of high production and massive migration. In 1956, for example, automakers insisted that those hired in 1955, and even in 1953, had been "temporary" employees and were not to be counted among Detroit's increasing jobless totals. Chrysler explained that most of those laid off were either newly hired and still in their ninety-day probationary periods or had low seniority. Many of them had only recently moved to Detroit, the company claimed, so the layoffs were not as severe as they seemed.[2] Yet few of the recent migrants or resident "fringe" workers thought of themselves as expendable. Once hired in the industry, most hoped to continue as autoworkers, whether or not the experts thought they should. Many of them spent as much time during the 1950s on, or looking for, secondary jobs—cab driving, waiting tables, posthole digging, cutting hair, and so forth—as they did in auto plants. It is not clear to what extent these workers, especially the emerging majority of younger ones, considered themselves to be primarily autoworkers at all during the 1950s. The categories of "autoworker" and "Detroiter" were obviously fluid and contested.

Although no one during the 1950s thought the auto industry was stable, a rough consensus exists today that these were prosperous times, especially for whites, when Detroit's autoworkers entered the middle class by virtue of their rising wages and benefits. How could there be such a discrepancy between autoworkers' actual experiences and what later generations have come to believe? Perhaps most significantly, aggregate economic data and wage figures in contracts do not necessarily tell us much about the lived experiences of ordinary autoworkers. Indeed, because there was a constantly fluctuating population of autoworkers, the aggregate data over time do not necessarily refer to the same people. Most importantly, as much as the Detroit Board of Commerce tried to convince the public that autoworkers' rising wages resulted in record incomes, their claims lost credibility by failing to account for chronic layoffs. As much as aggregate economic data show increasing prosperity over the course of the postwar boom, autoworkers had to pay bills in real time. Frequent layoffs often made this difficult or impossible, no matter how much their hourly wage rates increased.

There is a tendency as well to read history backward. If at some point autoworkers could afford to purchase new cars and own a cabin "up north," the thinking seems to go, then they must have been able to all along. But that was not the case. Few autoworkers in the 1950s were able to purchase new cars, and far more took advantage of Michigan's overcrowded state parks than their own properties, especially since they struggled to keep up with mortgages or rents.[3] Although those UAW members who survived the massive dislocations of the 1970s and 1980s—oil crises, foreign competition, outsourcing, and others—might have appeared to be prototypical post–World War II autoworkers, with their high wages, solid benefits, and financial protection against layoffs, they were the ones who, through interviews, emphasized most clearly that the earlier postwar years had been unstable and insecure. The dominance of the postwar boom framework is so strong that it took quite a few interviews to figure this out, in part because most retired autoworkers spoke with pride, for good reason, of their credited years of service that were used to determine pension eligibility. It was easy to assume, for example, that when someone mentioned thirty-six years of credited service it meant thirty-six continuous years of steady employment, when in reality for most people the number hid numerous, sometimes lengthy layoffs.

Given Detroit's decline, there is also a fair amount of nostalgia for a time when it was thriving, as the Arsenal of Democracy or the Motor City. This sense of the past is often fueled by middle-class perceptions of life in the region. The layoffs that frequently devastated working-class neighborhoods had far less impact on wealthier residents, as evidenced by solid sales at upscale department stores during this period. When I have presented versions of this research to metro-Detroit audiences, the argument generally has resonated with former autoworkers or those from blue-collar families, who recall these years as turbulent, while others have often been less convinced because that's not the way they remember things. Once a skeptic challenged my right to conduct this research, because I am not a native Detroiter and could not possibly understand how things really were, while another time a man whose family operated a bakery across from an auto plant in the 1950s noted that, because of how persistent layoffs affected their business, they always considered auto work to be part-time employment. My thesis was not news to him.[4]

Of course scholars have also reinforced the notion of a postwar boom for autoworkers. This has often served as the basis for criticism of Walter Reuther and top UAW leadership for abandoning militancy, workplace control, and broad social reforms in favor of larger paychecks, improved benefits, and entry for autoworkers into the consumer culture of the American middle class. More recently, as unionization rates have plummeted in the United States and income inequality has grown considerably, the 1950s have been seen as, if not the good old days, at least a time when collective bargaining gave industrial workers leverage to improve their lives.[5] Business-oriented scholars are more likely to see this period as the time when unionized autoworkers became so wealthy and powerful that they drove the industry overseas.[6] When looking at actual autoworkers and the availability of work in the industry, it is apparent that the boom was elusive. Autoworkers were indeed among the highest-paid blue-collar workers, if measured by hourly wages. People who were repeatedly tempted to return to the industry knew this to be true, confirming what can be found in contracts and from national wage data. The problem was a lack of steady work—sometimes, ironically, as a result of persistent worker militancy, whether through wildcat or authorized strikes, in either the auto industry or supply networks, especially for coal and steel. Despite unstable employment, Detroit autoworkers in the aggregate earned countless millions of dollars in this period. Almost all of it went directly to local shop owners, professionals, and landlords, in spasmodic torrents of "trickle-up" economics. Although businesses in working-class neighborhoods suffered from the volatility of the auto industry, wages and salaries from auto work appear to have helped create relatively stable employment and predictable incomes for many in the middle class. There was a postwar boom, but autoworkers were not the main beneficiaries of it.

What could the UAW have done to make auto work more stable and members' incomes more secure? Since it is widely believed that this is exactly what the union did, if more so for white men than for African Americans or white women, this question forces a reconsideration of the period, and there seems to be no ready answer unless one is willing to embrace counterfactual scenarios as plausible. As long as we think that the UAW was able to get most of what it wanted through negotiations in the early postwar years, it stands to reason that if the union's priorities had been different, instead of gaining higher wages, fringe benefits, and stable employment for its membership, it could have achieved other goals, such as greater control over the work process, or racial and gender equality. If we realize that UAW leadership was unable to achieve its highest negotiating priority in the fifties, stabilized employment and incomes through the guaranteed annual wage, then the era looks quite different. Instead of imagining hundreds of thousands of autoworkers rising steadily into the middle class, we see them being tossed and turned in a volatile industry, rarely able to make meaningful headway before the next round of layoffs, with many of them, disproportionately African American but lots of them white, chucked out of the industry for good, largely because of automation and decentralization.

Given how desperate autoworkers were for steady employment and wages after the 1954 recession, it would have been politically impossible to hold out for a full-fledged GAW in 1955, when times were good. And no other options existed besides the dead-on-arrival proposal of thirty hours of work for forty hours of pay. The GAW was always politically fraught, especially during the Cold War, as business leaders charged that the UAW wanted a planned economy and big money for autoworkers for as little work as possible. Despite gaining only an initially meager supplemental unemployment benefit plan instead of the GAW, UAW officials trumpeted their accomplishments in this period, and no doubt union members would have been in far worse shape without contractual gains. Automakers would certainly have preferred lower wages, no pensions, no health benefits, lower unemployment benefit premiums, and no ability for workers to file grievances. But union leaders were unable to compel automakers to rationalize production schedules to meet the most important needs of the industry's workers. Moreover, the UAW had little influence over the pace of automation and decentralization. Even if there had been steady employment in the fifties, autoworkers would have been on the lowest edge of middle-class status. Nevertheless, they were pilloried by automakers and business leaders for ruining the industry with their greed. So despite having a strong union, the best-positioned blue-collar workers in the nation—perhaps other than steelworkers—experienced job insecurity and economic instability during the heyday of the postwar boom.

Research projects in history rarely end up exactly where one thinks they will, and given the emergence of the dominant theme of insecurity and instability, this book ended up being more about access to auto work than about the lives of individual autoworkers. That was unexpected, especially since it was the interviewees that pointed the research toward those themes. It is worth mentioning in conclusion that despite experiencing such instability and insecurity, the people interviewed for this book did not necessarily consider these years to have been the worst of times. Most were not eager to relive them, for sure, but a sense of pride came through in having persevered through and having conquered tremendous challenges. In most cases, UAW membership in the fifties played a significant role in their lives, in part with negotiated wages and benefits, but more so by securing access to livelihoods through grievance procedures. Many would have been fired at some point early in their auto careers if not for successful union intervention, and this was often the first realization for relatively new hires that the UAW had a presence in the plants beyond claiming dues. During the fifties most of these interviewees were too preoccupied with trying to scratch out a living, raise kids, deal with marriages, and keep hopes and dreams alive to consider that they would someday be viewed as having ridden the crest of the postwar boom to comfortable, middle-class status. If they had paid attention to such talk at the time—for example, from leading economists or the Detroit Board of Commerce—they would have found it laughable. Indeed, interviews suggest that many younger autoworkers in the 1950s, at least those who managed to survive the industry's turbulence, did not experience stability and security until the 1970s, when they had high seniority, the postwar boom was over, and those with low seniority were most affected by that decade's volatility.[7]

Notes

Introduction

1. One exception is Lisa Fine's *The Story of Reo Joe: Work, Kin, and Community in Autotown, U.S.A.* (Philadelphia: Temple University Press, 2004), which focuses on workers in Lansing, Michigan. A good place to start when researching Detroit autoworkers is Steve Babson, with Ron Alpern, Dave Elsila, and John Revitte, *Working Detroit: The Making of a Union Town* (Detroit: Wayne State University Press, 1986). There were also a number of sociological studies conducted in the 1940s and 1950s, most of which tried to determine whether or not autoworkers were becoming middle-class citizens. See, for example, Charles R. Walker and Robert H. Guest, *The Man on the Assembly Line* (Cambridge, MA: Harvard University Press, 1952); Ely Chinoy, *Automobile Workers and the American Dream* (Garden City, NY: Doubleday, 1955); and Bennett M. Berger, *Working Class Suburb: A Study of Autoworkers in Suburbia* (Berkeley: University of California Press, 1960).

2. See especially Nelson Lichtenstein's *The Most Dangerous Man in Detroit: Walter Reuther and the Fate of American Labor* (New York: Basic Books, 1995), which takes a largely critical view of these developments; and John Barnard's *American Vanguard: The United Auto Workers during the Reuther Years, 1935–1970* (Detroit: Wayne State University Press, 2004), which takes a more positive view of the same evidence.

3. See Lichtenstein, *Most Dangerous Man*, 300; Barnard, *American Vanguard*, 264; and Frank Marquart, *An Auto Worker's Journal: The UAW from Crusade to One-Party Union* (University Park: Pennsylvania State University Press, 1975).

4. The propensity for wildcat strikes is particularly apparent in Steve Jefferys, *Management and Managed: Fifty Years of Crisis at Chrysler* (New York: Cambridge University Press, 1986). See also Lichtenstein, *Most Dangerous Man*, 291. Chad Berry challenges the generalization that Southern whites were more antiunion than others in *Southern Migrants, Northern Exiles* (Urbana: University of Illinois Press, 2000), 107–9.

5. The most significant example of this is the 1949 Ford speedup strike, covered most thoroughly in Robert Asher's "The 1949 Ford Speedup Strike and the Post War Social Compact, 1946–1961," in *Autowork*, ed. Robert Asher and Ronald Edsworth (Albany: State University of New York Press, 1995), 127–54.

6. Nelson Lichtenstein's critiques of bureaucratic grievance systems and of the 1950 UAW contracts that won higher wages and benefits, for example, seem to assume that there would have been rank-and-file assent if led in alternative directions. Jonathan Cutler, in *Labor's Time: Shorter Hours, the UAW, and the Struggle for American Unionism* (Philadelphia: Temple University Press, 2004), seems to assume widespread rank-and-file support for the thirty-hour week for forty hours of pay and criticizes Walter Reuther for failing to prioritize it in negotiations during the 1950s.

7. See, for example, Lisa Fine, "Rights of Men, Rites of Passage: Hunting and Masculinity at Reo Motors of Lansing, Michigan, 1945–1975," *Journal of Social History* (Summer 2000): 805–23; Stephen Meyer, "Work, Play, and Power: Masculine Culture on the Automotive Shop Floor, 1930–1960," *Men and Masculinities* 2, no. 2 (1999): 115–34; Stephen Meyer, *Manhood on the Line: Working-Class Masculinities in the American Heartland* (Urbana: University of Illinois Press, 2016); and Ryan Pettengill, "Fair Play in Bowling: Sport, Civil Rights, and the UAW Culture of Inclusion, 1936–1950," forthcoming, *Journal of Social History* 52, no. 4 (2018).

8. See Thomas Sugrue, *The Origins of the Urban Crisis: Race and Inequality in Postwar Detroit* (Princeton, NJ: Princeton University Press, 1996); and Kevin Boyle, "The Kiss: Racial and Gender Conflict in a 1950s Automobile Factory," *Journal of American History* 84, no. 2 (1997): 496–523.

9. See Sugrue, *Origins of the Urban Crisis*, particularly chapter 4, "'The Meanest and Dirtiest Jobs': The Structures of Employment Discrimination," and chapter 5, "'The Damning Mark of False Prosperities': The Deindustrialization of Detroit."

10. See Kevin Boyle, *The UAW and the Heyday of American Liberalism, 1945–1968* (Ithaca, NY: Cornell University Press, 1995), 107–31; and David M. Lewis-Colman, *Race against Liberalism: Black Workers and the UAW in Detroit* (Urbana: University of Illinois Press, 2008).

11. See Nancy Gabin, *Feminism in the Labor Movement: Women and the United Auto Workers, 1935–1975* (Ithaca, NY: Cornell University Press, 1990); and Dorothy Sue Cobble, *The Other Women's Movement: Workplace Justice and Social Rights in Modern America* (Princeton, NJ: Princeton University Press, 2004).

12. I kept in mind something Robert Zieger wrote in response to critics in a symposium on his landmark book *The CIO, 1935–1955* (Chapel Hill: University of North Carolina Press, 1995): "When it came time to assessing workers' views, I found little help in the existing literature. . . . Much of the writing on the CIO era seemed to posit, without ever quite documenting, the existence of an inherently militant rank and file, in contradistinction to an inherently bureaucratic labor leadership. . . . The problem of most oral history and autobiographical material is that it reflects the views and interests of activists and adds little first-hand evidence about truly ordinary workers." See "Robert Zieger's History of the CIO: A Symposium," *Labor History* (Spring 1996): 186.

13. Lizabeth Cohen, *A Consumers' Republic: The Politics of Mass Consumption in Postwar America* (New York: Vintage Books, 2003).

14. See Stephen Meyer, *The Five Dollar Day: Labor Management and Social Control in the Ford Motor Company, 1908–1921* (Albany: State University of New York Press, 1981); and Barnard, *American Vanguard*, 1–164.

15. The many important early works in oral history methodology include Ronald Grele, *Envelopes of Sound: Six Practitioners Discuss the Method, Theory, and Practice of Oral History and Oral Testimony* (Chicago: Precedent Publishing, 1975); Paul Thompson, *The Voice of the Past: Oral History* (New York: Oxford University Press, 1978); Michael Frisch, *A Shared Authority: Essays on the Craft and Meaning of Oral and Public History* (Albany: State University of New York Press, 1990); Alessandro Portelli, *The Death of Luigi Trastulli and Other Stories: Form and Meaning in Oral History* (Albany: State University of New York Press, 1990); and Daphne Patai and Sherna Berger Gluck, eds., *Women's Words: The Feminist Practice of Oral History* (New York: Routledge, 1991).

16. For an example of contested interpretation involving oral history, see Katherine Borland, "'That's Not What I Said': Interpretive Conflict in Oral Narrative Research," in Patai and Gluck, *Women's Words*, 63–75.

17. See, for example, Alessandro Portelli, "The Death of Luigi Trastulli: Memory and the Event," in Portelli, *Death of Luigi Trastulli*, 1–28; Alessandro Portelli, "What Makes Oral History Different," in Portelli, *Death of Luigi Trastulli*, 45–58 (quotes on pp. 50–51); and Mark Roseman, "Surviving Memory: Truth and Inaccuracy in Holocaust Testimony," *Journal of Holocaust Education* 8, no. 1 (1999): 1–20.

18. See, for example, Donald Ritchie, *Doing Oral History*, 3rd ed. (New York: Oxford University Press, 2015); and Valerie Yow, *Recording Oral History: A Guide for the Humanities and Social Sciences*, 3rd ed. (Lanham, MD: Rowman and Littlefield, 2014).

19. Recordings and transcripts of interviews for this project are available in the Metropolitan Detroit Autoworkers Oral History Collection, Walter Reuther Library, Archives of Labor and Urban Affairs, Wayne State University.

20. See Barnard, *American Vanguard*, 264.

21. Gerald Weales, "Small-Town Detroit: Motor City on the Move," *Commentary*, September 1, 1956. The third daily paper was the *Detroit Times*, which was purchased by William Randolph Hearst in the 1920s and which ceased publication in 1960.

22. For analysis of developments in journalism at the national level, see Michael Schudson, *Discovering the News: A Social History of American Newspapers* (New York: Basic Books, 1978), especially 3–11 and 160–94; and David T. Z. Mindich, *Just the Facts: How "Objectivity" Came to Define American Journalism* (New York: New York University Press, 1998). The quotes are from Mindich, 1.

23. James Fallows, *Breaking the News: How the Media Undermine American Democracy* (New York: Pantheon Books, 1996), 7.

24. See Boyle, "The Kiss"; Sugrue, *Origins of the Urban Crisis*; and Lewis-Colman, *Race against Liberalism*.

25. Although this idea is common wisdom among historians, this usage is a paraphrase of a point made by Christopher R. Browning in "Remembering Survival:

Inside a Nazi Slave-Labor Camp," excerpted in *The Oral History Reader*, 3rd ed., ed. Robert Perks and Alistair Thomson (New York: Routledge, 2016), 318.

26. Weales, "Small-Town Detroit."

27. See, for example, "Still Behind," *Fortune* (March 1948); "Materials Handling: The New Word in Industry," *Fortune* (June 1948); "The 'Used' Car Deal," *Fortune* (September 1948); "Chrysler's Hundred Days," *Fortune* (June 1950); "The Treaty of Detroit," *Fortune* (July 1950); "Confusion at the Rouge," *Fortune* (September 1950); "Detroit: Danger Ahead?" *Fortune* (May 1953); "Business Roundup: Cars, Cars, Cars," *Fortune* (August 1953); "Labor: Jitters in Detroit," *Fortune* (October 1953); "Labor: The Bumpy Road," *Fortune* (March 1954);"Chrysler Takes the Bumps," *Fortune* (April 1954); "Labor: No Basic Runaway," *Fortune* (July 1954); "Business Roundup: Cutbacks in Cars," *Fortune* (March 1955);"Labor: Stumbling Blocks to the G.A.W.," *Fortune* (August 1955); William B. Harris, "The Trouble in Detroit," *Fortune* (March 1958); "Labor: No Strike in Autos," *Fortune* (May 1958); William B. Harris, "Chrysler's Private Depression," *Fortune* (June 1958); and Daniel Bell, "The 'Invisible' Unemployed," *Fortune* (July 1958).

28. See, for example, memo from Local 600 Executive Board to Harry Truman, June 29, 1951, *Ford Facts Special Layoff Edition*, ca. July 1951; Vincent Mitchell, "Call Committeeman if You're Laid Off," *Ford Facts*, October 27, 1951; "The State of the Union," *Ford Facts*, September 27, 1952; John Orr, "Layoffs Continue," *Ford Facts*, February 11, 1956; Bill Collett, "The Mad Race, Then Layoffs," *Ford Facts*, February 18, 1956; Harold Becker, "What's Wrong with the Auto Industry?" *Ford Facts*, February 23, 1957; E. Plawecki, T. O'Neil, B. Hughes, "Outlook Bleak for Auto Workers," *Ford Facts*, January 4, 1958; Bill Collett, "The Jobless Our Major Concern," *Ford Facts*, May 10, 1958; and "Local 600 Supports UAW's Program to Put America Back to Work," *Ford Facts*, February 21, 1959. Issues of *Ford Facts* can be found at the Walter Reuther Library, Archives of Labor and Urban Affairs, Wayne State University, Detroit, Michigan.

29. See, for example, Charles Edwards, *Dynamics of the United States Automobile Industry* (Columbia: University of South Carolina Press, 1965), 16–44, 106–10; Lawrence White, *The Automobile Industry since 1945* (Cambridge, MA: Harvard University Press, 1971), 13–16; John Rae, *The American Automobile Industry* (Boston: Twayne Publishers, 1984), 96–100, 110; and James Rubenstein, *Making and Selling Cars: Innovation and Change in the U.S. Automotive Industry* (Baltimore: Johns Hopkins University Press, 2001), 214–18, 271.

30. Lichtenstein, *Most Dangerous Man*, 288; Barnard, *American Vanguard*, 260, 294. Barnard also discusses the collapse of Hudson and Packard production in Detroit, as well as the loss of crucial supplier firms like the Motor Products Corporation and Murray Corporation, but these are treated as relatively minor exceptions in a generally prosperous decade (296–98). Lizabeth Cohen relied on Lichtenstein's arguments for a qualifying paragraph about working-class prosperity in *Consumer's Republic*, 160. In a wide-ranging essay, Tami Friedman has pieced together examples like these from a number of industries and regions, including the auto industry in Detroit, to suggest that

the so-called post–World War II boom did not bring stability or prosperity for large numbers of American workers. See "'Acute Depression ... in ... the Age of Plenty': Capital Migration, Economic Dislocation, and the Missing 'Social Contract' of the 1950s," *Labor: Studies in Working-Class History of the Americas* 8, no. 4 (2011): 89–113.

31. Robert J. Gordon, *The Rise and Fall of American Growth: The U.S. Standard of Living since the Civil War* (Princeton, NJ: Princeton University Press, 2016), 379. Gordon cited no sources for this claim.

32. Marc Levinson, *An Extraordinary Time: The End of the Postwar Boom and the Return of the Ordinary Economy* (New York: Basic Books, 2016), 5, 7, 21–22.

33. Jefferson Cowie, *The Great Exception: The New Deal and the Limits of American Politics* (Princeton, NJ: Princeton University Press, 2016), 153, 158. For additional recent examples of historical literature extolling the postwar boom for autoworkers, see Louis Hyman, *Debtor Nation: The History of America in Red Ink* (Princeton, NJ: Princeton University Press, 2011), 132–37; David Maraniss, *Once in a Great City: A Detroit Story* (New York: Simon & Schuster, 2015), 212; and H. W. Brands, *America since 1945* (Upper Saddle River, NJ: Pearson, 2012), 62–63.

34. Tony Stellato, "Layoffs Continue: Ford Eng. Plant," *Ford Facts*, February 18, 1956.

35. Kenneth McCormick, "Paying the Unemployed of Michigan Is a Big Business," *Detroit Free Press* (hereafter cited as *DFP*), February 5, 1950; "No 'Normal' Seen for Unemployment," *DFP*, February 22, 1952; Geoffrey Howes, "How Jobless Are Checked," *DFP*, January 30, 1954.

36. Alessandro Portelli, *They Say in Harlan County: An Oral History* (New York: Oxford University Press, 2011), 3–12.

Chapter 1. Shortages and Strikes

1. Marvin Arrowsmith, "Auto Output for '45 Put at 500,000," *DFP*, August 13, 1945; Radford E. Mobley, "No Limit on Auto Output," *DFP*, August 16, 1945; and John B. Rae, *The American Automobile Industry* (Boston: Twayne Publishers, 1984), 96, 100.

2. Daniel Wells, "Huge Layoffs Head Host of Union Peace Problems," *DFP*, August 19, 1945; "Mass Layoffs Due Soon at War Plants," *DFP*, August 19, 1945; and Elwin Stouffer, "Housing Crisis Intensified as Few Workers Leave, Many Move to Detroit," *DFP*, September 23, 1945.

3. Katherine Lynch, "Working Future Not So Rosy for 'Rosie the Riveter,'" *DFP*, August 26, 1945; "Jobs Lag for Women in Detroit," *DFP*, August 18, 1950; and Nancy Gabin, *Feminism in the Labor Movement: Women and the United Auto Workers, 1935–1975* (Ithaca, NY: Cornell University Press, 1990), 111–42.

4. "Women Ford Plant Pickets Demand Seniority Rights," *DFP*, November 9, 1945.

5. Margaret Beaudry interview by Daniel Clark, June 24, 2002; Katie Neumann interview by Daniel Clark, March 18, 2002; and Dorothy Sackle interview by Daniel Clark, June 14, 2002.

6. Rae, *American Automobile Industry*, 96, 100; "Hayes Strike Perils Ford Production," *DFP*, August 30, 1945; "Strikers Stop New Cars in Two Plants," *DFP*, September

2, 1945; Arthur O'Shea, "Order Kelsey Strike Ended," *DFP*, September 13, 1945; Arthur O'Shea, "UAW Raps Kelsey Strikers as Ford Co. Lays Off 50,000," *DFP*, September 15, 1945; Fran Martin, "Strikers Refuse to Budge: Only 350 Hear Board's Aide," *DFP*, September 17, 1945; Fran Martin, "End of Kelsey Strike to Open Ford Plants," *DFP*, October 6, 1945; Arthur O'Shea, "Ford to Resume Full Production," *DFP*, October 13, 1945; and "Auto Output Lags at 26 Pct. of Goal," *DFP*, November 8, 1945. Nelson Lichtenstein emphasizes the militancy of the Kelsey-Hayes strike in *The Most Dangerous Man in Detroit: Walter Reuther and the Fate of American Labor* (New York: Basic Books, 1995), 217–18.

7. Leo Donovan, "Industry Now Gears for Peak Production," *DFP*, November 11, 1945; Leo Donovan, "GM Buys Plant in Kansas to Speed Auto Production," *DFP*, November 8, 1945; Leo Donovan, "Labor Strife Snags Production at GM," *DFP*, November 15, 1945; Leo Donovan, "Influence to Count in Getting New Cars," *DFP*, November 22, 1945; and "Glass Strike Slows Auto Production," *DFP*, December 14, 1945.

8. Leo Donovan, "GM Walkout Held Peril to Car Industry," *DFP*, November 20, 1945; "40,000 Made Idle by Shutdown at Ford," *DFP*, November 27, 1945; and "Ford Output Cut 50,000 by Parts Shortage," *DFP*, December 17, 1945. On GM as a major parts supplier, see James M. Rubenstein, *Making and Selling Cars: Innovation and Change in the U.S. Automotive Industry* (Baltimore: Johns Hopkins University Press, 2001), 210.

9. Arthur O'Shea, "GM Turns Down New Talks," *DFP*, November 27, 1945; "Complete List of Struck GM Plants in State," *DFP*, November 22, 1945; and "Glass Strike Deadlock Slows Auto Production," *DFP*, December 14, 1945.

10. Charles E. Edwards, *Dynamics of the Auto Industry* (Columbia: University of South Carolina Press, 1965), 26, 106–107; Arthur O'Shea, "GM Turns Down New Talks," *DFP*, November 27, 1945; Edwin A. Lahey, "Strikebound Flint Unlike City of '37," *DFP*, November 28, 1945; "City Will Ask State to Carry Full Relief Cost for 4 Months," *DFP*, January 23, 1946; and Lisa Fine, "Rights of Men, Rites of Passage: Hunting and Masculinity at Reo Motors of Lansing, Michigan, 1945–1975," *Journal of Social History* (Summer 2000): 805–23.

11. Warren Stromberg, "Zest Fades for Weary GM Strikers," *DFP*, January 17, 1946.

12. Letter to the editor from Ex-Sgt. F. L. Wolff, "Vet Blasts Labor Turmoil," *DFP*, March 3, 1946.

13. Bud Weber interview by Daniel Clark, May 15, 2003.

14. Gene Johnson interview by Daniel Clark, July 17, 2002.

15. "Glass Cuts Off Chrysler Jobs," *DFP*, January 19, 1946; and "Steel Crisis Hits Auto Jobs," *DFP*, January 25, 1946.

16. "Steel Mills Closing Up," *DFP*, January 20, 1946; Fran Marti, "Walkout Starts Early in Detroit," *DFP*, January 20, 1946; "57 Detroit Area Plants Closing in Steel Strike," *DFP*, January 21, 1946; and "Steel Crisis Hits Auto Jobs," *DFP*, January 25, 1946.

17. Arthur O'Shea, "GM Peace May Hinge on Steel Pact," *DFP*, January 27, 1946; Lichtenstein, *Most Dangerous Man*, 220–47; and John Barnard, *American Vanguard:*

The United Auto Workers during the Reuther Years, 1935–1970 (Detroit: Wayne State University Press, 2004), 212–19.

18. "9,000 Ordered Back Monday by Chrysler," *DFP*, February 1, 1946; Leo Donovan, "Auto Output Slowed by Parts Shortage," *DFP*, February 5, 1946; "Steel Strike Ends," *DFP*, February 16, 1946; and "Ford Calls 38,000 to Work," *DFP*, February 28, 1946.

19. Leo Donovan, "'46 Car Output to Be Half of Original Goal," *DFP*, March 14, 1946; Arthur O'Shea, "GM Workers Await Call Back to Jobs," *DFP*, March 14, 1946; "GM Balks at Recalling Men," *DFP*, March 20, 1946; "GM Calling Workers Back," *DFP*, March 26, 1946; "88,000 Back on Job at GM Plants Now," *DFP*, March 31, 1946; and "10,000 Await Recall to GM in Detroit," *DFP*, April 1, 1946.

20. "17,000 Idle Due to Strike at Briggs," *DFP*, April 6, 1946; and "Briggs Co. to Resume Work Today," *DFP*, April 8, 1946.

21. "Box to Sit on Missing, So 2,000 Are Idled," *DFP*, March 28, 1946; "Strike Vote Due Today at Briggs," *DFP*, May 3, 1946; and "Two Chrysler Plants Close," *DFP*, June 8, 1946.

22. "Ford Returns to Work," *DFP*, April 10, 1946; "Steel, Parts Shortages Close Ford for 3 Days," *DFP*, April 18, 1946; Leo Donovan, "Auto Output Hit by Mine Shutdown," *DFP*, April 21, 1946; Leo Donovan, "Auto Plants' Closing May Mark Jubilee," *DFP*, April 28, 1946; Leo Donovan, "Supplier Strikes Hit Auto Industry Heavily," *DFP*, May 3, 1946; and Leo Donovan, "Slack Says Controls Retard Auto Output," *DFP*, June 7, 1946.

23. Lawrence J. White, The *Automobile Industry since 1945* (Cambridge, MA: Harvard University Press, 1971), 10; "Coal Strike Closing Ford; Brownout Starts Tonight," *DFP*, May 8, 1946; "More Plants Hit; Lakes Ships Stop," *DFP*, May 10, 1946; "Idle Workers Stretch MUCC Lines," *DFP*, May 10, 1946; "Shortages Cut 10,000 off Job at Chrysler's," *DFP*, May 13, 1946; "Two Chrysler Plants Close," *DFP*, June 8, 1946; Leo Donovan, "Another Drop Likely in Auto Production," *DFP*, May 21, 1946; and "Ford Plants to Reopen June 24," *DFP*, June 5, 1946.

24. Leo Donovan, "New Depression Seen about to Hit Detroit," *DFP*, May 15, 1946; and Bud Weber interview.

25. Rae, *American Automobile Industry*, 101–2; Leo Donovan, "Kaiser-Frazer Far behind Schedule," *DFP*, May 5, 1946; Leo Donovan, "Auto Industry Needs Boogie-Woogie Pep," *DFP*, June 9, 1946; "Auto Industry Falls Far Short of Goal," *DFP*, June 27, 1946; and Leo Donovan, "Prices Seen as Crux of Auto Output Lag," *DFP*, September 15, 1946.

26. Leo Donovan, "Slack Says Controls Retard Auto Output," *DFP*, June 7, 1946.

27. "'Heat' Walkouts Idle 15,000 in City Plants," *DFP*, June 29, 1946; Fran Martin, "7,000 Idled at Chrysler and Briggs," *DFP*, July 12, 1946; "MESA Strikes 3 Plants to Get Doors on Toilets," *DFP*, July 26, 1946; and "Dodge Plant Is Closed by Celebration," *DFP*, August 15, 1946.

28. Other examples from just the next month include "Strikes Idle 22,200 in Auto Plants, *DFP*, September 12, 1946; Fran Martin, "13,050 Idle Following Firing of 2,"

DFP, September 17, 1946; Fran Martin, "2,050 Strike in Auto Plants; 50,000 Idled," *DFP*, September 18, 1946; "Strike Idle Total More Than 50,000," *DFP*, September 19, 1946; and "Strike at Briggs Settled," *DFP*, September 22, 1946.

29. Leo Donovan, "Auto Makers Timing Output during Crisis," *DFP*, November 26, 1946; "Railroad Embargo to Idle 500,000 Michigan Workers," *DFP*, December 4, 1946; Arthur O'Shea, "Ford Delays Layoffs of 20,000 More," *DFP*, December 7, 1946; "Hudson Shutdown to Last Two Days," *DFP*, December 14, 1946; "Yule Layoffs to Idle 82,000 Auto Workers," *DFP*, December 21, 1946; and "Workers Start Holiday Early; 20,000 Idled," *DFP*, January 1, 1947.

30. Leo Donovan, "Ford Output Totals 656,135 for Year," *DFP*, December 27, 1946; "County Survey Shows 444,000 in Factory Jobs," *DFP*, January 2, 1947; Leo Donovan, "Unfilled Chevrolet Orders Hit Million," *DFP*, January 3, 1947; "GM Auto Output Falls under Half of '41 Total," *DFP*, January 6, 1947; and "100,000 Laid Off in City in 3 Weeks," *DFP*, January 15, 1947.

31. Arthur O'Shea, "UAW Asks Guarantee of Full Week at GM," *DFP*, March 9, 1947.

32. Robert Zieger, *The CIO, 1935–1955* (Chapel Hill: University of North Carolina Press), 212–27.

33. Leo Donovan, "$400 Month Income Needed to Own Car?" *DFP*, March 30, 1947; and Leo Donovan, "1946 Auto Output Reaches 2,155,924," *DFP*, March 6 1947.

34. Arthur O'Shea, "UAW Accepts GM Offer: 11 1/2 Cts. Plus Holiday Pay," *DFP*, April 25, 1947; Arthur O'Shea, "Sign 2-Year Chrysler Pact," *DFP*, April 27, 1947; and Leo Donovan, "Chrysler Profits Hit Peak," *DFP*, May 2, 1947.

35. "30,000 Idled by Shortage of Steel," *DFP*, May 10, 1947; Leo Donovan, "Shortage of Steel Slows Auto Output," *DFP*, May 11, 1947; "Auto Output at Low in Steel Pinch," *DFP*, May 13, 1947; Leo Donovan, "Vast Black Market in Steel Is Charged," *DFP*, May 28, 1947; and Leo Donovan, "70,200 Face Layoff in 3 GM Plants," *DFP*, August 21, 1947.

36. "The 'Used' Car Deal," *Fortune* (September 1948); Leo Donovan, "Steel Circles Dislike Auto Output Plans," *DFP*, September 5, 1947; Leo Donovan, "Auto Makers Fail to Get More Steel," *DFP*, September 11, 1947; Leo Donovan, "Used-Car Market Seen Leveling Off," *DFP*, October 19, 1947; Leo Donovan, "Lack of Oil Hinges on Steel Shortage," *DFP*, November 11, 1947; and Leo Donovan, "3-Way Coal Pinch Cuts into Car Output," *DFP*, April 9, 1948.

37. "Still Behind," *Fortune* (March 1948); Leo Donovan, "Cars Growing Heavier," *DFP*, November 30, 1948; Warren Stromberg, "Even with GI Bill, Vets Can't Meet Home Costs, Survey Shows," *DFP*, March 30, 1947; Leo Donovan, "Used Car Sales Take Sharp Drop," *DFP*, October 8, 1947; Leo Donovan, "Used-Car Market Seen Leveling Off," *DFP*, October 19, 1947; and Leo Donovan, "Scrap-Iron Prices Worry Diemakers," *DFP*, December 30, 1947.

38. Arthur O'Shea, "Ford Output Periled by FAA Strike," *DFP*, May 22, 1947; "FAA Demands That Led to Ford Strike," *DFP*, May 22, 1947; "Ford Foremen End Strike," *DFP*, July 7, 1947; and Nelson Lichtenstein, "The Man in the Middle: A Social His-

tory of Automobile Industry Foremen," in *On the Line: Essays in the History of Auto Work*, ed. Nelson Lichtenstein and Stephen Meyer (Urbana: University of Illinois Press, 1989), 153–89.

39. "Auto Output at Low in Steel Pinch," *DFP*, May 13, 1947; and Leo Donovan, "Auto Workers Begin Returning to Jobs as Steel Pinch Eases," *DFP*, May 14, 1947.

40. "115,000 Return to GM Today," *DFP*, July 28, 1947; "Over 54,000 Are Idled in Auto Plants," *DFP*, July 31, 1947; "Murray OK's No-Suit Clause, Union Says," *DFP*, August 8, 1947; "Union Urges Return at Dodge Plant," *DFP*, August 16, 1947; Clyde Bates, "Long Murray Strike Ends," *DFP*, August 20, 1947; Leo Donovan, "70,200 Face Layoff in 3 GM Plants," *DFP*, August 21, 1947; Leo Donovan, "Stifling Heat Cuts into Auto Output," *DFP*, August 22, 1947; "Chevrolet Closes All City Plants," *DFP*, August 22, 1947; "GM Recalls 70,000 to Work Today," *DFP*, September 2, 1947; "Strike Idles 9,000 in Two Plants," *DFP*, November 14, 1947; "Strike at Briggs Ended," *DFP*, November 17, 1947; "12,000 Idled as 21 Quit Hudson," *DFP*, December 2, 1947; and "42 Drivers Case Short K-F Strike," *DFP*, December 20, 1947.

41. Leo Donovan, "Manpower Shortage Haunts Car Makers," *DFP*, August 26, 1947; and "Detroit Employment at Peacetime High," *DFP*, August 28, 1947.

42. Leo Donovan, "Workers' Output Reported Lower Than in 1930s," *DFP*, May 2, 1948; Paul Ish interview by Daniel Clark, June 18, 2002; and Joe Woods interview by Daniel Clark, June 28, 2002.

43. James Franklin interview by Daniel Clark, September 22, 2000.

44. L. J. Scott interview by Daniel Clark, October 27, 2003.

45. Don Hester interview by Daniel Clark, August 12, 2003.

46. "Still Behind," *Fortune* (March 1948): 136; Leo Donovan, "Automobile Industry Counts Blessings," *DFP*, December 25, 1947; "Unemployment in State Hits Peacetime Low," *DFP*, December 31, 1947; "Chrysler Net Earnings 67 Million in 1947," *DFP*, February 22, 1948; and Leo Donovan, "GM Rings Up Net of 287 Million in '47," *DFP*, March 16, 1948.

47. Leo Donovan, "Auto Makers Schedule Utmost in Production," *DFP*, January 18, 1947; Leo Donovan, "New Pontiac Models on Display Feb. 1," *DFP*, January 20, 1948; Leo Donovan, "Drop in Auto Sales Seen This Summer," *DFP*, January 28, 1948; and Leo Donovan, "New-Car Owners Greedy for Seconds," *DFP*, March 11, 1948.

48. "Plant Gas Off; 200,000 Idle," *DFP*, January 24, 1948; "Decision Due Today on Gas for Industry," *DFP*, February 1, 1948; Clyde Bates, "Gas Shortage Proves Greatest Blow to City's Industry since Depression," *DFP*, February 4, 1948; "Factory Figures," *DFP*, February 4, 1948; Clyde Bates, "Jobless Pay Claims Hit Record High," *DFP*, February 5, 1948; Clyde Bates, "Gas-Idled Workers Quick to Blame Industry," *DFP*, February 12, 1948; "Rouge Plant to Lay Off 25,000," *DFP*, March 5, 1948; Robert Sturgiss, "Depression Near, Says Ballenger," *DFP*, March 16, 1948; and "Auto Makers Blast Depression Forecast," *DFP*, March 17, 1948.

49. Leo Donovan, "Auto Industry Feels Coal Strike Pinch," *DFP*, April 7, 1948; Leo Donovan, "3-Way Coal Pinch Cuts into Car Output," *DFP*, April 9, 1948; "Rail Service Ordered Cut to 50 Per Cent," *DFP*, April 10, 1948; Leo Donovan, "Industry

Measures Cost of Coal Strike," *DFP*, April 13, 1948; "GM to Lay Off 200,000 Friday for 9 Days," *DFP*, April 17, 1948; Leo Donovan, "Coal Strike Seen Slowing Chrysler," *DFP*, April 21, 1948; "GM Layoff of 200,000 Starts Today," *DFP*, April 23, 1948; and "Steel Pinch to Close Chrysler," *DFP*, May 5, 1948.

50. "Auto Output to Slump 17,000 Units in Week," *DFP*, May 7, 1948; "Seek 50-Ct. Boost at Ford," *DFP*, May 4, 1948; and "Let's Cut Wage, Ford Tells UAW," *DFP*, May 16, 1948.

51. Arthur O'Shea, "Strike at Chrysler Seen Certain as Talks Fail to Break Pay Deadlock," *DFP*, May 11, 1948; Arthur O'Shea, "Chrysler Walkout to Hit 50,000 More," *DFP*, May 13, 1948; and "Chrysler Workers to Get Little Relief from State," *DFP*, May 14, 1948.

52. Jack Schermerhorn, "Wives Back Strikers, but See Grim Future," *DFP*, May 15, 1948; and Arthur O'Shea, "Work Stoppages Idle 100,000 in Detroit," *DFP*, May 22, 1948.

53. James J. Flink, *The Automobile Age* (Cambridge: Massachusetts Institute of Technology Press, 1988), 280; "How GM Formula Will Affect Workers," *DFP*, May 26, 1948; and Arthur O'Shea, "Quick Chrysler Peace Seen," *DFP*, May 26, 1948.

54. Arthur O'Shea, "13-Ct. Raise at Chrysler Ends Walkout of 75,000," *DFP*, May 29, 1948; "Briggs Plant Closed in New Strife," *DFP*, June 11, 1948; "GM Shuts for Week; Packard Raises Pay," *DFP*, June 11, 1948; "Briggs and UAW Agree on 13-Cent Pay Raise," *DFP*, June 13, 1948; and "Auto Layoffs in Detroit Increasing," *DFP*, June 13, 1948.

55. Leo Donovan, "Used-Car Market Seen Leveling Off," *DFP*, October 19, 1947; Leo Donovan, "Auto Dealers Get Warning on Credit," *DFP*, March 10, 1948; Leo Donovan, "Credit Curbs Seen Cutting Auto Prices," *DFP*, August 11, 1948; Leo Donovan, "Auto Producers Face Huge Backlog," *DFP*, August 19, 1948; "Reins on Credit Start Sept. 20," *DFP*, August 20, 1948; Leo Donovan, "Auto Output Still Short of Demand by Full Year," *DFP*, August 22, 1948; "K-F to Cut Car Output," *DFP*, January 10, 1949; and Leo Donovan, "Used Car Business at Standstill; Auto Values off 25 Per Cent," *DFP*, October 17, 1948.

56. "50,000 Out of Work as 170 Strike," *DFP*, September 9, 1948; "UAW Snubs Briggs' Bid to Reopen," *DFP*, September 12, 1948; "Briggs Talks Fail; UAW Intervenes," *DFP*, September 17, 1948; and Arthur O'Shea, "Briggs Settles; 100,000 Called Back," *DFP*, September 24, 1948.

57. "GM Profits Hit New High," *DFP*, October 28, 1948; "Chrysler Profits and Sales Reach New Peaks," *DFP*, November 3, 1948; and "City Reaches Peacetime High in Employment," *DFP*, November 21, 1948.

Chapter 2. *The Era of "The Treaty of Detroit"*

1. James J. Flink, *The Automobile Age* (Cambridge: Massachusetts Institute of Technology Press, 1988), 282; James M. Rubenstein, *Making and Selling Cars: Innovation and Change in the U.S. Automotive Industry* (Baltimore: Johns Hopkins University Press, 2001), 268; "Still Behind," *Fortune* (March 1948); "Joblessness Increasing in Michigan," *DFP*, January 30, 1949; "Dip in Employment Baffles U.S. Agencies," *DFP*,

February 1, 1949; "U.S. Calm as Jobs and Prices Fall," *DFP*, February 5, 1949; "MUCC Rolls Highest in 11 Months," *DFP*, February 9, 1949; Sigrid Arne, "Depression-Unemployment: Will They Return?" *DFP*, February 27, 1949; Leo Donovan, "Average Auto 9.3 Years Old," *DFP*, March 3, 1949; and Leo Donovan, "Car Inventories at Peak for Year," *DFP*, September 13, 1949.

2. "Chrysler Cars Moisture Proof," *DFP*, February 10, 1949; Leo Donovan, "Sales of Used Cars Fall Off," *DFP*, February 20, 1949; "Credit Curbs Eased," *DFP*, March 3, 1949; Leo Donovan, "Auto Circles Hail Eased Credit Curbs," *DFP*, March 3, 1949; Isaac Jones, "Unemployment Brings Scare to Detroit Area," *Michigan Chronicle*, March 5, 1949; and Leo Donovan, "Car Sales Surge Past 1948 Mark," *DFP*, April 14, 1949.

3. Flink, *Automobile Age*, 279, 284; Rubenstein, *Making and Selling Cars*, 209; Charles E. Edwards, *Dynamics of the United States Automobile Industry* (Columbia: University of South Carolina Press, 1965), 198–200; Leo Donovan, "For Five Cars, a New Job," *DFP*, March 12, 1950; Leo Donovan, "Auto Price War Seen Far Away," *DFP*, April 12, 1949; "Auto Industry Sees New Peak," *DFP*, April 16, 1949; Leo Donovan, "Plymouth Lines Moving Faster," *DFP*, April 20, 1949; Leo Donovan, "GM Profits at Record 136 Million," *DFP*, April 28, 1949; "Car Plant Sales at Postwar Peak," *DFP*, April 28, 1949; and Leo Donovan, "GM Production Near '41 Mark," *DFP*, May 5, 1949.

4. "Speed Up," *Fortune* (January 1949); Leo Donovan, "Kaiser to Lay Off 3,500 Monday," *DFP*, January 14, 1949; "Ford Division Lays Off 1,400," *DFP*, January 25, 1949; "14,000 Idled by Shortage and Strike," *DFP*, February 16, 1949; "Walkouts Idle 19,000 at Briggs and Hudson," *DFP*, February 19, 1949; "Hudson Shut Fourth Time in a Week," *DFP*, February 23, 1949; "5,500 Idled at Briggs by Standards Dispute," *DFP*, March 2, 1949; "It's Off Again, On Again at Hudson Motor Plant," *DFP*, March 16, 1949; "Strikes Idle 13,000 in Auto Plants," *DFP*, March 17, 1949; "9 Strikes Idle 29,000 in Detroit," *DFP*, March 23, 1949; and "36,000 Idled by Shortages at Auto Plants," *DFP*, March 26, 1949.

5. Arthur "O'Shea, "Auto Plant Strikes Laid to Competition," *DFP*, March 24, 1949.

6. Robert Asher, "The 1949 Ford Speedup Strike and the Post War Social Compact, 1946–1961," in *Autowork*, ed. Robert Asher and Ronald Edsworth (Albany: State University of New York Press, 1995), 127–54; "Union Council OK's Ford Strike Action," *DFP*, April 11, 1949; "Local 600 OK's Strike Poll at Rouge Plant," *DFP*, April 17, 1949; Arthur O'Shea, "Approval of Ford Strike Held Remote," *DFP*, April 24, 1949; Arthur O'Shea, "Rouge Strike Set for Thursday: UAW Backs Action by Local 600," *DFP*, May 4, 1949; Arthur O'Shea, "Ford Strikers Gird for Extended Siege," *DFP*, May 6, 1949; Arthur O'Shea, "Ford Strike Layoffs Rise," *DFP*, May 7, 1949; and "Ford Workers Preparing for Long Siege as Talks Resume," *Michigan Chronicle*, May 14, 1949.

7. Nelson Lichtenstein, *The Most Dangerous Man in Detroit: Walter Reuther and the Fate of American Labor* (New York: Basic Books, 1995), 292; "Strike to Idle 147,200 in 3 Weeks," *DFP*, May 6, 1949; Arthur O'Shea, "Ford Strike Layoffs Rise," *DFP*, May 7, 1949; Robert Perrin, "Ford Strike Costs Local $5,000 a Day," *DFP*, May 13, 1949; Charles J. Wartman, "On the Labor Line," *Michigan Chronicle*, May 14, 1949; and Robert Perrin, "Strike Nearly Over, Rouge Pickets Believe," *DFP*, May 25, 1949.

8. Arthur O'Shea, "Ford Strike Layoffs Rise," *DFP*, May 7, 1949; James Oliver Slade, "Keeping the Record Straight: Ford Strike Points to Danger Ahead," *Michigan Chronicle,* May 14, 1949; Arthur O'Shea, "U.S. Enters Ford Talks after Peace Moves Fail," *DFP*, May 15, 1949; Leo Donovan, "Ford Strike Closing All Assembly Plants," *DFP*, May 17, 1949; and "Strikers on Relief Take Big Pay Cut," *DFP*, May 24, 1949.

9. John Murray, "Detroit's Economy Showing Effects of Ford Strike," *DFP*, May 22, 1949; "Strike Ends as Ford and UAW Agree to Submit Grievances to Arbitration," *DFP*, May 29, 1949; Arthur O'Shea, "Return to Work Starts at Ford," *DFP*, May 30, 1949; and "Arbiters File Decision in Ford Speedup Row," *DFP*, July 9, 1949.

10. Fred Olmsted, "Prices Are Easing but You May Not Notice It in Detroit, *DFP*, May 29, 1949; Leo Donovan, "May Auto Sales 50 Pct. over 1948," *DFP*, June 9, 1949; Hub George, "Rise in Unemployment Worries State Officials," *DFP*, June 9, 1949; "Employment in County Up over 1948," *DFP*, June 10, 1949; "Auto Output in August Due to Pass All Marks," *DFP*, June 18, 1949; Leo Donovan, "Survey Shows Robust Market," *DFP*, June 21, 1949; "GM Output in June at Record Peak," *DFP*, July 2, 1949; Leo Donovan, "Now Who Buys All Those Cars?" *DFP*, July 3, 1949; Leo Donovan, "Car Demand Still Strong," *DFP*, July 7, 1949; "Auto Output for Week Is Highest Ever," *DFP*, July 16, 1949; Leo Donovan, "Truth about Tools," *DFP*, September 16, 1949; and Leo Donovan, "Just How Strong Is the Chain?" *DFP*, September 21, 1949.

11. Leo Donovan, "Body Shortage Slows Car Flow," *DFP*, August 18, 1949; "Plymouth Hit by Strike," *DFP*, September 3, 1949; "3,500 Idled at Lincoln in Work Dispute," *DFP*, September 6, 1949; Leo Donovan, "Technology's Pace Baffling," *DFP*, September 25, 1949; and Thomas Sugrue, The *Origins of the Urban Crisis: Race and Inequality in Postwar Detroit* (Princeton, NJ: Princeton University Press, 1996), 130–38.

12. Bud Weber interview; "63,000 Workers Idle as Unemployment Rises," *Michigan Chronicle*, February 12, 1949; and Isaac Jones, "Unemployment Brings Scare to Detroit Area," *Michigan Chronicle*, March 5, 1949.

13. "Ford Asks Freeze on Wages," *DFP*, June 19, 1949; and "Ford Pay-Freeze Plan a 'Fantasy,' Says UAW," *DFP*, June 23, 1949.

14. Harvey Campbell, "Some Workers Hold Two Jobs," *DFP*, August 12, 1949; Leo Donovan, "Auto Output Near 4,000,000," *DFP*, August 16, 1949; Leo Donovan, "Detroit's Riches Called Lasting," *DFP*, August 21, 1949; "Auto Worker Weekly Pay Sets Record," *DFP*, August 25, 1949; Leo Donovan, "Autos Feed Millions—," *DFP*, August 28, 1949; "Output Record Established by Auto Industry," *DFP*, September 1, 1949; and Fred Olmsted, "Detroit: Top-Paying City," *DFP*, October 2, 1949.

15. "A Compelling Argument," editorial, *Michigan Chronicle*, March 5, 1949; Sugrue, *Origins of the Urban Crisis*, 91–124; Charles Wartman, "On the Labor Line," *Michigan Chronicle*, February 4, 1949; Horace White, "Facts in Our News," *Michigan Chronicle*, March 5, 1949; quote from Charles J. Wartman, "On the Labor Line," *Michigan Chronicle*, July 2, 1949; "City Sets Up Board to Fight Unemployment," *DFP*, August 30, 1949; and Fred Olmsted, "Detroit: Prepared for a Depression?," *DFP*, September 11, 1949.

16. Arthur O'Shea, "Ford Accord Is Reached," *DFP*, September 29, 1949; Arthur O'Shea and Leo Donovan, "Industry Expects Chain Reaction in Ford Pension," *DFP*,

October 2, 1949; "Pensions Held Boon to Business," *DFP*, October 25, 1949; "Ford Pact Is OK'd," *DFP*, October 27, 1949; and James M. Haswell, "Retired Couple's Needs Set at $2,089 a Year," *DFP*, March 16, 1950.

17. Leo Donovan, "Just How Strong Is the Chain?" *DFP*, September 21, 1949; Leo Donovan, "Work Schedules Pose Problem," *DFP*, October 14, 1949; Leo Donovan, "Steel Strike Effects Felt," *DFP*, October 16, 1949; "State Acting to Assist Jobless; 300,000 New Layoffs Loom," *DFP*, October 23, 1949; and Leo Donovan, "Fear of Shutdown Grips Car Firms," *DFP*, October 30, 1949.

18. "Miners Back in Pits for Three Weeks," *DFP*, November 10, 1949; "U.S. Steel Strike Ends," *DFP*, November 12, 1949; "Auto Firms Heartened by Steel Peace," *DFP*, November 13, 1949; "Auto Layoffs Climbing Past 100,000," *DFP*, November 21, 1949; "Unemployment in Auto Plants to Reach New Peak," *DFP*, November 23, 1949; and "Jobless Total Hits Year's Peak in City," *DFP*, November 30, 1949.

19. Myrtle Gaskill, "Bitter and Puzzled, the Unemployed Agree: Fellows, It's Cold Outside," *Michigan Chronicle*, December 3, 1949.

20. Leo Donovan, "Auto Plants Call Thousands Back on Job Monday," *DFP*, December 3, 1949; and "Job Picture in State Improved," *DFP*, December 14, 1949.

21. John B. Rae, *The American Automobile Industry* (Boston: Twayne Publishers, 1984), 101–2; "1949 a Record Year, Chrysler Corp. Reports," *DFP*, March 3, 1950; "In 1949, GM Hit 2 Highs," *DFP*, March 11, 1950; Leo Donovan, "GM Reports Record 656-Million Profit," *DFP*, March 14, 1950; Leo Donovan, "2 Firms Report Drop in Profits," *DFP*, March 15, 1950; and "K-F Reveals Loss of 30 Million in '49," *DFP*, April 15, 1950.

22. Leo Donovan, "'49 Banner Year in Car Industry," *DFP*, December 20, 1949; and Hub George, "Retail Sales in Detroit Dip 10 Pct.," *DFP*, December 23, 1949. "Employes," not "employees," was standard usage in newspapers in this era.

23. Leo Donovan, "'49—Top Year in All Ways," *DFP*, January 15, 1950.

24. Lichtenstein, *Most Dangerous Man*, 283; John Barnard, *American Vanguard: The United Auto Workers during the Reuther Years, 1935–1970* (Detroit: Wayne State University Press, 2004), 276; Steve Jefferys, *Management and Managed: Fifty Years of Crisis at Chrysler* (New York: Cambridge University Press, 1986), 115–16; Arthur O'Shea, "Strike Notice Filed on Chrysler," *DFP*, January 19, 1950; Arthur O'Shea, "Chrysler Crews Poised to Strike," *DFP*, January 25, 1950; Arthur O'Shea, "UAW Looks Ahead to Long Strike," *DFP*, January 26, 1950; and "Chrysler Talks Set for Today," *DFP*, February 4, 1950.

25. "Chrysler's Hundred Days," *Fortune* (June 1950); Arthur O'Shea, "Chrysler Pension Rejected by UAW," *DFP*, January 18, 1950; Arthur O'Shea, "Strike Notice Filed on Chrysler," *DFP*, January 19, 1950; and Arthur O'Shea, "Behind the Strike at Chrysler: Principles Are Found at Stake," *DFP*, January 29, 1950.

26. Kenneth McCormick, "Paying the Unemployed of Michigan Is a Big Business," *DFP*, February 5, 1950; Kenneth McCormick, "MUCC Examines Claims with Care," *DFP*, February 6, 1950; "Chrysler Strike Hits Welfare," *DFP*, February 13, 1950; "City Speeds Relief to Strikers," *DFP*, February 21, 1950; and Fred Tew, "Cash Relief Is Denied to Chrysler Strikers," *DFP*, February 1, 1950.

27. "Jobs Scarce, Chrysler Workers Find," *DFP*, February 26, 1950.

28. Charles J. Wartman, "Idle Chrysler Co. Workers Prepared for Long Siege," *Michigan Chronicle*, February 4, 1950; Arthur O'Shea, "Chrysler Strikers Jam Meeting," *DFP*, March 8, 1950; letter to the editor from Chrysler striker John K. Evanoff, *DFP*, March 9, 1950; and Harold Schachern, "Striker's Family of 5 Fights to Keep Going," *DFP*, March 12, 1950.

29. Frank Beckman, "Depression-Era Army Answers DPW Job Call," *DFP*, February 14, 1950; and "Jobs Scarce, Chrysler Workers Find," *DFP*, February 26, 1950.

30. Fred Tew, "It Took a Strike: Now Detroit Housewife Has a Profitable Business," *DFP*, August 13, 1950.

31. Leo Donovan, "'Rat Race' Is On along Livernois," *DFP*, January 26, 1950; Arthur O'Shea, "Chrysler Picket Lines Continue Peacefully," *DFP*, January 28, 1950; "Chrysler Co. Workers Still Idle," *Michigan Chronicle*, February 4, 1950; "Old Ship Coaling Site Yields Supply of Fuel," *DFP*, February 19, 1950; "Coal Crisis at Hand as City's Stocks Vanish," *DFP*, February 22, 1950; and "300,000 Families in Area Burn Coal," *DFP*, February 22, 1953.

32. Harold Schachern, "Behind the Strike at Chrysler: Chrysler Strike Has Worker Tightening Belt," *DFP*, January 29, 1950; Harold Schachern, "Striker at Chrysler Has Job—As Picket," *DFP*, February 12, 1950; Harold Schachern, "Striking Worker Still Won't Get Discouraged," *DFP*, February 26, 1950; and "Food Problem Mounts as Strike Drags On," *DFP*, March 26, 1950.

33. Letter to the editor from "A CIO Member," *DFP*, February 22, 1950; and "7,000 Chrysler Strikers Hear Reuther at Rally," *DFP*, March 31, 1950.

34. Arthur O'Shea, "Chrysler Strikers Jam Meeting," *DFP*, March 8, 1950; and Harold Schachern, "Striker's Family of 5 Fights to Keep Going," *DFP*, March 12, 1950.

35. Harold Schachern, "Strike Family Splits Single Easter Basket," *DFP*, April 9, 1950; "Strike Won't Be Over for Months for Many," *DFP*, April 30, 1950; and Harold Schachern, "Easter Gloom Fades Fast at Striker's Home," *DFP*, April 10, 1950.

36. Fred Tew, "Long Strike Brings Out Tale of Family's Courage," *DFP*, May 1, 1950; and Fred Tew, "Sun Breaks through for Evicted Family," *DFP*, May 2, 1950.

37. "Chrysler's Hundred Days," *Fortune* (June 1950): 70; "MUCC Notes 199,000 Idle in Detroit," *DFP*, March 2, 1950; Fred Olmsted, "16,000 Jobs Lost to Detroiters as Factories Move Out of City," *DFP*, April 16, 1950; "Strike Ordeal Is Over but the Woes Linger," *DFP*, May 5, 1950; and "Everybody Pays Cost of Chrysler Strike," *DFP*, May 5, 1950.

38. Leo Donovan, "Ford Lines Work 5 Nine-Hour Days," *DFP*, March 2, 1950; Leo Donovan, "GM Output Pace Far Ahead of '49," *DFP*, March 3, 1950; Robert Sturgiss, "Coal Strike Settled: Daily Pay Up 70 Cents," *DFP*, March 4, 1950; Leo Donovan, "Car Output Is Speeded," *DFP*, March 7, 1950; and "Ford Plans 6-Day Week," *DFP*, March 17, 1950.

39. "GM's Divisions Set Records," *DFP*, April 4, 1950; Leo Donovan, "Ford-Chevrolet Battle Ever Hot," *DFP*, April 9, 1950; Leo Donovan, "Auto Output Still Zooming," *DFP*, April 27, 1950; "GM 3-Month Profit Again Sets Record," *DFP*, May 6, 1950; and Leo Donovan, "Hudson Sports Records Too," *DFP*, May 7, 1950.

40. "Peace Bid to Chrysler," *DFP*, April 18, 1950; Leo Donovan, "GM Runs Ahead of '49 Record," *DFP*, May 2, 1949; "Chrysler Bares Loss of 1.7 Million," *DFP*, May 5, 1950; and Harold Schachern, "Pact Doesn't End Worker's Troubles," *DFP*, May 5, 1950.

41. Arthur O'Shea, "$100-a-Month Pensions? Not Right Away," *DFP*, January 13, 1950; John Murray, "Ex-Ford Workers Praise Pension," *DFP*, February 19, 1950; Harold Schachern, "Pensioners Look Forward to a 'Soft' Life," *DFP*, March 1, 1950; "Summary of Pension at Chrysler," *DFP*, May 5, 1950; and "Worker, 85, to Get Pension from Chrysler," *DFP*, August 8, 1950.

42. Leo Donovan, "Greater Records Seen," *DFP*, May 5, 1950; Robert Perrin, "Chrysler Plants Hum Again as Strikers Return to Shops," *DFP*, May 9, 1950; "Chrysler Speeding Production," *DFP*, May 10, 1950; "Rail Row Hits Chrysler," *DFP*, May 11, 1950; "Rail Strike Has Brewed for 16 Years," *DFP*, May 11, 1950; "Auto Output Cracks All-Time Record," *DFP*, May 13, 1950; "Trucks Keep Auto Plants Running," *DFP*, May 14, 1950; Leo Donovan, "Auto Plants Still Plagued by 'Ifs,'" *DFP*, May 14, 1950; and "Rail Strike Ends on Note of Discord," *DFP*, May 17, 1950.

43. "The Treaty of Detroit," *Fortune* (July 1950); "The New Kind of Collective Bargaining," *Fortune* (January 1950); Russell Davenport, "Health Insurance Is Next," *Fortune* (March 1950); "UAW and GM Hail Pact," *DFP*, May 24, 1950; Robert Perrin, "UAW Turns Sights to Guaranteed Annual Wage," *DFP*, May 28, 1950; and C. E. Wilson, "Pact Working, Wilson Reports," *DFP*, July 9, 1950.

44. "Joblessness in State Hits Low Mark," *DFP*, June 11, 1950; "Factory Payrolls at County Record," *DFP*, June 13, 1950; Leo Donovan, "Auto Records Don't Last Long," *DFP*, June 2, 1950; Leo Donovan, "Ford Breaks Truck Record," *DFP*, June 9, 1950; Leo Donovan, "K-F Production Trails Demand," *DFP*, June 14, 1950; "Peacetime Employment at New High in State," *DFP*, July 1, 1950; "Chevrolet, Ford Set Records," *DFP*, July 2, 1950; "GM June Output Biggest of Any Month in History," *DFP*, July 6, 1950; "State Idle Shrinks to 100,000," *DFP*, August 9, 1950; and "UAW Blasts Story of State Labor Pinch," *DFP*, August 13, 1950.

45. Nancy Gabin, *Feminism in the Labor Movement: Women and the United Auto Workers, 1935–1975* (Ithaca, NY: Cornell University Press, 1990), 143–87; Dorothy Sackle interview; Joe Woods interview; Charles Wartman, "On the Labor Line," *Michigan Chronicle*, February 5, 1949; "A Compelling Argument," editorial, *Michigan Chronicle*, March 5, 1949; Charles Wartman, "On the Labor Line," *Michigan Chronicle*, October 8, 1949; Charles J. Wartman, "On the Labor Line," *Michigan Chronicle*, April 1, 1950; "NAACP Protests Bias in Factories," *Michigan Chronicle*, May 27, 1950; Edwin Lahey, "Jobs Fade for the Middle-Aged," *DFP*, June 7, 1950; and "Jobs Lag for Women in Detroit," *DFP*, August 18, 1950.

46. "801 Face Garnishment after Long Strike Siege," *DFP*, June 15, 1950; and "Detroit Is Rated Tops for Annual Factory Pay," *DFP*, July 3, 1950.

47. James M. Rubenstein, *Making and Selling Cars: Innovation and Change in the U.S. Automotive Industry* (Baltimore: Johns Hopkins University Press, 2001), 209; Rae, *American Automobile Industry*, 109; Lawrence J. White, *The Automobile Industry since 1945* (Cambridge, MA: Harvard University Press, 1971), 93; and Leo Donovan, "Who Buys Cars? GM Checks to See," *DFP*, February 24, 1950.

48. Edwards, *Dynamics of the Automobile Industry*, 28; White, *Automobile Industry since 1945*, 13; "Meat Prices Rising; No End in Sight," *DFP*, July 4, 1950; "Prices Up on Meat, Coffee, Sugar, Flour," *DFP*, July 19, 1950; Robert Perrin, "Public's Panic Buying Deplored by Dealers," *DFP*, July 20, 1950; Arthur O'Shea, "Warns War Industry Can't Sprout at Once," *DFP*, July 20, 1950; "Used-Car Sales Zoom in Detroit," *DFP*, July 6, 1950; and "Car Dealers Refusing to Take Orders," *DFP*, July 29, 1950.

49. Jefferys, *Management and Managed*, 118–20; "18 Walk Out, Idle 1,000 at Chrysler," *DFP*, June 16, 1950; "Vernor Plant of Briggs Shut by Walkout," *DFP*, June 30, 1950; "Dodge Runs in Spite of Wildcat Strike," *DFP*, July 8, 1950; "Strike of 24 at Briggs Idles 8,500," *DFP*, July 28, 1950; "Brief Strike Idles 5,000 at Chrysler," *DFP*, July 29, 1950; "Walkout at Briggs Idles 12,000," *DFP*, August 3, 1950; "Chrysler Crippled by Strike," *DFP*, August 22, 1950; and "23,700 Workers Idled by Detroit Strikes," *DFP*, August 24, 1950.

50. "K-F Layoff Today Will Idle 10,000," *DFP*, July 7, 1950; and "Pact Reached in Strike at Warner Gear," *DFP*, July 14, 1950.

51. "4-Day Strike Terminated at Hudson," *DFP*, September 30, 1950; and Les Coleman interview by Daniel Clark, August 29, 2000.

52. Nelson Lichtenstein, *Labor's War at Home: The CIO in World War II* (New York: Cambridge University Press, 1982), 89–94; Daniel Clark, *Like Night and Day: Unionization in a Southern Mill Town* (Chapel Hill: University of North Carolina Press, 1997), 125–26; Arthur O'Shea, "Umpire System Promotes Auto Peace," *DFP*, July 23, 1950; and Patricia Cayo Sexton, "A Feminist Union Perspective," in B. J. Widick, *Auto Work and its Discontents* (Baltimore: Johns Hopkins University Press, 1976), 21.

53. Sugrue, *Origins of the Urban Crisis*, 33–88; *Census of Population: 1950*, vol. 2: *Characteristics of the Population*, Part 22, Michigan (Washington, DC: U.S. Government Printing Office, 1952); George A. Hough III, "Housing Shortage Continues to Plague Many Detroiters," *DFP*, March 27, 1949; "No Houses to Rent, Workers Quit Detroit," *DFP*, October 29, 1950; James Ransom, "750,000 Found Ill-Housed in Detroit," *DFP*, December 7, 1950; and "'Bootleg' Landlords Called Threat to City," *DFP*, March 13, 1952.

54. Reprint of letter from Local 600 officers to President Truman, October 25, 1950, in *Ford Facts Special Layoff Edition*, ca. July 1951; "Credit Curbs Ordered," *DFP*, September 9, 1950; Leo Donovan, "Automotive Sales Tapering Off," *DFP*, October 3, 1950; "Credit Curb Hits Autos," *DFP*, October 14, 1950; "Car Dealers 'Shocked' by U.S. Order," *DFP*, October 14, 1950; Leo Donovan, "Credit Cut Hurts Dealers," *DFP*, October 17, 1950; Leo Donovan, "Defense Plans Stir Anxiety in Auto Industry," *DFP*, October 22, 1950; "Consumers Debts Soar as Income Drops Off," *DFP*, October 22, 1950; "Credit Curbs Slash Auto Sales," *DFP*, October 26, 1950; Leo Donovan, "New Car Sales Take Plunge," *DFP*, October 26, 1950; and Leo Donovan, "Auto Sales: New Credit Buying Controls Making Dealers Very Unhappy," *DFP*, November 26, 1950.

55. Leo Donovan, "Defense Plans Stir Anxiety in Auto Industry," *DFP*, October 22, 1950; Leo Donovan, "Wilson Raps Steel Pinch," *DFP*, October 31, 1950; "Reuther Hits Cutback Order in Metals," *DFP*, November 4, 1950; Leo Donovan, "Car Firms Face Steel

Shortage," *DFP*, November 16, 1950; Leo Donovan, "Copper Curb's Effect Uncertain," *DFP*, December 1, 1950; and "Workers in Demand as Year Closes," *DFP*, January 1, 1951.

56. "90,000 to Be Idled in Detroit," *DFP*, November 22, 1950; "Layoff Order Hits 50,000 at Ford Plant," *DFP*, November 30, 1950; "Changeover Idles 17,000 at Dodge," *DFP*, December 13, 1950; "17,500 More Being Idled at Chrysler," *DFP*, December 15, 1950; and "Chrysler to Cut Back 20 Per Cent," *DFP*, January 3, 1951.

57. Leo Donovan, "Auto Makers Hit All-Time Record," *DFP*, December 3, 1950; Leo Donovan, "Auto Records Go Sky High," *DFP*, December 21, 1950; "Detroit Production Up to 9.8 Billions," *DFP*, December 30, 1950; Leo Donovan, "Ford's '50 Output Totals 2 Million," *DFP*, December 31, 1950; and "Workers in Demand as Year Closes," *DFP*, January 1, 1951.

Chapter 3. No Longer the Arsenal of Democracy

1. Charles E. Edwards, *Dynamics of the United States Automobile Industry* (Columbia: University of South Carolina Press, 1965), 16; Earl F. Wegmann, "87,000 Idled in Auto Plants," *DFP*, February 2, 1951; Earl F. Wegmann, "Auto-Plant Layoffs Mushroom," *DFP*, February 3, 1951; "Rail Snarl to Idle 33,000 at Ford," *DFP*, February 8, 1951; "Unionist Asks UAW to Oust Local's Staff," *DFP*, March 23, 1951; and "DeSoto UAW Accuses 4 in Walkouts," *DFP*, April 11, 1951.

2. Norman Nicholson, "Job Seekers Warned against Expecting Work in Automobile Industry," *DFP*, January 14, 1951.

3. John Griffith, "Detroit Food-Price Spiral Continues Unabated," *DFP*, January 11, 1951; "'Delay Pay Lids,'—UAW," *DFP*, December 21, 1950; Earl F. Wegmann, "UAW Calls Price Lid an 'Outright Fraud,'" *DFP*, February 1, 1951; Leo Donovan, "Workers Find Car Payments Hard to Meet," *DFP*, February 23, 1951; Earl F. Wegmann, "Auto Worker's Wages Racing with Prices," *DFP*, March 12, 1951; and "Cost of Living Up 9.6 Pct. in Year," *DFP*, May 24, 1951.

4. Edwards, *Dynamics of the Automobile Industry*, 124; reprint of letter from Carl Stellato, Local 600 president, to Stuart Symington, National Security Resources Board, December 14, 1950, in *Ford Facts Special Layoff Edition*, ca. July 1951; reprint of memo from Local 600 Executive Board to President Truman, June 29, 1951, in *Ford Facts Special Layoff Edition*, ca. July 1951; "GM and Chrysler Get Huge War Contracts," *DFP*, December 23, 1950; "GM to Build Air Force Jet Planes," *DFP*, December 27, 1950; "Government Awards 2 More Defense Contracts to Detroit Companies," *DFP*, December 28, 1950; "Chrysler Given Contract to Produce Jet Engines," *DFP*, January 8, 1951; Leo Donovan, "Packard Gets Contract for Engines from Navy," *DFP*, February 20, 1951; "Ford Gets 195-Million Tank Order," *DFP*, March 7, 1951; and Leo Donovan, "Ford Awarded 3 New Contracts," *DFP*, May 2, 1951.

5. "U.S. Orders at GM Hit 3 Billion," *DFP*, March 3, 1951; "Pontiac Gets 57-Million U.S. Contract," *DFP*, March 22, 1951; and "Pontiac Gets Cannon Contract," *DFP*, April 19, 1951.

6. Elwin Brown interview by Daniel Clark, August 7, 2003.

7. L. J. Scott interview.

8. Reprint of memo from Local 600 to Walter Reuther and the UAW International Executive Board, in *Ford Facts Special Layoff Edition*, ca. July 1951; "10,500 Idled by Shortage," *DFP*, June 5, 1951; James M. Haswell, "Ask New Cuts in Auto Metals," *DFP*, May 19, 1951; and "U.S. Cuts Car Output 3 Pct.," *DFP*, June 3, 1951.

9. "10,000 Face Layoff at Ford in 60 Days," *DFP*, May 18, 1951; Leo Donovan, "More Automobile Layoffs Feared," *DFP*, May 20, 1951; Earl F. Wegmann, "Hudson Motor Lays Off 10,000," *DFP*, May 23, 1951; Leo Donovan, "More Layoffs to Follow New Cutback," *DFP*, June 3, 1951; "Ford to Idle 4,000 Friday at Rouge," *DFP*, June 27, 1951; and "Chrysler and Briggs to Lay Off 28,000," *DFP*, June 28, 1951.

10. "Budd Strike Idles 23,850 at Chrysler," *DFP*, May 1, 1951; "3,250 Idled at Chrysler," *DFP*, May 4, 1951; "Briggs Plant Again Shut by Walkout," *DFP*, May 12, 1951; "6,200 Idle as 30 Strike Briggs," *DFP*, May 16, 1951; "Dodge Workers Balk at Smocks; 10,000 Idled," *DFP*, May 26, 1951; Earl F. Wegmann, "Dodge Strike Idles 32,000 Workers at 8 Chrysler Plants," *DFP*, May 29, 1951; "Auto-Plant Rows Idle 21,000," *DFP*, July 7, 1951; "8,000 Idled in Disputes at Chrysler," *DFP*, July 9, 1951; "25,500 Idled by Auto Plant Work Dispute," *DFP*, July 12, 1951; "8,000 Idled in Disputes at Chrysler," *DFP*, July 19, 1951; "UAW Acts to Stop Walkouts," *DFP*, July 24, 1951; "Strike Idles 16,000 at Dodge Main," *DFP*, July 26, 1951; and David J. Wilkie, "Auto Makers Hit by Uncertainties," *DFP*, June 26, 1951.

11. "UAW Claims Hudson Plots Slowdown," *DFP*, July 21, 1951; "Unionist Hits Ford in Mass Layoffs," *DFP*, July 22, 1951; and "GM to Shut Plants a Week," *DFP*, July 24, 1951.

12. Leo Donovan, "Tool Business Really Rolling," *DFP*, August 2, 1951; and Leo Donovan, "Still Lining Up for the Cadillac," *DFP*, May 24, 1951.

13. Leo Donovan, "New U.S. Order to Cut Output," *DFP*, September 12, 1951; Leo Donovan, "Metals Worry Car Producers," *DFP*, November 12, 1950; and "Why an Auto Cutback? . . . 27 Cars Build a Tank," *DFP*, January 7, 1951.

14. Leo Donovan, "U.S. Order Irks Auto Makers," *DFP*, September 16, 1951; Robert Perrin, "Employment 'Squeeze' Is On," *DFP*, November 4, 1951; "Reuther Hits Cutback Order in Metals," *DFP*, November 4, 1950; "14,000 Ford Workers Face Indefinite Layoff," *DFP*, November 8, 1950; and Earl F. Wegmann, "Critical Labor Shortage Threatening Detroit," *DFP*, November 5, 1950.

15. Leo Donovan, "Eye State Plants for Scrap Metal," *DFP*, November 8, 1951; Leo Donovan, "Industry Relies on Scrap Iron," *DFP*, December 27, 1950; and "Whine of Diesels Replacing Old Iron Horses' Puff," *DFP*, December 12, 1954.

16. "Materials Handling: The New Word in Industry," *Fortune* (June 1948); Thomas Sugrue, *The Origins of the Urban Crisis: Race and Inequality in Postwar Detroit* (Princeton, NJ: Princeton University Press, 1996), 130–38; Leo Donovan, "Time Is Money, Industry Finds," *DFP*, October 11, 1951; "DeSoto's New Plant Is Opened," *DFP*, November 23, 1951; "Ford Engine Plant Nearly 'Automatic,'" *DFP*, March 31, 1952; and untitled graphic on front page, *Ford Facts*, September 27, 1952.

17. Vincent Mitchell, "Call Committeeman If You're Laid Off," *Ford Facts*, October 27, 1951; Charles J. Wartman, "On the Labor Line," *Michigan Chronicle*, December 22, 1951; and "Dodge Plant Closed by Walkout," *DFP*, August 9, 1951.

18. "NAACP Protests Bias in Factories," *Michigan Chronicle*, May 27, 1950; "Forty Women Fight to Save Jobs," *DFP*, July 25, 1951; "Women Ready Grievance in Ford Layoff," *DFP*, July 26, 1951; and Charles J. Wartman, "On the Labor Line," *Michigan Chronicle*, December 1, 1951.

19. Owen Deatrick, "Unemployed List at 135,000 in State," *DFP*, November 21, 1951; and Earl F. Wegmann, "Investigations Do Little to Cheer Detroit's 120,000 Jobless," *DFP*, December 23, 1951.

20. Open letter from Local 600 to UAW leadership, *Ford Facts*, October 27, 1951 (capitalization in the original); and "The State of the Union," *Ford Facts*, September 27, 1952.

21. Bill Collett, "Model Changeover Comes at Bad Time," *Ford Facts*, October 27, 1951; "DPW Denies Having 30,000 Jobs Open," *DFP*, November 28, 1951; and "Auto Plants to Lay Off 25,500," *DFP*, December 1, 1951.

22. "10,000 Sought for Mail Jobs," *DFP*, November 6, 1951; "10,000 Seek Postal Jobs," *DFP*, November 14, 1951; Geoffrey Howes, "3,000 Clamor for Shovel Jobs," *DFP*, December 21, 1951; and "3,500 Seek Jobs as Laborers," *DFP*, March 11, 1952.

23. "City, State Tackle Unemployment," *DFP*, January 4, 1952; Drew Pearson, "The Defense Battle for Detroit," *DFP*, January 6, 1952; "Wilson 'Regrets' City's Joblessness," *DFP*, January 7, 1952; Thomas S. Haney, "U.S. Acts to Aid City Job Crisis," *DFP*, January 13, 1952; "City Faces $1,200,000 Deficit," *DFP*, January 22, 1952; Robert Perrin, "Only 140,000 in State Now in Defense Work," *DFP*, February 13, 1952; and James M. Haswell, "City Gets Promises but No More Work," *DFP*, March 15, 1952.

24. "Raising of Car Quota to Save 70,000 Jobs," *DFP*, January 9, 1952; Leo Donovan, "Ford Declares Car Quota Stirs False Job Hopes," *DFP*, January 11, 1952; and Leo Donovan, "Aluminum Windfall Won't Reduce Idleness," *DFP*, February 11, 1952. There was long-standing frustration with Fleischmann among UAW members. See Local 600 Resolution on Jobs, *Ford Facts Special Layoff Edition*, ca. July 1951.

25. "Task Force Studies Shift of City's Idle," *DFP*, January 23, 1952; and Robert Perrin, "Tragedy of Errors Brought Job Pinch," *DFP*, February 10, 1952.

26. "Boom Threatens to Go BOOM in '52," *DFP*, January 5, 1952; and "Raising of Car Quota to Save 70,000 Jobs," *DFP*, January 9, 1952.

27. Robert Perrin, "How Workers without Jobs Weather Crisis," *DFP*, February 17, 1952; and Clint Wilkinson, "Things Aren't as Bad as They Seem," *DFP*, February 17, 1952.

28. Louis Cook, "Winter—And No Job," *DFP*, January 6, 1952; Louis Cook, "Available Jobs Don't Aid Jobless," *DFP*, January 8, 1952; and Robert Perrin, "How Workers without Jobs Weather Crisis," *DFP*, February 17, 1952.

29. Gene Johnson interview; Margaret Beaudry interview; Paul Ish interview; Paul Ross interview by Daniel Clark, May 20, 2003; and "Local Store Boycott: Community Aroused over Non-Employment," *Pontiac Herald*, October 14, 1957.

30. "Detroit Job Picture Labeled 'Normal'; Moody Objects," *DFP*, February 21, 1952; "No 'Normal' Seen for Unemployment," *DFP*, February 22, 1952; and "30,000 Fail to Seek Jobless Pay," *DFP*, May 27, 1951.

31. "Idle Rolls Increase by 13,000," *DFP*, January 8, 1952; Louis Cook, "Available Jobs Don't Aid Jobless," *DFP*, January 8, 1952; "Only 194 Jobs Lost, Ford Says," *DFP*, January 10, 1952; "Jobless Pay Exhausted by 20,000," *DFP*, January 17, 1952; and Russell Clanahan, "Job Hunter Visits 7 Plants in One Day, but Still No Work," *DFP*, March 14, 1952.

32. "114 Families Jam 3 Welfare Shelters," *DFP*, January 6, 1952; and Charles Weber, "Family of 10 Faces a Homeless Prospect," *DFP*, August 18, 1951.

33. "City Faces $1,200,000 Deficit," *DFP*, January 22, 1952; Robert Perrin, "How Workers without Jobs Weather Crisis," *DFP*, February 17, 1952; and Leo Donovan, "Influx of Out-of-Town Buyers Boosts Prices of Used Cars," *DFP*, February 22, 1952.

34. Dale Nouse, "Joblessness Again Ups City's Crime Curve," *DFP*, January 7, 1952; Charles E. Boyd, "New Layoffs Hit Squeezed Retailers," *DFP*, January 20, 1952; "Average Factory Wage Hits $2.04 Hourly Peak," *DFP*, May 3, 1952; and "Father of 10 Held in Grocery Holdup," *DFP*, July 17, 1952.

35. Norman Kenyon, "Recruiting Boom: Only Women Are a Problem," *DFP*, February 17, 1952; "1,600 Face Draft Call in County," *DFP*, November 8, 1951; and "State Draft Calls 2,200 for April," *DFP*, March 5, 1952.

36. Elwin Brown interview; Joe Woods interview; L. J. Scott interview; and Don Hester interview.

37. Robert Zieger, *The CIO, 1935–1955* (Chapel Hill: University of North Carolina Press, 1995), 300–304; Charles E. Egan, "Steel Firms to Fight Seizure; Strike Is Off," *DFP*, April 9, 1952; "Steel Workers Strike as Court Voids Seizure," *DFP*, April 30, 1952; "Steel Seizure Sticks til Top Court Rules," *DFP*, May 1, 1952; "Strike Grips Steel; Court Ends Seizure," *DFP*, June 3, 1952; and "Steel Strike Idles 18,000 in Detroit," *DFP*, June 3, 1952.

38. "Ford Orders 4-Day Week," *DFP*, June 19, 1952; "Ford Stays on 5-Day Week," *DFP*, June 20, 1952; Robert Perrin, "Ford to Shut 18 Plants in U.S. Monday," *DFP*, June 28, 1952; and Robert Perrin, "Ford to Halt All Assemblies for Week Beginning Monday," *DFP*, July 12, 1952.

39. "Steel Strike Idles 12,400 at Chevrolet," *DFP*, June 25, 1952; "Steel Strike Idling Thousands More Daily," *DFP*, June 27, 1952; "Chrysler Closing Monday Because of Steel Strike," *DFP*, July 10, 1952; Robert Perrin, "Layoffs Hit 16,000 at Briggs Today," *DFP*, July 11, 1952; Robert Perrin, "Chrysler Lays Off 14,500 More," *DFP*, July 19, 1952; and Leo Donovan, "Both Pontiacs Return to Normal," *DFP*, August 20, 1952.

40. Robert Perrin, "Steel Strike Perils State Economy," *DFP*, June 29, 1952; James McGuire interview by Daniel Clark, August 24, 2000; Leo Donovan, "Steel Priorities to Extend Famine," *DFP*, July 10, 1952; Leo Donovan, "Financiers Curb Buying Sprees," *DFP*, July 11, 1952; "Idle List Climbs to 240,000," *DFP*, July 16, 1952; Leo Donovan, "Future Black, Auto Men Agree," *DFP*, July 18, 1952; "Car Output Hits New Postwar Low," *DFP*, July 18, 1952; and Robert Perrin, "State Reels Out of Strike," *DFP*, July 25, 1952.

41. Leo Donovan, "Auto Industry Hopes for Relief," *DFP*, July 25, 1952; Robert Perrin, "State Reels Out of Strike," *DFP*, July 25, 1952; "Pact Ends Steel Strike," *DFP*, July

25, 1952; "Auto Layoffs Go On Despite Steel Peace," *DFP*, July 29, 1952; Robert Perrin, "Auto Plants Reopening," *DFP*, August 1, 1952; "Idle Rolls in State Top 350,000," *DFP*, August 5, 1952; Robert Perrin, "Ford to Shut 18 Plants for Week," *DFP*, August 8, 1952; Robert Perrin, "Ford Recalls 60,000 Next Week," *DFP*, August 15, 1952; "Strike Layoffs Due to End," *DFP*, August 24, 1952; and "50,000 Idled by Strike Called Back," *DFP*, August 27, 1952.

42. Letter to the editor from "Union Member," *DFP*, October 1, 1952.

43. "Auto Lines Up Despite Supply Gap," *DFP*, August 22, 1952; "Auto Output Hits 102,000," *DFP*, August 23, 1952; Leo Donovan, "Auto Industry to GO in April," *DFP*, September 7, 1952; "Manpower Pinch Hits Detroit," *DFP*, September 11, 1952; "Leo Donovan, "Auto Production Rising Sharply," *DFP*, September 19, 1952; Robert Perrin, "State Faces Acute Shortage of Manpower, Board Says," *DFP*, September 30, 1952; Leo Donovan, "Overtime Checks Seen for Detroit Auto Workers," *DFP*, October 3, 1952; and "State Faces Labor Shortage," *DFP*, October 19, 1952.

44. Ernie Liles interview by Daniel Clark, May 27, 2003.

45. C. E. Wilson, "Pact Working, Wilson Reports," *DFP*, July 9, 1950; Norman Kenyon, "Suburb Prepares to Attack Inflation," *DFP*, November 25, 1951; Leo Donovan, "Auto Wage Loss: $6,500,000 a Day," *DFP*, July 24, 1952; "Living Cost in Detroit Rises Again," *DFP*, July 25, 1952; "Auto Pay to Go Up," *DFP*, August 21, 1952; Robert Perrin, "Auto-Pay Boost to be 3 Cents," *DFP*, August 22, 1952; and letter to the editor from "Union Member," *DFP*, October 1, 1952.

46. "Renters Face Fast Gouging If Controls End Sept. 30," *Ford Facts*, September 13, 1952; "Detroit Rent Up 140% after Decontrol Vote," *Ford Facts*, September 27, 1952; James Ransom, "City Kills Rent Lids; DSR Increases Fares," *DFP*, September 17, 1952; "Rents Going Up 25 Per Cent, Complaining Tenants Report," *DFP*, September 18, 1952; "Courts See Deluge of Evictions," *DFP*, September 18, 1952; and letter to the editor from Irmgard Bobak, *Detroit News* (hereafter cited as *DN*), July 26, 1953.

47. Nelson Lichtenstein, *The Most Dangerous Man in Detroit: Walter Reuther and the Fate of American Labor* (New York: Basic Books, 1995), 294; Robert Perrin, "UAW Calls for GM Hike," *DFP*, September 18, 1952; and "GM Shows Full Job Recovery," *DFP*, October 28, 1952.

48. Robert Perrin, "Michigan Takes Job Crises in Stride," *DFP*, October 12, 1952.

49. Ed Winge, "U-M Portrays Social Profile of Detroit Area," *DFP*, November 2, 1952; Robert Perrin, "Serious Manpower Shortage Plagues Michigan's Industry," *DFP*, November 7, 1952; and "Chronicle Continues Probe into Plant Hiring Practices," *Michigan Chronicle*, January 17, 1953.

50. "Survey Indicates Job Picture Brightening in Detroit," *Michigan Chronicle*, August 30, 1952; Bill Lane, "Negro Employment Still a Mystery at Tank Arsenal," *Michigan Chronicle*, September 6, 1952; "Auto Plant Bias Under Attack by UAW-CIO," *Michigan Chronicle*, November 22, 1952; "Chronicle Continues Probe into Plant Hiring Practices," *Michigan Chronicle*, January 17, 1953; and Nancy Gabin, *Feminism in the Labor Movement: Women and the United Auto Workers, 1935–1975* (Ithaca, NY: Cornell University Press, 1990), 158–59.

51. Sugrue, *Origins of the Urban Crisis*, 91–123; "Non-Whites in City Put at 303,721," *DFP*, July 30, 1952; "UAW Opens Drive on Job Bias," *DFP*, November 22, 1952; letter to the editor from Earl Clemens, *DFP*, November 28, 1952; and Charles J. Wartman, "Study Reveals Little Change in Hiring Patterns since Riot," *Michigan Chronicle*, March 7, 1953.

52. Sam Petok, "Baffled Lad Seeks Sister in a Big City," *DFP*, January 27, 1950; Louis Cook, "Shoe Weather Came Too Soon," *DFP*, October 7, 1952; letter to the editor from Earl Clemens, *DFP*, November 28, 1952; and Gene Johnson interview.

53. Leo Donovan, "Chrysler's Vast Growth," *DFP*, October 20, 1952; Leo Donovan, "World of Wheels," *DFP*, November 14, 1952; "Factory Pay 42 Pct. of Michigan's Income," *DFP*, November 23, 1952; Leo Donovan, "World of Wheels," *DFP*, December 12, 1952; "State Cites Gains in Employment," *DFP*, December 25, 1952; "'52 Production of Big 3 Was 4,613,512 Units," *DFP*, January 3, 1953; "Chrysler Reports Plus Figures for 1952," *DFP*, February 12, 1953; "Jobs Hit Peak at Chrysler," *DN*, January 3, 1953; and "GM Payrolls Hit Record 2 Billion," *DFP*, March 6, 1953.

54. Leo Donovan, "Die Makers Toil 58 Hours a Week," *DFP*, June 10, 1952; Ed Winge, "U-M Portrays Social Profile of Detroit Area," *DFP*, November 2, 1952; and "The Skilled Worker Is King of the Roost," *DFP*, December 14, 1952.

Chapter 4. A Post–Korean War Boom

1. Charles E. Edwards, *Dynamics of the United States Automobile Industry* (Columbia: University of South Carolina Press, 1965), 29; John B. Rae, *The American Automobile Industry* (Boston: Twayne Publishers, 1984), 105; Leo Donovan, "Curtice Predicts High Employment for GM in 1953," *DFP*, January 17, 1953; "Employment at Ford Up," *DFP*, January 25, 1953; "Employment in Detroit Sets Record," *DFP*, January 31, 1953; "Jobs at Record High in Detroit Area," *DN*, February 1, 1953; Leo Donovan, "World of Wheels," *DFP*, February 4, 1953; "Auto Jobs Hit Record Peak," *DN*, February 15, 195; Leo Donovan, "World of Wheels," *DFP*, February 20, 1953; Ralph Watts, "Auto Output Climbs with New Models," *DN*, January 25, 1953; Ralph Watts, "Swift Rise Shown in Auto Production," *DN*, February 3, 1953; "Auto Quotas Die," *DFP*, February 14, 1953; Asher Lauren, "Auto Makers Cheer at End of Controls," *DN*, February 14, 1953; and "Auto Output Up Sharply," *DN*, February 20, 1953.

2. Robert Perrin, "Men Wanted! That's Detroit's Sign of Spring," *DFP*, March 1, 1953; and Ralph Watts, "Manpower Problem Perils Auto Goals," *DN*, March 24, 1953.

3. Kenneth Thompson, "'50,000 Youths, Idle in Streets, Hunt Trouble," *DFP*, April 16, 1948; Robert Perrin, "Jobs Are Available, but Employers Are Particular," *DFP*, September 6, 1949; and Leo Donovan, "Workers' Output Reported Lower Than in 1930s," *DFP*, May 2, 1948.

4. Robert Perrin, "Men Wanted! That's Detroit's Sign of Spring," *DFP*, March 1, 1953.

5. "More Wives Working Outside of Their Homes," *DFP*, May 28, 1952; "Manpower Pinch Hits Detroit," *DFP*, September 11, 1952; Robert Perrin, "State Faces Acute Shortage of Manpower, Board Says," *DFP*, September 30, 1952; "State Faces Shortage of

Labor," *DFP*, October 19, 1952; Robert Perrin, "Men Wanted! That's Detroit's Sign of Spring," *DFP*, March 1, 1953; Asher Lauren, "Employers Desperate as Worker Shortage Grows Worse," *DN*, March 8, 1953; "Job Boom Bypasses Women," *DN*, April 19, 1953; Nancy Gabin, *Feminism in the Labor Movement: Women and the United Auto Workers, 1935–1975* (Ithaca, NY: Cornell University Press, 1990), 143–87; and Stephen Meyer, *Manhood on the Line: Working-Class Masculinities in the American Heartland* (Urbana: University of Illinois Press, 2016), 112–209.

6. Edith Arnold interview by Daniel Clark, November 7, 2003; Margaret Beaudry interview; Nora Kay Bailey interview by Daniel Clark, August 8, 2003; and Edwin G. Pipp, "GM in Flint Hires Women as Labor Shortage Becomes Acute," *DN*, March 8, 1953.

7. "Job Boom Bypasses Women," *DN*, April 19, 1953.

8. Edith Arnold interview.

9. Margaret Beaudry interview; and Collins George, "Michigan Pushes Drive for Labor as Shortage Pinches State Industry," *DFP*, March 27, 1953.

10. Elwin Brown, Ernie Liles, Don Hester, and James Franklin interviews.

11. "Ford Upgrades First Negro Truck Driver," *Michigan Chronicle*, May 2, 1953; Charles J. Wartman, "On the Labor Line," *Michigan Chronicle*, May 2, 1953; and Charles J. Wartman, "The Spectator," *Michigan Chronicle*, May 2, 1953.

12. "Even with Pensions, Plant Workers Are Reluctant to Retire," *DFP*, November 30, 1952; Collins George, "Job Surplus a Break for Older Workers," *DFP*, March 31, 1953; and "Dixie Pool Drying Up; Seek New Workers Elsewhere," *DN*, April 1, 1953.

13. Edwards, *Dynamics of the Automobile Industry*, 172–74; Thomas Sugrue, *Origins of the Urban Crisis: Race and Inequality in Postwar Detroit* (Princeton, NJ: Princeton University Press, 1996), 127–30, 138–40; Leo Donovan, "See Decentralization Move by Auto Firms," *DFP*, January 20, 1946; Fred Olmsted, "16,000 Jobs Lost to Detroiters as Factories Move Out of City," *DFP*, April 16, 1950; Leo Donovan, "Chrysler Plant Starts Operating," *DFP*, February 8, 1952; Leo Donovan, "Chrysler's Vast Growth," *DFP*, October 20, 1952; "Ford to Build 2 New Plants," *DFP*, January 18, 1953; Collins George, "Michigan Pushes Drive for Labor as Shortage Pinches State Industry," *DFP*, March 27, 1953; Ralph Watts, "Auto Output Climbs Rapidly in California," *DN*, April 2, 1953; and "Ford Plans New Plant," *DFP*, April 27, 1953.

14. Robert S. Ball, "Auto Manufacturing Deep in the Throes of Significant Change," *DN*, February 22, 1953; Leo Donovan, "World of Wheels," *DFP*, February 5, 1953; Ralph Watts, "Auto Output Heads for 6-Month Record," *DN*, March 31, 1953; Leo Donovan, "World of Wheels," *DFP*, April 3, 1953; and "Expansion of Auto Industry Centers Mainly in Michigan," *DN*, May 26, 1953.

15. Fred Olmsted, "16,000 Jobs Lost to Detroiters as Factories Move Out of City," *DFP*, April 16, 1950; Ralph Watts, "Chevrolet to Build Factory in Livonia," *DN*, April 23, 1953; John Griffith, "Wayne Folks Harvest 5,000 Bushels of Corn," *DFP*, October 26, 1950; and Leo Donovan, "World of Wheels," *DFP*, October 9, 1952.

16. "Labor," *Fortune* (February 1953); Edwin G. Pipp, "Cancel 154 Million Ford Contract," *DN*, April 16, 1953; Robert Perrin, "Ike Tells UAW He'll Fight to Prevent

Any Job Pinch," *DFP*, April 26, 1953; Harold Tyler, "City Industrialists See No Recession Here," *DFP*, May 3, 1953; James M. Haswell, "Kaiser Shorn of Contracts by Air Force," *DFP*, June 25, 1953; "Save Jobs at Kaiser, UAW Pleads," *DFP*, June 25, 1953; Asher Lauren, "Job Hunt Speeded by State for 9,600 Kaiser Workers," *DN*, June 27, 1953; "Hope Wilts for Willow Villagers," *DN*, June 27, 1953; and "Slash in War Work Due to Hit Area Soon," *DN*, July 9, 1953.

17. "Business Roundup: Retail Boom," *Fortune* (February 1953); "How to Recognize a Recession," *Fortune* (March 1953); "Business Roundup," *Fortune* (March 1953); "Business Roundup: Detroit: Danger Ahead," *Fortune* (May 1953); Robert Perrin, "Auto Output Too High, Reuther Tells Industry," *DFP*, May 16, 1953; "Auto Layoffs Threatened, Reuther Says," *DN*, May 16, 1953; and "Automakers See Boom Continuing," *DFP*, May 27, 1953.

18. "Business Roundup: Cars, Cars, Cars," *Fortune* (August 1953); Edwards, *Dynamics of the Automobile Industry*, 29; "Inventories Increase 6 Billion," *DFP*, August 10, 1953; "Auto Plants Cut Down on Steel," *DFP*, August 10, 1953; Ralph Watts, "Dealers' Stocks at Postwar High," *DN*, August 27, 1953; Ralph Watts, "Auto Production Pace Slackens," *DN*, September 3, 1953; "77,571 Jobless in State," *DFP*, August 14, 1953; and "Economists Hit 'Depression Talk,'" *DFP*, August 14, 1953.

19. Nelson Lichtenstein, *The Most Dangerous Man in Detroit: Walter Reuther and the Fate of American Labor* (New York: Basic Books, 1995), 294; John Barnard, *American Vanguard: The United Auto Workers during the Reuther Years, 1935–1970* (Detroit: Wayne State University Press, 2004), 220; Robert Perrin, "UAW Gets 10 Ct. Hike in Fast Deal with GM," *DFP*, May 23, 1953; "Ford OK's 10-Ct. Hike and Record Pension," *DFP*, May 26, 1953; Asher Lauren, "GM, Chrysler Join in Pension Boost," *DN*, May 28, 1953; and Robert Perrin, "Chrysler Ups Benefits," *DFP*, May 28, 1953.

20. Jim Ransom, Jack Strohm, Arthur W. O'Shea Jr., Collins George, and Miller Hollingsworth, "$40,000,000 GM Fire Razes Plant, Kills 2: Fear More Dead in Ruins," *DFP*, August 13, 1953; "Drop Hose in Creek to Battle GM Blaze," *DN*, August 13, 1953; "10,000 Idled by Fire," *DN*, August 13, 1953; "GM Fire Ruins Yield 4th Body," *DFP*, August 15, 1953; and "GM Bids for K-F Plant," *DFP*, August 18, 1953.

21. "GM Sees No Layoffs at Burned-Out Plant," *DFP*, August 13, 1953; "10,000 Idled by Fire," *DN*, August 13, 1953; "50,000 Face Layoffs as Fire Result," *DFP*, August 14, 1953; "GM Bids for K-F Plant," *DFP*, August 18, 1953; Curt Haseltine, "GM Hopes Rise on Gear Output," *DFP*, August 19, 1953; "Negotiations Still On for Willow Run," *DFP*, August 20, 1953; and "GM Fire Seen Idling 65,000," *DFP*, September 18, 1953.

22. "GM Fire Slashes Output of Cars by 4,000 a Day," *DFP*, August 16, 1953; "Reuther Urges State Aid Stepup," *DFP*, August 16, 1953; Curt Haseltine, "GM Hopes Rise on Gear Output," *DFP*, August 19, 1953; Leo Donovan, "Fire to Idle 25,800 Next Week," *DFP*, August 22, 1953; "GM Recall of 7,000 Predicted," *DFP*, September 14, 1953; and Robert D'Arcy, "Savings, Temporary Jobs Support Thousands Hit by Livonia Fire," *DN*, September 27, 1953.

23. James McGuire interview.

24. Nick Smith, "10,000 Affected by Sale of Willow Run Plant to GM," *DN*, November 11, 1953.

25. Leo Donovan, "GM Closes Deal for Willow Run," *DFP*, November 11, 1953; and Robert Perrin, "Willow Run Purchase Held Blow to Workers," *DFP*, November 12, 1953.

26. "Leo Donovan, "K-F Deal Set with Willys," *DFP*, March 24, 1953; Strike Is Settled in GM Transfer," *DFP*, August 25, 1953; Robert Perrin, "GM Halts Shift of Machinery," *DFP*, August 26, 1953; and "Vital Jobs at Willow Run Open," *DFP*, September 4, 1953.

27. Ralph Watts, "Auto Production Pace Slackens," *DN*, September 3, 1953; "Hiring in July Hits Bottom," *DFP*, September 4, 1953; "Some Auto Firms Cut Production," *DFP*, September 13, 1953; Leo Donovan, "Ford Sales Please Boss," *DFP*, September 17, 1953; and "GM Fire Seen Idling 65,000," *DFP*, September 18, 1953.

28. "Labor: Jitters in Detroit," *Fortune* (October 1953); "22,000 Laid Off: Plymouth, Briggs Idle Workers," *DFP*, September 19, 1953; "Briggs to Call 14,000 Back Monday," *DFP*, September 22, 1953; Robert Perrin, "UAW Rips Chrysler for Overproduction," *DFP*, October 11, 1953; and Robert Perrin, "Labor: Reuther Makes a Point," *DFP*, October 11, 1953.

29. "Leo Donovan, "The Future Is Bright," *DFP*, September 1, 1953; "'Mr. Steel' Fails to See Any Recession," *DFP*, September 22, 1953; and Leo Donovan, "Don't Be Afraid," *DFP*, October 11, 1953.

30. Ralph Watts, "5,000,000th Car Rolls Off Line," *DN*, October 9, 1953; and Ralph Watts, "Auto Output Cut to Help Dealers," *DN*, November 3, 1953.

31. "A New Kind of Car Market," *Fortune* (September 1953); Frank Beckman, "Economy to 'Taper Off' in 1954, Expert Says," *DFP*, October 25, 1953; Ralph Watts, "Car Stocks Up, Output Drops," *DN*, November 17, 1953; "Jobless Rolls in Michigan Highest in Last 16 Months," *DFP*, November 29, 1953; "Jobs Hit 15-Month Low Here," *DN*, December 13, 1953; Ralph Watts, "Auto Cutbacks Mainly Seasonal," *DN*, December 11, 1953.

32. "10,000 Families to Go Homeless," *DFP*, August 20, 1953; Arthur O'Shea, Jr., "Progress Makes 'DPs' of Thousands in City," *DFP*, November 1, 1953; and James M. Haswell, "Detroit Rent Rise Tops Rest of U.S.," *DFP*, December 27, 1953.

33. "Any Home Looks Good to Evictees," *DFP*, August 21, 1953; and Sugrue, *Origins of the Urban Crisis*, 33–88.

34. Bud Goodman, "A Room Best Home Family of 4 Can Afford," *DFP*, August 25, 1953.

35. Letter to the editor signed "S.M.," *DN*, October 6, 1953.

36. Letter to the editor signed "Her Mother," *DN*, October 6, 1953.

37. "A Growing Crisis: Rapid Rise in Mortgage Foreclosures Perils Security of Laid-off Worker," *Michigan Chronicle*, February 20, 1954; "Foreclosures on Land Contracts Not Excessive," *Michigan Chronicle*, March 6, 1954; and Louis Tendler, "Foreclosures Rise on Land Contracts," *DN*, February 14, 1954.

38. Bud Goodman, "Slum Tenants Helpless against Landlords' Greed," *DFP*, August 22, 1953.

39. Ibid.

40. "Evictions Balked in Slum Dispute," *DFP*, March 16, 1954.

41. Bud Goodman, "8 in Family Live in Shelter Hall," *DFP*, August 26, 1953; Bud Goodman, "Families Down on Luck Crowd City's Shelters," *DFP*, August 27, 1953; R. Hollingsworth, "Many Bosses Shun Disabled Workers," *DFP*, September 13, 1953;

Robert Perrin, "Deafness Gets a Hearing," *DFP*, January 17, 1954; and Gene Johnson interview.

42. "A New Kind of Car Market," *Fortune* (September 1953).

43. "Reuther Hints World Depression," *DFP*, September 16, 1953; Miller Hollingsworth, "Auto Slump Due, Douglas Asserts," *DFP*, November 9, 1953; Leo Donovan, "Auto Supply Hits Peak," *DFP*, November 17, 1953; and "Michigan Idle Roll Increases," *DFP*, November 29, 1953.

44. Leo Donovan, "Sees Break for Buyers," *DFP*, November 10, 1953; and Leo Donovan, "Colbert Sees Gains," *DFP*, November 13, 1953.

45. "Ike Promises Fight to Keep Prosperity: It Doesn't Depend on War, He Says," *DFP*, January 5, 1954.

46. Kenneth A. Thompson, "Labor Level Slips Again," *DFP*, November 10, 1953; and "Auto Slump? Ford Derides Red's Forecast," *DFP*, November 29, 1953.

47. "Job Slash of 45,000 Seen in '54," *DFP*, November 14, 1953; Kenneth Thompson, "Detroit Has Most Jobless," *DFP*, December 10, 1953; Ralph Watts, "Value of Output, Pay at New High," *DN*, December 15, 1953; Jack Strohm, "High Employment in 1954 Predicted," *DFP*, December 27, 1953; and Jack Strohm, "Night Courses Develop Skills, Jobless Told," *DFP*, January 18, 1954.

48. Robert Perrin, "UAW Flays Chrysler Layoffs," *DFP*, December 17, 1953; "B of C Says Plant Pay Buys More," *DFP*, January 3, 1954; Robert Perrin, "Chrysler, Hudson to Idle 12,150," *DFP*, January 8, 1954; and "Reuther Demands Hiked Aid," *DFP*, February 26, 1954.

Chapter 5. A *"Painfully Inconvenient"* Recession

1. "Chrysler Takes the Bumps," *Fortune* (April 1954); Lawrence J. White, *The Automobile Industry since 1945* (Cambridge, MA: Harvard University Press, 1971), 15; James M. Rubenstein, *Making and Selling Cars: Innovation and Change in the U.S. Automotive Industry* (Baltimore: Johns Hopkins University Press, 2001), 214; Martin S. Hayden, "Jobs Here Periled by Army Cuts," *DN*, January 6, 1954; "UAW Lists Heavy Cost of Layoffs by Kaiser," *DN*, January 7, 1954; "100,000 Detroiters Idle, Union Tells Ike," *DFP*, January 7, 1954; Robert Perrin, "Chrysler, Hudson to Idle 12,150," *DFP*, January 8, 1954; Asher Lauren, "167,000 Out of Work in State, Says MESC," *DN*, January 10, 1954; "Packard Orders Layoff," *DFP*, January 15, 1954; and "Army's Orders Being Slashed," *DFP*, January 19, 1954.

2. Ed Winge, "107,000 Jobless in Detroit; More Layoffs Are Predicted," *DFP*, January 10, 1954; "Detroit Pinch Idles 82,000, State Reports," *DN*, January 7, 1954; Asher Lauren, "167,000 Out of Work in State, Says MESC," *DN*, January 10, 1954; Leo Donovan, "Ford Aide Chides Dealers for Chanting the Blues," *DFP*, January 11, 1954; Leo Donovan, "NADA Has a Program," *DFP*, January 15, 1954; and Asher Lauren, "Job Picture for Detroit Has Good and Bad Spots," *DN*, January 31, 1954.

3. Stewart Didzun, "Laid-off Workers Here Fearful of the Long Haul," *DN*, January 12, 1954.

4. Thomas Nowak interview by Daniel Clark, September 20, 2000; Emerald Neal interview by Daniel Clark, August 21, 2000; Don Hester, Margaret Beaudry, Gene Johnson, Elwin Brown, L. J. Scott, and James Franklin interviews.

5. Robert Perrin, "'Recession Has Set In'—Reuther," *DFP*, January 17, 1954; "Ford Sees 1,500,000 Auto Slash: Shouldn't Mean Layoffs, He Says," *DFP*, January 18, 1954; Leo Donovan, "GM to Put Billion in Expansion," *DFP*, January 20, 1954; Ed Winge, "Total at Work in Area Tops Boom of 1952," *DFP*, January 24, 1954; "Employment in Detroit," editorial, *DN*, February 4, 1954; "Wilson Disputes Detroit Job Need," *DN*, February 9, 1954; and Jack Strohm, "Job Pinch Here Seen at Peak," *DFP*, February 10, 1954.

6. James M. Haswell, "City's Jobless to Get U.S. Aid: Detroit Rated Area of Distress," *DFP*, February 9, 1954; and "Our Employment Pattern," *DN*, February 10, 1954.

7. Letter to the editor from Ted Kaleniecki, *DFP*, January 23, 1954.

8. Charles Manos, "We're the Unemployed," *DFP*, February 26, 1954.

9. "Survey Calls Pinch 'Moderate,'" *DFP*, January 26, 1954; Frank Beckman, "Worried Cobo Ponders Aid for Jobless," *DFP*, January 27, 1954; Leo Donovan, "Auto Output Cut 12 Pct.," *DFP*, January 28, 1954; "UAW Asks Local Action," *DFP*, February 3, 1954; "3,800 Face Week Off at Packard: Chevrolet to Idle 60,000 for a Day," *DFP*, February 5, 1954; and Jack Strohm, "UAW Official Attacks GM's '32-Hour Week,'" *DFP*, February 19, 1954.

10. Collins George, "Mother of 9 Finds Life Uphill Struggle," *DFP*, September 28, 1954.

11. Letter to the editor from Martin A. Larson, *DN*, March 12, 1953. For refutations of stereotypes associated with Southern white migrants, see Chad Berry, *Southern Migrants, Northern Exiles* (Urbana: University of Illinois Press, 2000); Bob Bowen interview by Daniel Clark, August 25, 2000, and August 28, 2000; Gene Johnson, Ernie Liles, James McGuire, Emerald Neal, and Paul Ross interviews. For evidence that could partially support Larson's position, with cautions against stereotyping, see Evelyn S. Stewart, "Third Ave. Opens Door to Southerners," *DFP*, August 28, 1957; and Gerald Weales, "Small-Town Detroit: Motor City on the Move," *Commentary*, September 1, 1956.

12. Dale Nouse, "Jobless Start Rush on Welfare," *DFP*, February 3, 1954.

13. Letter to the editor signed "A.V.F.," *DN*, October 5, 1953; letter to the editor from Walter F. Grogan, *DN*, February 18, 1954; letter to the editor signed "D.C.," *DN*, February 18, 1954; letter to the editor from Bill Thomson, *DN*, October 19, 1954; and letter to the editor from Henry Sommerfeld, *DN*, October 30, 1954.

14. "The Rich, Middle-Income Class," *Fortune* (May 1954); letter to the editor signed "Wage Earner," *DN*, February 1, 1954; Dorothy Sackle, Edith Arnold, and Katie Neumann interviews; letter to the editor signed "A Working Housewife," *DN*, February 26, 1954; Charles Manos, "We're the Unemployed," *DFP*, February 26, 1954; and Asher Lauren, "Jobs Kept by Women in Plants," *DN*, February 28, 1954.

15. George Bick, "Jobless Wives Forsake Hearth, Yearn for Return to Factory," *DN*, February 14, 1954; letter to the editor from Sarah Lovell, *DN*, October 28, 1954; and Boyd Simons, "Union Worked Up on Working Wives," *DN*, March 28, 1955.

16. Charles E. Edwards, *Dynamics of the United States Automobile Industry* (Columbia: University of South Carolina Press, 1965), 72; Asher Lauren, "Job Picture for Detroit Has Good and Bad Spots," *DN*, January 31, 1954; Leo Donovan, "Production Is Still High," *DFP*, February 5, 1954; Ralph Watts, "Ford, Chevrolet Set Pace in Race," *DN*, April 2, 1954; "Ford Outproduces Chevie in Quarter," *DFP*, April 3, 1954; "10-Hour Day to Lift Output of Cadillacs," *DN*, April 5, 1954; Dale Nouse, "Ford Hits 30-Year Sales Peak," *DFP*, April 8, 1954; Leo Donovan, "Ford Passed by Chevrolet," *DFP*, April 30, 1954; "Ford Output Soars Past Pace Last Year," *DN*, May 3, 1954; and Leo Donovan, "3rd Biggest Year Seen," *DFP*, May 7, 1954.

17. Robert S. Ball, "Ingenious New Machinery Cuts Toil in Auto Plants," *DN*, February 19, 1954.

18. Ralph Watts, "Chevrolet Line Rolls Over Gaps," *DN*, October 15, 1954; Leo Donovan, "The 'Most' in Plants," *DFP*, October 21, 1954; Leo Donovan, "Ford's Answer," *DFP*, October 22, 1954; Leo Donovan, "Automation at Pontiac," *DFP*, December 2, 1954; Leo Donovan, "Automation Will Grow," *DFP*, January 12, 1955; and "Ford Puts 625 Million into 3-Year Expansion," *DFP*, April 29, 1955.

19. Les Coleman interview; Robert S. Ball, "Ingenious New Machinery Cuts Toil in Auto Plants," *DN*, February 19, 1954; and Warren Stromberg, "Looking for a Trade? Factory Skills Spell Security," *DFP*, April 25, 1954.

20. Russell Clanahan, "How Does Worker Qualify Himself for Skilled Post?" *DFP*, March 16, 1952.

21. Ibid.; Don Vance, "Plenty of Jobs for Bright Apprentices?" *DFP*, November 3, 1953; Jack Strohm, "Are Skilled Men Cheated?" *DFP*, March 7, 1954; Warren Stromberg, "Looking for a Trade? Factory Skills Spell Security," *DFP*, April 25, 1954; Leo Donovan, "Let Junior Use Hands," *DFP*, September 24, 1954; and letter to the editor signed "Skilled Worker's Wife," *DN*, May 13, 1956.

22. L. J. Scott and Paul Ish interviews.

23. Joe Dowdall, "Burglaries Up 56 Pct. This Year," *DFP*, February 23, 1954; Jack Schermerhorn, "Crime in City Rises 100 Pct.," *DFP*, February 28, 1954; "One Buck Costs $25," *DFP*, March 4, 1954; "Rise in Hold-Ups Creating Serious Problem in Detroit," *Michigan Chronicle*, March 6, 1954; "140,000 in Area Lack Jobs," *DFP*, March 7, 1954; and Don Vance, "Sick, Idle, Broke; His Answer—a Gun," *DFP*, March 11, 1954.

24. "Women Foresake Homes for Odd Jobs as Clouds of Recession Lower," *Michigan Chronicle*, March 6, 1954; Richard B. Henry, "Negroes Hit Hard by Job Crisis," *Michigan Chronicle*, July 17, 1954; John Griffith, "8 Living in Hearse Would Like a Home," *DFP*, February 11, 1954; "Clan Living in Hearse Sad Again," *DFP*, February 12, 1954; "140,000 in Area Lack Jobs," *DFP*, March 7, 1954; and "Unemployed March on City Hall," *DFP*, April 14, 1954.

25. Ralph Watts, "Credit Backbone of Auto Market," *DN*, December 6, 1953; Ralph Watts, "Dealers' Stocks Stay Near Peak," *DN*, April 20, 1954; and Leo Donovan, "Hint Ceiling Reached in Auto Pay," *DFP*, May 16, 1954.

26. James M. Rubenstein, *Making and Selling Cars: Innovation and Change in the U.S. Automotive Industry* (Baltimore: Johns Hopkins University Press, 2001), 209; Lawrence J. White, *The Automobile Industry since 1945* (Cambridge, MA: Harvard University Press, 1971), 109–16; John B. Rae, *The American Automobile Industry* (Boston: Twayne Publishers, 1984), 109; Ralph Watts, "Ford, Chevrolet Set Pace in Race," *DN*, April 2, 1954; Leo Donovan, "Grim Days at Chevrolet," *DFP*, April 14, 1954; "Auto Sales Highest in 9 Months," *DFP*, April 21, 1954; Leo Donovan, "Styling Is a Gamble," *DFP*, May 18, 1954; Leo Donovan, "Output Hits 1954 Peak," *DFP*, May 21, 1954; Leo Donovan, "Dealers to Convene," *DFP*, May 23, 1954; Leo Donovan, "Rough Days for Dealers," *DFP*, May 25, 1954; Leo Donovan, "2nd Quarter Output Rises," *DFP*, June 15, 1954; Leo Donovan, "Somber Day for Dealers," *DFP*, June 18, 1954; and Leo Donovan, "Only Big 3 in Black," *DFP*, July 7, 1954.

27. White, *Automobile Industry since 1945*, 159–60; Edwards, *Dynamics of the Automobile Industry*, 30; Rubenstein, *Making and Selling Cars*, 324; Leo Donovan, "Dealers Alarmed by Bootlegging," *DFP*, January 31, 1950; "GM, Ford Warn 'Bootleg' Dealers," *DFP*, February 17, 1954; "Car Bootleg Increase Reported," *DFP*, February 19, 1954; Leo Donovan, "Chrysler Enters 'Bootleg' Battle," *DFP*, March 9, 1954; Ralph Watts, "Bootleg Autos Still Run Wild," *DN*, May 25, 1954; Leo Donovan, "Somber Days for Dealers," *DFP*, June 18, 1954; "Chrysler Dealers Told to Sell or Quit," *DN*, August 27, 1954; and Leo Donovan, "Bootlegging Rages Anew," *DFP*, November 9, 1954.

28. William B. Harris, "Last Stand of the Auto Independents," *Fortune* (December 1954); Edwards, *Dynamics of the Automobile Industry*, 13–14, 34–38, 109; Rae, *American Automobile Industry*, 100, 107; John Barnard, *American Vanguard: The United Auto Workers during the Reuther Years, 1935–1970* (Detroit: Wayne State University Press, 2004), 296; Robert Perrin, "Nash, Hudson Seal Merger," *DFP*, January 15, 1954; Leo Donovan, "Hudson Lines to Leave City," *DFP*, May 28, 1954; and Saul Pett, "Battle of the Giants," *DFP*, August 22, 1954.

29. Leo Donovan, "Hudson Lines to Leave City," *DFP*, May 28, 1954; Asher Lauren, "4,300 to Lose Jobs as Hudson Moves," *DN*, May 28, 1954; and "Hudson's Decision Stuns Work Force," *DN*, May 28, 1954.

30. Edwards, *Dynamics of the Automobile Industry*, 38–44, 75, 118; Barnard, *American Vanguard*, 296; Louis Cook, "Tri-County Area Gets 108 Plants," *DFP*, January 25, 1953; Ralph Watts, "Packard to Spend Millions to Expand," *DN*, February 8, 1954; "'54 Basically a Sound Year, Nance Says," *DFP*, March 16, 1954; Leo Donovan, "Loss Bared by Packard," *DFP*, May 4, 1954; David K. Wilkie, "Studebaker, Packard OK Merger," *DFP*, June 20, 1954; Leo Donovan, "Merger Seen Creating New Packard Jobs," *DFP*, June 23, 1954; "3,800 Idled by Moving at Packard," *DFP*, June 25, 1954; and "Packard Calls Back 4,800 at 2 Plants," *DFP*, July 13, 1954.

31. "Auto Suppliers Need Diversified Products," *DFP*, August 29, 1954; "Spring Firm Shuts Plant at Van Dyke," *DFP*, October 12, 1954.

32. Barnard, *American Vanguard*, 298; Geoffrey Howes, "2,500 Losing 'Life' at Murray," *DFP*, July 4, 1954; "7,000 Jobs Shrink to 50 at Murray's," *DN*, November 19, 1954; Bruce Tuttle, "Murray Ends Defense and Body Work," *DN*, November 19, 1954; and letter to the editor from Art Willcocke, *DN*, July 8, 1955.

33. "Chrysler Takes the Bumps," *Fortune* (April 1954); Rubenstein, *Making and Selling Cars*, 214; Ralph Watts, "Car Output Cut from Year Ago," *DN*, May 30, 1954; Leo Donovan, "Ford Sets New Marks," *DFP*, June 2, 1954; Ralph Watts, "Auto Forecast Proves Accurate," *DN*, June 30, 1954; "U.S. Job Picture Brighter in June," *DFP*, July 7, 1954; Leo Donovan, "Auto Sales in June Hit 4-Year Peak," *DFP*, July 10, 1954; and Ralph Watts, "Output to Rise Last Two Months," *DN*, August 3, 1954.

34. "How Teenagers Can Find Work," *DFP*, June 3, 1954; letter to the editor from A. M. Moakley, *DFP*, July 22, 1954; John McManis, "The Life Story of a Hoodlum," *DN*, July 28, 1954; letter to the editor from Mrs. Phyllis Robinson, *DN*, August 1, 1954; letter to the editor signed "40-Year News Reader," *DN*, August 30, 1954; and Marjorie Porter, "Teen-Age Gang Members Changed into Choirboys," *DN*, October 24, 1954.

35. "Labor: No 'Basic' Runaway," *Fortune* (July 1954); Edwards, *Dynamics of the Automobile Industry*, 172–74; Harold Schachern, "Plants Expected to Move Back to City from Suburbs," *DN*, November 15, 1954; and "High Stakes, High Hopes: Automobiles in Our Future," editorial, *DN*, September 2, 1954.

36. "6,000 Idled by 2 Auto Disputes," *DFP*, July 16, 1954; Asher Lauren, "Dodge Row Idles 30,000," *DN*, July 20, 1954; Jack Strohm, "32,000 Are Idled by Strike at Chrysler," *DFP*, July 21, 1954; Asher Lauren, "Strike at Dodge Boosts Jobless Total to 169,000," *DN*, July 22, 1954; "Strike Hits All Plants of Chrysler," *DFP*, July 23, 1954; "UAW Ends Chrysler Strike," *DFP*, July 24, 1954; and Asher Lauren, "Call Off Strike at Chrysler," *DN*, July 24, 1954.

37. "An Instance of Costly Cause and Effect Which Detroiters Should Weigh Soberly," editorial, *DFP*, July 26, 1954.

38. "Chrysler to Close All Plants," *DN*, July 19, 1954; Jack Strohm, "Chrysler to Lay Off 40,000," *DFP*, July 20, 1954; and "Auto Shutdown Longest since Before the War," *DN*, August 8, 1954.

39. Letter to the editor from W. A. Gallimore, *DFP*, July 30, 1954; and letter to the editor from Buddie Tidwell, *DN*, August 5, 1954.

40. "Colbert's Talk Stirs Workers' Hopes," *DFP*, August 27, 1954; and "Jobs in Detroit: Feast or Famine," editorial, *DN*, October 14, 1954.

41. Hub M. George, "Wilson Predicts 'Balancing Out' of Employment," *DFP*, October 12, 1954; and Robert Perrin, "Wilson Apologizes for 'Dog' Remarks," *DFP*, October 14, 1954.

42. "Ford's Fight for First," *Fortune* (September 1954); "Chrysler to Add 26,000 Jobs," *DFP*, September 12, 1954; "Record Job Total at Chrysler Seen," *DFP*, September 18, 1954; "306,000 to Draw Paychecks This Christmas," *DFP*, September 19, 1954; "New Cars Seen Hiking Employment," *DFP*, September 29, 1954; Leo Donovan, "Ford Takes Output Lead," *DFP*, October 3, 1954; Leo Donovan, "Nance Sees More Auto Jobs in City," *DFP*, October 5, 1954; Leo Donovan, "Chrysler Puts 250 Millions into 1955 Model Changes," *DFP*, October 12, 1954; Ralph Watts, "Floors Cleared for New Autos," *DN*, October 19, 1954; Leo Donovan, "Pontiac Eyes Lead in Its Field," *DFP*, October 20, 1954; and "Ford Shifts to '55s at Record Rate," *DFP*, October 20, 1954.

43. "Detroit Labeled Distressed Area," editorial, *DFP*, February 10, 1954.

44. Robert L. Wells, "Gain Is 383,000 as City Shrinks, Suburbs Boom," *DN*, November 14, 1954; Asher Lauren, "Warn Jobseekers Not to Flood City," *DN*, November 18, 1954; and "Job Hunters Told Not to Flock Here," *DN*, November 23, 1954.

45. Letter to the editor signed "B.H.," *DN*, October 19, 1954.

46. Emerald Neal interview; letter to the editor signed "What About It?" *DN*, December 1, 1954; and Charles J. Wartman, "On the Labor Line," *Michigan Chronicle*, December 4, 1954.

47. Steve Jefferys, *Management and Managed: Fifty Years of Crisis at Chrysler* (New York: Cambridge University Press, 1986), 127–30; Robert Perrin, "UAW Votes for Chrysler Strike," *DFP*, November 12, 1954; "Chrysler Faces 2nd Walkout," *DFP*, November 17, 1954; "Production, Orders Soar at Chrysler," *DFP*, November 24, 1954; M. M. Hollingsworth, "Chrysler Strike Called Tuesday," *DFP*, November 27, 1954; "Plymouth UAW Local Backs Strike Vote," *DFP*, November 29, 1954; Robert Perrin, "New Offer Seen Opening Way for Chrysler Peace," *DFP*, November 30, 1954; "Plymouth Strike Vote Called Off," *DFP*, December 9, 1954; Asher Lauren, "Job Timing Blamed in Threat of Lincoln-Mercury Strike," *DN*, December 15, 1954; and Ralph Watts, "Auto Big 3 Production Records Set," *DN*, December 17, 1954.

48. Leo Donovan, "Auto Lines Humming," *DFP*, November 30, 1954; Leo Donovan, "GM Doubles Its Output," *DFP*, December 3, 1954; Ralph Watts, "Auto Big 3 Production Records Set," *DN*, December 17, 1954; Leo Donovan, "Autos, Autos Everywhere," *DFP*, December 19, 1954; Leo Donovan, "Output Peak at Chevrolet," *DFP*, December 21, 1954; and Leo Donovan, "Ford Sights First Place," *DFP*, December 22, 1954.

49. Barnard, *American Vanguard*, 263–64; letter to the editor signed "Perplexed," *DN*, November 30, 1954; letter to the editor signed "A Worker's Wife," *DN*, November 30, 1954; letter to the editor from Robert W. McGill, *DN*, December 3, 1954; and letter to the editor signed "A Worker?" *DFP*, January 30, 1955.

50. Robert Perrin, "Reuther Urges U.S. to Work for Full Employment," *DFP*, December 6, 1954; letter to the editor from Jim Basden, *DN*, December 22, 1954; and "Auto Chiefs See Big Year in '55," *DFP*, January 1, 1955.

Chapter 6. "The Fifties" in One Year

1. William Cronin, "AMA Has a Smile," *DFP*, January 9, 1955; A. W. Zelomek, "Consumption to Determine Whether Level Is Sustained," *DFP*, January 9, 1955; "Production Loss Seen by Reuther," *DFP*, January 17, 1955; "A Well Qualified Prophet Sees 1955 as Best Year," editorial, *DFP*, January 18, 1955; Robert Perrin, "Auto World Keeps Eye on Chrysler's Comeback," *DFP*, January 30, 1955; "Late Rally Gives Chrysler '54 Profit," *DFP*, February 11, 1955; Leo Donovan, "'55 Output to Hit New Peak—Curtice," *DFP*, January 18, 1955; and Leo Donovan, "More Fords, Dealers Ask," *DFP*, February 11, 1955.

2. Leo Donovan, "Gay Tempo at Plymouth," *DFP*, February 16, 1955; "Auto Output Near 200,000 a Week," *DFP*, February 19, 1955; "Car Sales Peak for First Quarter Seen by Expert," *DFP*, February 23, 1955; "Auto Sales Records Chalked Up by Big 3," *DFP*, February 26, 1955; Ralph Watts, "Car Production at Record Pace," *DN*, March

30, 1955; Ralph Watts, "Auto Market Fools Skeptics," *DN*, April 1, 1955; "Auto Sales for March Set Record," *DFP*, April 2, 1955; "Ford Reports Record Sales, Production," *DFP*, April 6, 1955; and "Chrysler Sets Record," *DFP*, April 6, 1955.

3. "Jobless Rolls in Detroit Drop 15,000," *DFP*, January 6, 1955; letter to the editor signed "Ed J.," *DFP*, January 18, 1955; "Jobless Down 50% in City, U.S. Reports," *DFP*, January 22, 1955; letter to the editor signed "Independent," *DFP*, January 24, 1955; letter to the editor signed "Florence M.," *DFP*, January 24, 1955; letter to the editor from Mary Evans, *DN*, March 4, 1955; Asher Lauren, "Auto Boom Increases Jobs Here," *DN*, March 6, 1955; "Jobless Roll Cut Slightly, State Says," *DFP*, March 6, 1955; letter to the editor from Edward Klien, *DN*, March 9, 1955; and Geoffrey Howes, "At 40, Jobs Are Scarce, Experts Admit," *DFP*, May 8, 1955.

4. "UAW Sees Jobless Rise in Late '55," *DFP*, January 28, 1955; and Leo Donovan, "Can Sales Keep Pace?" *DFP*, February 9, 1955.

5. Robert Perrin, "Unions Training for Annual Wage Fight," *DFP*, March 22, 1953; Nat Weinberg, "UAW Has a Frown," *DFP*, January 9, 1955; "UAW Sees Jobless Rise n Late '55," *DFP*, January 28, 1955; "Curtice Says GM Is Not Stockpiling," *DFP*, February 4, 1955; "Labor," *Fortune* (January 1955); "Business Roundup: Cutbacks in Cars," *Fortune* (March 1955): 34; and Daniel Bell, "Beyond the Annual Wage," *Fortune* (May 1955).

6. Robert Perrin, "Reuther Calls for Teamwork," *DFP*, November 29, 1953; Jack Strohm, "UAW to Bid for Job Guarantees," *DFP*, March 24, 1954; Jack Strohm, "Can Industrial Unions Survive?" *DFP*, April 25, 1954; and Frank Woodford, "Fear: Industrial By-product," *DFP*, May 9, 1955.

7. Robert Perrin, "Reuther Insists Annual Wage Precede Short Week," *DFP*, December 7, 1953; "Reuther Objects to 30-Hour Week," *DFP*, March 24, 1954; and "Guaranteed Jobs Goal—Reuther," *DFP*, April 28, 1955. For a sustained argument in favor of the thirty-hour week and opposed to Reuther and the GAW, see Jonathan Cutler, *Labor's Time: Shorter Hours, the UAW, and the Struggle for American Unionism* (Philadelphia: Temple University Press, 2004).

8. Tom Nicholson, "Rank and File Back Yearly Pay in Quiz," *DFP*, January 17, 1955; letter to the editor signed "H.J.S.," *DFP*, April 16, 1955; and Horace White, "Facts in the News: Guaranteed Annual Wage," *Michigan Chronicle*, May 21, 1955.

9. Letter to the editor from Charlie Buber, *DFP*, January 28, 1955; "National Labor Group Backs Reuther's Annual Wage Campaign," *DFP*, February 23, 1955; Edwin Lahey, "UAW Ties Stand for Annual Wage to Principle," *DFP*, March 8, 1955; and Leo Donovan, "Wage Drive Is Given Impetus by Automation," *DFP*, March 27, 1955.

10. "National Labor Group Backs Reuther's Annual Wage Campaign," *DFP*, February 23, 1955; "GM Paid Curtice $686,000," *DFP*, February 18, 1955; "The Mutual Aims of Religion and Labor," in *Walking Together: Religion and Labor*, pamphlet distributed by the National Religion and Labor Foundation, ca. 1950, in author's possession; Adrian Fuller, "Methodists Laud Full GAW," *DFP*, June 17, 1955; and Arthur O'Shea Jr., "Father Coughlin Returns, Backs Annual Wage," *DFP*, December 5, 1953.

11. Tom Nicholson, "Rank and File Back Yearly Pay in Quiz," *DFP*, January 17, 1955; Ed Winge, "GAW Hit, Praised in Debate," *DFP*, March 14, 1955; and letter to the editor signed "Guy in the Middle," *DFP*, April 11, 1955.

12. "Business Hits Annual Wage Plan," *DFP*, October 11, 1953; Leo Donovan, "Chrysler Chief Cool to Annual Auto Pay," *DFP*, November 13, 1953; "UAW, C. of C. Clash on Annual Pay Plan," *DFP*, December 29, 1953; Jack Strohm, "Vital Annual Wage Question," *DFP*, May 23, 1954; "Bugas Spikes Ford Annual Wage Rumor," *DFP*, January 23, 1955; "The Guaranteed Annual Wage Issue," editorial, *DFP*, February 1, 1955; "Industrialist Sees Bad Labor Year," *DFP*, March 12, 1955; and William Sudomier, "Sligh Raps GAW as a Potential 'Disaster' to U.S.," *DFP*, April 26, 1955.

13. Robert Perrin, "State Job Rate 'High' Compared with Past," *DFP*, March 27, 1955.

14. Leo Donovan, "Chrysler Net Already Tops '54," *DFP*, March 25, 1955; Leo Donovan, "Plymouth to Boost Capacity," *DFP*, April 15, 1955; "Detroit Area Payrolls Hit Record High," *DN*, April 17, 1955; Leo Donovan, "GM Divisions Report Peak Output," *DFP*, April 21, 1955; Leo Donovan, "GM Pay, Profits Hit Peak," *DFP*, April 22, 1955; Leo Donovan, "Suppliers Are Pressed," *DFP*, May 6, 1955; "Earnings Set Record at Chrysler," *DFP*, May 6, 1955; "Jobless Total Dips to 3.5 Pct.," *DFP*, May 6, 1955; Leo Donovan, "Best Month in 14 Years," *DFP*, May 10, 1955; Leo Donovan, "Plymouth After Another Record," *DFP*, May 18, 1955; "GM Sales in Early May Set Record," *DFP*, May 27, 1955; Leo Donovan, "Five Months of Records," *DFP*, June 2, 1955; and "Plymouth Sales Soar," *DFP*, July 12, 1955.

15. L. J. Scott, Thomas Nowak, Joe Woods, Elwin Brown, James Franklin, Edith Arnold, Margaret Beaudry, Katie Neumann, Dorothy Sackle, and Paul Ross interviews.

16. "Ford Puts 625 Million into 3-Year Expansion," *DFP*, April 29, 1955; Frank Beckman, "Ford Seen as First Target for GAW," *DFP*, April 30, 1955; and "Free Loans Form Part of Ford Plan," *DFP*, May 27, 1955.

17. "Workers Comment on Proposal," *DFP*, May 27, 1955; "How the UAW Answers Ford's Offer," *DFP*, May 28, 1955; and Charles Manos, "The People Speak—and Today's Subject Is the Ford Offer," *DFP*, May 28, 1955.

18. Letter to the editor signed "Worker's Wife," *DFP*, June 3, 1955; letter to the editor signed "Capitalist," *DFP*, June 3, 1955; Robert Perrin, "UAW to Ford: Let Vote Settle Pact," *DFP*, May 31, 1955; Robert Perrin, "UAW Ultimatum to Ford: Pact Monday—or Strike," *DFP*, June 2, 1955; "4,800 Idle in Ford Walkouts," *DFP*, June 2, 1955; Ted Shurtleff, "Ford Workers Boo Extension of Talks," *DFP*, June 2, 1955; and "Ford Gets Rejections on Overtime," *DFP*, June 4, 1955.

19. "Labor," *Fortune* (July 1955); "FORD PEACE!" *DN*, June 6, 1953; Robert Perrin, "GM Can Give Us More, Says UAW," *DFP*, June 7, 1955; and Miller Hollingsworth, "Ford Would Pick Up Entire Idle-Pay Tab," *DFP*, June 9, 1955.

20. "What's the Story behind Ford Jobless Pay Plan?" *DFP*, June 7, 1955; Miller Hollingsworth, "Jobless Aid Laws Facing Changes," *DFP*, June 7, 1955; and Lyall Smith and Leo Donovan, "Fight Over, Bugas 'Hangs Up Gloves,'" *DFP*, June 7, 1955.

21. "NAM President 'Disappointed' at Ford Contract," *DFP*, June 7, 1955; "Reuther Hands the UAW a Fat Economic Package," editorial, *DFP*, June 7, 1955; Sylvia Porter, "GAW Means Price Hikes," *DFP*, June 7, 1955; Leo Donovan, "Crystal Ball Mighty Busy," *DFP*, June 7, 1955; and Dale Nouse, "Ford Contract Called Buffer to Depression," *DFP*, June 8, 1955.

22. "Labor: Stumbling Blocks to the G.A.W.," *Fortune* (August 1955); Ted Shurtleff, "Stellato Booed at Rouge Plant," *DFP*, June 7, 1955; Lyall Smith and Leo Donovan, "Fight Over, Bugas 'Hangs Up Gloves,'" *DFP*, June 7, 1955; "Contract 'Flaws' Cited by Workers," *DFP*, June 7, 1955; and "Walkout at Rouge," *DN*, June 7, 1955.

23. Saul Pett, "But This Worker Is Leery—He May Vote Against It," *DFP*, June 12, 1955; and Saul Pett, "The Profile of a Ford Worker: Jim's Not Strong for New Pact," *DN*, June 12, 1955.

24. Sylvia Porter, "America's New Aristocracy Comes Off Assembly Lines," *DFP*, June 10, 1955; and "The Rich, Middle-Income Class," *Fortune* (May 1954).

25. Robert Perrin, "10,000th Worker Gets Ford Pension," *DFP*, January 11, 1955. On rising prices after wage increases, see Bill Collett, "The Jobless Our Major Concern," *Ford Facts*, May 10, 1958.

26. Robert Perrin, "Strikes Idle 60,000," *DFP*, June 10, 1955; "GM Skilled Aides Seek Own Local," *DFP*, June 12, 1955; "Skilled Men at GM Seek UAW Charter," *DFP*, June 13, 1955; Robert Perrin, "GM-UAW AGREEMENT!" *DFP*, June 13, 1955; "Craftsmen Map Drive for Local," *DFP*, June 14, 1955; and Edwin A. Lahey, "Big Auto Strikes Are Dead," *DFP*, June 14, 1955.

27. "Curtain Going Up," editorial, *DFP*, June 14, 1955; "Employers See 'Doom' in GAW," *DFP*, June 16, 1955; "Curtain Going Up," editorial, *DFP*, June 17, 1955; and "What Is UAW Thinking on GAW, Future Plans?" *DFP*, June 17, 1955.

28. "GM Back-to-Work Move Growing," *DFP*, June 14, 1955; "GM Pickets Feel Strike Is Legal," *DFP*, June 16, 1955; "GM's Idle at 65,900 in Strike Wave," *DN*, June 17, 1955; Ralph Nelson, "UAW Chiefs to Settle GM Strike," *DFP*, June 17, 1955; and "2 GM Plants Still Struck," *DN*, June 18, 1955.

29. Ralph Watts, "Rise Is Halted in Auto Output," *DN*, May 13, 1955; Ralph Watts, "Auto Production Bound to Drop," *DN*, May 20, 1955; "Booming Car Sales Start to Taper Off," *DN*, May 25, 1955; Leo Donovan, "Inventories Set Record," *DFP*, June 21, 1955; Leo Donovan, "World of Wheels," *DFP*, June 23, 1955; Ralph Watts, "Drop Expected in Auto Output," *DN*, June 23, 1955; Leo Donovan, "Is 4 Million 55 Pct.?" *DFP*, June 28, 1955; and "Unemployed Up for June," *DFP*, July 9, 1955.

30. James J. Flink, *The Automobile Age* (Cambridge: Massachusetts Institute of Technology Press, 1988), 281–82; Ralph Watts, "Auto Cleanup Drive Mapped," *DN*, July 9, 1955; "Ford Offers Safety Belts on Cars," *DFP*, July 12, 1955; Ralph Watts, "GMAC Cautions on Easy Credit," *DN*, August 11, 1955; "Are Autos Running on Debt?" *DFP*, August 11, 1955; Don Whitehead, "U.S. Lives It Up on Credit," *DN*, September 18, 1955; and Kenneth Thompson, "How High Can It Go?" *DFP*, October 2, 1955.

31. "Payrolls in Area Set Record," *DFP*, April 16, 1955; "406,631 Employed by GM," *DFP*, June 13, 1955; "Take-Home Pay Hits New Peak," *DFP*, June 24, 1955; Sterling R. Green, "U.S. Sees '55 as Best Year in All History," *DFP*, July 3, 1955; "Recession of '54 Is Minimized," *DFP*, July 12, 1955; Asher Lauren, "Auto Workers Reaping Fat Overtime Payments," *DN*, July 24, 1955; David J. Wilkie, "5-Millionth Auto Is Due Next Week," *DFP*, July 26, 1955; "Ford Motor Weekly Pay Held Record," *DFP*, August 9, 1955; Leo

Donovan, "Detroit Merchants Escape Annual 'Summer Slump,'" *DFP*, August 10, 1955; and "Store Sales in Detroit Up 10.6 Pct.," *DFP*, October 1, 1955.

32. Asher Lauren, "Chrysler Pay Up in Accord," *DN*, September 1, 1955; "Comparing Chrysler Pact with Ford, GM Contracts," *DN*, September 1, 1955; Robert Perrin, "Auto Pacts Worth Billion," *DFP*, September 2, 1955; Robert Perrin, "Half of UAW Is Covered by GAW," *DFP*, September 18, 1955; John S. Knight, "What Makes Detroit Tick Told in Chrysler Story," *DFP*, September 18, 1955; "Chrysler Plans Huge Parts Plant," *DFP*, October 2, 1955; "Chrysler Sales Set High Mark," *DFP*, October 8, 1955; Asher Lauren, "Packard Pact Gives Idle Pay," *DN*, November 10, 1955; and James M. Rubenstein, *Making and Selling Cars: Innovation and Change in the U.S. Automotive Industry* (Baltimore: Johns Hopkins University Press, 2001), 214.

33. John B. Rae, The *American Automobile Industry* (Boston: Twayne Publishers, 1984), 108; Lawrence J. White, *The Automobile Industry since 1945* (Cambridge, MA: Harvard University Press, 1971), 15; Bruce M. Tuttle, "$9.5 Billion Sales Sets GM Record," *DN*, October 27, 1955; Leo Donovan, "Car Output Is Record," *DFP*, January 17, 1956; "'55 Payroll of Ford Co. Tops Billion," *DFP*, January 25, 1956; "3 1/2 Billion in Sales Set Chrysler Mark," *DFP*, February 10, 1956; Bruce M. Tuttle, "Chrysler Net Quadruples on All-Time Record," *DN*, February 10, 1956; "GM Weekly Pay Up $11 to $102.41," *DN*, February 20, 1956; "Big 3's Payrolls Exceeded 5 Billion," *DFP*, February 21, 1955; Bruce M. Tuttle, "Ford Net Up 92 Pct. Over '54," *DN*, February 21, 1956; and Leo Donovan, "Ford's Profits Hit 437 Million," *DFP*, February 21, 1956.

34. Asher Lauren, "Skilled UAW Workers Plan to Form Own Union," *DN*, July 13, 1955; "2,000 Skilled UAW Workers Plan Union of Their Own," *DFP*, July 18, 1955; "Craftsmen Protest UAW Policy," *DFP*, October 24, 1955; Asher Lauren, "275 Craftsmen Vote on Leaving UAW," *DN*, November 3, 1955; "Skilled Tradesmen Vote for Own Union," *DN*, November 7, 1955; and Asher Lauren, "Nation's Boom Shows Need for More Skilled Workers," *DN*, November 20, 1955.

35. Jean Sharley, "Working Gal Lets Jobs Go Begging," *DFP*, August 1, 1955; and Asher Lauren, "391,000 Women Defying Men to Keep Jobs in Detroit Area," *DN*, August 7, 1955.

36. "State Jobless Drop 13,000 to 143,000," *DFP*, October 7, 1955; Robert Perrin, "Plymouth Line Cut," *Detroit Reporter*, December 17, 1955 (the *Detroit Reporter* was a temporary newspaper published during a strike that shut down the city's daily newspapers); Ralph Watts, "Production Falls Off," *DN*, January 16, 1956; and Ralph Watts, "Auto Production Sales Tops in '55," *DN*, January 22, 1956.

Chapter 7. "A Severe and Prolonged Hangover"

1. Miller Hollingsworth, "2,450 Facing Layoff," *Detroit Reporter*, January 4, 1956; Thomas Nowak interview; Miller Hollingsworth, "Chevrolet Tops Ford by 65,504," *Detroit Reporter*, January 4, 1956; M. M. Hollingsworth, "Ford to Idle 1,657," *Detroit Reporter*, January 10, 1956; and "Chrysler to Slash Production 10 Pct.," *Polish Daily News* (English edition), January 13, 1956. The *Polish Daily News* published several editions in English during a strike that shut down Detroit's daily newspapers in late 1955 and early 1956.

2. Walter Rosser, "One-Day Layoff," *Ford Facts*, February 18, 1956; Bill Collett, "The Mad Race, Then Layoffs," *Ford Facts*, February 18, 1956; Leo Donovan, "GM Plans to Spend a Billion," *DFP*, January 17, 1956; Ralph Watts, "GM Allots Billion for '56 Spending," *DN*, January 16, 1956; "1,500 More to Be Idled at Chrysler," *DN*, February 3, 1956; "Chrysler, Ford Reveal New Layoffs," *DFP*, February 14, 1956; and "Chrysler, Ford Go on 4-Day Week," *DN*, February 14, 1956.

3. John Orr, "Layoffs Continue," *Ford Facts*, February 11, 1956; Tony Stellato, "How Can We Stop Layoffs?" *Ford Facts*, February 11, 1956; "Car Dealers Hit Factory Pressure," *DN*, January 19, 1956; Ed Winge, "Outlook for '56: Year of the Hard Sell," *DFP*, February 19, 1956; "'Easy' Auto Deals Spark Credit Boom," *DN*, January 25, 1956; Ralph Watts, "Auto Industry Backs Credit," *DN*, January 26, 1956; Ralph Watts, "Further Decline in Output Seen," *DN*, February 2, 1955; and Harry Golden Jr., "Here's the Car I Would Make," *DFP*, February 19, 1956.

4. Ralph Watts, "Inventories Set Auto Record," *DN*, February 21, 1956; Tom Nicholson and Harry Golden Jr., "Layoffs Reflect Season Lag," *DFP*, March 4, 1956; Leo Donovan, "Inventories Hit Peak," *DFP*, March 20, 1956; "Jobs Down 10 Per Cent in Detroit," *DFP*, April 6, 1956; "Hangover Lasts for Auto Men," *DN*, June 5, 1956; and "Did Industry Make Too Many Cars?" *DN*, June 10, 1956.

5. Carl Stellato, "Lay-Offs Show Need for GAW & 30 Hr. Week," *Ford Facts*, February 18, 1956; Sylvia Porter, "GAW Picture Far from Rosy," *DFP*, April 21, 1956; and Asher Lauren, "Idle Benefits Protested on Eve of Start," *DN*, May 25, 1956.

6. "Output Cuts by Big 3 Idle 26,000," *DFP*, January 22, 1956; Tom Joyce, "Business Hums in City Despite Auto Cutbacks," *DN*, February 5, 1956; "Detroit Layoffs Jam Jobless Pay Offices," *DFP*, February 15, 1956; "Relief Up 25 Pct. in City," *DFP*, May 1, 1956; Harry Golden Jr., "Busy City in Land of Play," *DFP*, May 6, 1956; and L. J. Scott and Dorothy Sackle interviews.

7. Tom Nicholson and Harry Golden Jr., "Layoffs Reflect Season Lag," *DFP*, March 4, 1956; Sylvia Porter, "Dilemma of Vanished Income," *DFP*, April 26, 1955; and letter to the editor from William Mazinkowski, *DFP*, November 30, 1956.

8. Sylvia Porter, "Dilemma of Vanished Income," *DFP*, April 26, 1955; and Robert Perrin, "This Prosperity Worries Pierre," *DFP*, September 18, 1955.

9. Kenneth A. Thompson, "Supplier's Number Up?" *DFP*, March 23, 1956; Kenneth A. Thompson, "Motor Prod. Loses Out," *DFP*, April 4, 1956; Ralph Watts, "Jobbers Lost Out to Car Makers," *DN*, April 8, 1956; "4,000 Face Loss of Jobs if Motor Products Closes," *DN*, May 18, 1956; "Mack Plant Idles 4,000," *DN*, September 1, 1956; and Leo Donovan, "Sharp Cuts Detailed," *DFP*, September 5, 1956.

10. Charles E. Edwards, *Dynamics of the United States Automobile Industry* (Columbia: University of South Carolina Press, 1965), 172–74; John Barnard, *American Vanguard: The United Auto Workers during the Reuther Years, 1935–1970* (Detroit: Wayne State University Press, 2004), 297; Leo Donovan, "World of Wheels," *DFP*, April 11, 1956; Leo Donovan, "We Must Be Efficient," *DFP*, May 2, 1956; and Leo Donovan, "Stress Ideas at Bendix," *DFP*, May 3, 1956.

11. Charles J. Wartman, "On the Labor Line," *Michigan Chronicle*, April 7, 1956; Charles Weber, "Industry Shifts to Be Studied," *DFP*, April 29, 1956; and Thomas Sug-

rue, *The Origins of the Urban Crisis: Race and Inequality in Postwar Detroit* (Princeton, NJ: Princeton University Press, 1996), 76–77, 140–41.

12. Edwards, *Dynamics of the Automobile Industry*, 118; Leo Donovan, "Studebaker-Packard Near Merger with Curtiss Firm," *DFP*, May 9, 1956; Earl Wegmann, "Congressmen Act to Help Packard," *DN*, May 9, 1956; "Workers Await Fate in Move by Packard," *DN*, May 9, 1956; "Job Rise Prediction 'Hoax,' Reuther Says," *DN*, July 4, 1956; Leo Donovan, "Details of S-P Deal Revealed," *DFP*, August 5, 1956; Ralph Watts, "Packard Dismantling Ends Plant Operations," *DN*, August 15, 1956; Leo Donovan, "Packard Motor Hits End of Road in Detroit," *DFP*, August 16, 1956; Robert D'Arcy, "Hopes Die as Packard Passes Out," *DN*, August 16, 1956; Tom Nicholson, "Government, Unions to Aid Laid-Off Older Workers," *DFP*, September 9, 1956; "Reuther Urges Hike for Jobless," *DFP*, September 19, 1956; and "Older Workers And New Work," editorial, *DFP*, September 24, 1956.

13. "Employment Up Despite Layoffs," *DFP*, April 25, 1956; "Living Cost Rise Here Tops Nation," *DFP*, April 26, 1956; "Jobs in April Set Record," *DN*, May 8, 1956; "Auto Pay Rises 7 Cents," *DFP*, May 25, 1956; "'56 Seen as Best Year Yet," *DFP*, June 25, 1956; "Boom Records Set Despite Soft Spots," *DN*, July 1, 1956; "U.S. Jobs Hit Record High in June," *DFP*, July 10, 1956; Asher Lauren, "Auto Pay to Go Up 4 Cents," *DN*, August 24, 1956; and Tom Nicholson, "Living Cost Brings Raise to Workers," *DFP*, August 25, 1956. Harvey Swados emphasized the discrepancy between America's prosperous middle class and the lives of autoworkers in "The Myth of the Happy Worker," *The Nation* (August 17, 1957): 65–66.

14. Bill Collett, "Mad Race, Then Layoffs," *Ford Facts*, February 18, 1956; "Ford Profit Near Peak," *DN*, April 23, 1956; Ralph Watts, "Defense Contracts Off at GM," *DN*, April 26, 1956; Tom Nicholson, "More Join Idle Ranks in Detroit," *DFP*, May 2, 1956; "Union Aide Seeks to Halt Auto Layoffs," *DFP*, May 4, 1956; Bruce Tuttle, "Chrysler's Profits Decline 66 Pct. for First Quarter," *DN*, May 4, 1956; and Leo Donovan, "GM Lines Close Today," *DFP*, May 11, 1956.

15. "But Job Sag Here Is Called Critical," *DFP*, May 9, 1956; "Governor Asks U.S. Aid after New Auto Layoffs," *DN*, May 9, 1956; "6,500 Face 2-Day Layoff at Chrysler," *DFP*, May 10, 1956; "Chrysler Extends Layoffs," *DFP*, May 12, 1956; Tom Nicholson, "U.S. Plans Detroit, Flint Job Aid," *DFP*, May 24, 1956; and Asher Lauren, "Label Detroit, Flint Critical Job Areas," *DN*, May 24, 1956.

16. Harold Becker, "What's Wrong with the Auto Industry?" *Ford Facts*, February 23, 1957; "McNamara: Auto Men Ignored," *DFP*, June 14, 1956; Leo Donovan, "Car Backlog Being Cut," *DFP*, July 6, 1956; "Ford to Start Changeover in Late July," *DFP*, July 14, 1956; David J. Wilkie, "Car Output Holds Low, but Level," *DFP*, July 24, 1956; and Ralph Watts, "Car Production to Drop 20 Pct.," *DN*, August 3, 1956.

17. Elwin Brown, James McGuire, and Emerald Neal interviews; Asher Lauren, "Jobs, Work Force Fluctuate Together," *DN*, June 24, 1956; and Carl Rudow, "A Look at Detroit, State Economy," *DN*, July 2, 1956. For more on autoworkers' secondary support networks in this period, see Swados, "Myth of the Happy Worker," 65–66.

18. Tom Joyce, "Business Hums in City Despite Auto Cutbacks," *DN*, February 5, 1956; Tom Nicholson and Harry Golden Jr., "Layoffs Reflect Season Lag," *DFP*, March

4, 1956; "Merchants Rejoice as Workers Return," *DN*, March 9, 1956; Frank Beckman, "Despite Auto Lag, Faith in Future Is Strong," *DFP*, July 1, 1956; "Job Rise Prediction 'Hoax,' Reuther Says," *DFP*, July 4, 1956; John R. Stewart, "Detroit Trends Distorted," *DFP*, January 13, 1957; and William F. Chapman, "Store Blight Widespread," *DFP*, February 10, 1957.

19. "Job Picture Brighter, State Says," *DFP*, October 5, 1956; Tom Nicholson, "Ford, GM Report Hike in Jobs," *DFP*, October 11, 1956; and "GM's Payroll Climbs 42,000 in Michigan," *DN*, October 22, 1956.

20. Carl Stellato, "Job Runaway Plagues Chrysler, Ford, General Motors Workers," *Ford Facts*, February 23, 1957; Asher Lauren, "139,500 Now at Work for Ford in Job Upswing," *DN*, October 11, 1956; "Auto Output Up Sharply," *DN*, October 19, 1956; "New Model Pickup Increases Auto Jobs," *DFP*, October 20, 1956; Leo Donovan, "'Leftovers' Help Score," *DFP*, December 19, 1956; "Auto Slump Shown in '56 Figures," *DFP*, January 3, 1957; and "'56 Car and Truck Production 2 Million Below '55 Record," *DN*, January 3, 1957.

21. "Wildcatters Idle 8,000 at Chrysler," *DFP*, February 24, 1956; "1,400 End Walkout at Ford Plant," *DN*, May 10, 1956; "12,000 Idled by Dispute at Dodge," *DFP*, May 16, 1956; "11,000 Idle in Walkout at Chrysler," *DN*, June 11, 1956; "New Strikes Idle 16,000 at Chrysler," *DN*, June 14, 1956; "New Strike Idles 13,500 at Chrysler," *DN*, June 15, 1956; and "Walkout Continues at DeSoto," *DFP*, July 26, 1956.

22. "Wildcatters Ordered to Return," *DFP*, October 24, 1956; "Chrysler Strike Idles 35,000," *DFP*, October 25, 1956; "Wildcat Strike Ends at Chrysler," *DFP*, October 26, 1956; "Chrysler Plant Workers Vote to End Tie-Up," *DN*, October 25, 1956; "35,000 Back at Chrysler," *DN*, October 26, 1956; "Chrysler Fires Strike Ringleaders," *DFP*, October 27, 1956; and letter to the editor signed "Laid-Off Worker's Wife," *DN*, December 5, 1956.

23. "Labor: The Bumpy Road," *Fortune* (March 1954); Margaret Beaudry, Edith Arnold, Katie Neumann, Don Hester, and Bud Weber interviews; and Tom Agorgianitis interview by Daniel Clark, January 21, 2002.

24. Elwin Brown, Les Coleman, and Ernie Liles interviews.

25. Asher Lauren, "UAW Denies Refugees Get Idled Men's Jobs," *DN*, November 29, 1956; and James K. Anderson, "Refugees Finding Niche in Detroit," *DN*, December 11, 1956.

26. Letter to the editor signed "Proud American," *DN*, December 5, 1956; letter to the editor signed "G. N.," *DN*, December 11, 1956; and letter to the editor signed "L. C.," *DN*, February 4, 1957.

27. Andy Yesta, "The Truth about Layoffs," *Ford Facts*, February 25, 1956; Pauline Sterling, "Rosie Is Still with Us," *DFP*, October 27, 1957; letter to the editor from Frank Winn, *DN*, November 8, 1956; and letter to the editor from Kenneth Filary, *DN*, December 17, 1956.

28. John R. Stewart, "Detroit Trends Distorted," *DFP*, January 13, 1957; Charles Schmidt, "1956 Economy Reached New High," *DFP*, January 13, 1957; "Spokesman Says Work Is 'Deferred,'" *DFP*, January 22, 1957; and Miller Hollingsworth, "State Finds It Hard to Lure Plants," *DFP*, May 1, 1957.

29. "UAW Seeks DeSoto Strike OK," *DFP*, January 21, 1957; Tom Joyce, "Vast Chrysler Shakeup in Plants," *DN*, March 7, 1957; Tom Nicholson, "Here's Story behind Spurt in Chrysler Profits, Sales," *DFP*, March 8, 1957; and Leo Donovan, "Firm Now Getting 19 Per Cent of Market," *DFP*, March 8, 1957.

30. "5,500 Idled by Dodge Wildcatters," *DFP*, January 16, 1957; and "UAW Says Chrysler Gives 'False Picture,'" *DN*, March 8, 1957.

31. Roberta Mackey, "How Your Neighbor Lives," *DFP*, February 16, 1957; letter to the editor from Leo Orsage, *DN*, April 3, 1957; and Geoffrey Howes, "1,400,000 to Get 2-Cent Hike," *DFP*, May 25, 1957.

32. Ralph Watts, "Auto Sales Boom Linked to Growth of Middle Class," *DN*, January 30, 1957.

33. Ruth Weiss, "Deserting Husbands Take Easy Way Out," *DN*, February 16, 1957; Robert Kirk, "Foreclosures on Land Contracts Rising," *DN*, April 10, 1957; and John Orr, "Layoffs Continue," *Ford Facts*, February 11, 1956. See also Swados, "Myth of the Happy Worker," 65–66.

34. James M. Rubenstein, *Making and Selling Cars: Innovation and Change in the U.S. Automotive Industry* (Baltimore: Johns Hopkins University Press, 2001), 214; Ralph Watts, "Delay Now Seen in Auto Boom," *DN*, April 25, 1957; "Car Output Holds Firm, but Sales Dip," *DFP*, April 27, 1957; "Auto Output Due to Boom This Month," *DN*, May 3, 1957; "Car Output Moves Up 5.2 Per Cent," *DFP*, May 10, 1957; "Curtice Sees 1957 Sales at '56 Level," *DFP*, May 25, 1957; Ralph Watts, "Car Distribution Is Top Problem," *DN*, June 21, 1957; "Half-Year Auto Output 2nd Highest," *DN*, June 28, 1957; Fred Olmsted, "'57s Do Well for Chrysler," *DFP*, July 2, 1957; and Bruce Tuttle, "Chrysler's Sales and Net Hit All-Time Peaks for Half Year," *DN*, July 26, 1957.

35. Miller Hollingsworth, "Industry Jobs Fall Sharply in Michigan," *DFP*, June 28, 1957; Owen Deatrick, "Auto Jobs Shrink 153,000," *DFP*, July 30, 1957; Carl Rudow, "Williams Traces Jobless Rise in Michigan to Auto Industry," *DN*, July 30, 1957; and "Machines Held Small Job Factor," *DFP*, August 14, 1957.

36. John Griffith, "'The Box' Baffles 5,000 Seeking Jobs," *DFP*, August 4, 1957; "Women, Older Workers Face Obstacles," *DFP*, June 16, 1957; and Tom Nicholson, "The 16-Hour Day," *DFP*, September 24, 1957.

37. "Ford Executive Assails Unions' Wage Inflation," *DN*, October 11, 1957; and "You're Almost Broke," *DFP*, October 19, 1957.

38. Lawrence J. White, *The Automobile Industry since 1945* (Cambridge, MA: Harvard University Press, 1971), 93; Fred Olmsted, "Auto Costs $775 a Year?" *DFP*, October 30, 1957; Ralph Watts, "Family Budgets, Autos Analyzed," *DN*, October 30, 1957; "'Need New Labor Policy,'" *DFP*, November 1, 1957; "Jobless Problem Still Here," *DFP*, November 10, 1957; and "October Industrial Output Off," *DFP*, November 16, 1957.

39. Kenneth Thompson, "Current 'Recession' Third since World War II," *DFP*, November 10, 1957; Tom Nicholson, "AFL-CIO Demands Big Raise in 1958,'" *DFP*, December 12, 1957; "NAM Chief Attacks AFL-CIO," *DFP*, December 13, 1957; "Cost of Living Soars to Record," *DFP*, December 21, 1957; "UAW Aide Fires Back at Curtice," *DFP*, December 29, 1957; and Tony Stellato, "How Can We Stop Layoffs?" *Ford Facts*, February 11, 1956.

40. Ralph Watts, "Some Makers Curtail Output," *DN*, December 11, 1957; "Ford Calls for Layoff of 3,333," *DFP*, December 12, 1957; Tom Nicholson, "Layoffs Slated for 70,000," *DFP*, December 21, 1957; and Harry Salsinger, "No Jobs and No Parking," *DN*, December 24, 1957.

41. Edwards, *Dynamics of the Automobile Industry*, 202–204; Fred Olmsted, "Auto Makers End Fourth-Best Year," *DFP*, January 1, 1958; Fred Olmsted, "Ford Claims Auto Lead for 1957," *DFP*, January 1, 1958; Fred Olmsted, "Chevy '57 Output Leads by 132 Cars," *DFP*, January 3, 1958; "Ford Boasts of Record Jobs, Pay," *DFP*, January 22, 1958; "Chrysler Hits 20% of Market," *DFP*, January 4, 1958; and "What's So Bad About 7,207,304," editorial, *DFP*, January 8, 1958.

42. "Job Picture Gloomy in Detroit," *DFP*, January 1, 1958; Tom Joyce, "State Unemployment Higher during 1957," *DN*, January 1, 1958; and "Plus and Minus Signs," editorial, *DFP*, January 3, 1958.

Chapter 8. The Nadir

1. E. Plawecki, T. O'Neil, and B. Hughes, "Outlook Bleak for Auto Workers," *Ford Facts*, January 4, 1958; William B. Harris, "The Trouble in Detroit," *Fortune* (March 1958); Hub M. George, "Jobless Pay Overdrawn," *DFP*, January 3, 1958; "Chrysler Layoff Hits 1,000," *DFP*, January 4, 1958; "Auto Sales Set Record: 55 Billion," *DFP*, January 5, 1958; Tom Nicholson, "UAW Sees Big Layoffs at Chrysler," *DFP*, January 8, 1958; James M. Haswell, "Jobs Are Detroiters' Chief Concern, Dingell Finds," *DFP*, January 8, 1958; Ralph Watts, "Output Slashed for 1st Quarter," *DN*, January 9, 1958; "Auto Plant Layoffs Spreading," *DFP*, January 10, 1958; "Auto-Output Off 16 Pct. from 1957," *DN*, January 10, 1957; "Million a Day Paid by MESC," *DFP*, February 2, 1958; Hub George, "Jobless Pay Expected to Rise," *DFP*, February 6, 1958; and "4,000 More at Ford to Be Laid Off," *DN*, February 22, 1958.

2. Charles Weber, "Vacant Stores All over Detroit Are Headache for Our Planners," *DFP*, January 13, 1958; "Prices That Rise Despite Recession," editorial, *DFP*, February 27, 1958; "Bad Checks on Increase," *DFP*, March 1, 1958; Kenneth Thompson, "How Stores Suffered in February," *DFP*, April 1, 1958; Tom Nicholson, "UAW Is in Red, May Need Loan," *DFP*, April 20, 1958; Tom Nicholson, "UAW Pay Cuts and Layoffs Outlined," *DFP*, April 25, 1958; "Reuther Tells How UAW Cuts Its Costs," *DN*, May 2, 1958; "Local 600 Asks Members to Pay Extra $1 a Month," *DFP*, May 17, 1958; and Roy Courtade, "Chrysler Peace Brightens Jefferson Business Outlook," *DN*, October 2, 1958.

3. "Labor: End of the Quiet Time," *Fortune* (January 1958); William B. Harris, "The Trouble in Detroit," *Fortune* (March 1958); Miller Hollingsworth, "Hint UAW to Drop 4-Day Week Bid," *DFP*, January 12, 1958; and Tom Nicholson, "UAW Locals Like Profit Sharing—And!" *DFP*, January 19, 1958.

4. "Labor: End of the Quiet Time," *Fortune* (January 1958); William B. Harris, "The Trouble in Detroit," *Fortune* (March 1958); Charles J. Wartman, "UAW Plan Becomes Hot Issue," *Michigan Chronicle*, January 18, 1958; "New Proposals Necessary to Maintain Progress," *Michigan Chronicle*, January 25, 1958; Asher Lauren, "UAW's Demands,"

DN, January 13, 1958; "What UAW Wants in 1958 Contracts," *DFP*, January 14, 1958; Tom Nicholson, "New GAW Proposal Will Be Big Point in Auto Bargaining," *DFP*, January 19, 1958; Tom Nicholson, "UAW Locals Like Profit Sharing—And!" *DFP*, January 19, 1958; Asher Lauren, "UAW to Ask 80 Per Cent Jobless Pay," *DN*, January 20, 1958; "UAW Asks 80% Idle Pay," *DFP*, January 20, 1958; and Tom Nicholson and Tom Craig, "UAW OK's Profit-Split Demand," *DFP*, January 24, 1958.

5. "Auto Executives Assail UAW Profit-Split Plan," *DFP*, January 14, 1958; Earl Wegmann, "Big 3 to Fight UAW Profit Plan," *DN*, January 14, 1958; and "Breech Cites 'Fishhooks' in UAW Plan," *DFP*, January 24, 1958.

6. "Priced Out of Jobs," editorial, *DN*, January 2, 1958; "UAW's Big Package," editorial, *DN*, January 14, 1958; "What Walter Reuther Is Really Asking For," editorial, *DFP*, January 15, 1958; and David Lawrence, "Why Doesn't Reuther Offer to Share Loss?" *DFP*, January 17, 1958.

7. Tom Craig, "Reuther Accuses Big 3 of Distortion," *DFP*, January 15, 1958; Asher Lauren, "UAW to Ask 80 Percent Jobless Pay," *DN*, January 20, 1958; and James Haswell, "Big 3 'Rigs' Car Prices, Reuther Says," *DFP*, January 29, 1958.

8. Miller Hollingsworth, "226,000 on Jobless 'Payroll,' in Michigan," *DFP*, February 13, 1958; "U.S. Must Act Now in Job Crisis: An Editorial," *Michigan Chronicle*, March 8, 1958; letter to the editor signed "Unemployed," *DN*, April 2, 1958; and letter to the editor from B. E. Pierson, *DN*, April 6, 1958.

9. "Seek More Arms Jobs for State," *DFP*, January 8, 1958; Asher Lauren, "Chrysler Starts Hiring for Big Missile Job," *DN*, January 9, 1958; "Chrysler Creates Missile Division," *DFP*, January 25, 1958; James Bellows, "Detroit Can Lead World in Missiles," *DFP*, February 2, 1958; "Thor IRBM Undercuts Jupiter," *DFP*, February 18, 1958; "Army Work to Open 200 Jobs in Area," *DFP*, March 5, 1958; "Reuther to U.S.: Rush Contracts," *DN*, March 19, 1958; "New Contracts Seen Spurring Jobs in City," *DN*, March 20, 1958; "State Gets 211 Millions in Boosts," *DFP*, March 20, 1958; and "Chrysler Gets New Missile Job," *DFP*, April 2, 1958.

10. "Layoffs Spell Upturn in Ranks of Teachers," *DN*, January 25, 1958; Earl Wegmann, "Plenty of Jobs Available, but There's a Catch," *DN*, January 26, 1958; Miller Hollingsworth, "226,000 on Jobless 'Payroll' in Michigan," *DFP*, February 13, 1958; "Eye Jobs for 2,600 in Parks," *DN*, February 19, 1958; John Carlisle, "City Spurs Projects to Increase Jobs," *DN*, March 20, 1958; Douglas Larsen, "Women Workers Survive Slump Better Than Men, Facts Show," *DN*, May 7, 1958; letter to the editor signed "An Old Maid," *DFP*, June 1, 1958; and Frank Beckman, "Mayor Cries for U.S., State Aid in Crisis," *DFP*, October, 16, 1958.

11. James B. Glyn, "Detroit's Jobless 'Have Had It,'" *DFP*, March 23, 1958; L. J. Scott and James McGuire interviews.

12. Elwin Brown, Les Coleman, Emerald Neal, Gene Johnson, Margaret Beaudry, and Edith Arnold interviews.

13. Tom Joyce, "Idled Workers Return to Dixie," *DN*, March 16, 1958; Ray Courage, "State Jobless Leave—$1 1/2 Million Follows," *DFP*, June 15, 1958; and "Jobless Workers Return to Mountains from Detroit," *DN*, September 28, 1958.

14. "Pontiac UAW to Protest Short Weeks," *DFP*, March 20, 1958; "Pontiac UAW Parades to Protest Work Cuts," *DN*, March 23, 1958; "Paraders Hit Short Work Week," *DFP*, March 23, 1958; Frank Tripp, "Is Jobless Pay Developing New 'Willingly Idle' Class?" *DFP*, June 29, 1958; and letter to the editor from Mrs. T. White, *DN*, August 12, 1958.

15. Jane Schermerhorn, "Union Wives Long for Year-Round Security," *DN*, February 23, 1958.

16. Ibid.; letter to the editor from Leona McCabe, *DFP*, March 14, 1958; and Ruth Carlton, "A Wife's Salary: Where Does It Go?" *DN*, October 26, 1958.

17. Letter to the editor from A. Dunn, *DFP*, March 21, 1958; Kenneth Thompson, "How Stores Suffered in February," *DFP*, April 1, 1958; and Earl Wegmann, "Buyers, Tipplers, Jailbirds All Feel Recession Woes," *DN*, April 13, 1958.

18. Samuel Lubell, "Washington Worries Most about Slump," *DFP*, April 8, 1958; "450,000 Jobless in State," *DFP*, April 10, 1958; Samuel Lubell, "Own Status Guides Ideas on Recession," *DFP*, April 15, 1958; Samuel Lubell, "Young Ask over 50 to Retire," *DFP*, April 16, 1958; "Living Cost Soars to New Peak," *DFP*, April 24, 1958; and "Cost of Living Index Hits New High," *DFP*, May 23, 1958.

19. Joseph Alsop, "'Wait and See' on Recession? You Can See in Detroit NOW," *DFP*, April 15, 1958; and Joseph Alsop, "Debts Crush Jobless," *DFP*, April 17, 1958.

20. Joseph Alsop, "'Wait and See' on Recession? You Can See in Detroit NOW," *DFP*, April 15, 1958; Joseph Alsop, "Debts Crush Jobless," *DFP*, April 17, 1958; "Chronicle Urges Moratorium on Mortgage Payments," *Michigan Chronicle*, March 15, 1958; and "Unemployed Now 205,000 in Detroit," *Michigan Chronicle*, March 22, 1958.

21. Fred Olmsted, "Says 'Hesitancy' Adds to Dip," *DFP*, December 31, 1957; James M. Haswell, "Colbert Frowns on Car Price Cut," *DFP*, February 7, 1958; "Buy More, Hall Urges," *DN*, March 3, 1958; "Idle Rolls Soar; Action Demanded," *DFP*, March 15, 1958; "Idle Pay Offices to Open," *DFP*, March 16, 1958; Asher Lauren, "'Drive Out of Slump in a New Car' Urged," *DN*, March 21, 1958; Geoffrey Howes, "Split on How to End Slump," *DFP*, June 3, 1958; and Carl Rudow, "Labor Peace, New Cars Called Recovery Keys," *DN*, July 15, 1958.

22. "Inventory of New Cars Dips," *DFP*, April 15, 1958; "GM to Shut 2 Plants for a Week," *DFP*, March 29, 1958; Fred Olmsted, "Sales Lowest Since '52," *DFP*, April 1, 1958; "Chevy to Shut Willow Run Truck Plant," *DFP*, April 5, 1958; "One in 7 Unemployed in Pontiac," *DFP*, April 9, 1958; "Jobs, Pay, and Sales Fall Again," *DFP*, April 12, 1958; "Chevy to Shut Nine Plants for a Week," *DFP*, April 12, 1958; William Sudomier, "People Feel the Slump's Cause Is Making too Many Cars too Fast," *DFP*, April 13, 1958; Kenneth Thompson, "Industrial Output Nears 1954 Low," *DFP*, April 15, 1958; "24 Auto Plants Shut to Trim Inventories," *DN*, April 15, 1958; "60,000 Hit as 24 Auto Plants Shut," *DN*, April 21, 1958; and "April Auto Production Cut Sharply," *DFP*, May 3, 1958.

23. "Jobless Mark Hits 18 Pct. in City, 15.9 Pct. in State," *DFP*, May 3, 1958; "Michigan Jobless at Peak of 465,000," *DN*, May 3, 1958; Fred Olmsted, "History Repeating Itself, Says Benson Ford," *DFP*, May 7, 1958; and Carl Rudow, "Labor Peace, New Cars Called Recovery Keys," *DN*, July 15, 1958.

24. "Labor: No Strike in Autos," *Fortune* (May 1958); Tom Nicholson, "No Strike; Better SUB; A 7¢ Raise," *DFP*, May 18, 1958; Tom Craig, "How Reuther Figures to Outwit Big 3," *DFP*, May 24, 1958; Ralph Watts, "Half-Year Output Is Down 31.5 Pct.," *DN*, July 1, 1958; Ralph Watts, "Billion Gambled on 1959 Autos," *DN*, July 9, 1958; Fred Olmsted, "Ford Loses 17.3 Million in Quarter," *DFP*, July 22, 1958; "Chrysler Loss $2.89 a Share," *DFP*, July 25, 1958; and letter to the editor from J. H. Bohl, *DFP*, June 13, 1958.

25. Tom Nicholson, "GM-UAW Pact Is Dead," *DFP*, May 30, 1958; Tom Craig, "UAW, Ford Also Get Nowhere," *DFP*, May 31, 1958; Tom Nicholson, "Ford, Chrysler Refuse to Yield," *DFP*, June 1, 1958; Tom Nicholson, "UAW Contracts Die at Chrysler, Ford," *DFP*, June 2, 1958; Asher Lauren and Tom Joyce, "Plants Stay Normal as Auto Pacts Die," *DN*, June 2, 1958; and Tom Craig, "We'll Work This Week, UAW Says," *DFP*, June 8, 1958.

26. Steve Jefferys, *Management and Managed: Fifty Years of Crisis at Chrysler* (New York: Cambridge University Press, 1986), 135–42; Tom Nicholson and Charles Weber, "Chrysler-UAW Row Flares," *DFP*, June 6, 1958; Asher Lauren, "2,700 Idled in Dispute at Plymouth," *DN*, June 6, 1958; and "UAW Talk Seeks Chrysler Peace 5,400 Are Idled," *DN*, June 7, 1958.

27. Bill Collett, "Unemployed Demand Action," *Ford Facts*, April 26, 1958; "'Spring Upsurge' Brings Rise in Unemployment," *Ford Facts*, April 26, 1958; Bill Collett, "The Jobless Our Major Concern," *Ford Facts*, May 10, 1958; William B. Harris, "Chrysler's Private Depression," *Fortune* (June 1958); Ralph Watts, "Chrysler Local Leaders Boo Back-to-Job Plea," *DN*, June 8, 1958; Tom Nicholson, "Chrysler Plant Walkouts End," *DFP*, June 10, 1958; Tom Nicholson, "Wildcat Strike Closes Dodge Truck Plant," *DFP*, June 11, 1958; Jerome Hansen, "Industry Begins Model Changeover," *DFP*, June 27, 1958; and Asher Lauren and Tom Joyce, "Row Idles 5,400 at Plymouth," *DN*, June 28, 1958.

28. Robert Boyd, "'If We Could Only Get Out of Hock,'" *DFP*, July 8, 1958.

29. Asher Lauren and Tom Joyce, "13,000 UAW Old-Timers Hear Reuther at Picnic," *DN*, July 16, 1958; "UAW Retirees Plan Slow March at GM," *DN*, July 20, 1958; Asher Lauren, "5,000 Retirees Picketing GM over Pensions," *DN*, July 23, 1958; Roy Courtade, "Backyard Farmers Reap Their Harvest," *DN*, August 3, 1958, "Welfare Rolls Still Climbing," *DFP*, October 16, 1958; and Louis Cook, "Garden of Eatin,'" *DFP*, August 1, 1959.

30. "Strike Shuts Chrysler's Mound Plant," *DFP*, August 7, 1958; "Detroit May Feel Ohio Strike," *DFP*, August 14, 1958; "Chrysler Twinsburg Strike Ends," *DFP*, August 19, 1958; "Walkouts Peril Output of '59 Cars," *DN*, August 22, 1958; Tom Nicholson, "5 Strikes Slow Lines at Big 3," *DFP*, August 23, 1958; "Pontiac Factory and Dodge Truck Shut by Strikes, *DN*, August 26, 1958; Tom Craig, "'Cold War' Auto Strikes Increase," *DFP*, August 27, 1958; "9,000 Strikers Delaying 1959 Cars," *DFP*, August 28,1958; Tom Craig, "Wildcat Strikes Idle over 18,500," *DFP*, August 29, 1959; Tom Craig, "Car Strikes Boost Idled to 12,000," *DFP*, August 30, 1958; "Every Day Is Labor Day," editorial, *DN*, September 1, 1958; and Asher Lauren, "Car Strikes Idle 26,100 as Talks Near Climax," *DN*, September 7, 1958.

31. "Pontiac Factory and Dodge Truck Shut by Strikes," *DN*, August 26, 1958; and Tom Joyce, "New Strike Boosts Idle Past 18,000," *DN*, August 29, 1958.

32. Tom Nicholson, "3-Year Pact at Ford Improves Wages, SUB," *DFP*, September 18, 1958; "Highlights of Ford Pact with UAW," *DN*, September 18, 1958; and "Ford-UAW Contract Terms," *DFP*, September 18, 1958.

33. Tom Craig, "'This Is It, Boys': Ford Local Strikes, Then Peace Comes," *DFP*, September 18, 1958; James Sullivan, "Skilled Workers Fear a 'Sellout,'" *DFP*, September 15, 1958; "Ford Paralyzed as Rebels Strike," *DN*, September 19, 1958; Tom Craig, "UAW Rejects GM Proposal," *DFP*, September 21, 1958; "Skilled Units at Rouge Vote to Continue Strike," *DFP*, September 22, 1958; "Pickets Return to Ford Rouge," *DN*, September 22, 1958; "Rouge Open; Talks at Chrysler Stalled," *DN*, September 24, 1958; and Tom Nicholson, "23,000 Returning at Rouge," *DFP*, September 24, 1958.

34. Tom Craig, "Chrysler Pact Ok'd; GM Faces Deadline," *DFP*, October 2, 1958; Asher Lauren and Tom Joyce, "GM Shut by Strike," *DN*, October 2, 1958; Tom Nicholson and Tom Craig, "GM, UAW Settle," *DFP*, October 3, 1958; "Highlights of UAW, GM Pact," *DFP*, October 3, 1958; and Boyd Simmons, "What the UAW Asked and Benefits It Got," *DN*, October 3, 1958.

35. Letter to the editor signed "Disgusted Member," *DN*, September 7, 1958; letter to the editor from Gene Hoffman, Chairman, and Irving Canter, Secretary, representing the Rank and File Citywide Committee of UAW Skilled Workers, *DN*, October 8, 1958; "Tradesmen Seek UAW Jobless Aid," *DFP*, October 20, 1958; Tom Joyce, "Tool, Die Industry Warns Union on Pay Demands," *DN*, October 28, 1958; "Job Shops Ask Help of UAW," *DFP*, October 28, 1958; letter to the editor from James L. Ward, Chief Steward, Local 157, Consolidated Tooling Co., *DN*, October 31, 1958; letter to the editor signed "Voice of Experience," *DN*, November 5, 1958; "Tool-Die Workers OK Strike," *DFP*, November 10, 1958; and Kenneth Thompson, "Tool and Die Industry Put in Peril," *DFP*, November 16, 1958.

36. Letter to the editor signed "Unemployed Skilled Worker," *DN*, November 10, 1958; letter to the editor signed "Another Worker," *DN*, November 14, 1958; "Union OK's Pay Cut to Keep Firm Open," *DN*, December 14, 1958; and Tom Nicholson, "Negro Workers Seeking Opportunities in Skilled Trades," *DFP*, December 27, 1960.

37. "Auto Pay to Soar in Overtime Spurt," *DN*, November 7, 1958; letter to the editor from Mrs. J. E. Bennett, *DN*, November 12, 1958; letter to the editor from W. F. Scott, *DFP*, November 23, 1958; and Fred Olmsted, "More Overtime Set Next Month by Ford," *DFP*, November 27, 1958.

38. "Pickets Halt Dodge Output," *DFP*, November 9, 1958; "Pickets Cut Production at Chrysler," *DN*, November 22, 1958; Asher Lauren, "Chrysler Unemployed Hold Firm on Protest," *DN*, November 23, 1958; "Jobless Pickets Halt Two Plants," *DFP*, November 23, 1958; and "Hire More of Jobless, UAW Asks," *DFP*, November 26, 1958.

39. Ralph Watts, "Output Trails '57 by 2 Million," *DN*, December 16, 1958; William Sudomier, Tom Nicholson, and John Mueller, "'Tis the Season to Be . . .," *DFP*, December 23, 1958; "How Grim Was Job Picture?" *DFP*, December 28, 1958; and "Recession Struck Detroit Hardest of All U.S. Areas," *DFP*, July 3, 1960.

40. Tom Nicholson, "Some Jobs Gone for Good," *DFP*, November 2, 1958; "Detroit Business Picture Bright," *DFP*, December 16, 1958; and Daniel Bell, "The 'Invisible' Unemployed," *Fortune* (July 1958): 109.

41. "Breech Sounds a Warning of Rising Danger to America," editorial, *DFP*, December 21, 1958.

Chapter 9. *"What IS happening? Which way ARE we headed?"*

1. Fred Olmsted, "Chevrolet, Ford Wage Hot Battle," *DFP*, February 7, 1959; "Ford Has Record Profits; U.S. Economy Zooms," *DFP*, April 20, 1959; Fred Olmsted, "Chrysler Earnings, Sales Rise," *DFP*, April 22, 1959; and "GM Sales, Earnings Up Sharply," *DFP*, April 30, 1959.

2. "Jobs and the Jobless," editorial, *DN*, July 18, 1957; "Machines Held Small Factor," *DFP*, August 14, 1957; "Unemployed Employables," editorial, *DFP*, January 7, 1959; Don Schram, "500 Jobless Hold Rally in City Hall," *DFP*, January 13, 1959; Fred Olmsted, "Chevrolet, Ford Wage Hot Battle," *DFP*, February 7, 1959; James Haswell, "Reuther Asks U.S. to Aid Idle," *DFP*, February 10, 1959; Jerry Johnson, "State Idle Decline by 37,000," *DFP*, April 10, 1959; "Ford Has Record Profits," *DFP*, April 20, 1959; Fred Olmsted, "Chrysler Earnings, Sales Rise," *DFP*, April 22, 1959; "GM Sales, Earnings Up Sharply," *DFP*, April 30, 1959; and "7,300 Jobs at $12 a Day," *DFP*, July 17, 1959.

3. Tom Nicholson, "Auto Plants Hit by Glass Strike," *DFP*, January 13, 1959; "Chrysler Lines to Close Friday," *DFP*, January 14, 1959; "Chrysler Moves to Get Glass," *DFP*, January 24, 1959; "Auto Glass Strike Near Settlement," *DFP*, January 29, 1959; "Glass Strike Talks Recess, Chrysler's Hopes Dashed," *DFP*, January 30, 1959; "Glass Union Settles," *DFP*, February 12, 1959; "Chrysler to Recall Thousands," *DFP*, February 17, 1959; Fred Olmsted, "Chrysler Earnings, Sales Rise," *DFP*, April 22, 1959; and Fred Olmsted, "Chrysler's Profit Tops 15 Million," *DFP*, May 1, 1959.

4. "UAW Cuts Staff and Services," *DFP*, January 15, 1959; "UAW Will Lay Off 70," *DFP*, February 7, 1959; "UAW Rolls Dip 289,411 in 1958," *DFP*, March 17, 1959; and Tom Nicholson, "Even the MESC Lays Off People," *DFP*, March 28, 1959.

5. William Sudomier, "75 Store Jobs Available, 600 Line Up to Apply," *DFP*, January 28, 1959.

6. Jean Sharley, "My Husband Is Out of a Job," *DFP*, March 15, 1959.

7. Tom Nicholson, "I Got a Job," *DFP*, April 26, 1959.

8. "'59 Detroit Boom Seen as Auto Output Rises," *DFP*, February 22, 1959; Ray Moseley, "Life Tough, but Oldsters Laugh," *DFP*, December 10, 1959; Ray Moseley, "'We Look All Over for Jobs—No Luck,' Say Oldsters," *DFP*, December 11, 1959; "Packard Retirees Win Millions," *DFP*, December 12, 1959; and "Where Are Packard's 4,000?" *DFP*, January 24, 1960.

9. "200 Women Rally for Job Rights," *DFP*, April 16, 1959; and "Stellato: No Favors for Women," *DFP*, April 16, 1959.

10. Lawrence J. White, *The Automobile Industry since 1945* (Cambridge, MA: Harvard University Press, 1971), 183; James J. Flink, *The Automobile Age* (Cambridge: Massachusetts Institute of Technology Press, 1988), 319–26; and John B. Rae, *The*

American Automobile Industry (Boston: Twayne Publishers, 1984), 120. The only American automaker to specialize in small, fuel-efficient vehicles in the mid- to late 1950s was Nash, which produced the Rambler and continued to do so after its merger with Hudson to form American Motors. Nash/American Motors produced the Rambler in Kenosha, Wisconsin. See White, *Automobile Industry since 1945*, 180; Flink, *Automobile Age*, 284; Charles E. Edwards, *Dynamics of the United States Automobile Industry* (Columbia: University of South Carolina Press, 1965), 50–69; and Rae, *American Automobile Industry*, 109.

11. Edwards, *Dynamics of the Automobile Industry*, 127–41; White, *Automobile Industry since 1945*, 177–87; Rae, *American Automobile Industry*, 117–29; Fred Olmsted, "Volks Is a 'Hot' Little Car," *DFP*, June 16, 1957; James Haswell, "Car Imports Top U.S. Export Sales," *DFP*, October 10, 1957; Tom Nicholson, "Jobs and Small Cars," *DFP*, April 5, 1959; Samuel Lubell, "Despite 'Boom,' Many Workers Are Worried," *DFP*, May 4, 1959; and Fred Olmsted, "Small Cars Bring New Boost for 6's," *DFP*, June 21, 1959.

12. "9 Centers to Aid Idle in Detroit," *DFP*, March 12, 1959; "Ford Pickets Protest Ohio Small Car Job," *DFP*, May 16, 1959; Tom Nicholson, "Local 600 Fights for Falcon Work," *DFP*, June 2, 1959; "1,700 Workers Protest Layoffs, Strike Ford Plant," *DFP*, July 7, 1960; and Collins George, "Quit City, Dodge Men Told," *DFP*, July 13, 1959.

13. "Auto Output Zooms, Far Surpasses 1958," *DFP*, June 2, 1959; Tom Nicholson, "State Industry Masses Steel Stockpile," *DFP*, June 28, 1959; Fred Olmsted, "June Auto Sales Best since 1955," *DFP*, July 8, 1959; Kenneth Thompson, "Steel Stockpiled but Strike Feared," *DFP*, July 9, 1959; "Ford Co. Earnings Hit All-Time High," *DFP*, July 22, 1959; Kenneth Thompson, "GM Sales Hit 6.5 Billion," *DFP*, July 30, 1959; "July Output of Autos Is 3rd Best," *DFP*, August 1, 1959; "Auto Output Near 4 Million Mark," *DFP*, August 4, 1959; and Tom Nicholson, "GM Faces Near Total Shutdown," *DFP*, October 22, 1959.

14. The best account of the 1959 steel strike is Jack Metzgar's *Striking Steel: Solidarity Remembered* (Philadelphia: Temple University Press, 2000). "McLouth Tied Up over Safety," *DFP*, January 30, 1959; "Safety Plan Ends McLouth Strike," *DFP*, January 31, 1959; "First Crews Go Back at McLouth," *DFP*, February 1, 1959; Tom Nicholson, "McLouth Workers Jump Gun," *DFP*, July 15, 1959; Tom Nicholson, "Pickets' Motto: Don't Let Them Take It Away," *DFP*, July 16, 1959; and "Area Steel Output Slows to Trickle," *DFP*, July 22, 1959.

15. Jerry Johnson, "Strike Fails to Disturb Ecorse Calm," *DFP*, July 26, 1959; "U.S. Steel Profits Highest in History," *DFP*, July 29, 1959; "Head of USW Rallies Detroit Steel Workers," *DFP*, August 15, 1959; Gerald Johnson, "Strike Blights Business in Steel Towns," *DFP*, August 23, 1959; and Jean Sharley, "'We Can Hold Out Another 75 Days,'" *DFP*, September 27, 1959.

16. "Detroit Area to Feel Steel-Strike Pinch in 14 Days," *DFP*, September 15, 1959; "Shortage of Steel Hits GM," *DFP*, September 22, 1959; "Auto Firms Feeling Steel Pinch," *DFP*, September 27, 1959; Curt Haseltine, "Ore Ready If Steel Strike Ends," *DFP*, September 27, 1959; "Chevrolet Layoffs to Idle 9,000," *DFP*, October 13, 1959;

"40,500 Idle at GM from Steel Strike," *DFP*, October 16, 1959; "32,000 Idled in Michigan as Steel Shortage Grows," *DFP*, October 17, 1959; Tom Nicholson, "GM Faces Near Total Shutdown," *DFP*, October 22, 1959; "Steel Strike Puts GM at Standstill," *DFP*, October 30, 1959; "Auto-Plant Layoffs Hit 199,530," *DFP*, November 6, 1959; Fred Olmsted, "Auto Sales Soaring—Now, No Steel," *DFP*, November 6, 1959; "Steel Trickles in Too Late for GM," *DFP*, November 11, 1959; "GM Halts Production of Autos," *DFP*, November 12, 1959; "GM Sales Plunge by 40 Pct.," *DFP*, November 17, 1959; "All Workers Back at Great Lakes," *DFP*, November 21, 1959; Fred Olmsted, "Auto Sales to Top 4th Quarter Output," *DFP*, December 10, 1959; and Fred Olmsted, "Strike Cost Autos Output of 600,000," *DFP*, January 5, 1960.

17. "Ford Profits Soar to $8.24 a Share," *DFP*, February 4, 1960; and "GM's '59 Profit Near Record," *DFP*, February 5, 1960.

18. Tom Nicholson, "Auto Industry Sets Stage for Record First Quarter," *DFP*, January 5, 1960; "Car Output Highest since 1955," *DFP*, January 15, 1960; Tom Nicholson, "Dodge Local 3 Boss Sees Blue Skies Ahead," *DFP*, January 18, 1960; Tom Nicholson, "Car Output Up, Job List Down, Survey Shows," *DFP*, January 21, 1960; James Ransom, "Auto Output Sets January Record," *DFP*, February 2, 1960; Sylvia Porter, "Auto Pattern Changed? Too Early to Say," *DFP*, February 8, 1960; "Car Output Hits Low for 1960," *DFP*, February 12, 1960; "Car Output Declines 4th Week," *DFP*, February 13, 1960; "Ford to Idle 4,400 for One Week," *DFP*, February 26, 1960; and "667,900 Car Output Forecast," *DFP*, March 19, 1960.

19. "Chrysler Warns It May Leave City," *DFP*, February 19, 1960; and "Here's What Haber Group Discovered," *DFP*, March 20, 1960.

20. Edwards, *Dynamics of the Automobile Industry*, 47–69; Tom Craig, "Ex-Hudson Men Happy in Kenosha," *DFP*, June 28, 1959; Fred Olmsted, "Dart Success Story of 1960 Car Market," *DFP*, March 24, 1960; James Ransom, "Auto Production Up 23 Per Cent in First Quarter," *DFP*, April 2, 1960; "Willow Run GM Plants Still Closed," *DFP*, April 5, 1960; James Ransom, "AMC Sales Up 37 Pct. This Year," *DFP*, April 6, 1960; James Ransom, "575,847 Car Sales in March Boost Industry's Hopes," *DFP*, April 7 1960; Fred Olmsted, "Compact Boom Sparks Best Spring since '55," *DFP*, May 6, 1960; "Car Output Up 7 Pct. for Week," *DFP*, May 21, 1960; Fred Olmsted, "Output Edge over 1959 Due to New Compacts," *DFP*, June 1, 1960; Fred Olmsted, "Compacts Boost Share of State's Production," *DFP*, July 1, 1960; and "Chevrolet Will Add 2,600 Jobs," *DFP*, September 1, 1960.

21. "Reuther Fights Ford Rouge Layoffs," *DFP*, April 12, 1960; Fred Olmsted, "Record Profits for Ford," *DFP*, April 21, 1960; Fred Olmsted, "1st-Quarter GM Profits a Record," *DFP*, April 28, 1960; and Kenneth Thompson, "Another Auto Supplier, Peninsular, Drops Out," *DFP*, June 17, 1960.

22. "Here's What Haber Group Discovered," *DFP*, March 20, 1960; and Tom Nicholson, "Job Outlook Still Dim for Three Months," *DFP*, April 17, 1960.

23. Tom Nicholson and Ray Courage, "Their Big Fear: Unemployment," *DFP*, May 1, 1960; Tom Nicholson, "Spread Out Factory Jobs, Union Men Here Plead," *DFP*, May 5, 1960; and "Detroit Listed by U.S. for Lack of Jobs," *DFP*, June 7, 1960.

24. "1960 Auto Output Nears '59 Total," *DFP*, June 25, 1960; Fred Olmsted, "First Half Only 6 Pct. Off Record 1955 Pace," *DFP*, June 28, 1960; "Car Output in Early '60 Near Peak," *DFP*, July 2, 1960; Fred Olmsted, "GM Sales Hit All-Time High for 6 Months," *DFP*, July 28, 1960; Fred Olmsted, "Chrysler Sales, Earnings Rise," *DFP*, July 29, 1960; "AMC Sales Set Record for Quarter," *DFP*, July 29, 1960; "Detroit Idle Roll Up 30,000," *DFP*, August 10, 1960; "Michigan Economy Plugs Along," *DFP*, August 14, 1960; and "Auto Output Hits Three-Year High," *DFP*, September 10, 1960.

25. "1,700 Workers Protest Layoffs, Strike Ford Plant," *DFP*, July 7, 1960; "Row Halts All Ford Compacts," *DFP*, July 8, 1960; "Progress Made in Ford Talks," *DFP*, July 10, 1960; "Rift Shuts Four More Ford Plants," *DFP*, July 12, 1960; "Cleveland Strike Settled," *DFP*, July 14, 1960; "Walton Hills Ford Strike Ends as Workers Ratify Pact," *DFP*, July 15, 1960; "Chevrolet Will Add 2,600 Jobs," *DFP*, September 1, 1960; "Production of Autos Up, Down," *DFP*, November 12, 1960; and Tom Kleene, "Corvair Plant Expanded 50 Pct.," *DFP*, December 7, 1960.

26. "Cut to Idle 1,900 at Chrysler," *DFP*, November 16, 1960; Tom Nicholson, "Car Output and Sales Soaring," *DFP*, November 29, 1960; "Great Lakes Steel to Shut Down Production for 10 Days," *DFP*, December 8, 1960; Fred Olmsted, "Car Sale Lag Is Forecast," *DFP*, December 8, 1960; Fred Olmsted, "Sales Placed at 6,740,000," *DFP*, December 21, 1960; "New Rise in Jobless Is Reported," *DFP*, December 28, 1960; and Fred Olmsted, "Car Sales Are Off 11.5 Pct.," *DFP*, December 29, 1960.

Conclusion

1. "Detroit Job Picture Labeled 'Normal'; Moody Objects," *DFP*, February 21, 1952; "No 'Normal' Seen for Unemployment," *DFP*, February 22, 1952; and Charles Weber, "B of C Secretary Hall Calls Senator Moody Puppet of CIO," *DFP*, February 26, 1952.

2. "Chrysler to Slash Production 10 Pct.," *Polish Daily News* (English edition), January 13, 1956; and "Output Cuts by Big 3 Idle 26,000," *DFP*, January 22, 1956.

3. Bert Stoll, "Michigan's Popular State Parks about to Burst Seams," *DFP*, February 13, 1957.

4. Presentation to the Rochester Older Persons Commission, October 28, 2008, Rochester, Michigan; and presentation as part of the Oakland University History Department's "History Comes Alive" lecture series, January 14, 2014, Rochester, Michigan.

5. For recent depictions of the early postwar years as relative boom times for organized labor generally, and autoworkers in particular, see David Maraniss, *Once in a Great City: A Detroit Story* (New York: Simon & Schuster, 2015), 212; and Jefferson Cowie, *The Great Exception: The New Deal and the Limits of American Politics* (Princeton, NJ: Princeton University Press, 2016), 153–54, 156–60.

6. See, for example, James J. Flink, *The Automobile Age* (Cambridge: Massachusetts Institute of Technology Press, 1988), 280.

7. Evelyn Rogers, interview by Daniel Clark, June 21, 2002; Edith Arnold, Elwin Brown, Les Coleman, James Franklin, Don Hester, Paul Ish, Gene Johnson, Ernie Liles, James McGuire, Emerald Neal, Katie Neumann, Thomas Nowak, Paul Ross, Dorothy Sackle, L. J. Scott, and Joe Woods interviews.

Selected Bibliography

Interviews by Author

Recordings and transcripts are located in the Metropolitan Detroit Autoworkers Oral History Collection, Walter Reuther Library, Archives of Labor and Urban Affairs, Wayne State University.

Agorgianitis, Tom. Pontiac, Michigan, January 21, 2002.
Arnold, Edith. Pontiac, Michigan, November 7, 2003.
Bailey, Nora Kay. Pontiac, Michigan, August 8, 2003.
Beaudry, Margaret. Waterford, Michigan, June 24, 2002.
Bowen, Bob. Ypsilanti, Michigan, August 25, 2000, and August 28, 2000.
Brown, Elwin. Pontiac, Michigan, August 7, 2003.
Coleman, Les. Ypsilanti, Michigan, August 29, 2000.
Franklin, James. Ypsilanti, Michigan, September 22, 2000.
Hester, Donald K., Sr. Pontiac, Michigan, August 12, 2003.
Ish, Paul. Pontiac, Michigan, June 18, 2002.
Johnson, Arthur E. (Gene). Pontiac, Michigan, July 17, 2002.
Liles, Ernie. Sterling Heights, Michigan, May 27, 2003.
McGuire, James. Ypsilanti, Michigan, August 24, 2000.
Neal, Emerald. Ypsilanti, Michigan, August 21, 2000.
Neumann, Katie. Shelby Township, Michigan, March 18, 2002.
Nowak, Thomas. Ypsilanti, Michigan, September 20, 2000.
Rogers, Evelyn. Pontiac, Michigan, June 21, 2002.
Ross, Paul. Pontiac, Michigan, May 20, 2003.
Sackle, Dorothy. Westland, Michigan, June 14, 2002.
Scott, L. J. Detroit, Michigan, October 27, 2003.
Weber, Ambrose (Bud). Pontiac, Michigan, May 15, 2003.
Woods, Joe, Jr. Pontiac, Michigan, June 28, 2002, and March 2, 2004.

Newspapers, Periodicals, Pamphlets, and Government Documents

Census of Population: 1950, vol. 2: *Characteristics of the Population*, part 22, Michigan. Washington, DC: U.S. Government Printing Office, 1952.

Detroit Free Press, 1945–1960

Detroit News, 1953–1958

Ford Facts Collection, Walter Reuther Library, Archives of Labor and Urban Affairs, Wayne State University.

Fortune, 1948–1959

Michigan Chronicle, 1949–1959

National Religion and Labor Foundation. "Religion and Labor: Walking Together," New Haven, Connecticut, ca. 1950.

Books and Articles

Asher, Robert, and Ronald Edsworth, eds. *Autowork*. Albany: State University of New York Press, 1995.

Babson, Steve, et al. *Working Detroit: The Making of a Union Town*. Detroit: Wayne State University Press, 1986.

Barnard, John. *American Vanguard: The United Auto Workers during the Reuther Years, 1935–1970*. Detroit: Wayne State University Press, 2004.

Berger, Bennett. *Working-Class Suburb: A Study of Auto Workers in Suburbia*. Berkeley: University of California Press, 1960.

Berry, Chad. *Southern Migrants, Northern Exiles*. Urbana: University of Illinois Press, 2000.

Boyle, Kevin. "The Kiss: Racial and Gender Conflict in a 1950s Automobile Factory." *Journal of American History* 84, no. 2 (1997): 496–523.

———. *The UAW and the Heyday of American Liberalism, 1945–1968*. Ithaca, NY: Cornell University Press, 1995.

Chinoy, Ely. *Automobile Workers and the American Dream*, 2nd ed. Urbana: University of Illinois Press, 1992. (Originally published by Doubleday in 1955.)

Cobble, Dorothy Sue. *The Other Women's Movement: Workplace Justice and Social Rights in Modern America*. Princeton, NJ: Princeton University Press, 2004.

Cohen, Lizabeth. *A Consumer's Republic: The Politics of Mass Consumption in Postwar America*. New York: Vintage Books, 2003.

Cowie, Jefferson. *The Great Exception: The New Deal and the Limits of American Politics*. Princeton, NJ: Princeton University Press, 2016.

Cutler, Jonathan. *Labor's Time: Shorter Hours, the UAW, and the Struggle for American Unionism*. Philadelphia: Temple University Press, 2004.

Edwards, Charles E. *Dynamics of the United States Automobile Industry*. Columbia: University of South Carolina Press, 1965.

Fallows, James. *Breaking the News: How the Media Undermine American Democracy*. New York: Pantheon Books, 1996.

Fine, Lisa. "Rights of Men, Rites of Passage: Hunting and Masculinity at Reo Motors of Lansing, Michigan, 1945–1975." *Journal of Social History* (Summer 2000): 805–23.

———. *The Story of Reo Joe: Work, Kin, and Community in Autotown, U.S.A.* Philadelphia: Temple University Press, 2004.

Flink, James J. *The Automobile Age.* Cambridge: Massachusetts Institute of Technology Press, 1988.

Friedman, Tami J. "'Acute Depression . . . in . . . the Age of Plenty': Capital Migration, Economic Dislocation, and the Missing 'Social Contract' of the 1950s." *Labor: Studies in Working-Class History of the Americas* 8, no. 4 (2011): 89–113.

Frisch, Michael. *A Shared Authority: Essays on the Craft and Meaning of Oral and Public History.* Albany: State University of New York Press, 1990.

Gabin, Nancy. *Feminism in the Labor Movement: Women and the United Auto Workers, 1935–1975.* Ithaca, NY: Cornell University Press, 1990.

Gordon, Robert J. *The Rise and Fall of American Growth: The U.S. Standard of Living since the Civil War.* Princeton, NJ: Princeton University Press, 2016.

Grele, Ronald. *Envelopes of Sound: Six Practitioners Discuss the Method, Theory, and Practice of Oral History and Oral Testimony.* Chicago: Precedent Publishing, 1975.

Hyman, Louis. *Debtor Nation: The History of America in Red Ink.* Princeton, NJ: Princeton University Press, 2011.

Jefferys, Steve. *Management and Managed: Fifty Years of Crisis at Chrysler.* New York: Cambridge University Press, 1986.

Levinson, Marc. *An Extraordinary Time: The End of the Postwar Boom and the Return of the Ordinary Economy.* New York: Basic Books, 2016.

Lewis-Colman, David M. *Race against Liberalism: Black Workers and the UAW in Detroit.* Urbana: University of Illinois Press, 2008.

Lichtenstein, Nelson. *Labor's War at Home: The CIO in World War II.* New York: Cambridge University Press, 1982.

———. *The Most Dangerous Man in Detroit: Walter Reuther and the Fate of American Labor.* New York: Basic Books, 1995.

Lichtenstein, Nelson, and Stephen Meyer, eds. *On the Line: Essays in the History of Auto Work.* Urbana: University of Illinois Press, 1989.

Maraniss, David. *Once in a Great City: A Detroit Story.* New York: Simon & Schuster, 2015.

Marquart, Frank. *An Auto Worker's Journal: The UAW from Crusade to One-Party Union.* University Park: Pennsylvania State University Press, 1975.

Metzgar, Jack. *Striking Steel: Solidarity Remembered.* Philadelphia: Temple University Press, 2000.

Meyer, Stephen. *The Five Dollar Day: Labor Management and Social Control in the Ford Motor Company, 1908–1921.* Albany: State University of New York Press, 1981.

———. *Manhood on the Line: Working-Class Masculinities in the American Heartland.* Urbana: University of Illinois Press, 2016.

———. "Work, Play, and Power: Masculine Culture on the Automotive Shop Floor, 1930–1960," *Men and Masculinities* 2, no. 2 (1999): 115–34.

Mindich, David T. Z. *Just the Facts: How "Objectivity" Came to Define American Journalism.* New York: New York University Press, 1998.

Patai, Daphne, and Sherna Berger Gluck, eds. *Women's Words: The Feminist Practice of Oral History*. New York: Routledge, 1991.

Pettengill, Ryan. "Fair Play in Bowling: Sport, Civil Rights, and the UAW Culture of Inclusion, 1936–1950," *Journal of Social History* 52, no. 4 (Summer 2018).

Portelli, Alessandro. *The Death of Luigi Trastulli and Other Stories: Form and Meaning in Oral History*. Albany: State University of New York Press, 1990.

———. *They Say in Harlan County: An Oral History*. New York: Oxford University Press, 2010.

Rae, John B. *The American Automobile Industry*. Boston: Twayne Publishers, 1984.

Rubenstein, James M. *Making and Selling Cars: Innovation and Change in the U.S. Automotive Industry*. Baltimore: Johns Hopkins University Press, 2001.

Schudson, Michael. *Discovering the News: A Social History of American Newspapers*. New York: Basic Books, 1978.

Sugrue, Thomas. *The Origins of the Urban Crisis: Race and Inequality in Postwar Detroit*. Princeton, NJ: Princeton University Press, 1996.

Swados, Harvey. "The Myth of the Happy Worker." *The Nation* (August 17, 1957): 65–66.

Thompson, Paul. *The Voice of the Past: Oral History*. New York: Oxford University Press, 1978.

Walker, Charles R., and Robert H. Guest. *The Man on the Assembly Line*. Cambridge, MA: Harvard University Press, 1952.

Weales, Gerald. "Small-Town Detroit: Motor City on the Move." *Commentary* (September 1, 1956). www.commentarymagazine.com/articles/small-town-detroitmotor -city-on-the-move.

White, Lawrence J. *The Automobile Industry since 1945*. Cambridge, MA: Harvard University Press, 1971.

Widick, B. J. *Auto Work and Its Discontents*. Baltimore: Johns Hopkins University Press, 1976.

Zieger, Robert. *The CIO, 1935–1955*. Chapel Hill: University of North Carolina Press, 1995.

Index

DANIEL J. CLARK is an associate professor of history at Oakland University, Michigan. He is the author of *Like Night and Day: Unionization in a Southern Mill Town.*

The Working Class in American History

The University of Illinois Press
is a founding member of the
Association of American University Presses.

University of Illinois Press
1325 South Oak Street
Champaign, IL 61820-6903
www.press.uillinois.edu